Modernizing Legal Services in Common Law Countries

Modernizing Legal Services in Common Law Countries

Will the US Be Left Behind?

Laura Snyder

LEXINGTON BOOKS
Lanham • Boulder • New York • London

Published by Lexington Books
An imprint of The Rowman & Littlefield Publishing Group, Inc.
4501 Forbes Boulevard, Suite 200, Lanham, Maryland 20706
www.rowman.com

Unit A, Whitacre Mews, 26-34 Stannary Street, London SE11 4AB

British Library Cataloguing in Publication Information Available

Library of Congress Cataloging-in-Publication Data

Library of Congress Control Number: 2017945439

ISBN 978-1-4985-3006-4 (cloth: alk. paper)
ISBN 978-1-4985-3007-1 (electronic)

Printed in the United States of America

For my big brother Paul,
who taught me to swim
and
who would have had an opinion on everything in this book

We'll miss you forever

Paul Andrew Snyder
1952–2017

Contents

List of Figures and Tables

FIGURES

TABLES

Preface

The first draft of the manuscript for this book was completed in spring 2016. At that time, Donald Trump's victory in the US presidential election still seemed far-fetched. The final manuscript was completed in spring 2017. What a difference one year made.

During as well as after his campaign, Trump did not seem to have a single kind word for regulation. Headlines read along the lines of "Donald Trump Says 70% of Federal Regulations 'Can Go,'"[1] and "Donald Trump Promises to Eliminate Two Regulations for Every One Enacted."[2] Trump nominated to his Cabinet people whose primary objective appeared to be, for each of their Departments, to dismantle as much of the existing regulatory framework as possible with little in mind to replace it.[3]

Further, by all appearances, Trump holds in contempt at least some of the six essential elements of regulatory policy discussed in this book. For example, his Cabinet selections mock the concept of regulatory independence and freedom from conflicts of interest.[4] His rejection of intelligence briefings suggests a comparable rejection of evidence-based regulatory impact assessments.[5] His refusals both to disclose his tax returns and to place his assets in a blind trust fly in the face of accountability and transparency in decision-making.[6]

With respect to legal services, this book takes an entirely opposite approach. This book calls not for existing regulation (of which, in terms of quantity, there is in fact very little) to be dismantled, but for it to be re-assessed, and for a new regulatory framework to be developed. Especially, this book calls for a new regulatory environment to be created, one that ends the current rejection of the OECD's elements of good governance, and instead fully embraces, and fully implements them. In sum, this book calls for more—and better—regulation of legal services.

With Trump's election, it is fair to ask: What's the point? In the current political environment—one that presumably will prevail for at least four years—is there any realistic possibility that the arguments made in this book can actually find a receptive audience? Optimism seems naïve.

That's certainly one way of looking at it. Another way to look at it is this: if the Trump Administration attempts to dismantle multiple regulatory frameworks in the way Trump suggests that it will, there may be a backlash. Certainly most people don't care about the regulation of legal services. Few people make a connection between how legal services are regulated and how difficult it is for them to access legal services. But people do make this kind of connection when it comes to other kinds of regulation. That is, most people understand that environmental regulations have a direct bearing upon their access to clean air and water. Most people understand that labor regulations have a direct bearing upon their access to safe working environments. Perhaps attempts to dismantle regulations such as those will lead to an increased awareness of and sensitivity to the direct bearing that regulation has on many other aspects of our lives, not the least of which is access to legal services. At that point, perhaps the mention of the words "regulation of legal services" will no longer cause eyes to glaze over but instead to fire up; perhaps.

NOTES

1. "Donald Trump Says 70 Percent of Federal Regulations 'Can Go,'" *The Telegraph*, October 7, 2016, http://www.telegraph.co.uk/news/2016/10/07/donald-trump-says-70-percent-of-federal-regulations-can-go/.

2. Clyde Wayne Crews, "Donald Trump Promises to Eliminate Two Regulations for Every One Enacted," *Forbes*, November 22, 2016, http://www.forbes.com/sites/waynecrews/2016/11/22/donald-trump-promises-to-eliminate-two-regulations-for-every-one-enacted/#413314902b87.

3. New York Times Editorial Board, "How a Budget Chief Can Wreak Havoc," *New York Times*, December 27, 2016, http://www.nytimes.com/2016/12/27/opinion/how-a-budget-chief-can-wreak-havoc.html?_r=0.

4. See, for example, Oleg Kashin, "Rex Tillerson's Special Friend in the Kremlin," *New York Times*, December 22, 2016, http://www.nytimes.com/2016/12/22/opinion/rex-tillersons-special-friend-in-the-kremlin.html?_r=0.

5. Maxwell Tani, "Trump: I'm a 'Smart Person,' Don't Need Intelligence Briefings Every Single Day," *Business Insider UK*, December 11, 2016, http://uk.businessinsider.com/donald-trump-intelligence-briefings-skip-2016-12?r=US&IR=T.

6. Susanne Craig, "Trump's Empire: A Maze of Debts and Opaque Ties," *New York Times*, August 20, 2016, http://www.nytimes.com/2016/08/21/us/politics/donald-trump-debt.html; Richard C. Paddock et. al, "Potential Conflicts Around the Globe for Trump, the Businessman President," *New York Times*, November 26, 2016, http://www.nytimes.com/2016/11/26/us/politics/donald-trump-international-business.html.

Acknowledgments

This book is entirely my own, and, especially, any errors are entirely my own.

That being said, I owe a huge debt of gratitude to Lisa Webley, Richard Devlin, John Flood, Paddy Oliver, Mark Haney, Elaine Tan, Alberto Treviño, John Chisholm, Steve Mark and Tahlia Gordon. Without your highly precious help and support, this book would have been impossible.

I am also indebted to the anonymous peer reviewer, who made invaluable suggestions for improving this book.

Introduction

Alternative business structure (ABS) Omnia Strategy LLP offers a multidisciplinary expertise in law, strategy, policy, business and communications. It serves governmental, corporate and individual clients located around the globe.

ABS Proelium Law is a multidisciplinary practice that offers legal and business advice to companies, individuals and governmental agencies that seek to operate in complex, high-risk and hostile environments (such as Syria, Afghanistan and Iraq). Proelium Law's partnership includes Richard Stephens, a former Special Forces officer with expertise in the areas of surveillance, reconnaissance and problem-solving in complex environments. Proelium's clients are based both within and outside of the UK.

ABS Schillings International LLP offers multidisciplinary expertise in reputation management and defense combining the disciplines of legal services, risk consulting and information security. It serves "prominent individuals and businesses wherever they are in the world."[1] Schillings has won a number of awards, including in 2015 Legal Week's Legal Innovation Award for "Marketing and Business Development Innovation" and was highly commended in the category of "Future of Legal Services Innovation."[2] In 2016 Schillings's COO, Christopher Mills (who is not a lawyer), won Legal Week's Outstanding Individual Innovator award for his "instrumental" role in reinventing the firm from a defamation boutique to a reputation defense business.[3]

ABS Radiant Law offers the application of technology and managed processes to shorten the negotiations and sales cycle for companies with large volumes of commercial contracts. Radiant's non-executive chair (and a minority shareholder) is Greg Tufnell, who formerly served as managing director at retailers Mothercare and at Burton Menswear, and who currently also serves as the non-executive director for the investment group The House of Britannia and as chair of leather accessories company Zachels. Radiant Law serves a number of clients outside the United Kingdom, including clients based in the United States. In 2015 Radiant won the Managing Partners' Forum "Mold Breaking Firm"[4] award and came in second in the category "Most Innovative Client Service."[5] In addition, it was shortlisted for the African Legal Awards 2015, in the category "Innovation."[6]

ABS Riverview Law offers the application of technology and managed processes to improve the efficiency and the quality of the work of in-house legal departments. Riverview is owned (i) by the managed HR advisory service company Adviserplus, (ii) by the international law firm DLA Piper and (iii) by a variety of individuals, including the management team of Riverview Law. Riverview's Chief Executive, Karl Chapman, was the founder of Adviserplus and remains its principal shareholder; he is not a lawyer. Riverview serves a number of clients outside the United Kingdom, including clients based in the United States. Riverview has won a number of awards, including in 2013 the US-based College of Law Practice Management's InnovAction award for its innovative law firm model.[7]

ABS Keystone Law offers a range of corporate and commercial legal services to corporate clients. Its lawyers are independent contractors—they are not required to meet billing targets or to work from any particular physical location. The recipient of £3.15 million of private equity,[8] the firm provides IT, marketing and administrative support together with professional liability insurance to its lawyers. The firm retains 30% of client fees, with the remaining 70% paid to the relevant lawyer(s). Keystone has created an Australia-based joint venture, ILP Keypoint Law, which operates under the same model as Keystone. Keystone has won a number of awards, including in 2015 Legal Week's Legal Innovation Award for "Recruitment Innovation."[9]

ABS Judicare Law International Limited provides "specialist global legal advice" in connection with investments in property and land overseas, in the areas of conveyancing, property disputes, mortgages, wills and inheritance and immigration. The company's in-house lawyers assist both UK-based and international buyers in a wide range of countries, including the United States, Spain, Portugal, Italy, France, Turkey, Poland, Barbados, Brazil and United Arab Emirates.

ABS Thomas Miller Law Limited offers legal services in the areas of shipping, transport and specialist insurance. In doing so, it expands the spectrum of services offered by its owner Thomas Miller, which provides specialist insurance, investment and professional services to clients around the world.[10]

ABS Ascent Performance Group Limited, having acquired five debt services businesses between 2012 and 2015,[11] offers services in debt collection, outsourced collections, recovery and legal debt litigation to businesses on both a national and international basis. Ascent is a member of the

Irwin Mitchell group, which offers legal services to both individuals and businesses, as well as, through two other subsidiaries, financial and asset management and claims management.

ABS YangTze Law offers corporate and commercial advice to Chinese corporate clients investing in the UK and Europe. The firm caters to the clients of YangTzejiang Legal Network, which has forty independent law firm members throughout China with more than 3,000 lawyers.[12] YangTze Law is entirely owned by two Chinese lawyers—Winston Gao and Steve Ng—Ng is also the secretary general of the YangTzejiang Legal Network. The UK firm Michelmores has gained access to this market of Chinese corporate investors via an agreement with YangTze Law to provide back office legal and regulatory support, and Michelmores's Managing Partner (an English solicitor) also serves as Compliance Officer for Legal Practice (COLP) of YangTze Law.[13]

ABS Foran Glennon (UK) LLP is 80% owned by Foran Glennon Palandech Ponzi & Rudloff (FGPPR), the remaining 20% shared between two UK solicitors.[14] FGPPR is a US-based law firm that serves insurance company and other corporate clients in a variety of practice areas, and notably international litigation. Foran Glennon has described itself as a "professional services company" rather than a "traditional partnership," and it has stated that two advantages of its ABS status are that it will permit the company (i) to develop an in-house forensic accountancy capability, notably by merging with an accounting firm (the accountants can become partners of the UK-based ABS) and (ii) to receive external investment through private equity "at an appropriate time."[15]

ABS Leyton UK Partners LLP offers employment legal services to the corporate and individual clients of its parent company, management consulting firm Leyton UK Ltd.[16] Leyton's London offices are one of fifteen offices worldwide, including offices in Canada, Belgium, Ireland, Spain and Morocco, and nine offices in France, where Leyton is headquartered.

ABS RM Company Services Limited offers business information and registration services, including: (i) United Kingdom and international company registrations (including the United States), (ii) access to corporate reports and credit checks on over 200 million companies in more than 220 countries and access to worldwide company documents from over 1000 registries, (iii) worldwide trademark search and registration together with brand protection and advice, (iv) creating trusts and offshore corporate structures, and (v) worldwide assistance with opening bank accounts.[17] Most of the company's services are offered online, and it claims that its aRMadilo company and credit report app was the world's first B2B app.[18] The company was awarded an ABS license in September, 2015; Emmanuel Cohen, Chair of the RM Group, stated that the company sought an ABS license in order to "offer clients a complete range of corporate services all under one roof," and namely to offer the drafting of corporate documents and agreements and general commercial legal advice, together with accounting and bookkeeping services.[19]

Incorporated legal practice (ILP) TST Partners Group offers to individuals and businesses multidisciplinary services in accounting, tax, legal and finance brokering. Its clientele is focused in Australia, but includes a number of Asia-based clients.

For sure these fourteen companies have many differences. They use a large range of delivery models, and they cover a large range of subject matters: maritime, defamation and reputation defense, security, insurance litigation, debt collection, international investment, human resources, high-volume contracts, international diplomacy and dispute resolution, real property and intellectual property.

But they also share fundamental commonalities:

The first commonality of these companies is that they are all taking advantage of the modernized regulatory environments of England and Wales or Australia (if not both) to develop and offer products and services that would be far more difficult to develop and offer in a more restrictive regulatory environment. It would not be impossible—companies like the US-based Axiom demonstrate that—but it would be significantly more difficult and that is the reason why these companies have few close counterparts or competitors based in the United States (or in any other country).

How are they taking advantage of the liberal regulatory environments? By doing one or more of these:

- By combining legal services with non-legal goods and services, in order to craft unique combinations of goods and services that, together, address not just an isolated legal issue but the client's larger, multidisciplinary matter in its entirety;
- By obtaining third party capital, in these cases in the form of private equity, in order to invest the money to develop new processes and technology for the provision of legal services;
- By bringing in as partner or shareholder persons who have expertise in areas other than law, but which are complementary to law and critical in crafting an effective legal good or service, in order to fully motivate them with a stake in the company's success.

The second commonality of these companies is that they are all actively seeking—and finding—clients outside of their home countries—in many cases the United States and other countries where the regulatory environments are more restrictive. And why wouldn't they? Why wouldn't the unique products and services that they have developed have appeal outside their home countries? The competitive advantages that these companies offer have nothing to do with knowledge of local laws or, in most of their cases, with the personality or rainmaking capabilities of any particular lawyer or lawyers. Instead, their competitive advantages lie in their unique combinations of legal and non-legal expertise and in their unique processes and technology, all of which offer value independently of the country where a client is located.

In sum, the competitive advantages of these companies lie in their business models and the appeal of those models is not limited by borders. In this manner, by taking advantage of their respective home country's more liberal regulatory environment to develop unique goods and services and offer them outside their home countries, these companies have enormous advantages as well as a head start over anyone who might seek to compete with them but who are subject to more restrictive regulations in their own home countries. And this advantage is true not only in the home countries of their would-be competitors, but also in all countries. In other words, by modernizing their regulatory environments, England and Wales and Australia have in many respects opened up the global market for their home-grown legal service providers. At the same time, the United States (and other countries), in choosing to maintain a restrictive regulatory environment, are making it very difficult for their own legal services providers to access that same global market (not to mention their difficulties in accessing their own national market).

The third commonality of these companies is that they attract investment, create jobs and bring tax revenue to their home countries of England and Wales and of Australia. In many respects the manner by which they do so is obvious: the investments are made in English or Welsh and/or in Australian legal entities, the bulk (if not all) of the work is done by persons domiciled in England or Wales or in Australia, and/or income tax on any company profit is paid in England and Wales or in Australia.

But in other respects the benefits these companies bring to their home countries may be less obvious. For example, it would be natural to assume that most if not all of the jobs created would be jobs for lawyers. However, the examples of these companies demonstrate that jobs are equally created for specialists in strategy, management, IT, marketing, finance, accounting and human resources. Another example: by helping the Chinese investor to feel more comfortable with English legal matters, the ABS YangTze Law also helps the Chinese investor to feel more comfortable with investing in England more generally, encouraging the investor to invest in England instead of in another European or Western country.

In whatever respect it may be, the bottom line is that the liberal regulatory environments of England and Wales and of Australia work to attract investment, create jobs and generate tax revenue in ways that are difficult if not impossible in countries with more restrictive regulatory environments.

The fourth commonality of these companies is that their clientele is composed principally of large organizations—governmental agencies, corporations or other law firms (and, in some cases, wealthy or prominent individuals).

What is the significance of this commonality? Is it a coincidence that of these fourteen ABSs and ILPs serving clients overseas, all fourteen serve principally large organizations (and in some cases wealthy or prominent individuals) rather than ordinary individuals? Why should we care that this is the case?

We should care because the United States suffers from a huge unmet need for legal services—a need so great that some consider it to be a human rights crisis.[20]

While large organizations in the United States certainly do face challenges in obtaining legal services,[21] those challenges pale in comparison to those of lower and middle-income individuals (as well as small businesses and start-ups). It is the challenges they face that constitute the human rights crisis: This is reflected in the World Justice Project Rule of Law Index[22] which, on the question of affordable and accessible civil justice, ranks the United States 94th out of a total of 113 countries, and which, out of the regional group of North America and Western Europe, ranks the United States last (behind countries like Romania and Bulgaria).[23]

It would be tempting to see this commonality as proof that alternative structures do not improve access to justice—that instead they operate simply to produce more options for the part of the market that is already adequately served (large organizations), while doing little for the part of the market that is desperately underserved (low and middle-income individuals, small businesses and start-ups).

But the significance of this commonality is more complex than that. The complexity is this: The very reason that these fourteen companies are able to offer their goods and services to clients outside their home countries is because their clients principally are large organizations, rather than low and middle-income individuals or small businesses. That is because rules in those other countries restricting who may provide legal services are applied differently depending upon the identity of the client. In the United States in particular, we have carved out exceptions when the decision maker for the client is a licensed lawyer, either in a law firm or a member of an in-house legal department. This fact explains why companies like Axiom Law (legal placement and outsourcing), Lex Machina (legal data analytics), KCura (web-based e-discovery) and Anaqua (intellectual property asset management)—all US based—have been able prosper: because the decision-makers for their clients are, in most if not in all cases, lawyers.[24]

A number of ILPs in Australia and ABSs in England and Wales serve individuals and small businesses. Some operate as for-profit companies; others operate as not-for-profit or community interest companies. Examples of for-profit businesses include Australia's Shine Lawyers and Maurice Blackburn (both personal injury and consumer services), and the UK's Stephensons Solicitors (full service), Roberts Jackson (industrial diseases), Kings Court Trust (probate services), and BPIF Legal (legal needs of small businesses in printing and graphics industry). Examples of not-for-profit or community interest companies include Australia's Salvos Legal Humanitarian (range of services including family law, housing, social security and migration, all free of charge), and the UK's Aspire Law (spinal cord injuries, 50% of its profits are used to provide housing, funding and other support for people with spinal cord injury), as well as Castle Park Solicitors (family law and immigration, offered at a reduced charge to low-income clients). None of these companies may seek to expand their businesses to countries such as the United States, nor may their models be replicated in the United States, because their low and middle-income and small business clients do not have a lawyer intervening on their behalf.

In sum, the restrictive regulatory environment of the United States operates to completely shut out of its market companies like Shine Lawyers, Salvos Legal Humanitarian and Aspire Law (which serve individuals and small businesses), while merely restricting the activities of companies like Radiant and Riverview (which serve large organizations), without shutting them out completely.

This is a complex discussion—it requires a significant intellectual investment—one that many people are not willing to make. What is the bottom line?

The bottom line is that as long as the United States maintains its restrictive regulatory environment for legal services, the consequences will be twofold:

Firstly, companies like the fourteen listed above will continue to be created and to be active across the globe, including, for many of the companies, in the United States and for clients based in the United States. In doing so, they will continue to augment the variety and the accessibility of legal services for large companies, wealthy individuals and governmental organizations across the globe.

US-based law firms will need to compete with them. Some will succeed—especially large corporate firms with significant resources—but many others will find it difficult, both in the United States and in other countries, because of the inflexibility of US firms' singular business and service delivery model (partnership using the professional consultancy model to deliver legal services only), and because of their lack of access to resources such as investment capital and management and other kinds of expertise.

Secondly, and perhaps most importantly, low and middle-income individuals and small businesses in the United States will continue to suffer from lack of access to legal services. The restrictive regulatory framework will operate to severely limit not only the development of home-grown alternative business and service delivery models, but also the entry into the United States of foreign companies offering alternate models to low and middle-income individuals.

If the United States does not succeed in modernizing its regulatory environment for legal services, will it simply be left behind?

WHY THIS BOOK

The World Justice Project Rule of Law Index for 2016 ranks the United States 18th out of 113 countries on an overall basis. This is respectable, even if it is behind our common law sisters, the UK (10th), Australia (11th) and Canada (12th). These overall rankings are based upon nine factors, such as constraints on government powers, absence of corruption and openness of government. However, as mentioned above, when one element is singled out—affordable and accessible civil justice—the rank of the United States falls to 94th (yes, 94th) of 113.[25] This ranking is behind countries such as Albania, Belarus, Kyrgyzstan, Myanmar, Russia and Zimbabwe. To be clear—this means that the persons living in those countries have better access to civil justice than Americans do. In most if not all aspects of their lives, they are better able to learn their rights and obligations, and better able to assure their rights and obligations are respected. Let's repeat that list: Albania, Belarus, Kyrgyzstan, Myanmar, Russia and Zimbabwe.

By way of comparison, for this same element Australia ranks 42nd, Canada ranks 48th and the UK ranks 46th.[26] While these rankings are not stellar, they are a vast improvement over that of the United States. Given the similarities among the legal systems of the four countries, we would be missing a trick if we did not take a close look at how legal services in those countries are regulated. That is, if we didn't consider what elements of their governance make their systems, even if far from perfect, nevertheless so much better than ours when it comes to affordable and accessible civil justice.

A comprehensive examination of how legal services are regulated in each of these countries would require far more space than the pages of just one book, and it would likely cause eyes to glaze over. In an attempt to avoid that fate, this book selects just one topic, and examines how each of the four countries has dealt with just that topic. This approach allows for the countries to be compared and contrasted in a meaningful as well as focused manner.

The topic selected is that of alternative structures. This topic was not selected randomly. To the contrary, it was selected because it lends itself to this task in a way that few other topics do: It has recently been the subject of either actual or proposed regulatory reform in all four countries. As a (highly) controversial topic, it has received considerable media attention and a lot of information is publicly available. Finally, of all the recently adopted or proposed regulatory reforms with respect to legal services common to these four countries, many believe that alternative structures offer one of the most significant vehicles for addressing the shortfall (or, in the United States, the dearth) of affordable and accessible civil justice.[27] (Of course, as just stated, the topic is a controversial one and many lawyers are opposed to alternative structures. Their arguments are cited on various occasions throughout this book).

This examination will teach us what each country has done right, and what each has done wrong. We'll be able to discern patterns and commonalities, and learn which reform activities are productive and which are not. Most especially, by means of this focused examination, we'll gain insight into the regulatory environments of each country, and we'll understand what the consequences of those environments are.

This is a journey that we as a country must make. As mentioned above, the United States today is facing an unmet need for legal services so acute and widespread, it has been described as a human rights crisis. It would be absurd to suggest that there is just one, or even just a small number of "silver bullet" solutions to the crisis. To the contrary, actions are required at all levels, such as simplifying and streamlining court procedures, and the wider development of automation. But we cannot fool ourselves into believing that large, structural changes are not also required. We cannot fool ourselves into believing that the United States can solve its access to justice crisis in the absence of the modernization of its entire regulatory environment for legal services.

That is the essential purpose of this book: to shine a spotlight on the current regulatory environment for legal services in the United States. To understand what that environment is, and, as an important part that understanding, how it compares to the regulatory environments of other countries, our closest common law sisters.

While attaining this understanding has always been important, today it is especially so, in the context of the United Nations 2030 Agenda for Sustainable Development.[28] As a signatory of this document, the United States has committed to implement certain goals and targets by 2030, including these:

> Goal 16: Promote peaceful and inclusive societies for sustainable development, provide access to justice for all and build effective, accountable and inclusive institutions at all levels. …
>
> 16.3: Promote the rule of law at the national and international levels and *ensure equal access to justice for all.* …
>
> 16.6: *Develop effective, accountable and transparent institutions at all levels.*[29]

No one would argue that the availability of legal services is not an important component of ensuring equal access to justice for all.[30] No one would argue that the manner by which legal services are regulated does not have a direct bearing on the availability of legal services.[31]

With respect to the regulation of legal services in the United States, do we have effective, accountable and transparent institutions—the ones that are required in order to ensure equal access to justice for all? This book will demonstrate that we do not, not by a long shot. And that if we do not radically change—if we do not modernize—our regulatory environment in its entirety, it is highly doubtful that we ever will.

THE APPROACH OF THIS BOOK

This book begins, in part I, by setting the stage: What is the purpose of regulation generally, and what is the purpose of the regulation of legal services? Why are legal services regulated, who are the regulators, and with what instruments and methods do they regulate? What criteria will be used for comparing the four countries? The book continues, in parts II and III, with close examinations of England and Wales, on the one hand, and of Australia, on the other. Each examination first explores the institutions and processes (the regulatory environment) that led to the adoption of a new regulatory framework, describes the most salient aspects of the regulatory framework in place today, then gauges the current political environment surrounding the new regulatory framework, and, finally, discusses the additional reforms that are under consideration for the future.

Part IV takes a close look at Canada. First Nova Scotia, Manitoba and the other Prairie provinces, and British Columbia: a description of their relevant institutions, of how each province has approached its work, the progress each has made, and what remains to be done. This part then contrasts these provinces with the province of Ontario, which, after a false start, is following in their path: What explains the significant differences between Nova Scotia, Manitoba and British Columbia, on the one hand, and Ontario on the other? To what extent have the new (and still evolving) regulatory frameworks of England and Wales and Australia influenced the work being done in Canada?

Next, in part V, this book comes back to the United States. This part begins by exploring the historical context of the country's ban on the corporate practice of law and on the unauthorized practice of law more generally before exposing in detail each of the significant challenges that have been made (or might have been made) to the ban since the early 1980s. Then, this part examines three outliers: why and how the rules in Washington DC, Colorado, and Illinois are different. This part finishes with an explanation of the effect of Model Rule 5.4 and the current regulatory framework on the development of new models for the delivery of legal services in the United States.

Using the criteria established in part I, part VI makes a final assessment of the four countries and asks how the United States can modernize its regulatory environment for legal services. Part VI takes special care to distinguish the modernization of the country's regulatory environment (what is advocated in this book) from a very different concept: the privatization of regulation.

Finally, as part of my research for this book I interviewed a number of persons who either play or have played a significant role in the regulation of legal services in England and Wales, Australia, Canada or the United States. References to those interviews appear through this book. Excerpts from selected interviews are provided in the Appendix, together with information about how the interviews were conducted. Full versions of all the interviews are available online at *www.notjustforlawyers.com.* The interviews offer unique, first-hand insight into the outlook and approach of a modern (or a modernizing) regulator.

NOTES

1. "Law at the Speed of Reputation," Schillings, accessed on March 20, 2017, https://www.schillings.co.uk/our-approach.

2. "The Legal Innovation Awards 2015: Winners," The Legal Innovation Awards, accessed September 7, 2015, http://www.thelegalinnovationawards.com/ehome/index.php?eventid=188946&.

3. "Legal Week Innovation Awards: Celebrating Creative Excellence in the Legal Profession," May 27, 2016, http://www.thelegalinnovationawards.com/ehome/index.php?eventid=188946&.

4. "Mould Breaking Firm," Managing Partners' Forum Global, accessed on March 20, 2017, http://www.mpfglobal.com/awards/2015/Mould_Breaking_Firm.aspx.

5. "Most Innovative Client Service," Managing Partners' Forum Global, accessed March 20, 2017, http://www.mpfglobal.com/awards/2015/Most_innovative_client_service.aspx.

6. "The African Legal Awards 2015: The Shortlist," African Legal Awards, accessed September 11, 2015, http://www.africanlegalawards.com/static/2015-shortlist.

7. Karen Rosen, "Announcing the InnovAction Award 2013 Winners," College of Law Practice Management, August 15, 2013, http://collegeoflpm.org/announcing-the-innovaction-award-2013-winners/.

8. Neil Rose, Keystone Law Takes Private Equity Investment, *Legal Futures*, October 23, 2014, http://www.legalfutures.co.uk/latest-news/keystone-law-takes-private-equity-investment.

9. "The Legal Innovation Awards 2015: Winners," The Legal Innovation Awards, accessed September 7, 2015, http://www.thelegalinnovationawards.com/static/winners-2015.

10. Nick Hilborne, "International Insurance Group to Launch ABS for Corporate Clients," *Legal Futures*, January 29, 2015, http://www.legalfutures.co.uk/latest-news/international-insurance-group-launch-abs-corporate-clients.

11. "Irwin Mitchell Completes Seventh Acquisition as Expansion Continues," *Legal Futures*, July 2, 2015, http://www.legalfutures.co.uk/associate-news/irwin-mitchell-completes-seventh-acquisition-as-expansion-continues.

12. Lindsay Fortado, "Chinese-Owned Law Firm Seeks Deals in West with London Launch," *Financial Times*, May 31, 2015, http://www.ft.com/cms/s/0/e05e603e-077f-11e5-a58f-00144feabdc0.html#axzz3l4xbNHRH.

13. Neil Rose, "Unique ABS Aims to Capitalise on Push by Chinese Companies to Invest Overseas," *Legal Futures*, June 1, 2015, http://www.legalfutures.co.uk/latest-news/unique-abs-aims-to-capitalise-on-push-by-chinese-companies-to-invest-overseas.

14. Tom Moore, "Targeting London: Locke Lord Duo Depart to Launch Boutique Foran Glennon in the City," *Legal Business*, April 2, 2015, http://www.legalbusiness.co.uk/index.php/lb-blog-view/3926-targeting-london-locke-lord-duo-depart-to-launch-foran-glennon-in-the-city.

15. Nick Hilborne, "Exclusive: American ABS Considering Merger with Accountants, *Legal Futures*, June 12, 2015, http://www.legalfutures.co.uk/latest-news/exclusive-american-abs-considering-merger-with-accountants.

16. Dan Bindman, "ABS News: R&D Experts Plot Expansion, PI Firm Set to Launch Second ABS and Plans Third," Legal Futures, June 30, 2015, http://www.legalfutures.co.uk/latest-news/abs-news-rd-experts-plot-expansion-pi-firm-set-to-launch-second-abs-and-plan-third.

17. "About the RM Group," RM Online, accessed on March 17, 2017, http://www.rmonline.com/about-us.html.

18. "aRMadillo Mobile Application—World's First Company & Credit Report App!," RM Online, accessed March 20, 2017, http://www.rmonline.com/armadillo-app.html.

19. Dan Bindman, "Business Services Pioneer Launches ABS to Extend Offering to Clients," *Legal Futures*, September 18, 2015, http://www.legalfutures.co.uk/latest-news/business-services-pioneer-launches-abs-to-extend-offering-to-clients.

20. Carrie Johnson, "Rights Advocates See 'Access to Justice' Gap in U.S.," NPR, March 10, 2014, http://www.npr.org/sections/thetwo-way/2014/03/10/288225649/rights-advocates-see-access-to-justice-gap-in-u-s; see also Laura Snyder, *Democratizing Legal Services: Obstacles and Opportunities* (Lanham, Maryland: Lexington Books, 2016), 185–194.

21. Gillian Hadfield offers fascinating insight on the challenges that companies like Google, Mozilla and Cisco Systems face in obtaining legal services: Gillian Hadfield, "Legal Infrastructure and the New Economy," *I/S: A Journal of Law and Policy for the Information Society* 8 (2012): 1–59, http://ssrn.com/abstract=1567712.

22. The World Justice Project, *Rule of Law Index 2016*, 2016, 5, 144, http://worldjusticeproject.org/sites/default/files/media/roli_withcover.pdf.

23. The World Justice Project, *Rule of Law Index 2016*, http://worldjusticeproject.org/historical-data. This ranking is derived from the data (xls) that is available for download from the World Justice Project website.

24. Laura Snyder, "Does the UK Know Something We Don't About Alternative Business Structures?" *ABA Journal*, January 1, 2015, http://www.abajournal.com/magazine/article/does_the_uk_know_something_we_dont_about_alternative_business_structures"; Snyder, *Democratizing Legal Services*, 40–41.

25. The World Justice Project, *Rule of Law Index 2016*, http://worldjusticeproject.org/historical-data.

26. See Laura Snyder, "WJP Rule of Law Index: Rankings for Four Subfactors," *Not Just for Lawyers*, April 17, 2017, http://notjustforlawyers.com/wjp-rule-of-law-index-rankings/.

27. A number of persons have written on this topic, perhaps most notably Gillian Hadfield. See, for example: Gillian K. Hadfield, "The Cost of Law: Promoting Access to Justice through the (Un)Corporate Practice of Law," *International Review of Law and Economics* 38 (2014): 43–63, http://ssrn.com/abstract=2333990; Gillian K. Hadfield and Jamie Heine, "Life in the Law-Thick World: The Legal Resource Landscape for Ordinary Americans," USC CLASS Research Papers Series No. CLASS15–2; USC Law Legal Studies Paper No. 15–2, January 9, 2015, http://dx.doi.org/10.2139/ssrn.2547664; Gillian Hadfield, "Legal Barriers to Innovation: The Growing Economic Cost of Professional Control Over Corporate Legal Markets," *Stanford Law Review* 60 (2008): 101–146, http://ssrn.com/abstract=1104902. See also, for example, Renee Newman Knake, "Democratizing the Delivery of Legal Services," *Ohio State Law Journal* 73 (2012): 1–46, http://dx.doi.org/10.2139/ssrn.1800258; Edward S. Adams and John H. Matheson, "Law Firms on the Big Board?: A Proposal for Nonlawyer Investment in Law Firms," *California Law Review* 86 (1998): 1–40, http://scholarship.law.umn.edu/cgi/viewcontent.cgi?article=1100&context=faculty_articles; Thomas M. Gordon, "Comments on: Alternative Business Structures," May 31, 2011, http://www.americanbar.org/content/dam/aba/administrative/ethics_2020/ethics_20_20_comments/responsivelaw_issuespaperconcerningalternativebusiness-structures.authcheckdam.pdf; Thomas M. Gordon, "Comments on: Alternative Law Practice Structures," January 30, 2012, http://www.americanbar.org/content/dam/aba/administrative/ethics_2020/ethics_20_20_comments/responsivelaw_alpsdiscussion-draft.authcheckdam.pdf; Thomas Gordon, "Comments On: Issues Paper Regarding Alternative Business Structures," May 2, 2016, http://www.americanbar.org/content/dam/aba/images/office_president/responsive_law_abs.pdf; Laura Snyder, *Democratizing Legal Services*.

28. "UN Adopts New Global Goals, Charting Sustainable Development for People and Planet by 2030," United Nations News Centre, September 25, 2015, http://www.un.org/apps/news/story.asp?NewsID=51968#.Vgo773qqqko.

29. United Nations Summit for the Adoption of the Post-2015 Development Agenda, "Transforming Our World: The 2030 Agenda for Sustainable Development," October 21, 2015, 25–26, http://www.un.org/ga/search/view_doc.asp?symbol=A/RES/70/1&Lang=E (hereinafter, "Agenda for Sustainable Development").

30. Columbia Law School Human Rights Institute and Northeastern University School of Law Program on Human Rights and the Global Economy, "Equal

Access to Justice: Ensuring Meaningful Access to Counsel in Civil Cases, Including Immigration Proceedings—Response to the Seventh and Ninth Periodic Reports of the United States to the Committee on the Elimination of All Forms of Racial Discrimination," July, 2014, http://web.law.columbia.edu/sites/default/files/microsites/human-rights-institute/files/equal_access_to_justice_-_cerd_shadow_report.pdf; John Levi, "Civil Legal Aid: Ensuring Equal Access to Justice," Legal Services Corporation Blog, January 26, 2015, http://www.lsc.gov/media-center/blog/2015/01/26/civil-legal-aid-ensuring-equal-access-justice.

31. See, for example, Noel Semple, "Access to Justice: Is Legal Services Regulation Blocking the Path?" *International Journal of the Legal Profession*, 20 (2013): 267–283, http://scholar.uwindsor.ca/cgi/viewcontent.cgi?article=1004&context=lawpub.

Part I

REGULATION: WHY, WHAT, WHO AND HOW

This book examines in detail how certain elements of legal services are regulated in England and Wales, Australia, Canada and the United States. This part I sets the stage for that detailed examination by first exploring regulation more generally: What is its purpose, why does it matter, and, especially, what is required for good regulation? And then more specifically: Why and how are legal services regulated? Who are the regulators of legal services, and with what instruments and methods do they regulate?

As a comparative work, this book needs criteria for assessment. For this purpose, I have selected those of the Organization of Economic Cooperation and Development (OECD). The OECD has published extensively in the area regulatory policy and reform, including a number of publications identifying the essential elements of an effective regulatory policy. This part I, and especially chapter 1, draws heavily from these publications in order to establish six criteria for assessment.

Chapter 1

Good Regulation

What It Takes

A number of persons have offered explanations for the purpose of regulation.[1] Perhaps the most general and as well as succinct is this one: regulation is a "key lever of state power"[2] and a critical tool used by governments to shape the welfare of economies and societies.[3] The objective of regulation is to support economic growth and development as well as the achievement of broader societal objectives, such as social welfare, environmental sustainability and the respect of the rule of law.[4] Modern economies and societies need effective regulation for growth, investment, innovation, market openness, to support the rule of law and to promote better lives.[5] A poor regulatory environment undermines social welfare, business competitiveness and citizens' trust in government and it encourages corruption in public governance.[6]

This does not, however, mean that all regulation is good regulation. Sometimes the expected benefits do not manifest, in whole or in part. Sometimes the costs do not justify the benefits.[7] Sometimes (often) it's hard to adequately understand the full extent of a regulation's cost and/or benefits. It is because regulation can sometimes be bad regulation that the Organisation for Economic Co-operation and Development (OECD) promotes the importance for its member countries to develop a consistent and coherent regulatory policy, the objective of which is to ensure that the country's "regulatory lever" works effectively, and so that regulations and regulatory frameworks are in the public interest.

Based on OECD documents, six essential elements of an effective regulatory policy include (among other elements): (i) independent regulators who are free from conflicts of interest,[8] (ii) accountability and transparency in regulatory decision-making,[9] (iii) the placement of regulatory oversight bodies "at the center of government,"[10] (iv) making regulatory stakeholders, including businesses but also, notably, citizens and consumers, part of the regulatory process and paying attention to their voices;[11] (v) the use of evidence-based regulatory impact assessments[12] and (vi) the use of a risk-based approach to regulation.[13]

Let's look at each of these elements, in turn.

INDEPENDENCE

The OECD explains that regulators operate in a complex environment and their actions have repercussions for many different types of persons and organizations. In this context, regulators necessarily interact with a number of actors, and most notably with public authorities, members of the regulated industry and citizens. These interactions are inevitable and desirable[14] (indeed, as the discussion below regarding citizen engagement evidences, they are essential). At the core of independence, the OECD explains, is the balance between the appropriate—as opposed to the undue—influence that can be exercised through these interactions. For these reasons, regulators must behave and act objectively, impartially and consistently, without conflict of interest, bias or undue influence.[15] Regulators must act and make decisions in a manner that is disinterested and without regard for personal gain.[16] Independence means freedom from undue influence not only of governmental authorities (the executive as well as the legislature) but also from the regulated industry and from consumer groups and other special interest organizations. Regulators should act in the public interest, and undue influence from any of these actors makes regulation in the public interest very difficult, if not impossible.[17]

With respect to independence from governmental authorities, the OECD states that in certain situations there is a need for the regulatory agency to be seen as independent in order to maintain public confidence.[18] In those situations, regulators should have sufficient autonomy to conduct their functions without political interference from the executive or legislature. However, the long-term strategy and policy goals of the regulator should be in line with the broad strategic national priorities as set by elected representatives in the executive and legislature.[19] While there are different manners of protecting a regulator from undue political pressure or interference, some of the most important include requiring specific procedures and criteria for agency head and board appointments and dismissals,[20] autonomy in managing human and financial resources,[21] and setting clear and transparent boundaries on who does what and who is accountable to whom.[22]

The OECD explains that undue pressure can be exercised at different points in the life of a regulatory agency. For that reason, independence cannot be taken for granted, but must be translated into practice in a number of ways, most notably in the regulator's structure and in the way that the regulator attracts, motivates and retains staff.[23]

Further, regulators should engender an organizational culture that is "intolerant of conflicts of interest."[24] This is because public office is held as a trust, and a public servant's primary obligation is to the public interest. This means, the OECD explains, that the essence of public office is to uphold the general good above sectional interests. In relation to financial interests it is generally held that a public servant should not have any financial stake or relationship with the private corporations that he or she is responsible for regulating. Form and substance do matter: "public officials must be, *and clearly be seen to be*, independent of the interests they regulate."[25]

In sum, independence is an essential element of an effective regulatory policy. In this context, "independence" encompasses not only from public authorities but also from the regulated industry and other private interests.

ACCOUNTABILITY AND TRANSPARENCY

The OECD briefly defines accountability as the requirement for the regulator to report on set issues, usually backed by sanctions. Equally briefly, the OECD defines transparency as "the openness of process to external scrutiny."[26]

The United Nations Economic and Social Commission for Asia and the Pacific has offered more extensive explanations of these terms: Transparency means that: (i) decisions taken and their enforcement are done in a manner that follows rules and regulations, (ii) information is freely available and directly accessible to those who will be affected by such decisions and their enforcement, and (iii) enough information is provided and it is provided in easily understandable forms and media. As regards accountability, not only governmental institutions but also the private sector and civil society organizations must be accountable to the public and to their institutional stakeholders. In general, an organization or an institution is accountable to those who will be affected by its decisions or actions.[27]

The OECD explains that, in particular, independence must be tied to accountability. Regulators who are given significant power and autonomy in their operations and decision-making also need to be accountable to government and the legislature for the ways in which they have exercised that power. Strong accountability mechanisms for independent regulators, who are neither elected nor directly managed by elected officials, allow ministers and the legislature to assess whether the objectives set for them are being achieved efficiently and their powers exercised with integrity.[28]

The OECD observes that regulators are generally accountable to three groups of stakeholders: the minister and the legislature, regulated entities and the public. For each kind of stakeholder, specific principles for accountability and transparency apply. For example, with respect to the minister and the legislature, the expectations for each regulator should be clearly outlined by the appropriate oversight body (discussed below), and they should be published. Further, regulators should report to ministers or legislative oversight committees on all major measures and decisions and on a regular basis. With respect to regulated entities, regulators should establish and publish processes for arm's length internal review of significant delegated decisions. Finally, with respect to the public, all major decisions made by the regulator should be accompanied by publicly stated reasons.[29]

In sum, accountability is the flip—and essential—side of independence. At the same time, transparency and accountability go hand in hand, not the least because accountability requires transparency. Accountability also requires the next essential element of an effective regulatory policy under the OECD documents: regulatory oversight bodies.

REGULATORY OVERSIGHT BODIES

An OECD working paper explains that while regulation can solve social problems, it can also impose its own problems. For this reason, regulation requires effective oversight, in order to reduce the costs and side effects of regulation, promote efficiency in standard setting and instrument choice, encourage consistency and transparency, and improve the overall social outcomes of regulation. It is in this context that regulatory oversight bodies have become an integral part of reform programs in many countries, and, in doing so, have significantly affected the functioning of markets and governments.[30]

A regulatory oversight body (or a "regulator of regulators") commonly serves one or more four core functions, as follows: (i) coordination and supervision (the implementation and monitoring of a regulatory policy or initiative), (ii) training, advice and technical support (assisting regulators in improving the quality of their regulations), (iii) advocacy (helping to identify opportunities for reform and to support and argue for the development and progress of reform measures) and (iv) challenge and scrutiny (appraising, on technical grounds, the quality of the regulator's existing or new regulations and providing an opinion if not a veto on the regulator's proposed new regulations).[31]

The same working paper points out that the fourth function, challenge and scrutiny, is the most resented and controversial. At the same time, however, it is considered to be essential because at the core of the oversight concept is the idea that self-assessment and self-improvement by regulators are required but not sufficient to prepare high-quality regulations.[32]

An oversight body must be properly "located" among other public authorities.[33] In most cases, the best location is at the "center of government," be it the executive (most common), legislative or judicial branch. Such a location enables the oversight body to exercise its functions in a manner that is coherent with other regulatory policies. It also contributes to the credibility of the oversight body in assuring regulatory quality.[34]

The creation and growth of an oversight body will likely be met with resistance from different types of actors. Regulators may perceive it as reducing their levels of autonomy and discretion as well as instituting "confrontational" oversight and external control in an environment that prioritizes cooperative and consensual traditions. Further, regulatees (the individuals/organizations who are the subject of the regulation) can show a lack of enthusiasm for, if not outright opposition to regulatory oversight, because they perceive it a threat to "cozy" arrangements they may have with the regulator.[35] In other words, effective regulatory oversight can serve to end or at least diminish undue influence on the regulator, if not regulatory capture itself. From this perspective it would be rational for those exercising undue influence to object to the creation of a regulatory oversight body.

Given the nature of the functions of a regulatory oversight body, and especially given its function to challenge and scrutinize, it is difficult to imagine that it could escape criticism, if not from those claiming it is playing a "gatekeeping" role too zealously, then from those claiming it is not playing that same role zealously enough. Nevertheless, once an oversight body is established, no one (or nearly no one) calls for its abolishment. To the contrary, they are seen to function as an essential link between society's needs, political demand, and economic and social outcomes.[36] In sum, regulatory oversight bodies, warts and all, play a vital if not indispensable role in assuring effective regulatory policy.

CITIZEN ENGAGEMENT (OPEN AND INCLUSIVE POLICYMAKING)

One commentator has defined citizen engagement as all measures and/or institutional arrangements that link citizens more directly into the decision-making process of a State as to enable them to influence the public policies and programs in a manner that impact positively on their economic and social lives.[37] For the OECD, citizen engagement in the development, implementation and evaluation of regulatory policy is not just necessary but indispensable to the survival of open, democratic government.[38] This is because, the OECD explains, given the complexity and scale of emerging governance challenges, governments cannot hope to design effective policy responses, or to strengthen legitimacy and trust, without the input, ideas and insights of as wide a variety of citizens' voices as possible.[39] It is with that input, ideas and insight that two better regulatory outcomes are achieved: They are more responsive and equitable and better suited to diverse needs,[40] and trust and confidence in the regulatory process itself is improved.[41] Further, the OECD perceives citizen engagement as an essential element in the development of inclusive policy outcomes[42] (that is, of policies that promote economic growth and opportunities for all segments of the population and distribute the dividends of increased prosperity fairly across society[43]).

Canadian Donald G. Lenihan perhaps stated it the most bluntly:

> [E]ffective governance requires a new relationship between citizens, communities and stakeholders, on the one hand, and government, on the other. The basic reason is that many public goals—such as protecting the environment, ensuring safer streets, renewing the workforce, or building healthy communities—cannot be achieved by government alone. The public have a role to play. If they do not assume a new role in making choices, developing plans and taking action, goals such as these will not be achieved. *Public engagement therefore is not just desirable; it is a condition of effective governance.*[44] [emphasis in original]

In order for citizen engagement to succeed, it must, as mentioned above, include as wide a variety of citizen's voices as possible.[45] This means going beyond the highly selective and unrepresentative "usual suspects."[46] That is, this means going beyond highly resourced industry and other special interest groups to include all the stakeholders as well as those who have specific knowledge or expertise with respect to the subject at hand. Because many of those who are the "least equipped" for public participation are often those from whom input is important if not vital, the OECD states that policymakers must make extra efforts to reach out and ensure they are included.[47] Merely creating a "level playing field" which allows for passive access to information, consultation and participation is not enough because it will not result in the needed diversity of voices.[48]

In making those extra efforts, policymakers have to overcome the "many good reasons" that people have for not participating in policymaking. As one French commentator observed, "many people continue to perceive public authorities as distant from their concerns and do not dare imagine that their opinion, even if it is very personal or noninstitutional, could legitimately be heard in a public decisionmaking process."[49]

The OECD identifies two broad groups of persons who have "many good reasons" for not participating: On the one hand, there are those who are "willing but unable" to participate, for a variety of reasons, such as cultural or language barriers, geographical distance, disability or socioeconomic status.

On the other hand, there are those who are "unwilling but able" to participate, typically because they are not interested, they do not have the time, or they do not trust the policymakers to make good use of their input.[50] In the case of the former, the OECD states that policymakers must lower the barriers, such as making information multilingual. In the case of the latter, policymakers must make participation more attractive, such as by providing multiple channels for participation, including face-to-face, online and mobile options. Often, the OECD observes, people lack confidence in their knowledge and their ability to express themselves. In this context, the challenge for policymakers is to create an enabling environment which ensures people that they can participate if they want to. To this end, the OECD states, policymakers must build capacity, skills and knowledge to participate effectively.[51] Above all, policymakers must "go where the people are" when seeking to engage with them, rather than expecting people to come to them.[52]

There are obstacles to public engagement, and both resources and careful planning are required.[53] Nevertheless, the obstacles to successful citizen engagement must be overcome both in order to build open and democratic institutions and as a condition to effective governance.

EVIDENCE-BASED REGULATORY IMPACT ASSESSMENTS

Evidence-based regulatory impact assessments (RIA) has been defined in a number of ways, and those definitions continue to evolve. For our context, a useful definition is offered by Andrea Renda: a systemic approach to critically assessing the positive and negative effects of proposed and existing regulations and non-regulatory alternatives.[54]

For the OECD, RIA is important both as an administrative and decision-making tool and as a regulatory quality process that helps policymakers to design policies which are evidence based and fit-for-purpose. The process assists integrity and trust in the regulation-making system through levers of transparency and accountability by disclosing the historical design of the regulation. A well-functioning RIA system can assist in promoting policy coherence by making transparent the trade-offs inherent in regulatory proposals and by identifying who is likely to benefit from a given regulation. Further, RIA can reveal how risk reduction in one area may create risks for another area of government policy. RIA improves the use of evidence in policymaking and reduces the incidence of regulatory failure arising from regulation when there is no case for doing so, or failing to regulate when there is a clear need.[55]

RIA can be performed both prior to (ex ante) the adoption of regulation and after a period of time subsequent to its adoption (ex post). As Renda explains, the key steps for an ex ante RIA include defining the problem, identifying alternative options (such as self- and co-regulation), collecting data, assessing alternative options (including "no change"), identifying the preferred policy option (which should be the subject of a more in-depth assessments, notably a quantitative one), and monitoring and evaluating over time.[56]

As regards ex post RIAs, the OECD explains that it is only after implantation that the effects and impacts of regulations can be fully assessed, including direct and indirect incidences and unintended consequences. Regulations may also become outdated as result of a change in societal preferences or technological advancement. Consequently, regular reviews are needed to ensure that regulations are still necessary, relevant and fit-for-purpose.[57]

The OECD further explains that different approaches can be used in conducting ex post RIAs. A common approach is to base them on a single principal, such as to promote competition or to reduce regulatory burdens. In addition, the OECD recommends that they be used even more strategically and systematically, by conducting comprehensive reviews that assess the cumulative impact of laws and regulations in a sector as a whole, with a particular focus on the policy outcomes. This could entail, the OECD points out, "*the evaluation of an entire regulatory framework*"[58] (emphasis added).

The benefits of RIAs are not automatic. For example, an RIA that is designed to stress economic benefits or efficiency may create tension if the regulation's underlying objectives are not primarily economic.[59] Further, some costs as well as benefits are difficult to identify and to measure, and those responsible for conducting the RIA may lack the time and resources to fully address them. The factors that are easier to identify and measure may be given undue precedence over those that are difficult. The regulated industry may offer its own information in its place, but this information may be subject to bias. If care is not taken, the end result may be that the public interest is not sufficiently taken into account.[60]

In sum, RIAs oblige the regulator to conduct fact-based, empirical research in order to justify the adoption, the amendment, the revocation and, in many cases, the mere maintenance, of any one or more regulations, if not an entire regulatory framework. In order to do this, the regulator must involve a wide range of stakeholders—including those with traditionally low rates of participation in customary consultation processes—and proceed in an unbiased, accountable and fully transparent manner.

A RISK-BASED APPROACH

While the concept of a risk-based approach to regulation has been described in a variety of manners,[61] the most salient for our purposes is the one offered by Julia Black: it is the use of "systematized frameworks of supervision or inspection" which are primarily designed to manage regulatory or institutional risk, and notably risks to the regulatory agency itself that it will not achieve its objectives. Risk-based regulation involves the development of decision-making frameworks and procedures to prioritize regulatory activities and deploy resources, based upon an assessment of the risks that regulated firms pose to the regulator's objectives.

Importantly, risk-based regulation is *not* focused on the potential risks that individuals or firms may present to their customers, to the public or to the economy. Instead, risk-based regulation is focused on the risks the regulator faces in failing to achieve its objectives. In this context, risk-based regulation requires the regulator to define its regulatory objectives[62] (the risks "to what" it is concerned to control[63]) and to translate its statutory mandates into operational objectives (this, in turn, requires clear statutory objectives for the regulator[64]). In doing so, the regulator establishes a means to identify what matters to it and what does not, and, on that basis, how it should allocate its necessarily limited resources. In sum, Black explains: the key element of risk-based frameworks for allocating resources is that the starting point is risks not rules. Risk-based frameworks require regulators to begin by identifying the risks that it is seeking to manage, not the rules it has to enforce.[65]

One kind of risk-based regulation is referred to as "management-based regulation." Its underlying concept is to deploy regulatory authority in a way that leverages the private sector's knowledge about its particular circumstances and engages firms in developing their own internal procedures and monitoring practices that respond to risks.[66] Under management-based regulation, firms are not mandated to adopt specific risk protection technologies or practices. Instead, firms are mandated to study their operations comprehensively and develop their own management strategies and plans suited to the risks they identify in their operations. Unlike traditional forms of regulation that treat a firm as a "black box"—with the regulator not particularly caring what goes on inside as long as the firm uses the means prescribed by the regulator, management-based regulation "seeks to shape the actual operations of a firm, imposing requirements for systematic planning with respect to public risks and the adoption of internal procedures, training and management practices."[67]

A risk-based approach to regulation explicitly acknowledges that it is not possible to regulate to remove all risks and that regulatory action, when taken, should be proportionate, targeted and based on an assessment of the nature and magnitude of the risks and of the likelihood that regulation will be successful in achieving its aims.[68]

With a risk-based approach, the regulator must be willing to take risks, including the risk of erring, which the regulator is bound to do.[69] On the one hand, the risk of error may lie on the side of caution, in that the regulator assumes something is riskier than it actually is. On the other hand, the risk of error may lie on the side of risk, in that the regulator assumes something is safer than it actually is. The regulator must determine its risk appetite—that is, the types of risks it is prepared to tolerate and at what level.[70] As Black explains, the higher the political salience (that is, its prominence or visibility) is the lower will be the regulator's tolerance of failure in that area. As a result, the regulator may allocate resources not where its risk model says it should, but rather where there is the most political sensitivity.[71]

No one would claim that risk-based regulation is infallible.[72] This fact does not make it any less an essential element of an effective regulatory policy.

CONCLUSION

In this chapter, we have seen that while regulation is necessary to protect and shape the welfare of economies and societies, not all regulation is good regulation. For this reason, the OECD promotes the importance for each country to develop a consistent and coherent regulatory policy, the objective of which is to ensure that the country's "regulatory lever" works effectively, so that regulations and regulatory frameworks are in the public interest.

For the OECD, an effective regulatory policy includes these six essential elements (among other elements): (i) independent regulators who are free from conflicts of interest (ii) accountability and transparency in regulatory decision-making, (iii) the placement of regulatory oversight bodies "at the center of government," (iv) making regulatory stakeholders, including businesses but also, notably, citizens and consumers, part of the regulatory process and paying attention to their voices; (v) the use of evidence-based RIAs, both before and after adoption and (vi) the use of a risk-based approach to regulation.

These elements are the criteria we will use in our detailed examination of how legal services are regulated in England and Wales, Australia, Canada and the United States. More specifically, these are the criteria we will use to compare and assess their respective regulatory environments.

However, before moving on to that examination, we'll first explore regulation in another manner: the specific context of legal services.

NOTES

1. See, for example, Robert Baldwin, Martin Cave and Martin Lodge, *Understanding Regulation: Theory, Strategy and Practice* (Toronto: Oxford University Press, 2011), 15–24, https://webcampus.unamur.be/claroline/backends/download.php?url=

L0EuX0Rlc21ldF9fMV9CYWxkd2luXyZhbXA7X2NvX1VuZGVyc3RhbmRpbmdf cmVndWxhdGlvbi0xLnBkZg%3D%3D&cidReset=true&cidReq=ECONM864.

2. OECD, “Regulatory Policy and the Road to Sustainable Growth,” 2010, 5, https://www.oecd.org/regreform/policyconference/46270065.pdf (hereinafter “OECD Road to Sustainable Growth”).

3. OECD CleanGovBiz, “Regulatory Policy: Improving Governance,” July, 2012, 3, http://www.oecd.org/cleangovbiz/toolkit/49256979.pdf.

4. Ibid.

5. OECD, *Regulatory Policy and Governance: Supporting Economic Growth and Serving the Public Interest* (Paris: OECD Publishing, 2011), 15, http://www.oecd.org/gov/regulatory-policy/regulatorypolicyandgovernancesupportingeconomicgrowthandservingthepublicinterest.htm (hereinafter “OECD Supporting the Public Interest”).

6. David Parker and Colin Kirkpatrick, “Measuring Regulatory Performance – The Economic Impact of Regulatory Policy: A Literature Review of Quantitative Evidence,” OECD Expert Paper No.3, August, 2012, 9, https://www.oecd.org/gov/regulatory-policy/3_Kirkpatrick%20Parker%20web.pdf; OECD Road to Sustainable Growth, 7.

7. Parker and Kirkpatrick, “Measuring Regulatory Performance,” 9.

8. OECD Supporting the Public Interest, 9; Parker and Kirkpatrick,”Measuring Regulatory Performance,” 11.

9. Parker and Kirkpatrick, “Measuring Regulatory Performance,” 11; OECD CleanGovBiz, “Regulatory Policy,” 3–4, 6–7.

10. Parker and Kirkpatrick, “Measuring Regulatory Performance,” 11; OECD CleanGovBiz, “Regulatory Policy,” 6–7.

11. Parker and Kirkpatrick, “Measuring Regulatory Performance,” 11; OECD CleanGovBiz, “Regulatory Policy,” 4,6; OECD Road to Sustainable Growth, 39–40.

12. Parker and Kirkpatrick, “Measuring Regulatory Performance,” 11, 27–32; OECD CleanGovBiz, “Regulatory Policy,” 6; OECD Road to Sustainable Growth, 3, 8.

13. Parker and Kirkpatrick, “Measuring Regulatory Performance,” 11; OECD CleanGovBiz, “Regulatory Policy,” 14; See generally OECD, *Risk and Regulatory Policy: Improving the Governance of Risk* (Paris: OECD Publishing, 2010), http://dx.doi.org/10.1787/9789264082939-en (hereinafter “OECD Risk and Regulatory Policy”).

14. OECD, *Being an Independent Regulator* (Paris: OECD Publishing, 2016), 3, http://dx.doi.org/10.1787/9789264255401-en (hereinafter “OECD Being an Independent”).

15. Ibid.

16. OECD, *Managing Conflict of Interest in the Public Service: OECD Guidelines and Overview* (Paris: OECD Publishing, 2003), 25, http://www.oecd.org/corruption/ethics/48994419.pdf, (hereinafter “OECD Managing Conflict of Interest”); OECD Public Governance And Territorial Development Directorate Public Governance Committee, “Revolving Doors, Accountability and Transparency—Emerging Regulatory Concerns and Policy Solutions in the Financial Crisis,” Expert Group on Conflict of Interest Discussion Paper, May 5, 2009, 10, http://www.oecd.org/officialdocuments/publicdisplaydocumentpdf/?cote=GOV/PGC/ETH(2009)2&docLanguage=En (hereinafter, “OECD Revolving Doors”).

17. OECD Revolving Doors, 50. Scott Hempling emphasizes that regulators must not see their role as balancing competing interests To the contrary, the regulator's mission is to protect and promote the public interest, and an important part of the regulator's job is to be able to identify when the interests of certain actors (public authorities, members of the regulated industry, even consumer groups) deviates from the public interest, in spite of their arguments to the contrary. Scott Hempling, *Preside or Lead? The Attributes and Actions of Effective Regulators* (Silver Spring, MD: Scott Hempling Attorney at Law LLC, 2013), 51–54.

18. OECD Supporting the Public Interest, 84.

19. OECD Being an Independent, 41.

20. OECD Being an Independent, 17; OECD, *The Governance of Regulators* (Paris: OECD Publishing, Paris, 2014), 60–61, http://dx.doi.org/10.1787/9789264209015-en (hereinafter "OECD The Governance of Regulators").

21. OECD Being an Independent, 18, 44.

22. OECD Being an Independent, 18.

23. OECD Being an Independent, 4.

24. OECD Managing Conflict of Interest, 27; OECD Revolving Doors, 10.

25. OECD Revolving Doors, 50.

26. OECD, Regulatory Policy in Perspective: A Reader's Companion to the OECD Regulatory Policy Outlook 2015 (Paris: OECD Publishing, 2015), 25, http://dx.doi.org/10.1787/9789264241800-en (hereinafter "OECD Reader's Companion"). But also see Christopher Carrigan, "Captured by Disaster? Reinterpreting Regulatory Behavior in the Shadow of the Gulf Oil Spill," in *Preventing Regulatory Capture: Special Interest Influence and How to Limit It*, ed. Daniel Carpenter and David A. Moss (New York: Cambridge University Press, 2014), 239–291.

27. United Nations Economic and Social Commission for Asia and the Pacific, "What is Good Governance?" 2009, http://www.unescap.org/sites/default/files/good-governance.pdf.

28. OECD The Governance of Regulators, 51.

29. Ibid., 80.

30. Cesar Cordova-Novion and Stéphane Jacobzone, "Strengthening the Institutional Setting for Regulatory Reform: The Experience from OECD Countries," OECD Working Papers on Public Governance, No. 19, OECD Publishing, 2011, 7, http://dx.doi.org/10.1787/5kgglrpvcpth-en.

31. Ibid., 9–12.

32. Ibid., 11.

33. Ibid., 21.

34. Ibid., 38–39, 49.

35. Ibid., 13–14.

36. Ibid., 48.

37. Jocelyne Bourgon, "Why Should Governments Engage Citizens in Service Delivery and Policy Making?" in *Focus on Citizens: Public Engagement for Better Policy and Services*, OECD Studies on Public Engagement (Paris: OECD Publishing, 2009), 201, http://www19.iadb.org/intal/intalcdi/pe/2009/03785.pdf.

38. OECD Studies on Public Engagement, *Focus on Citizens: Public Engagement for Better Policy and Services* (Paris: OECD Publishing, 2009), 13, 22,

http://www19.iadb.org/intal/intalcdi/pe/2009/03785.pdf (hereinafter, "OECD Studies on Public Engagement").

39. Ibid., 24; OECD Post-2015, "Building More Effective, Accountable, and Inclusive Institutions for All," Element 6, Paper 1, n.d., 3–4, http://www.oecd.org/dac/_POST-2015%20effective%20and%20accountable%20institutions.pdf (hereinafter "OECD Post-2015").

40. OECD Post-2015, 2.

41. OECD Studies on Public Engagement, 13; OECD Initiative on Inclusive Growth, *All On Board: Making Inclusive Growth Happen* (Paris: OECD Publishing, 2014), 162, 174, https://www.oecd.org/inclusive-growth/All-on-Board-Making-Inclusive-Growth-Happen.pdf (hereinafter "OECD Initiative on Inclusive Growth").

42. OECD Initiative on Inclusive Growth, 162.

43. OECD Initiative on Inclusive Growth, 80.

44. Donald G. Lenihan, "Public Engagement Is a Must in a Multi-Stakeholder World," in *Focus on Citizens: Public Engagement for Better Policy and Services*, OECD Studies on Public Engagement (Paris: OECD Publishing, 2009), 208, http://www19.iadb.org/intal/intalcdi/pe/2009/03785.pdf.

45. OECD Studies on Public Engagement, 13; OECD Initiative on Inclusive Growth, 162.

46. OECD Studies on Public Engagement, 14; Archon Fung, "Participate, but Do so Pragmatically," in *Focus on Citizens: Public Engagement for Better Policy and Services*, OECD Studies on Public Engagement (Paris: OECD Publishing, 2009), 228, http://www19.iadb.org/intal/intalcdi/pe/2009/03785.pdf.

47. OECD Studies on Public Engagement, 14.

48. OECD Studies on Public Engagement, 46; OECD Initiative on Inclusive Growth, 175.

49. OECD Studies on Public Engagement, 50.

50. Ibid., 14.

51. Ibid., 49.

52. Ibid., 14, 46–54.

53. Ibid., 15; Edward Andersson and Richard Wilson, "Globalised Democracy," in *Focus on Citizens: Public Engagement for Better Policy and Services*, OECD Studies on Public Engagement (Paris: OECD Publishing, 2009), 302, http://www19.iadb.org/intal/intalcdi/pe/2009/03785.pdf.

54. Andrea Renda, "Regulatory Impact Assessment and Regulatory Policy," in Regulatory Policy in Perspective: A Reader's Companion to the OECD Regulatory Policy Outlook 2015, OECD (Paris: OECD Publishing, 2015), 36, http://dx.doi.org/10.1787/9789264241800-en.

55. OECD, *OECD Regulatory Policy Outlook 2015* (Paris: OECD Publishing, 2015), 96, http://dx.doi.org/10.1787/9789264238770-en (hereinafter "OECD Regulatory Policy Outlook").

56. Renda, "Regulatory Impact Assessment," 36–37.

57. OECD Regulatory Policy Outlook, 120.

58. Ibid.

59. Baldwin, Cave and Lodge, *Understanding Regulation*, 320.

60. Ibid., 322–323; see also James Goodwin, "Racism, Cost-Benefit Analysis, and Trump Advisor Steve Bannon," *CPR Blog*, November 29, 2016, http://www.progressivereform.org/CPRBlog.cfm?idBlog=BD292079-CA1F-3304-A41D96F4C6D2A68F.

61. See, for example, Baldwin, Cave and Lodge, *Understanding Regulation*, 281–283.

62. Julia Black, "Risk-Based Regulation: Choices, Practices and Lessons Being Learnt," in *Risk and Regulatory Policy: Improving the Governance of Risk*, OECD (Paris: OECD Publishing, 2010), 187–188, http://dx.doi.org/10.1787/9789264082939-en.

63. Julia Black and Robert Baldwin, "Really Responsive Risk-Based Regulation," *Law & Policy* 32 (2010): 184, http://ssrn.com/abstract=1571808.

64. Black, "Risk-Based Regulation," 187–188, 194.

65. Ibid., 190.

66. Cary Coglianese, "Management-Based Regulation: Implications for Public Policy," in *Risk and Regulatory Policy: Improving the Governance of Risk*, OECD (Paris: OECD Publishing, 2010), 159, http://dx.doi.org/10.1787/9789264082939-en.

67. Ibid, 170.

68. OECD Risk and Regulatory Policy, 16.

69. Black, "Risk-Based Regulation," 186, 193.

70. Ibid., 190.

71. Ibid., 194; Black and Baldwin, "Really Responsive," 184. The public often demonstrates a willingness to accept certain risks, especially when the benefits to accepting them are well understood. At the same time, however, the public as well as regulators themselves often demonstrate a tendency to overestimate events associated with lower-probability events, such as botulism and floods, and to underestimate the risks associated with higher-probability events, such as the risk of being killed in a car accident, or risks of cancer, heart disease and stroke. This can lead to regulators making decisions on the basis of biased perceptions rather than the best available estimates of the true level of risk. In this manner, public perceptions influence the regulator, who in then influences public perceptions, leading to what now US Supreme Court Justice Stephen Breyer has termed a "vicious circle." For this reason, Breyer has argued in favor of "depoliticizing" the regulatory process in order to break this circle, notably by creating an independent super agency that would build a coherent risk-regulating system adaptable to different risk-related programs. OECD Risk and Regulatory Policy 96, 121–122. See also Stephen Breyer, *Breaking the Vicious Circle: Toward Effective Risk Regulation* (Cambridge, Massachusetts: Harvard University Press, 1993).

72. Baldwin, Cave and Lodge take a highly cautious approach to risk-based regulation, stating that, among other dangers, it can cause regulators to focus on certain firms to the neglect of others and that is can be difficult to apply effectively if regulatory authority is shared among different bodies. Baldwin, Cave and Lodge, *Understanding Regulation*, 284, 287.

Chapter 2

The Regulation of Legal Services

As discussed in chapter 1, not all regulation is good regulation. Further, and as OECD documentation points out, sometimes it is better not to regulate a given activity than it is to regulate it. If, as stated in chapter 1, the objective of regulation is to support economic growth and development as well as the achievement of broader societal objectives, in certain situations regulation might not be the most appropriate means to meet that objective. From this perspective, the decision to regulate or to otherwise intervene with respect to any given activity should be well considered and based upon explicit evidence that regulation or other intervention is justified.[1]

Further, once the conclusion is made that intervention of some kind is warranted, the OECD recommends that a wide range of options be taken into account.[2] That is, in addition to "traditional command and control" regulation, that alternative policy instruments also be considered. Such instruments can include, the OECD specifies, co-regulation and self-regulation, incentive and market-based instruments (the use of taxes and/or subsidies), and simple information and guidance.[3] The choice of the right instrument(s) is important, the OECD explains, because the use of an inferior policy instrument may have significant implications for competition, economic performance and may be less effective in meeting wider social objectives.[4]

It is in this context that this chapter examines the regulation of legal services. More specifically, this chapter examines firstly the rationale for the regulation of legal services and secondly the rationale for the manner in which lawyers have traditionally been regulated in common law countries and continue to be regulated in the United States today.

WHY REGULATE LEGAL SERVICES?

Many (many) have offered rationales for the need to regulate legal services.[5] In his book *Legal Services at the Crossroads: Justitia's Legions*, Noel Semple provides a useful synthesis as well as categorization of those various—but nevertheless consistent—rationales:[6]

Rationale Number 1: Legal services must be regulated in order to protect the interests of clients. Semple begins by explaining that in certain respects legal services are not significantly different from other goods or services, in that it is in the client's (or consumer's) interest to have higher quality, lower price and greater choice. However, Semple continues, legal services offer a greater potential for market failure, and thus require regulation, because information asymmetry renders consumers unable to protect their own interests. Asymmetry exists because lawyers are in a better position than most consumers are to judge the value of their services. Most consumers are unable to judge their need for legal services, to evaluate the quality of the alternatives available to them, even to judge quality after purchase. Further, often legal services are purchased during times of great personal stress, making it even more difficult for the consumer to protect his/her interests. For these reasons, clients must trust their legal services provider. If not, they will not purchase the services and their needs for legal services will not be met.[7] While regulation may not guarantee trust, it can, at least arguably, foster it.

Rationale Number 2: Legal services must be regulated in order to protect third parties from bad legal services. Semple explains that deficient legal services can harm not only the client, but also third parties. A classic example is a deficient will, which might not harm the client at all, but could subject the will's beneficiaries to painful and expensive years of personal strife. Another example is opposing parties in litigation: an overzealous lawyer could cause the opposing party to expend unjustified amounts in time and energy to defend itself, and could also result in a malfunctioning of the court.[8]

Rationale Number 3: Legal services must be regulated to assure good legal services because good legal services can benefit the public as a whole. This rationale is more esoteric in its explanation but is no more or less compelling than the previous two. According to this rationale, in a common law legal system, good legal services (or, at least, good lawyering) increases the quality of legal arguments and, subsequently, of the law itself. It also can work to reduce the incidence of fraud and other crimes, because lawyers can be (and, by regulation, are) prevented from assisting clients with fraudulent or other criminal behavior.[9]

In addition to these three commonly cited rationales, Semple also mentions a few more. For example, Stephen Mayson argues that there is a "values-based or moral foundation" for the regulation of legal services. More specifically, protecting the "democratic fabric of society" and facilitating societal rights and participation are reasons to regulate. Additionally, Alice Woolley argues that regulation is justified in order to assure that lawyers fulfill their special public role of counseling, dispute resolution and preventing miscarriages of justice. If these roles are not fulfilled or are fulfilled negligently, "the pluralist compromise of democracy" itself is put at risk.[10]

To be clear, while there is considerable consistency in these rationales offered in support of regulation of legal services, not everyone agrees with them. One vocal critic is Benjamin Barton. He argues that neither information asymmetry nor irremediable harms are present in most areas of legal practice.[11] For this reason, he states, regulation is appropriate only for those limited "sub-sections" of the market (such as criminal matters) where these problems are more likely to exist, rather than for the legal market as a whole.[12] Further, Barton accords, courts have a legitimate need for competent practitioners who know how to efficiently and effectively shepherd cases through procedural and conceptual hurdles, thus limited, specifically tailored regulation for that purpose is also appropriate.[13] However, beyond those purposes, Barton argues, regulation of legal services is neither needed nor appropriate. In particular, he emphasizes that maintaining lawyers' status as "professionals" (that is, as he explains, "to perpetuate or raise the social or economic status of the group as a profession") cannot justify the costs associated with regulatory entry barriers.[14]

WHY SELF-REGULATION?

Having exposed, in summary form, the rationales most commonly offered for the regulation of legal services, the next question is how are legal services traditionally regulated (using the word of the OECD, what "instrument"[15] is used), and why?

Over the course of the late 19th and early 20th centuries, the bars (that is, the population of lawyers) in most (if not all) common law countries had achieved self-regulation in one form or another.

In the United States today, the extent to which the legal profession is, in fact, self-regulated, is a subject of academic dispute.[16] Those that see a self-regulated profession point to the facts that:

- State supreme courts, who have the authority to adopt rules of professional conduct and the responsibility to enforce discipline, are made up of lawyers,[17]
- Most state supreme courts adopt the Model Rules of Professional Conduct promulgated and amended from time to time by the American Bar

Association (ABA) with limited and, in many cases, no modifications. In this manner, the ABA, a voluntary association of practicing lawyers, plays a key role in the regulation of the legal profession. (Further, to the extent the rules are adopted with modifications, those modifications are generated by the state and local bar associations and other groups of practicing attorneys rather than by the state supreme courts themselves).
- State supreme courts have delegated disciplinary enforcement to bodies that are also made up of lawyers. And, most notably, in twenty-one states the supreme court has delegated disciplinary authority to a state bar association whose members are practicing lawyers and that exercises both representative and regulatory functions.[18]

On the other hand, those that do not see a self-regulated profession point to the facts that:

- While the members of state supreme courts are lawyers, they are not practicing attorneys. They have the authority to make decisions in a manner that is independent of national and state bar associations. While state supreme courts (usually after consultation with the ABA via the Conference of Chief Justices and with state and local bar associations) often adopt the ABA's Model Rules and while they often delegate disciplinary authority to a state bar association, there is no legal requirement that they do either, and they may at any time stop doing so, and
- Other bodies have exercised authority over the legal profession. Examples include the US Supreme Court (such as by striking down bans on attorney advertising), federal regulatory authorities, such as the Federal Trade Commission (FTC) and the Securities and Exchange Commission (SEC), and Congress (most notably with Sarbanes-Oxley).

The debate in academia over whether or not the legal profession in the United States is or is not self-regulated may never be resolved. Outside of academia, however, by all appearances the debate has been long resolved. Most notably, the Preamble to the ABA's Model Rules of Professional Conduct makes reference to self-regulation or self-governance no fewer than four times, including the phrases "The legal profession is largely self-governing," and "The legal profession's relative autonomy carries with it special responsibilities of self-government. The profession has a responsibility to assure that *its* regulations are conceived in the public interest and not in furtherance of parochial or self-interested concerns of the bar" [emphasis added].[19]

Certainly persons who have played key roles with the ABA have perceived those roles to be regulatory in nature. The most telling, perhaps, are comments made by Andrew Perlman, the vice-chair of the ABA's Commission on the Future of Legal Services. In April, 2016, a few months before the Commission issued its final report, he was asked "whether the commission is looking at regulating e-discovery companies and other companies that provide products and services to the legal industry."[20] In responding, Perlman did not challenge the characterization of the commission's activities as "regulating." To the contrary, he reinforced it, stating: "It was not intended to address and we never even discussed regulating the entire legal technology industry. That's much broader than anything that's ever been discussed." As well as: "Probably the most common concern raised so far is the breadth of the regulatory opportunities being considered. . . . I wanted to take this opportunity to allay some of those concerns. We are not thinking about regulating the entire legal tech industry."[21]

Taking both the Preamble to the Model Rules and Perlman at their word (that is, that in the United States the legal profession is self-regulated to a certain if not to a great extent), then the question becomes, of the different kinds of regulation that are possible, why is the legal profession self-regulating? Why has this traditionally been the case in most if not all common law countries, and why is it still the case in the United States today?

The Preamble offers a beginning of a response. It states:

> To the extent that lawyers meet the obligations of their professional calling, the occasion for government regulation is obviated. Self-regulation also helps maintain the legal profession's independence from government domination. An independent legal profession is an important force in preserving government under law, for abuse of legal authority is more readily challenged by a profession whose members are not dependent on government for the right to practice.[22]

In essence, this paragraph states, self-regulation is important to preserve the independence of the legal profession from the influence of the government—that is, from political pressure. If a lawyer is dependent upon a government-controlled entity to have the right to practice, this argument continues, that lawyer is less likely to challenge that government when it should be challenged, thus undermining the rule of law, if not democracy itself.[23]

But, again, this is just a beginning of a response to the question of why the legal profession is self-regulated. Indeed, in addition to the Preamble's relatively practical and succinct explanation, a number of commentators have offered additional explanations, some of which are more theoretical, multifaceted and considerably less succinct. Here are three of the more commonly cited:

1. Efficiency: According to this explanation for self-regulation, there is information asymmetry not only between lawyers and consumers, but also between lawyers and regulators. That is, there is a cost for external regulation by a governmental agency to acquire the information it needs

to regulate.[24] This is particularly the case with respect to the information it needs to regulate questions of quality: members of the legal profession are in a better position to observe the quality supplied by other members more easily and at a lower cost.[25] As Camille Chaserant and Sophie Harnay argue:

> Self-regulation may help to achieve high quality in the market for legal services when the collective rent accruing to the legal profession grants lawyers with high-powered incentives to build and maintain a good collective reputation and, therefore, to supply high quality in a market where clients are unable to detect cheating.[26]

In sum, according to this explanation, lawyers know better than anyone else about how they should be regulated, and they are in a better position than anyone else to actually exercise that regulation. For this reason, regulation by anyone else is inefficient and does not make sense.[27]

2. Contract: According to this explanation for self-regulation—most commonly ascribed to Alan Paterson—self-regulation is an element of the "professionalism contract." More specifically, Paterson explains, the nature of professionalism, at least in its "traditional model," is that it carries certain obligations for the profession in exchange for which it also provides to them certain benefits. The obligations that it carries include competence (or expertise), a service ethic, public protection and access. In counterpart, the profession is accorded status, "reasonable rewards," restricted competition and autonomy (or self-regulation).[28] Seen from this perspective, self-regulation is an integral if not essential element of what it means to exercise a profession. Put another way, without autonomy (or self-regulation), there is no profession.
3. A Means to Control the Market: Commonly ascribed to Richard Abel, this explanation for self-regulation is a cynical, if not mercenary, twist on the contract explanation. According to this explanation, controlling the market is an essential element of professionalism, and self-regulation is a key means of that control. More specifically, self-regulation allows the legal profession "to control of the production of and by the producers."[29] This control includes both the supply side (as in who offers legal services and how they do so) and the demand side (such as how legal services may be advertised or solicited, and the extent to which pro bono work is encouraged).[30] In the words of Abel, "from a structural perspective, a profession must seek to control its market or else commit collective suicide."[31] In sum, for Abel, even if self-regulation does not enable the profession to achieve a perfect or total control over the market,[32] it nevertheless enables it to achieve some, and for that reason self-regulation is essential to the survival of the legal profession.

For Abel, the ABA's Model Rules of Professional Conduct are a crucial means by which the legal profession exercises self-regulation, and, in doing so, market control. Of course, he clarifies, this is not and cannot be the declared purpose of the Rules. Further, it is a latent, not a manifest function of them. Specific Model Rules that operate for this purpose include, for example, those that define conflicts of interest (while they have an ethical purpose, they also serve to spread business among lawyers and limit the capacity of firms to concentrate business), and restrictions on how lawyers may advertise and otherwise solicit business.[33]

Abel argues that the Model Rules also exercise market control by maintaining two kinds of hierarchy: the hierarchy of the legal profession in relation to other professions, as well as the hierarchy with the profession itself. With respect to other professions, Abel cites Model Rule 5.4 and explains that it enables the legal profession to "resist subordination to other occupational categories." With respect to the hierarchy within the profession itself, Abel argues that the content of the Model Rules is shaped in such a way that those at the bottom of the professional pyramid are likely, and those at the top unlikely, to violate them. Once the substance of the rules has been "subtly biased" in this manner, it is possible to enforce them evenhandedly, thereby appearing to respect the rule of law while still scapegoating non-elite lawyers and justifying the hierarchy of status, wealth and power as a reflection of moral worth.[34]

Abel cites a number of instances of such "implicit bias." For example, Model Rule 7.3 places greater restrictions on solicitation when it involves "one-shot" work and the clients are individuals.[35] This is because, the comments to that rule explain, "there is far less likelihood that a lawyer would engage in abusive practices against a former client. . . . Nor is there a serious potential for abuse when the person contacted is a lawyer."[36] For these reasons, lawyers of corporate clients are given almost free rein in soliciting work, in part because so much of their work comes from former clients and in part because most if not all of their potential clients have in-house counsel. At the same time, other lawyers, who are lower in the professional hierarchy because they serve individuals rather than corporations, must, for example, explicitly label their written solicitations as "Advertising Material."[37] As a further example of "implicit bias," Model Rule 1.5(d) places significant restrictions on how lawyers in different firms may share fees, and notably it requires either that the division is proportionate to the services performed by each lawyer, that each lawyer assumes joint responsibility for the representation, or the client expressly agrees in writing to the fee arrangement.[38] In contrast, lawyers in the same firm are free to share fees as they see fit, without the need to inform the client let alone receive the client's consent.[39] Abel explains that this rule penalizes firms that are lower in the professional hierarchy, and notably small firms that may work together—for example, one, as a generalist, obtaining business for another, a specialist. At the same time, this rule places no restrictions on large firms—who are higher in the professional hierarchy—from hiring "rainmakers" who do little or no legal work but who generate business for their partners and take a large share of the profits.[40]

In this manner, Abel provides specific examples of how the legal profession uses self-regulation, and the Model Rules in particular, as a means to maintain professional hierarchies and thereby to exercise control over the market.

MUCH ADO ABOUT SELF-REGULATION

In light of Abel's explanation for self-regulation of the legal profession, it is not at all surprising that self-regulation has become a controversial topic. Indeed, in recent years the topic has been the focus of a number of commentators, notably arguing it is at the origin of many if not most (or even all) of the problems in the market for legal services today. Here is just a sampling:

1. In his 2005 article "Occupation Code 541110: Lawyers, Self-Regulation, and the Idea of a Profession," Jonathan Macey begins by deploring the decline in civility and "professionalism" among lawyers. While, on its face, this might seem of limited importance (no one has the right to be free of incivility),[41] he argues that it is a symptom of a larger and more significant problem. That problem is that the "economies" of practicing law no longer make sense. On the one hand, there are high barriers to entry into the profession, requiring those seeking to become lawyers to spend a considerable amount of time and money. On the other hand, once they enter the profession, they enter into what has become a highly competitive environment where the professional opportunities and monetary rewards are much less than what they expected, obliging them to compete intensely, if not ferociously, with other lawyers as well as with nonlawyers for work.[42] In this environment, Macey argues, lawyers face an "ethical prisoner's dilemma" in that while it is in the interest of all lawyers, collectively, to act civilly and ethically, it is in the interest of each lawyer, individually, to act uncivilly if not unethically, in order to gain advantages over other lawyers, and especially over those who do act civilly and ethically. At the same time, because the profession is self-regulated, lawyers face limited to no sanctions when they do act uncivilly, and even often when they act unethically. This is because, Macey explains, lawyers are reluctant to sanction each other or to impose particularly stiff penalties in those rare instances where lawyers are sanctioned.[43]

Macey blames this state of affairs, if not in whole than in large part, upon self-regulation. This is because, he argues, the bar associations that hold regulatory power attract support from individual lawyers whose interests, as participants in an ethical prisoners' dilemma, sharply diverge from the overall best interests of the legal profession. For these reasons, Macey argues against self-regulation, questioning whether it is "still in the public interest, if indeed it ever was." At the same time, he is not optimistic about it ending, stating that it is highly unlikely that it will be replaced "any time soon" and that it is not even clear that a superior alternative exists. Instead, Macey argues, courts and legislatures should "end the anticompetitive and ultimately ineffectual regulations that pass for self-regulation of the bar."[44]

2. In her 2008 article "Legal Barriers to Innovation: The Growing Economic Cost of Professional Control Over Corporate Legal Markets," Gillian Hadfield argues that self-regulation (what she refers to as "professional" regulation) has consequences not only with respect to ethics and access to justice, but also with respect to its economic costs for corporations and other business entities. Lawyers, she argues, use their "legitimately unique" roles in political and democratic fields to illegitimately protect the production and distribution of a service that is fundamental, and fundamentally economic.[45] "Professional regulation of legal markets dampens, even extinguishes, at every turn the energy of market creativity that, as we increasingly recognize in most other markets, drives the modern economy forward."[46]

   For Hadfield, self-regulation of the legal profession has four major effects on innovation in legal services:

   i. It forces the standardization of legal services (what Hadfield calls the "legal product") in ways that result in inefficient and unnecessarily costly transactions. Self-regulation does this by focusing on the means of delivering legal inputs rather than on the ends.
   ii. It results in the "homogeneity of the idea pool." Self-regulation does this by restricting the pool of talent from which the market can draw, and by ensuring that only those who have gone through extensive induction into the conventional practice of law may be included in that pool.
   iii. It restricts the capacity for scaling up new legal ideas: self-regulation of legal markets inhibits "the extension into legal markets of the large-scale information processing that underlies much of the revolution in the modern economy." Self-regulation does this by limiting the potential to exploit economies of scale and scope.
   iv. It restricts the methods for financing legal innovation. Self-regulation does this by prohibiting the corporate practice of law. As a result, risks

> in legal innovation cannot be spread through the mechanisms essential to the modern economy: diversified portfolios, large-scale and liquid capital markets, and tailored financial instruments.[47]

In sum, repeating an anecdote told by Richard Susskind, Hadfield explains that self-regulation forces the legal profession to focus on building more and more elaborate drills, rather than on what clients really need, which is holes in walls.[48]

3. In their 2008 article "The End(s) of Self-Regulation?" Richard Devlin and Porter Heffernan begin by observing that in Canada, it seems that "the status quo of self-regulation is entrenched and unassailable." Not only it is "the only game in town," but also, consideration of alternatives appears pointless.[49] However, the authors argue, this complacency about self-regulation is unwarranted. They offer ten examples in support of their argument that in Canada, "all is not well," such as the rising number of unrepresented litigants in court and the dearth of pro bono services.[50] Yet, Devlin and Heffernan are quick to point out that they are not arguing that self-regulation is entirely unsalvageable. Instead, they encourage the adoption of what they call "calibrated regulation," where regulatory power is shared between the profession, on the one hand, and an independent body of some kind, on the other.[51] The authors explain that "pure self-regulation is both normatively indefensible in a liberal democratic society and strategically ineffective in achieving its goals." At the same time, they continue, the traditional alternative—the conventional state-centered command and control model of regulation—is too blunt an instrument to work effectively. As a result, some form of shared regulatory power is the only viable alternative.[52]
4. In his 2011 book *The Lawyer-Judge Bias in the American Legal System*, Benjamin Barton states that "lawyers covet the opportunity to govern themselves." The best way to do that, he continues, is to convince judges to take over the regulation. This is because, he explains, judges are highly sympathetic to the lawyers' point of view: judges are lawyers themselves, judges are open and highly vulnerable to informal lobbying by lawyers, and elected judges are dependent upon lawyers for donations and political support. In contrast, when a state's legislature has a say in the regulation of a profession (such as the medical profession), it serves as a check should its regulatory board (usually dominated by members of the profession in question) overreach. Because the legal profession (and, indeed, legal services as a whole) are regulated without any such check, the result is a litany of rules and policies that favor the legal profession over the public in need of legal services: high barriers to entry, multiple restrictions on competition, lax enforcement of rules relating to incompetence and neglect.[53]

5. In their 2012 article "Comparative Perspectives on Lawyer Regulation: An Agenda for Reform in the United States and Canada," Deborah Rhode and Alice Woolley explore why problems in American and Canadian legal regulation persist, and how they can be reformed in light of recent innovations, most notably from England and Wales and Australia. In both countries (the United States and Canada), they explain, the problems are structural, and they stem from self-regulation: "No matter how well intentioned," they state, "no occupational group is situated to take a disinterested perspective on matters that implicate its own status and livelihood. Nothing in the history of bar self-governance suggests that lawyers are an exception."[54]

The authors explain that in the United States this occurs by reason of the courts' delegation of their regulatory authority to the organized bar with respect to professional discipline. In doing so, the courts engage in little oversight over the bar when it exercises this authority. At the same time, lawyer discipline is not a subject of priority for the general public. The public's access to information on the topic is limited, and they have little incentive to mobilize on the issue. The result is a system that is closely aligned to the interests of the organized bar. This explains, the authors continue, why bar oversight processes are almost entirely reactive and generally respond only to complaints of serious professional misconduct or criminal convictions. It also explains why even though almost all jurisdictions have ethical rules requiring lawyers to report evidence of misconduct, these mandates are widely ignored and rarely enforced. Further, the system fails to respond when clients benefit from the misconduct, as in abusive litigation practices or complicity in fraud, or when victims lack information or incentives to file complaints.[55]

In Canada, the authors explain, the self-regulatory nature of the system is more straightforward. Provincial law societies, established by statute, have a wide range of regulatory powers, including the authority to determine the standards for admission and discipline, to make rules, and to investigate and sanction lawyer misconduct. The law societies are governed by elected members of the profession called "benchers," together with a small number of appointed "lay" (nonlaywer) benchers. Benchers serve part-time (all or nearly all are otherwise employed) and in most cases, they either are unpaid or are paid modest amounts to serve as benchers.[56] In contrast to the United States, in Canada courts have only highly limited regulatory authority over lawyers, and notably they cannot suspend or disbar lawyers, cannot impose consequences for patterns of conduct, and cannot sanction conduct that occurs outside of the litigation context. In this light, it is not surprising that Canada has been referred to as the "last bastion of unfettered self-regulation of the legal profession in the common law world."[57]

The resources of the law societies are limited, if not scarce. It is for that reason they have been accused of focusing their regulatory resources on discipline cases deemed to be "high reward" while neglecting those deemed to be "high risk." Most lawyers who get disbarred are guilty of misappropriation of client funds or other obvious wrongdoing, or have shown themselves unwilling to respect law society authority; very few lawyers are disciplined for incompetence or other more ambiguous types of professional misconduct. In addition, disciplinary sanctions tend to disproportionately target lawyers practicing alone or in small firms. While this might at least in part be because those lawyers engage in "higher risk" types of practice or lack "collegial supports and controls," Rhode and Woolly suggest that, more disturbingly, it "may be because they are at the margins of the profession in power and status."[58]

Rhode and Woolley attribute these problems in large part to a highly autonomous regulatory structure:

> It may well be that any lawyer regulatory structure will be vulnerable to capture by its subjects on at least some issues. In the Canadian system, however, no capture is necessary. Lawyers control every aspect of the governance process, and have the statutory authority to regulate in their own interests. No countervailing forces have a meaningful voice. No elaborate conspiracy theory is required to suggest that such a regulatory structure is likely to privilege professional over public interests, and to focus attention on contexts where those interests align: clear moral misconduct by the least powerful members of the bar.[59]

In sum, for Rhode and Woolley, the self-regulatory structures of the United States as well as of Canada are not working. The authors argue that they should be reformed along the models of England and Wales and of Australia. Most notably, the United States and Canada should adopt co-regulatory structures in which the bar shares authority with other, more publicly accountable entities. Focusing on disciplinary matters, the authors recommend, for example, the use of lay ombudsman to mediate disputes. The authors also recommend that disciplinary procedures become more transparent and that the concerns of public protection figure more prominently. The authors conclude by stating that the examples of England and Wales and Australia demonstrate that the independence of the legal profession from "government domination" can be preserved with a co-regulatory structure. At the same time, they point out, a co-regulatory structure can provide greater checks on professional self-interest and greater responsiveness to consumer concerns.[60]

Again, the articles described above are just a few examples of the many arguments against self-regulation that have been made. In sum, these arguments object to self-regulation as a highly flawed regulatory structure and support its significant modification if not replacement with a new structure.

How have these arguments been received? To say they have been "received" might be going too far. Given the numerous and unquestioning—if not categorical—defenses of self-regulation that have been asserted recently and continue to be asserted today, one could be forgiven for thinking that the arguments against self-regulation described above have not been heard at all.

These defenses of self-regulation can, in particular, be found in comments submitted to the ABA's Commission on Ethics 20/20 and Commission on the Future of Legal Services. When each of these commissions (in 2011/12 and 2016, respectively) called for comments in response to the question of whether or not the United States should allow for alternative structures, in both cases the large majority of the comments submitted expressed objections to them. In a certain number of those submissions, the objections were supported at least in part upon the prediction that allowing for alternative structures would more or less necessarily lead to the end of self-regulation, and that such a result was unacceptable. Here are examples of those arguments:

> As one scholar has noted, "[i]n comparison to all other professions, the legal profession is the most free of external governmental control." This absence of external control is a good not because it allows lawyers to avoid regulations, but because it allows lawyers to shape their professional norms, be responsive to lawyers' practical experiences, and serve the public good by teaching and guiding members of their own profession. By opening law firms to non-lawyer ownership . . . there is a very real concern that legislatures or non-judicial entities might claim a right to regulate this new form of practice. If law firms are no longer made up of solely lawyer partners, it will be that much harder to resist the argument that lawyers should be subject to regulation by non-lawyers, rather than by the state bars and judicial institutions that understand the ethical norms upon which the profession has been built. The legal profession's independence—which allows it to put the good of both clients and the profession itself first—is a virtue that should be maintained, not undermined.[61]
>
> Hasn't the ABA had a long standing policy against regulation of law firms by the Executive branch? I know The Florida Bar has. Are we going to give up that independence for non-lawyer partners?[62]
>
> The adoption of [alternative structures] would be disastrous and would facilitate the destruction of . . . the judicial branch of government . . . due to the involvement of non-lawyers, [the adoption] would encourage legislative rather than judicial control of the practice of law. . . . The alleged activity in other jurisdictions demonstrates the important differences for the better in our self-governance in the United States and what happens when legislatures get involved in other countries.[63]
>
> Allowing non-lawyer ownership of law firms would put our ability to self-govern at risk. Once the legal profession is no longer viewed as independent, we will no longer be allowed the privilege of self-governing.[64]
>
> At present, our profession is self-regulating by way of licensing by the various state supreme courts. We have procedures to enforce the various codes of

> professional responsibility, up to and including disbarment. The businessmen owning the ABS entities are neither trained nor obligated to follow the professional rules of responsibility. If the states should take this path of allowing ABS, they will have to create a means to regulate the nonlawyer owners. As a result we will likely lose our ability to regulate our own profession, and we lawyers become little more than employees.[65]

In sum, in the United States, the debate over how to regulate the legal profession—and, by virtue of the lawyer monopoly on legal services, legal services as a whole—is in large part focused upon the question of self-regulation. On the one hand, there are those that contend that the legal profession is self-regulating, and, on the other hand, there are those that contend it is not. Further, on the one hand, there are those who contend that self-regulation is at the root of many problems relating to legal services and to access to justice itself. And, on the other hand, there are others who, failing to even acknowledge much less address such arguments, contend that self-regulation is an essential characteristic of the legal profession without which the profession would fall prey to undue influence by the state and might even lose its status as a profession.

But in the debate over how to regulate the legal profession—and legal services as a whole—is this nearly exclusive focus on the question of self-regulation the right focus?

As discussed in detail in chapter 1, the OECD promotes six essential elements of an effective regulatory policy (among other elements): (i) independent regulators who are free from conflicts of interest, (ii) accountability and transparency in regulatory decision-making, (iii) the placement of regulatory oversight bodies "at the center of government," (iv) making regulatory stakeholders, including businesses but also, notably, citizens and consumers, part of the regulatory process and paying attention to their voices; (v) the use of evidence-based regulatory impact assessments, both before and after adoption, and (vi) the use of a risk-based approach to regulation. If we accept that at least some, if not all, of these elements are pertinent for the regulation of the legal profession and for legal services as a whole, then whether or not the legal profession in the United States is, or should be, self-regulating is a false debate. Engaging in that debate distracts us (disables us) from engaging in the real debate, which is, self-regulation or not, how do we create a regulatory environment that incorporates the OECD's essential elements of effective regulation, in order improve regulation of the legal profession as well as of legal services as a whole? In sum, self-regulation—or not—does not obviate the need for good regulation.

With this part I, the stage is now set for an examination of the development of legal services regulation in England and Wales, Australia, Canada and the

United States. As explained in the Introduction, rather than attempting to cover legal services regulation as a whole, this examination will focus upon the aspects of regulation that are most relevant to the adoption—or not—of alternative structures.

For each country, the examination concludes with an assessment. Drawing from the examination, the assessment exposes in a summary format the extent to which that country has (or has not) implemented the OECD's six elements of good governance in the regulation of legal services. The last part of this book (part VI) begins with a chapter that brings these assessments together, enabling a comparison of the four countries with respect to each element. The assessments provide unique insight into the regulatory environment of each country and, especially, they help to explain why some countries' regulatory environments are more open, more vibrant and more productive—in sum, more modern—than others.

NOTES

1. Glen Hepburn, "Alternatives to Traditional Regulation," OECD Report, 2006, 15, http://www.oecd.org/gov/regulatory-policy/42245468.pdf.
2. "Alternatives to Regulation," OECD, accessed on March 20, 2017, http://www.oecd.org/gov/regulatory-policy/alternativestoregulation.htm.
3. Hepburn, "Alternatives to Traditional Regulation," 10.
4. "Alternatives to Regulation," OECD.
5. Just a few of the others include: Deborah L. Rhode and Alice Woolley, "Comparative Perspectives on Lawyer Regulation: An Agenda for Reform in the United States and Canada," *Fordham Law Review* 80 (2012): 2762–64, http://ir.lawnet.fordham.edu/cgi/viewcontent.cgi?article=4808&context=flr; Amy Salyzyn, "From Colleague to Cop to Coach: Contemporary Regulation of Lawyer Competence," *Canadian Bar Review* forthcoming, Ottawa Faculty of Law Working Paper No. 2016–43, October 24, 2016, https://ssrn.com/abstract=2858332; Laurel S. Terry, "Trends in Global and Canadian Lawyer Regulation," *Saskatchewan Law Review* 76 (2013): 145–184, http://www.personal.psu.edu/faculty/l/s/lst3/Terry_Canada_Trends_Lawyer_Regulation.pdf.
6. Of course a number of others have written on the same topic. See, for example, Gillian K. Hadfield and Deborah L. Rhode, "How to Regulate Legal Services to Promote Access, Innovation, and the Quality of Lawyering," *Hastings Law Journal* 67 (2016): 1196–1200, http://www.hastingslawjournal.org/wp-content/uploads/Hadfield_Rhode-67.5.pdf.
7. Noel Semple, *Legal Services Regulation at the Crossroads: Justitia's Legions* (Cheltenham, UK: Edward Elgar Publishing, 2015), 20–27.
8. Ibid., 28.
9. Ibid., 29–32.
10. Ibid., 32–33.

11. Benjamin Hoorn Barton, "Why Do We Regulate Lawyers?: An Economic Analysis of the Justifications for Entry and Conduct Regulation," *Arizona State Law Journal* 33 (2001): 439.

12. Ibid., 441.

13. Ibid., 456.

14. Ibid., 453, 435.

15. "Alternatives to Regulation," OECD.

16. On this topic generally, see Fred C. Zacharias, "The Myth of Self-Regulation," *Minnesota Law Review* 93 (2009): 1147–1190, http://www.minnesotalawreview.org/wp-content/uploads/2012/01/Zacharias_MLR.pdf.

17. See, for example, Benjamin H. Barton, "Do Judges Systematically Favor the Interests of the Legal Profession?" University of Tennessee Legal Studies Research Paper No. 1, October, 2007, 8–9, http://ssrn.com/abstract=976478.

18. Judith L. Maute, "Global Continental Shifts in a New Governance Paradigm in Lawyer Regulation and Consumer Protection: Riding the Wave," in *Alternative Perspectives on Lawyers and Legal Ethics: Reimagining the Profession*, ed. Francesca Bartlett, Reid Mortensen and Kieran Tranter (London: Routledge, 2011), 30.

19. American Bar Association, "Model Rules of Professional Conduct: Preamble & Scope," accessed on March 20, 2017, http://www.americanbar.org/groups/professional_responsibility/publications/model_rules_of_professional_conduct/model_rules_of_professional_conduct_preamble_scope.html.

20. Bob Ambrogi, "Perlman: ABA Future Commission Not Out to Regulate 'Entire Legal Tech Industry,'" Catalyst, April 26, 2016, https://www.catalystsecure.com/blog/2016/04/perlman-aba-future-commission-not-out-to-regulate-entire-legal-tech-industry/.

21. Ibid.

22. American Bar Association, "Model Rules of Professional Conduct: Preamble & Scope."

23. On the topic of self-regulation and the independence of the bar from government influence or control, see, for example: Richard F. Devlin and Porter Heffernan, "The End(S) Of Self-Regulation?" *Alberta Law Review* 45 (2008): 186–188, 191–193, http://ssrn.com/abstract=2101801; see also Noel Semple, "Legal Services Regulation in Canada: Plus Ça Change?" Invited submission to international volume on comparative legal services regulation, ed. Andy Boon. Hart Publishing, 2017 Forthcoming, (September 1, 2016): 3, 5–6, https://ssrn.com/abstract=2833336.

24. Camille Chaserant and Sophie Harnay, "The Regulation of Quality in the Market for Legal Services: Taking the Heterogeneity of Legal Services Seriously," *The European Journal of Comparative Economics* 10 (2013): 278, 284, http://eaces.liuc.it/18242979201302/182429792013100208.pdf. See also Baldwin, Cave and Lodge, *Understanding Regulation*, 140–141.

25. Chaserant and Harney, "The Regulation of Quality in the Market for Legal Services," 284.

26. Ibid., 285.

27. Also on the topic of self-regulation and efficiency and expertise, see Devlin and Heffernan, "The End(s) Of Self-Regulation?"

28. See: Alan A. Paterson, "Professionalism and the Legal Services Market," *International Journal of the Legal Profession* 3 (1996): 140; Alan Paterson, Lindsay Farmer, Frank Stephen and James Love, "Competition and the Market for Legal Services," *Journal of Law and Society* 15 (1988): 361; Alan Paterson, *Lawyers and the Public Good* (New York: Cambridge University Press, 2012), 16.

29. Richard L. Abel, "Why Does the ABA Promulgate Ethical Rules?" *Texas Law Review* 59 (1981): 653; see also Richard L. Abel, *American Lawyers* (New York: Oxford University Press, 1989), 40–73, 112–157; Richard L. Abel, "United States: The Contradictions of Professionalism," in *Lawyers in Society: The Common Law World*, ed. Richard L. Abel and Philip S.C. Lewis (Washington DC: Beard Books, 2005), 205–222.

30. Abel, "Why Does the ABA Promulgate Ethical Rules?" 657–660.

31. Ibid., 654.

32. Abel says that the profession's struggle for market control is "*waged*," not that it is necessarily "*won*." Ibid.

33. Ibid., 660, 662–664.

34. Ibid., 664–665.

35. Ibid., 665–666.

36. American Bar Association, "Comment on Rule 7.3," accessed on March 17, 2017, http://www.americanbar.org/groups/professional_responsibility/publications/model_rules_of_professional_conduct/rule_7_3_direct_contact_with_prospective_clients/comment_on_rule_7_3.html.

37. American Bar Association, "Model Rule 7.3: Direct Contact with Prospective Clients," accessed on March 17, 2017, http://www.americanbar.org/groups/professional_responsibility/publications/model_rules_of_professional_conduct/rule_7_3_direct_contact_with_prospective_clients.html.

38. American Bar Association, "Model Rule 1.5: Fees," accessed on March 17, 2017, http://www.americanbar.org/groups/professional_responsibility/publications/model_rules_of_professional_conduct/rule_1_5_fees.html.

39. American Bar Association, "Comment on Rule 1.5," accessed on March 17, 2017, http://www.americanbar.org/groups/professional_responsibility/publications/model_rules_of_professional_conduct/rule_1_5_fees/comment_on_rule_1_5.html.

40. Abel, "Why Does the ABA Promulgate Ethical Rules?" 666–667.

41. Jonathan Macey, "Occupation Code 541110: Lawyers, Self-Regulation, and the Idea of a Profession," *Fordham Law Review* 74 (2005): 1079–1081, http://digitalcommons.law.yale.edu/cgi/viewcontent.cgi?article=2352&context=fss_papers.

42. Ibid., 1098–1099.

43. Ibid., 1082–1085.

44. Ibid., 1081, 1096.

45. Hadfield, "Legal Barriers to Innovation," 107.

46. Ibid., 131.

47. Ibid., 131–141.

48. Ibid., 133, 141.

49. Devlin and Heffernan, "The End(s) of Self-Regulation?" 171.

50. Ibid., 181–182.

51. Ibid., 196–206.

52. Ibid., 196–197.

53. Benjamin H. Barton, *The Lawyer-Judge Bias in the American Legal System* (New York: Cambridge University Press 2011), 129–159.

54. Rhode and Woolley, "Comparative Perspectives on Lawyer Regulation," 2762.

55. Ibid., 2766.

56. Ibid., 2773.

57. Ibid., 2774.

58. Ibid., 2775, citing Harry W. Arthurs, "Why Canadian Law Schools Do Not Teach Legal Ethics," in *Ethical Challenges to Legal Education and Conduct* (Kim Economides et al. eds., 1998), 115.

59. Rhode and Woolley, "Comparative Perspectives on Lawyer Regulation," 2776.

60. Ibid., 2781–2790.

61. Mark Chandler et al., "Comments of Nine General Counsel on the ABA Commission on Ethics 20/20's Discussion Paper on Alternative Law Practice Structures," February 29, 2012, 5–6, http://www.americanbar.org/content/dam/aba/administrative/ethics_2020/ethics_20_20_comments/ninegeneralcounselcomments_alpschoiceoflawinitialdraftproposal.authcheckdam.pdf.

62. Larry D. Murrell, "Ethics 20/20 Non-lawyer Ownership of Law Firms," March 2, 2012, 2, http://www.americanbar.org/content/dam/aba/administrative/ethics_2020/ethics_20_20_comments/murrell_alpsdiscussiondraft.authcheckdam.pdf.

63. Richard L. Thies, Letter to the ABA Commission on Ethics 20/20, February 23, 2012, 4, http://www.americanbar.org/content/dam/aba/administrative/ethics_2020/ethics_20_20_comments/thies_alpsdiscussiondraft.authcheckdam.pdf.

64. DRI—The Voice of the Defense Bar, "Issues Paper Regarding Alternative Business Structures," May 4, 2016, 5, https://www.americanbar.org/content/dam/aba/images/office_president/dri_the_voice_of_the_defense_bar_abs.pdf.

65. Texas Association of Defense Counsel et al, "Comment and Opposition by Texas Association of Defense Counsel, Texas Trial Lawyers Association, and Texas Chapters of the American Board of Trial Advocates on Alternate Business Structures," May 4, 2016, 1, http://www.americanbar.org/content/dam/aba/images/office_president/texas_association_of_defense_counsel_abs.pdf.

Part II

ENGLAND AND WALES: AN EARTHQUAKE

Before 2007, England and Wales was quite similar to the United States in many ways, notably in that representative and regulatory functions were combined in the same bodies (the Law Society for solicitors and the Bar Council for barristers, to name two), lawyers were regulated only in a reactive manner and only at an individual level (not proactively and not at the level of the entity or organization), and alternative structures were not permitted (only lawyers could own and operate law firms). However, the 2007 UK Legal Services Act radically changed all of those, together with the entire regulatory landscape of England and Wales.

Chapter 3

A Great Big Mess

Few would dispute the enduring success of the English legal system. For several centuries it has served as the example for a number of legal systems around the world, not the least of which are those of Australia, Canada and the United States. England has a well-developed common law and an independent and respected judiciary. England has litigation procedures that are considered fair and effective and its judgments are respected and easily enforceable outside the UK. England is a global leader in arbitration and well as in corporate legal services, its global leadership position reinforced by its low barriers to entry for foreign lawyers and firms.

Yet, in spite of its centuries as a beacon for other legal systems, few would dispute that, by the early 2000s,[1] in many ways the English legal system was a mess. A big mess.

In just what ways was it a mess? That would depend on who you asked.[2]

If you asked the Legal Services Ombudsman, you would hear that there were an unacceptably high number of complaints—there was one complaint for every five practicing solicitors and for every twenty-two practicing barristers. And these complaints demonstrated recurrent failings in service delivery: excessive delays, excessive costs, poor responsiveness to communications, failure to follow instructions, failure to act in the client's best interest and failure to clarify the implications of proposed actions. In addition, the multistepped and multilayered complaints process placed "an unacceptable and disproportionate burden" on complainants—it required a "degree of patience, tenacity and endurance" such that only "the most determined complainants" would not be deterred from seeking redress.[3]

If you asked Lord Falconer (then secretary of state for Constitutional Affairs), you would hear that the regulatory system for legal services was a mess: there were at least twenty-two regulatory and oversight bodies. And the problem wasn't just their number, but also their complexity. They had overlapping powers and responsibilities, and they lacked transparency and public accountability. The regulatory system did not meet "the demands of a modern, changing legal services market."[4]

Exacerbating this problem was the fusion in the same regulatory body of both regulatory and representative functions, which created an "inevitable conflict of interest" with the body driven by the interests of its members rather than by the interests of consumers.[5]

If you asked the Office of Fair Trading ("OFT," comparable to the US Federal Trade Commission), you would hear that methods of supply of legal services

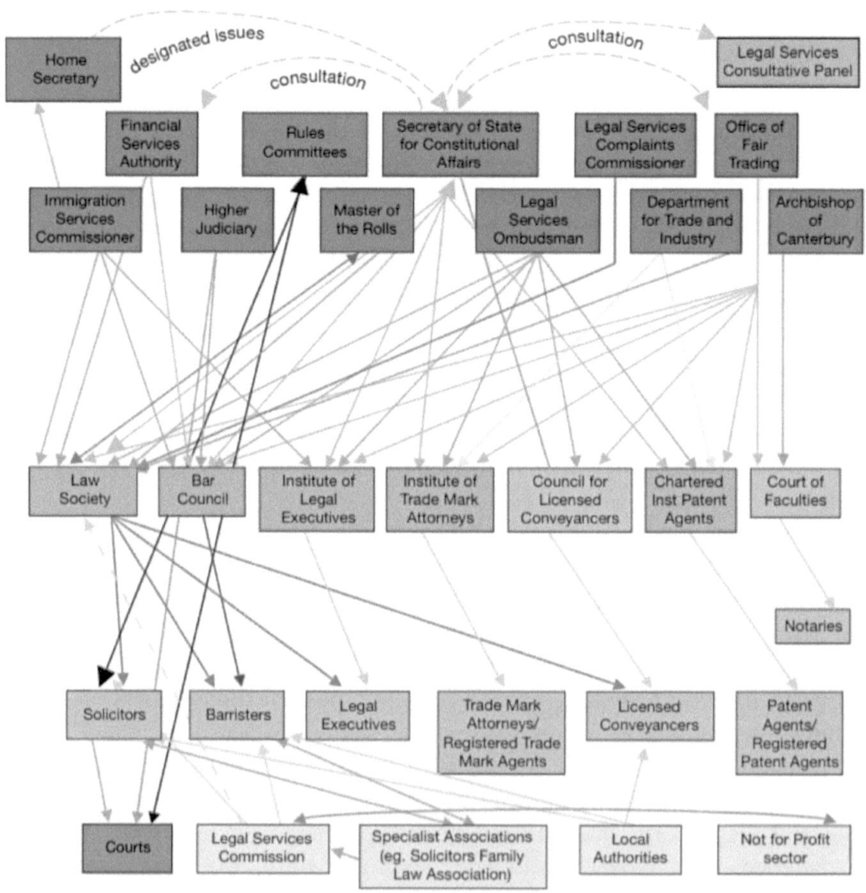

Figure 3.1 The system for the regulation of legal services in England and Wales prior to the implementation of the 2007 Legal Services Act. *Source*: Department for Constitutional Affairs, "The Future of Legal Services: Putting Consumers First," October, 2005, 11, http://webarchive.nationalarchives.gov.uk/+/http://www.dca.gov.uk/legalsys/folwp.pdf.

were a mess: that they resulted in unacceptable restrictions on competition that could not be justified for reasons of public interest or economic efficiency. While, in a 2001 report, the OFT cited many restrictions, they most notably pointed to restrictions on multidisciplinary practices (MDPs) and on lawyers employed by nonlawyers from providing services to third parties. For example, the OFT stated that if MDPs were allowed, they might "achieve advantages in branding, overhead cost savings, and the ability to transfer resources in response to fluctuations in demand and to give a seamless service to clients." Further, the opportunity to provide combinations of different kinds of professional services from the same structure "should unlock potential cost efficiencies and enhance customer choice and convenience."[6] In addition, allowing solicitors to be employed by non-solicitors "could allow competition from those suitably qualified working in different business structures," and concerns about regulating solicitors employed by non-solicitors could be met by a system where business structures rather than individual practitioners were regulated.[7]

If you asked (Tony Blair's) Government, you would hear that there were too many messes to count, not the least of which were the number of complaints and the complaint handling system, the regulatory framework and the restrictions on delivery methods. In a July 2003 report, the Government questioned whether the general regulatory framework for legal services was in the public interest and operated to meet client's needs. Not only did the self-regulatory system remove accountability, but also "The current framework is out-dated, inflexible, over-complex and insufficiently accountable or transparent. . . . The fact that the current framework cannot accommodate new business structures or embrace new ways of doing business bodes ill for the future in what is a fast changing and dynamic service sector. Nothing short of a fundamental revision can, we believe, address these issues."[8]

THE CLEMENTI REPORT

It was in this context that the Government decided that "a thorough and independent investigation without reservation" was needed. The purpose of the investigation was multifold: (i) to consider what regulatory framework would best promote competition, innovation, and the public and consumer interest in an efficient, effective and independent legal sector, (ii) to recommend a framework which will be independent in representing the public and consumer interest, comprehensive, accountable, consistent, flexible, transparent, and no more restrictive or burdensome than is clearly justified, (iii) to review how business entities such as MDPs and corporate bodies can operate in the legal services market and how such entities are best regulated, and, more generally, to examine more efficient ways of liberalizing the market.[9]

The Government was particular about who was to conduct the investigation, or, rather, who was *not* to conduct it. It was to be conducted by an independent person "who commands public confidence" but who is neither a practicing lawyer nor a judge."[10]

The person selected to conduct the investigation was Sir David Clementi. Trained as an accountant, he was a respected former deputy governor of the Bank of England, and was then serving as chairman of Prudential plc.

Appointed in July 2003, Clementi published a consultation paper in March 2004.[11] In the paper, he asked respondents to comment on a range of topics, including:

- What were the appropriate objectives of a regulatory system for legal services?
- Whether a regulatory system should see a clear distinction between the regulatory and the representative role of a professional body?
- Whether the mechanism for handling consumer complaints is better organized within the professional bodies or outside, reporting to an independent regulator?
- What demand and what advantages and disadvantages exist in respect of alternative business structures?[12]

Clementi received 265 written responses to his consultation paper, including, without surprise, from the Law Society of England and Wales and from the Bar Council (which, at that time, served in both representative and regulatory functions of solicitors and barristers, respectively).[13]

Clementi met the deadline for the completion of his investigation, issuing what is now referred to as the "Clementi Report" in December 2004.[14]

The organization of Clementi's 139-page report neatly mirrored the three principal issues mentioned above—namely, reform of the regulatory framework, reform of the complaints system and reform of the restrictive nature of business structures.

In addressing the issue of the regulatory framework, Clementi began with the question of what the objectives of a regulatory regime should be. He stated that clarification of regulatory objectives is "critical" for those charged with regulatory responsibility, since the objectives represent the criteria against which they must determine the appropriate regulatory action, and the criteria against which they will be held accountable.[15]

In its response to the consultation paper, the Bar Council stated that, for it, the basic purposes of regulation were to seek to ensure that members of a professional body are suitably qualified and observe appropriate ethical standards.[16]

But Clementi rejected this narrow description as being "a rather profession centric view."[17] Instead, in his report, Clementi listed six objectives for legal service regulators and recommended that they provide the core around which a regulatory framework for legal services be built.

As can be quickly understood from the list below, the objectives that Clementi recommended for legal service regulators go far beyond merely assuring that services providers are qualified and act ethically:

Maintaining the rule of law

> The rule of law embodies the basic principles of equal treatment of all people before the law, fairness, and a guarantee of basic human rights. A predictable and proportionate legal system with fair, transparent, and effective judicial institutions is essential to the protection of both citizens and commerce against any arbitrary use of state authority and unlawful acts of both organizations and individuals. . . . [T]hose charged with regulating legal service providers should have an important part to play in ensuring the rule of law by creating conditions necessary for its delivery.[18]

Access to justice

> Access to justice has [a variety of dimensions but it is critically] an issue about access for those who are disadvantaged and in particular those who cannot afford to pursue their legal rights.[19]

Protection and promotion of consumer interests

> [T]he regulator of legal services should have a twin duty in respect of consumers: first to ensure that consumers have sufficient information about the standards of the services provided so that they are able to take informed decisions about these services; and second, given that consumers may not always be 'informed,' to have powers to act in the market, for example, to prohibit oppressive marketing practices, raise or set standards, develop information/awareness programs, resolve disputes and protect vulnerable groups.[20]

Promotion of competition

> [A]ny Regulator of legal services should have as an objective the prevention of unjustified restrictions on the supply of, and encourage competition in, the provision of legal services and the promotion of choice in both the number and type of providers, subject to the proper safeguard of consumers' interests.[21]

Encouragement of a confident, strong and effective legal profession

> The regulatory objective of maintaining a strong and effective legal profession (including setting appropriate entry standards and supporting new entrants to the market) [will] help to ensure access to justice, the maintenance of a healthy

> supplier base for publicly funded work and continued support for pro bono initiatives, thereby serving the public interest. It would also underpin the international efforts of our legal sector. [Clementi considered that the Bar Council's limited objectives would be covered by this one].

Promoting public understanding of the citizen's legal rights

> [The] regulator should maintain the professional obligation on lawyers to set out for clients their rights and the consequences of different options.[22]

Having explained his recommendations for the objectives of a regulatory regime, Clementi then turned to the regulatory model itself.

He began by agreeing that "the current system is flawed." For him, this was due to a number of reasons, not by any means limited to the large number of regulatory bodies and their overlapping functions that others had cited. For Clementi, the problem was much larger than that: The regulatory system had no clear objectives or principals, and it had insufficient regard to the interest of consumers.[23]

Clementi agreed that the complaints system was also flawed, as regards its efficiency, as regards the overlapping powers of the oversight bodies and as regards the principle of the system itself, questioning whether a system for complaints against lawyers that is run by lawyers themselves could achieve consumer confidence.[24]

Finally, Clementi's third area of concern was about the restrictive nature of the permitted business structures for legal services. He observed that they had changed little over a long period of time, with its most easily recognizable structure as the sole practitioner or partnership of lawyers. But business practices have changed, he argued. Notably, the skills necessary to run a modern legal practice have developed; but while those with finance or IT skills may sit on the management committee of a legal firm, they were not permitted to be principals in the business.[25]

Clementi observed that the concerns he outlined are related to each other. Notably, he pointed out, one of the difficulties which stands in the way of new business structures is that the current framework does not easily allow for their regulation.[26]

Before finally setting out his suggestions for reform in relation to his three areas of concern, Clementi made some additional observations. For Clementi:

- Each type of "economic unit" that can embody a legal service has its own advantages and disadvantages. He rejected the suggestion that any one type of economic unit, be it a sole practitioner, unlimited partnership, limited liability partnership or company, would be better than another for serving the interests of consumers and the public. To the contrary, he favored a regulatory framework which permits a high degree of choice: choice both for the consumer in where he goes for legal services and for the lawyer in the type of structure he works for.

- It is wrong to see a conflict between lawyers as professionals and lawyers as business people. For him, access to justice requires that not only the legal advice given is sound, but also the presence of the business skills necessary to provide a cost-effective service in a consumer-friendly way. Citing complaints about the delays experienced when lawyers are involved and frustration over the uncertainty of costs, Clementi observed that "complaints arise as much from poor business service as from poor legal advice. If certain lawyers continue to reject the notion that they are in business, such complaints will continue until they are indeed out of business."
- It is wrong to assume that high-quality legal services can or should only be provided at high cost. Clementi stated high-quality legal services are important to society, but of limited value if available only to the very rich or those paid for by the government. In developing business systems to minimize costs while maintaining high standards, there is no reason why lawyers should not work alongside those with other skills, for example in finance or IT. Reforms can be developed that encourage cost-effective practices while maintaining both quality and ethical standards.[27]

With this preface, Clementi's most salient recommendations for reform were as follows:

Regulatory Bodies

Clementi made two principal recommendations with respect to regulatory bodies:

His first principal recommendation was that representative and regulatory functions should be clearly separated into different bodies. Clementi stated that this change was needed to protect public and consumer interest, to promote competition and to encourage innovation. For Clementi, it was not possible that the same body could effectively regulate a profession at the same time representing itself and lobbying for its interests: "There is a conflict of interest between the two roles which should be tackled." Specifically, in a regulatory body the public interest should have primacy, and issues such as changes in practice rules should be examined, not against the wishes of the membership, but against the test of public interest. Further, he stated, it is particularly difficult for professional bodies that combine both regulatory and representative roles to deal with competition issues. Regulatory bodies should be expected to encourage open competition, subject to maintaining quality standards; representative bodies have a legitimate right to fight their corner, warning that the public may suffer if the market is opened too widely. This is a difficult set of conflicting issues for one body to balance. Indeed, Clementi observed, both the Law Society and the Bar Council had demonstrated difficulty in getting significant practice rule changes approved by their representative councils.[28]

Clementi's second principal recommendation with respect to regulatory bodies was the establishment of a Legal Services Board (LSB), charged with the oversight of the "front-line" regulatory bodies. Clementi called this structure Model B+. In making this recommendation Clementi also considered an alternative, called Model A, where all regulatory power and authority across all legal professions (solicitors, barristers, etc.) would be invested into one single authority. However, Clementi rejected Model A in favor of Model B+, for a variety of reasons, notably, in his opinion: (i) leaving day-to-day rule making and oversight as far as possible at the practitioner level is more likely to increase the commitment of practitioners to high standards—so they see rules as aids to raise standards and not as constraints to be circumvented; (ii) leaving day-to-day rule making and oversight at the practitioner level more clearly demonstrates the independence of the legal profession from the government; (iii) consistency among rules can be sufficiently guaranteed by the LSB setting minimum standards—this then permits for appropriate variations in standards depending upon the legal profession in question, (iv) Model B+ provides greater flexibility for the LSB to be empowered to, for example, authorize new regulatory bodies to come into existence and/or to modify their mandates.[29]

With respect to representative bodies, Clementi further recommended firstly that regulatory bodies should have lay involvement in their decision-making functions, and secondly that a one-year term for a Chair of a regulatory body is too short. Such a short term, he stated, is "long enough for the incumbent to want to ensure that no damage is sustained 'during his watch' but not long enough to see through difficult change."[30]

Complaints Handling Process

Clementi recommended that the complaints handling process be simplified and streamlined by the creation of a single complaints handling body for all consumer complaints, which he called the Office for Legal Complaints (OLC). He listed these benefits of such a process:

- Independent of the legal profession
- Simplification for consumers, due to a single system with one point of entry,
- Greater consistency and clarity of process,
- Greater flexibility, notably in order to accommodate alternative business structures.[31]

Clementi recommended that the LSB have oversight over the OLC, but that such oversight should be limited to systemic and policy issues, without encompassing individual complaints. Finally, Clementi recommended that the OLC have a board structure, the majority of which, as well as the Chair, should be nonlawyers.[32]

Alternative Business Structures

Clementi's recommendations in this regard were to move forward in two stages. The first, arguably modest, stage should be to permit lawyers regulated by different professional bodies (notably, but not exclusively, solicitors and barristers) to practice together as equals in the same structure (at the time the Clementi Report was issued, this was not permitted). Clementi referred to these structures as Legal Disciplinary Practices (LDPs), and further argued that outside ownership of them should be permitted, subject to certain regulatory verifications that such owners are fit to own, and, especially, that their managers are fit to manage. Clementi recommended that in regulating LDPs, the focus should be on the economic unit rather than on individual lawyers, and a determination of the LDPs authorization to practice would include an examination of its governance and administrative arrangements.[33]

It is only once a regulatory system for LDPs has been established, Clementi stated, that regulatory authorities should then consider moving to the second step, of authorizing MDPs (practices that bring lawyers together with other professionals to provide a combination of legal and nonlegal services to third parties).[34]

Clementi explains these recommendations as follows:

In the context of a market where restrictive practices operate as a barrier to innovative forms of service delivery, the absence of an articulated consumer demand is not, in itself, a persuasive argument that other forms of service delivery should not be permitted. Further, even if consumer demand is not articulated directly as such, it can be observed in the attitudes and fears that many people have with respective to lawyers and legal services: that legal services are too expensive, that lawyers are often difficult to approach and to understand and that lawyers provide poor customer service.[35]

Further, such changes can also benefit legal service providers. For example, they will permit adequate reward for non-solicitors who play a key role in the success of the business—people such as IT, HR and finance specialists. In addition, they will open new opportunities for those in the legal profession who feel excluded from the partnership role in a traditional legal practice—because they are not able to put up the required capital, because they are members of ethnic minorities who feel they do not "fit" into a traditional partnership role and/or because due to personal commitments are not able to undertake the work commitment required of a traditional partnership role. Such changes, Clementi stated, "would broaden access to capital, reduce the need for practitioners to put in equity capital, and accommodate varied work styles to suit a broader range of people wishing to work in the profession."[36]

Clementi cited existing examples of different types of legal professionals already working together with nonlawyers in management positions, in a manner that did not compromise professional standards. The examples he cited were the many legal practices where professionals with IT, HR and finance skills already sat on the Executive Committees of their firms, and also Law Centers (organizations that provide legal assistance to persons in the UK who cannot afford a lawyer).[37]

Finally, Clementi argued that it should be possible to address ethical concerns through regulation, and notably by shifting emphasis toward regulation of the economic unit rather than of the individual practitioner.[38]

Clementi rejected arguments that "widening the net of ownership" led to greater risk. To the contrary, he responded that many shareholders would bring business practices to firms that would improve the standards of many firms, and notably higher levels of internal controls. That being said, Clementi recommended that prospective outside shareholders be subject to a "fit to own" test. While he deferred to the regulator to fix the parameters of such a test, he suggested that it would consider honesty, integrity and reputation, competence and capability, and financial soundness. He further suggested that the regulator would be entitled to look at the business plan of the prospective owner and to understand what type of practice it wished to run and why. Further, in a group context, Clementi stated that the regulator should have the right to look beyond the immediate shareholder, for example to the ultimate beneficial owner.[39]

Clementi rejected the Bar Council's argument that "a conflict would inevitably rise between the commercial interests of the owners and the ethical duties on which the practice of law is based." Clementi stated that with proper safeguards in place, it is not at all inevitable that this would happen. Further, he continued, clients are not fully protected from unethical actions as it is today, as witnessed by the reports of the Solicitors Disciplinary Tribunal, which lists the names of those who have been struck from the Roll for malpractice and criminal behavior.[40]

AFTER THE CLEMENTI REPORT

Immediately after Clementi submitted his report in December 2004, the Government "warmly" welcomed it, and stated that it "broadly" accepted the report's main recommendations, as well as the arguments for change that it set out.[41]

In October 2005, the Government issued its own White Paper, in which it described more fully its reaction to the Clementi Report, and explained the Government's agenda for reforming the regulation and delivery of legal services in England and Wales.[42]

Finally, in May 2006, the Government circulated its draft Legal Services Bill, together with explanatory notes and a regulatory impact assessment. The Bill was the subject of the extensive scrutiny and debate, and as a result it exploded in size: In its first incarnation, the Bill contained 159 clauses and 15 Schedules, but by the time it emerged from Parliament in 2007, it had grown to 214 sections and 24 Schedules, filling up 389 pages.[43]

Perhaps surprisingly, the debate did not focus on the fundamental changes that Clementi had recommended in his report. Instead, most of the commentators on the draft Bill, and most notably the Law Society and the Bar Council, expressed general support for Clementi's recommendations. For example, the Law Society stated that Clementi's recommendations "have the potential to improve the way in which the legal services market operates for consumers and practitioners alike,"[44] and the Bar Council stated that it is "in favor of the liberalization of services."[45]

In fact, both the Law Society and the Bar Council implemented certain of Clementi's recommendations even before the circulation of the Bill. Notably, each of them split their regulatory and representation functions, with the creation of the Solicitors Regulation Authority (SRA) in 2005 and the Bar Standards Board (BSB) in 2006.[46] (However, the separation was only operational, and yet today both the SRA and the BSB remain housed under the Law Society and the Bar Council, respectively. As explored below, this incomplete independence remains today a point of contention.)

The elements of the Bill that sparked the most concern and discussion were those considered to have diverged too far from Clementi's recommendations. The most notable debates centered on the extent to which the independence of the legal profession from government would be assured, and the process for complaint handling.

With respect to the independence of the legal profession, for example, the Law Society objected that the first draft Bill gave the Lord Chancellor (a high-ranking government function) the sole power to make appointments to the LSB without consultation. And both the Law Society and the Bar Council complained that the first draft Bill gave the LSB wide powers to intervene in the work of the frontline regulators, in contrast to the "light touch" recommended by the Clementi Report. Presumably in response to these comments, the final draft Bill provided that the Lord Chancellor may make appointments to the LSB only upon consultation with the Lord Chief Justice (a person selected by the nondepartmental public body called the Judicial Appointments Commission), and it clarified both that primary regulatory responsibility rests with the frontline regulators, and that the LSB may interfere only when their actions are unreasonable.[47]

Additional questions for debate were:

i. The impact that Alternative Business Structures (ABSs) were predicted to have on access to justice: Some argued that ABSs would decrease access to justice because they would cherry-pick the most profitable work, leaving the less profitable work to existing firms, driving them out of business. It was considered that this concern would be mitigated by requiring the frontline regulator to take account of the regulatory objective of access to justice in considering an application for an ABS license.
ii. The cost of regulation: There was strong debate over who should cover the costs to establish the new regulatory bodies, and who would pay for their operation. The Government's position, and the position that prevailed, was that it would be the legal service providers, via fees levied by the regulators.[48]

On the topic of ABS, the Law Society stated that it: "supports the development of new business structures for the delivery of legal services to the public. The Law Society believes that, provided the necessary consumer protection can be put in place, there should be no restrictions on the entities through which legal services can be provided to the public."[49]

Less enthusiastic but nevertheless supportive, the Bar Council stated: "The proposed new ABSs may well provide improved ways for consumers to access legal services and provide new sources of work for barristers."[50]

Their support of ABSs was not without reserve—for example, the Law Society emphasized that ABSs should be subject to the same regulations as other structures,[51] and the Bar Council stressed that the regulations should assure proper standards of conduct by lawyers and nonlawyers alike.[52]

In spite of the more or less tepid support of the Law Society and the Bar Council, not all lawyers were in favor of the Bill, and notably not in favor of ABSs. For example, Clive Sutton, of the Solicitors Sole Practitioners Group, said that given the changes had only previously been adopted by two states in Australia, they were "untried and untested innovation," and they would "[put] at risk the independence of legal advice, via the profit interests of commercial owners."[53]

First-hand perspective

Sir David Clementi (online): Clementi explains why he was chosen to prepare a report on the regulatory system for lawyers, and his approach in preparing the report.

NOTES

1. Some efforts to reform were attempted even sooner, in 1989. See: Richard Devlin and Ora Morison, "Access to Justice and the Ethics and Politics of Alternative Business Structures," *The Canadian Bar Review* 91 (2012): 508–511, http://ssrn.com/abstract=2437035. This article also contains an excellent review of the larger historical and political context in England and Wales. Ibid., 508–525.

2. Paul Paton has provided a succinct review of the events that led to the adoption of the Legal Services Act. See Paul D. Paton, "Between a Rock and a Hard Place: The Future of Self-Regulation—Canada between the United States and the English / Australian Experience," *Journal of the Professional Lawyer* (2008): 97–104, https://ssrn.com/abstract=1226802.

3. Michael McLaren and Marianne Butler, "Origins of the Legal Services Act 2007," in *Guide to the Legal Services Act 2007*, ed. James Thorne and Iain Miller (UK: LexisNexis, 2009), 2.

4. Ibid., 1.

5. Department for Constitutional Affairs, "The Future of Legal Services: Putting Consumers First," October, 2005, 8, 94, http://webarchive.nationalarchives.gov.uk/+/http://www.dca.gov.uk/legalsys/folwp.pdf.

6. Director General of Fair Trading, "Competition in Professions," March, 2001, 30, http://webarchive.nationalarchives.gov.uk/20140402142426/http:/www.oft.gov.uk/shared_oft/reports/professional_bodies/oft328.pdf.

7. Ibid., 13. This phrase actually reads "by a system where individual practitioners rather than business structures were regulated." Presumably this construction was a mistake and the intended sentence was "Concerns about regulating solicitors employed by non-solicitors could be met by a system where business structures rather than individual practitioners were regulated."

8. "Government Conclusions—Competition and Regulation in the Legal Services Market: A Report Following the Consultation 'In the Public Interest?'" July 2003, http://webarchive.nationalarchives.gov.uk/+/http://www.dca.gov.uk/consult/general/oftreptconc.htm.

9. Ibid.

10. Ibid.

11. David Clementi, "Consultation Paper on the Review of the Regulatory Framework for Legal Services in England and Wales," March, 2004, http://webarchive.nationalarchives.gov.uk/+/http://www.legal-services-review.org.uk/content/consult/review.htm.

12. McLaren and Butler, "Origins of the Legal Services Act 2007," 3–4.

13. Ibid., 4.

14. David Clementi, "Review of the Regulatory Framework for Legal Services in England and Wales: Final Report," December, 2004, http://webarchive.nationalarchives.gov.uk/+/http://www.legal-services-review.org.uk/content/report/report-chap.pdf.

15. Ibid., 14–15.

16. Ibid., 18.

17. Ibid.

18. Ibid., 15.

19. Ibid., 16.
20. Ibid.
21. Ibid., 17.
22. Ibid.
23. Ibid., 1–2.
24. Ibid.
25. Ibid., 2–3.
26. Ibid., 3.
27. Ibid., 5–6.
28. Ibid., 27–30.
29. Ibid., 32, 34–35.
30. Ibid., 36–37.
31. Ibid., 64.
32. Ibid., 73.
33. Ibid., 138–139.
34. Ibid., 139.
35. Ibid., 108–109.
36. Ibid., 110.
37. Ibid., 114.
38. Ibid., 112.
39. Ibid., 117.
40. Ibid., 116–118.
41. Lord Falconer of Thoroton, "Legal Services: Clementi Report," written statement to House of Lords, December 15, 2004, http://hansard.millbanksystems.com/written_statements/2004/dec/15/legal-services-clementi-report#column_83ws.
42. Department for Constitutional Affairs, "The Future of Legal Services," 94.
43. McLaren and Butler, "Origins of the Legal Services Act 2007," 10.
44. "Memorandum by the Law Society of England and Wales," *Joint Committee on the Draft Legal Services Bill Minutes of Evidence*, June 2006, http://www.publications.parliament.uk/pa/jt200506/jtselect/jtlegal/232/6060802.htm ("Law Society Memorandum").
45. "Memorandum by the General Council of the Bar," *Joint Committee on the Draft Legal Services Bill Minutes of Evidence*, June, 2006, http://www.publications.parliament.uk/pa/jt200506/jtselect/jtlegal/232/6060812.htm ("Bar Council Memorandum").
46. McLaren and Butler, "Origins of the Legal Services Act 2007," 10.
47. Ibid., 10–11.
48. Ibid., 11.
49. Law Society Memorandum.
50. Bar Council Memorandum.
51. Law Society Memorandum.
52. Bar Council Memorandum.
53. "Supermarket 'Law Shops' to Sell Legal Services," *BBC News*, October 6, 2011, http://www.bbc.co.uk/news/uk-15187154.

Chapter 4

The Seismic Shift (with Survivors)

Adopted by the UK Parliament on October 30, 2007, the Legal Services Act entered into effect in stages, with the final elements relating to alternate business structures (ABSs) entering into effect in 2011 and the SRA issuing the first ABS licenses in March, 2012.[1]

With the full entry into effect of the Act, here is what the regulatory environment of England and Wales looks like today—not just the new, but also some of the old that survived and which, in light of the new, has taken on new significance.[2]

THE NEW

The new Legal Services Board (LSB) acts as an oversight regulator, whose primary role is to regulate the approved regulators. Each approved regulator is, in turn, responsible for "frontline" regulation. Responsibility for all complaints across all legal professions is vested in the single body, the OLC or Legal Ombudsman. All regulators are required to act in conformity with defined regulatory objectives.

It is no longer only individual lawyers, but also entities that are subject to regulation. Both must be authorized in order to carry on reserved legal activities. Regulated entities include traditional lawyer-owned law firms as well as "licensable bodies," otherwise referred to as ABSs. ABSs may be owned or managed, in whole or in part, by nonlawyers. In regulating both entities and individuals, rules are shifting away from proscriptive, "tick-the-box" approach toward an "outcomes" approach, where the focus is on the outcomes achieved rather than on the processes used to achieve them.

Let's look at each of these elements, in turn:

LSB as Oversight Regulator

The LSB is an independent body that is accountable to the Parliament, through the Lord Chancellor, and with sponsorship by the Ministry of Justice.[3] The LSB is responsible for overseeing the regulation of lawyers in England and Wales, and, in that role, it regulates ten "frontline" legal regulatory authorities in England and Wales—those authorities are discussed below.

The LSB consists of a chairman, appointed by the Lord Chancellor, and between seven and ten "ordinary" members, appointed by the Lord Chancellor in consultation with the Lord Chief Justice. The chairman and a majority of the ordinary members must be laypersons[4] (that is, they may not be lawyers, nor may they have been lawyers in the past).

In appointing ordinary members, the Lord Chancellor is to seek persons who, between them, have expertise or knowledge in the areas of not only the provision of legal services, legal education and training and the workings of courts, but also in a wide range of other areas: consumer affairs, competition matters, the maintenance of professional standards outside the legal profession, the handling of complaints, commercial affairs, the differing needs of consumers and the provision of claims management services.

The period for which an ordinary member is appointed cannot exceed five years, and members cannot be reappointed more than once.

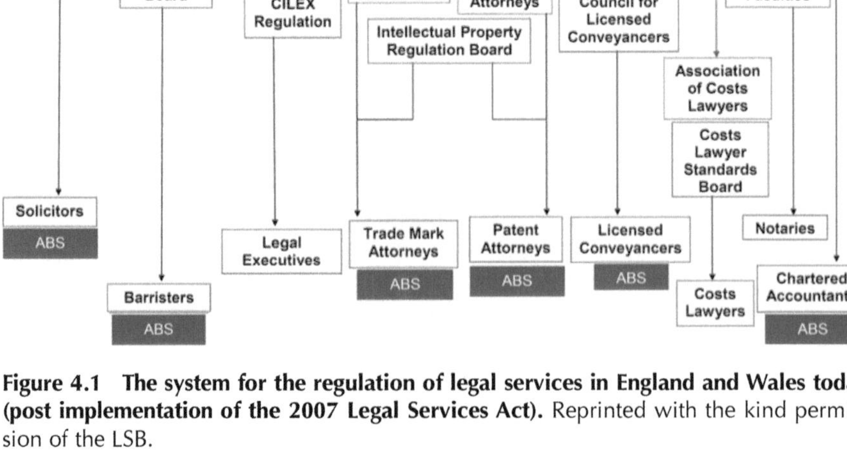

Figure 4.1 The system for the regulation of legal services in England and Wales today (post implementation of the 2007 Legal Services Act). Reprinted with the kind permission of the LSB.

In its principal role as "the regulator of regulators," the LSB has what has been described as "draconian"[5] powers. These include setting standards for and providing guidance to each frontline regulator, overseeing the OLC, recommending to the Lord Chancellor changes to the scope of reserved legal services (discussed below) and to the functions of approved regulators and exercising control over the funding of the regulatory system. However, except in exceptional circumstances, the LSB does not have any direct control over regulated individuals or entities—those powers are reserved for the frontline regulators.[6]

In 2016, the International Bar Association (IBA) issued a draft report in which it questioned the LSB's independence from government by describing the LSB as an example of "external involvement in the regulatory scheme."[7] The LSB immediately rejected that claim, stating that it was "entirely misconceived." This is because, the LSB stated, "the appointments process for the members of the LSB takes place under rigorous independent scrutiny" including judicial representation, and, once appointed, the members take their decisions "without fear or favour from government." Indeed, the LSB stated, "No decision made by the LSB and its executive has ever been at the 'control,' behest of or subject to any improper influence whatsoever by the government."[8] Since the statement in the IBA's draft report was false, the LSB concluded, the IBA should remove it from its final report.

Frontline Regulators and Regulatory Competition

Save for a small number of exemptions (notably including, as discussed below, European lawyers), any individual as well as entity that seeks to carry out a reserved legal activity must be authorized by an approved frontline regulator (at which time they are referred to as "authorised persons").[9] Given the fragmentation of the legal services profession in England and Wales, there exist over fifteen of them, of which nine fall under the remit of the LSB as follows:[10]

In most cases, it is the regulatory body listed in the right column (not the representative body listed in the left) that has the power to authorize individuals and entities to carry out reserved activities, and that also has the power to take disciplinary action in relation to those same persons. The two principal regulatory bodies for lawyers are the SRA and the Bar Standards Board (BSB). Like the chair of the LSB itself, the chairs of the SRA and the BSB are laypersons.

Frontline regulators have the right to make their own rules, but they must conform to the rules and guidelines fixed by the LSB, and certain rules require the prior approval of the LSB. A frontline regulator must first seek approval from the LSB before being able to act as a licensing authority. To date, five authorities have requested and have received the authority to license ABSs.

Table 4.1 Frontline regulators which fall under the remit of the LSB

Profession	*Approved regulator (representative body)*	*Independent Regulatory Body*
Solicitors	Law Society	SRA
Barristers	Bar Council	BSB
Legal Executives	Chartered Institute of Legal Executives	CILEx Regulation
Licensed Conveyancers	[no representative body]	CLCs
Patent Attorneys	Charted Institute of Patent Attorneys	Intellectual Property Regulation Board
Trade Mark Attorneys	Chartered Institute of Trade Mark Attorneys	
Costs Lawyers	Association of Costs Lawyers	Costs Lawyer Standards Board
Notaries	[no representative body]	Master of the Faculties
Chartered Accountants	Institute of Charted Accountants in England and Wales	[decisions regarding legal activities are delegated to independently chaired Probate Committee]

Those five authorities are: the SRA, the Council for Licensed Conveyancers (CLC), the Institute of Charted Accountants in England and Wales (ICAEW), the Intellectual Property Regulation Board (IPReg), and the BSB.

In the event that a frontline regulator fails in any of its duties and obligations under the Act, the LSB is empowered to take a number of actions, including issuing directions to the frontline regulator to correct the deficiency, publishing a public censure, imposing a financial penalty, appointing a different person to perform the regulatory function and recommending that the Lord Chancellor cancel the regulator's approval.[11]

This complex regulatory framework, which has its origins in the fragmentation of the legal services market in England and Wales, has led to a seemingly novel result: regulatory competition, or competitive regulation. In essence, in certain contexts and notably with respect to ABSs, legal service providers in England and Wales are not required to work with one regulator—they can select one from a panel of approved regulators.

At the time the Legal Services Bill was under debate, some argued that regulatory competition may lead to a relaxation of professional standards—that there would be a "race to the bottom" with regulators competing to impose the least stringent rules.[12] However, these arguments were overruled by the belief that, instead, regulatory competition would lead to better regulation because it "will help ensure that those bodies operate a licensing regime efficiently, in a user friendly manner and without unnecessary restrictions. Oversight by the LSB will help ensure that in making the necessary rules the licensing bodies balance objectives appropriately."[13]

In fact, the phenomena of regulatory competition found in the regulatory framework for legal services in England and Wales is not novel—a number of examples have preceded it, such as that of corporate law in the United States, and notably the choices available to companies as regards state of incorporation. However, even if the phenomenon is not novel to England and Wales, its development there nevertheless seems to have sparked an increased interest in the phenomenon and its potential for use in other regulatory contexts. The best example of this increased interest is probably Gillian Hadfield's 2016 book *Rules for a Flat World: Why Humans Invented Law and How to Reinvent It For a Complex Global Economy*.[14] The phenomenon, and Hadfield's book in particular, is discussed in greater detail in part VI.

Research programs

The LSB conducts research in accordance with a 2010 document that establishes the LSB's research strategy. According to that document, "The LSB is committed to using research to ensure all the work we do is underpinned by robust relevant evidence."[15] The LSB has established internally a Research Section charged with establishing and assuring the fulfillment of the LSB's research program. The LSB makes available on its website its annually updated research program[16] as well as its research reports.[17]

In addition to the LSB, the frontline regulators have also established research programs. Most notable among them is the SRA, which publishes its research program each year, as well as a multitude of research reports.[18] In announcing the SRA's research program for 2016, Crispin Passmore, Executive Director for Policy, described the "ambitious" program as focused on issues "critical to the public interest and expanding and growing our evidence base," in order to help the SRA to continue making informed decisions. Passmore also stressed the importance for the SRA of understanding the impact of its regulation and of identifying ways to improve and refine its work.[19]

Office for Legal Complaints/Legal Ombudsman

The OLC is the board of the Legal Ombudsman. The OLC is a body subject to the regulatory oversight of the LSB. Through the Legal Ombudsman, this body provides a single, independent avenue for the resolution of complaints against authorized persons (regulated legal service providers).[20]

The OLC consists of a chairman and between six and eight additional "members." The chair is appointed by the LSB, with the approval of the Lord Chancellor, and the members are appointed by the LSB, after consultation with the chairman. The chair as well as the majority of the members must be laypersons (nonlawyers).[21]

Under the "scheme" of the Legal Ombudsman, frontline regulators must require authorized persons to have a complaints procedure and to inform their clients of the procedure. In turn, a complainant must first resort to that procedure before it can bring a claim before the Legal Ombudsman.[22]

The Legal Ombudsman has the power to "determine" a complaint, and notably, if the Legal Ombudsman decides the complaint is founded, to order redress in a variety of forms (to apologize, to pay monetary compensation, to correct an error, etc.). The Legal Ombudsman does not, however, have the power to take disciplinary action—that falls under the exclusive remit of the frontline regulators.[23]

Legal Services Consumer Panel

The Legal Services Act requires the LSB to establish and maintain a Consumer Panel for the purpose of representing the interests of consumers to the LSB. This panel is housed at the premises of the LSB, but it is operated independently of the LSB. The Panel consists of eight laypeople with a range of expertise (e.g., consumer services, consumer protection, competition, market research)[24] each appointed by the LSB subject to the approval of the Lord Chancellor. The Panel is supported by a policy secretariat.[25]

The Panel is mandated to represent the interests of a variety of consumers of legal services, including not only individuals, but also businesses and not-for-profit organizations. The Panel has the right to publish its advice to the LSB, and it does so regularly. The LSB is not obliged to follow the advice of the Panel but, in the event it disagrees with the Panel's advice, the LSB is obliged to explain its reasons.[26]

Two of the Panel's most important activities are its issuance of a Tracker Survey and a Consumer Impact Report. The Tracker Report is issued on an annual basis—each year the Panel surveys 3,000 members of the general public and consumers of legal services. Each year, the Panel asks the same questions, in order to determine what is and is not changing for them. The Consumer Impact Report is issued every other year. It combines evidence from the Tracker Survey with information from other parts of the sector, in order to shed additional light on what is and is not changing for consumers, where there have been improvements and where more improvement is needed.[27]

Regulatory Objectives

All regulators—the LSB, the frontline regulators, the OLC—are required to operate in furtherance of eight regulatory objectives. These objectives include protecting and promoting the public interest, supporting the constitutional principle of the rule of law, improving access to justice, protecting and promoting the interests of consumers of legal services, and promoting competition in the provision of legal services.[28]

Firm-based Regulation and the SRA's Authorization Requirements

As Clementi recognized, in permitting ABSs, the regulation of legal services would need to shift, in order to encompass the regulation of not just individuals, but of firms or entities as well. Accordingly, the SRA has modified its regulations to encompass entities as well as individuals (the BSB, the CLC, the ICAEW and the IPReg have also done so, but we will focus here on the SRA, as the largest frontline regulatory body for England and Wales). Notably, the SRA requires recognition and approval of "authorised persons" at two levels: at the level of the individual, and the level of the firm or entity.

The SRA's firm-based authorization requirements begin with the completion of a written application form. The SRA amends the form from time to time; as of the time this book went to press, the form was fourteen pages in length. In addition to items like the names of the applicant's address and expected areas of work (by subject matter), it also requires information such as the applicant's managers and owners (names), ownership and management structure, expected turnover and sources of funding (capital or debt).

The same 14-page application form is required for all applicants, regardless of whether they intend to operate as an ABS, a traditional law firm or as a sole practitioner. However, approximately 1.5 of the fourteen pages is reserved for "licensed bodies" or ABSs. These pages request, in part and in addition to the above:

- Details regarding the applicant's ultimate beneficial owner(s),
- The steps the applicant has taken to identify and resolve any potential conflicts of interest with respect to any nonlawyer owner or manager,
- A list of the persons entitled to exercise or control the exercise of voting power,
- A list of nonlawyers who will have significant influence over the management of the applicant, and
- Whether any nonlawyer has the right to impose directions or financial policies on the applicant.

The full application form is available on the SRA's website.[29]

Interestingly, prior to October, 2015, the application form was thirty pages in length, and it asked for a much greater volume of information and documentation from all applicants, not only ABSs. That information and documentation included:

- A business plan,
- An operating plan,
- Plans to outsource any work, including legal work,
- A description of systems and controls for protecting client monies and assets,
- Plans for financing and debt management,
- Profit/loss forecast and cash flow,
- Risk analysis (operational, breaches of confidentiality and conflicts of interest, firm viability, financial management, procedural, marketing, client service), and
- Plans to assure equal opportunity and diversity.[30]

Equally interestingly, the SRA did not issue a formal announcement of or explanation for its adoption of a remarkably shorter and simpler application form. The likely explanation is that it was adopted as a part of the SRA's larger efforts, at the urging of the LSB and others, to simplify and accelerate the application process, in part by getting "rid of some of the bureaucracy."[31]

Indeed, in the SRA's first years, it was heavily criticized for taking too long to approve applications, and, in particular for taking too long to approve novel structures, against which the SRA was accused of having "an inherent cognitive bias."[32] During those years, while "simple" applications might (or might not) have been processed quickly, the novel or complex ones took anywhere from five to twelve months for the SRA to process, with some taking as long as two years.[33] Today the average processing time is 2.5 months, with the longest taking about six months.[34]

In fact, the application form is just a first step in a laundry list of ongoing regulatory requirements. Under the SRA's new rules, all firms, regardless of their size and including sole practitioners, must meet the following requirements:

1. Compliance Plan: Every firm must have in place formal systems and plans to ensure that the firm complies with applicable ethical, professional and accounting standards.[35]
2. Compliance Officer for Legal Practice (COLP) and a Compliance Officer for Finance and Administration (COFA): Every firm must at all times have a designated COLP as well as COFA. The COLP is responsible for ensuring that the firm has in place the systems and controls needed to comply with the applicable ethical and professional standards (as set forth in the Handbook). These persons bear principal (but not sole) responsibility for

the firm's compliance and they are obliged to report to the SRA material noncompliance.[36]

Both the COLP and the COFA must be "fit and proper" to undertake their roles. In addition, the COLP must be either a lawyer of England or Wales, or a Registered European Lawyer (or certain other kinds of European lawyers but a Registered Foreign Lawyer does not qualify).[37] The COFA is responsible for ensuring that the firm complies with the SRA's accounting rules.[38]

3. Qualified to Supervise: At least one manager of the firm must be "qualified to supervise." A person is deemed to be qualified to supervise if he/she: (i) has been entitled to practice and has practicing as a lawyer for at least thirty-six months within the past ten years, and (ii) has completed training specified by the SRA.[39]
4. Professional Indemnity Insurance: All firms are required to carry professional indemnity insurance:[40] ABSs and incorporated firms in the minimum of £3 million per claim, and unincorporated firms and sole practitioners in the minimum amount of £2 million per claim. There are no mutual or group policies available. Each firm must secure its insurance for itself. The SRA has defined minimum terms and conditions for the coverage—for example, insurers may not reject a claim on the basis of fraud.[41] Insurers are not obliged to provide coverage, but, if they do, the coverage must meet those minimum terms. (As a result, many small firms considered to be high risk have experienced difficulty obtaining insurance, whereas larger firms considered lower risk typically experience little difficulty.[42])

Outcomes-focused Regulation

In regulating both entities and individuals, the SRA has shifted its rules away from a proscriptive, "tick-the-box" approach toward "outcomes-focused regulation" (OFR), described as an approach focused on the outcomes achieved rather than on the processes used to achieve them, and as a rejection as a "one size fits all" approach to regulation.

The SRA defends this approach as one which provides to firms the power "to implement the right systems and controls for your clients and type of practice. You will have more flexibility in how you achieve the right outcomes for your clients, which will require greater judgment on your part."[43]

The SRA explains that changes are reflected, not only in the Code of Conduct, but also in its approach to authorization, supervision and enforcement: "This will be risk based, proportionate and targeted and will involve a more open and constructive relationship between the SRA and those we regulate.

Firms that are already well-managed and providing a good service to their clients should have nothing to fear from this approach."[44]

Under OFR, for each issue addressed by the Code of Conduct, there are two lists: one of "outcomes" and the other of "indicative behaviors."

The SRA describes these as follows:

> "Outcomes" . . . describe what you are expected to achieve . . . in specific contexts. . . . The outcomes are mandatory.
>
> "Indicative behaviors" . . . provide non-mandatory examples of the kind of behaviors which may establish whether you have achieved the relevant outcomes.[45]

As an example, the Code of Conduct contains a list of sixteen outcomes on the topic of client care, followed by a list of twenty-eight indicative behaviors. One of those outcomes is "you treat your clients fairly" and the corresponding indicative behaviors include "agreeing an appropriate level of service with your client, for example the type and frequency of communications," "explaining your responsibilities and those of the client" and "ensuring that the client is told, in writing, the name and status of the person(s) dealing with the matter and the name and status of the person responsible for its overall supervision."[46]

As an additional example, the Code of Conduct contains a list of thirteen outcomes on the topic of management and supervision of the firm, followed by a list of six indicative behaviors. One of the outcomes is "you maintain systems and controls for monitoring the financial stability of your firm and risks to money and assets entrusted to you by clients and others." The corresponding indicative behaviors include "safekeeping of documents and assets entrusted to the firm," "controlling budgets, expenditure and cash flow" and "identifying and monitoring financial, operational and business continuity risks including complaints, credit risks and exposure."[47]

As a further example, the Code of Conduct contains a list of five outcomes on the topic of confidentiality and disclosure, followed by a list of seven indicative behaviors. One of the outcomes is "you keep the affairs of clients confidential unless disclosure is required or permitted by law or the client consents," and another outcome is "you have effective systems and controls in place to enable you to identify risks to client confidentiality and to mitigate those risks." The corresponding indicative behaviors include "your systems and controls for identifying risks to client confidentiality are appropriate to the size and complexity of the firm or in-house practice and the nature of the work undertaken, and enable you to assess all relevant circumstances."[48]

Investigation, Revocation and Intervention

The SRA has the power to investigate misconduct by an ABS, and to require explanations and documentation in that regard. If the SRA determines that the ABS or someone in connection with it has not respected the terms of its license or has engaged in dishonesty, and if the SRA deems that it is necessary to take action in order to protect the interests of the clients or the public, then the SRA may revoke the ABS's license and "intervene" in the ABS. In intervening, the SRA appoints an intervention agent, who is responsible for liquidating the ABS in an orderly manner.[49]

Registry of ABSs

Frontline regulators that act as licensing authorities for ABSs are required to maintain and publish a registry of the ABSs that they have authorized. Each of the SRA,[50] the CLC[51] and the ICAEW[52] maintain these registries on their respective websites. Each of IPReg and the BSB, respectively, maintain a separate registry.[53]

THE OLD, BUT WITH NEW SIGNIFICANCE

The Legal Services Act clearly changed the landscape for legal services in England and Wales. But certain elements of the old framework survived—two of those elements are worth noting here, because they take on a new significance in light of the new landscape:

Six Reserved Activities (No General Monopoly on Legal Services)

In England and Wales, non-legally qualified persons have always been, and today they continue to be able to provide legal services. The only restriction has been that they may not provide any of the six "reserved activities." Only these six activities may be performed by qualified lawyers: the exercise of rights of audience (appearing as an advocate before a court); the conduct of litigation (issuing proceedings before a court and commencing, prosecuting or defending those proceedings); reserved instrument activities (notably the conveyancing of real property); probate activities; notarial activities and the administration of oaths.[54]

The activities that appear on this list are far less interesting than the activities that do not appear on it. Notably, activities such as preparing contracts and providing legal analysis and advice do not appear. There is no need to be a qualified lawyer to be able to perform those, or, indeed, any other "legal" activity that is not one of the six reserved activities. In other words, outside of a narrow list of restricted activities, there is no lawyer monopoly on the provision of legal services in England or Wales.

European and Foreign Lawyers

In addition to being open to nonlawyers performing legal activities, England and Wales has for a long time been open to foreign lawyers. Their rules permit lawyers from nearly anywhere in the world to establish themselves and be regulated there, as Registered Foreign Lawyers, or, if they are members of the bar of a Member State of the European Union, then as Registered European Lawyers.[55] These lawyers can do so without attending law school or taking a bar exam in England and Wales. Their only restrictions are that they cannot claim to be solicitors or barristers (or other kind of UK lawyer) and, in the case of Registered Foreign Lawyers, they cannot engage in any of the six reserved activities.

The lack of a general monopoly on the provision of legal services and the ease with which foreign lawyers may work in England and Wales are additional evidence of the openness of the English and Welsh legal services market. As a result of this openness, from a base in England or Wales, it is not just possible but relatively easy to offer legal services in the law of pretty much any country in the world.

First-hand perspectives

Crispin Passmore, Executive Director, Solicitors Regulation Authority (Appendix): Passmore explains how the SRA inherited a "traditional and old-fashioned" regulatory system driven by the needs of the legal profession, and the SRA's ongoing journey to transform the system to one focused on consumers of legal services.

Elisabeth Davies, Chair, Legal Services Consumer Panel (online): Davies explains why it is important that the Legal Services Act requires the establishment of the Panel and the vital contributions the Panel makes toward an understanding the needs of consumers of legal services.

NOTES

1. "SRA Unveils Its First Three ABSs," *Legal Futures*, March 28, 2012, http://www.legalfutures.co.uk/latest-news/breaking-news-sra-unveils-its-first-three-abss.

2. For another overview of the current regulatory framework in England and Wales, see Hadfield and Rhode, "How to Regulate Legal Services," 1204–1211.

3. Framework Document: Agreement between the Ministry of Justice and the Legal Services Board," June, 2011, 8, http://www.legalservicesboard.org.uk/about_us/lsb_framework_document/pdf/moj_framework_agreement_june_2011.pdf.

4. Ibid., 8.

5. "LSB Could Pose Risk to Independence of Legal Profession, Warns Law Society President," *Legal Futures*, May 25, 2010, http://www.legalfutures.co.uk/latest-news/lsb-could-pose-risk-to-independence-of-legal-profession-warns-law-society-president.

6. Patricia Robertson and Katherine Watt, "The Regulatory Framework," in *Guide to the Legal Services Act 2007*, ed. James Thorne and Iain Miller (UK: Lexis-Nexis, 2009), 16.

7. Michael Cross, "IBA 2016: Legal Independence in E&W Under Attack," *The Law Society Gazette*, September 22, 2016, https://www.lawgazette.co.uk/news/iba-2016-legal-independence-in-eandw-under-attack/5057851.article.

8. Neil Buckley, Letter to David W. Rivkin, September 23, 2016, http://www.legalservicesboard.org.uk/news_publications/speeches_presentations/2016/20160923_LSB_Letter_Re_Draft_Report_IBA_Pres_Task_Force_Independance_Of_Legal_Prof.pdf.

9. Robertson and Watt, "The Regulatory Framework," 25.

10. "Approved Regulators," Legal Services Board, accessed on March 20, 2017, http://www.legalservicesboard.org.uk/can_we_help/approved_regulators/.

11. Robertson and Watt, "The Regulatory Framework," 13.

12. Frank H. Stephen, *Lawyers, Markets and Regulation* (Cheltenham, UK: Edward Elgar, 2013), 119. For a more detailed discussion of the potential advantages and disadvantages of regulatory competition, see Baldwin, Cave and Lodge, *Understanding Regulation*, 356–369.

13. Frank H. Stephen, *Lawyers, Markets and Regulation*, 118–119.

14. Gillian Hadfield, *Rules for a Flat World: Why Humans Invented Law and How to Reinvent It For a Complex Global Economy* (New York: Oxford University Press, 2016).

15. Legal Services Board, "Research Strategy," June 14, 2010, 2, http://www.legalservicesboard.org.uk/what_we_do/Research/pdf/lsb_research_strategy_2010_formatted_version.pdf.

16. "About LSB Research: LSB research programme," Legal Services Board, accessed on March 20, 2017, https://research.legalservicesboard.org.uk/about-lsb-research/lsb-research-programme/.

17. "Reports," Legal Services Board, accessed on March 20, 2017, https://research.legalservicesboard.org.uk/reports/.

18. "Research and Reports," Legal Services Board, last modified on October 25, 2016, http://www.sra.org.uk/sra/how-we-work/reports.page.

19. "News Release: Research Projects to Inform the Work of the SRA," Legal Services Board, January 4, 2016, http://www.sra.org.uk/sra/news/press/research-programme-2016.page.

20. Patricia Robertson and Katherine Watt, "The LSB's Role in the Regulatory Framework," in *Guide to the Legal Services Act 2007*, ed. James Thorne and Iain Miller (UK: LexisNexis, 2009), 46–51.

21. "Office for Legal Complaints (OLC) Operating Framework," July, 2012, 2, http://www.legalombudsman.org.uk/wp-content/uploads/2014/08/OLC-Operating-framework-20121.pdf.

22. Robertson and Watt, "The Regulatory Framework," 21.

23. Nicholas Peacock, "The Office for Legal Complaints," in *Guide to the Legal Services Act 2007*, ed. James Thorne and Iain Miller (UK: LexisNexis, 2009), 82–85.

24. "Panel Members," Legal Services Consumer Panel, accessed on March 17, 2017, http://www.legalservicesconsumerpanel.org.uk/aboutus/panel_members/index.html.

25. "Welcome to the Legal Services Consumer Panel," Legal Services Consumer Panel, accessed on March 17, 2017, http://www.legalservicesconsumerpanel.org.uk/index.html.

26. Robertson and Watt, "The LSB's Role," 54.

27. For more information, see "Consumer Impact Report," Legal Services Consumer Panel, accessed on March 17, 2017, http://www.legalservicesconsumerpanel.org.uk/ourwork/consumerwelfareindex.html.

28. Legal Services Board, "The Regulatory Objectives: Legal Services Act 2007," undated, http://www.legalservicesboard.org.uk/news_publications/publications/pdf/regulatory_objectives.pdf

29. The form can also be downloaded from this page: "New Applicants," Solicitors Regulation Authority, accessed on March 17, 2017, http://www.sra.org.uk/solicitors/firm-based-authorisation/authorisation-recognition.page.

30. Form FA1 v19 dated July 23, 2015. It appears that this version of the form is no longer available online. A copy is on file with the author.

31. Monidipa Fouzder, "SRA Says 'Sorry' Over ABS Application Delays," *The Law Society Gazette*, April 27, 2015, http://www.lawgazette.co.uk/practice/sra-says-sorry-over-abs-application-delays/5048340.fullarticle.

32. Robert Cross, "Balancing Regulatory Risk," (presentation at UCL International Access to Justice Conference, London, England, June 20, 2014), 25, https://research.legalservicesboard.org.uk/wp-content/media/UCL-AtoJ-Conference-presentation-20-June-2014.pdf; see also Neil Rose, "SRA's Approach to Licensing ABSs 'Damaging Competition, Consumers and Access to Justice,'" *Legal Futures*, April 9, 2014, http://www.legalfutures.co.uk/latest-news/sras-approach-licensing-abss-damaging-competition-consumers-access-justice.

33. Dan Bindman, "Cypriot Construction Consultancy Becomes ABS for its International Kudos," *Legal Futures*, January 17, 2014, http://www.legalfutures.co.uk/latest-news/cypriot-construction-consultancy-becomes-abs-international-kudos.

34. Neil Rose, "SRA Finally Taken Off Report Over Way It Handles ABS Applications," *Legal Futures*, May 20, 2015, http://www.legalfutures.co.uk/latest-news/sra-finally-taken-off-report-over-way-it-handles-abs-applications. See also Nick Hilborne, "Not So Slow: SRA Approving Alternative Business Structures in Only Two Weeks," *Legal Futures*, February 17, 2016, http://www.legalfutures.co.uk/latest-news/not-so-slow-sra-approving-alternative-business-structures-in-only-two-weeks.

35. See SRA Code of Conduct, Chapter 7, "Management of Your Business," November 1, 2015, http://www.sra.org.uk/solicitors/handbook/code/content.page. See also SRA Authorisation Rules for Legal Services Bodies and Licensable Bodies 2011, Rule 8.2, "Suitable Arrangements for Compliance, http://www.sra.org.uk/solicitors/handbook/authorisationrules/content.page.

36. See generally, "COLPs and COFAs," Solicitors Regulation Authority, accessed on March 20, 2017, http://www.sra.org.uk/solicitors/colp-cofa.page.

37. "What is a COLP and COFA?" Solicitors Regulation Authority, last modified May 13, 2013, http://www.sra.org.uk/solicitors/colp-cofa/ethos-roles.page#roles.

38. "Responsibilities of COLPs and COFAs," Solicitors Regulation Authority, last modified on September 10, 2014, http://www.sra.org.uk/solicitors/colp-cofa/responsibilities-record-report.page.

39. See Practice Framework Rules, Rule 12, "Persons Who Must Be 'Qualified to Supervise,'" November 1, 2015, http://www.sra.org.uk/solicitors/handbook/practising/part3/rule12/content.page.

40. See Indemnity Insurance Rules, Rule 4, "Obligation to Effect Insurance," November 1, 2015, http://www.sra.org.uk/solicitors/handbook/indemnityins/part2/content.page.

41. See SRA Indemnity Insurance Rules 2013—Appendix 1, "SRA Minimum Terms and Conditions of Professional Indemnity Insurance," http://www.sra.org.uk/solicitors/handbook/indemnityins/appendix-1/content.page.

42. Frank Maher, "PII Renewal: The Insurance Issues Facing Law Firms," *LexisNexis Future of Law Blog*, May 28, 2013, http://blogs.lexisnexis.co.uk/futureoflaw/2013/05/pii-renewal-the-insurance-issues-facing-law-firms/.

43. Solicitors Regulation Authority, "Outcomes-Focused Regulation at a Glance: Your Quick Guide to Getting Started with OFR and the New Handbook," undated, http://c.ymcdn.com/sites/ncbp.org/resource/collection/F9556696-FF20–442A-B922–0FE6CFD2FB3E/Outcomes_focused_regulation_Redacted.pdf.

44. Ibid.

45. Ibid.

46. See SRA Code of Conduct, Chapter 1, "Client Care," November 1, 2016, http://www.sra.org.uk/solicitors/handbook/code/part2/content.page.

47. See SRA Code of Conduct, Chapter 7, "Management of Your Business," November 1, 2016, http://www.sra.org.uk/solicitors/handbook/code/part3/rule7/content.page.

48. See SRA Code of Conduct, Chapter 4, "Confidentiality and Disclosure, November 1, 2016, http://www.sra.org.uk/solicitors/handbook/code/part2/rule4/content.page.

49. ""The following entities are registered with IPReg as at 30 May 2017," IPReg, http://ipreg.org.uk/wp-content/files/2017/05/Registered-Bodies-List-170530.pdf; Bar Standards Board, "Entities, Including Alternative Business Structures," accessed June 19, 2017, https://www.barstandardsboard.org.uk/regulatory-requirements/entities,-including-alternative-business-structures/.

50. "Search for a Licensed Body (ABS), Solicitors Regulation Authority, accessed on March 17, 2017, http://www.sra.org.uk/solicitors/firm-based-authorisation/abs/abs-search.page.

51. "ABS Register," Council for Licensed Conveyancers, accessed on March 20, 2017, http://www.conveyancer.org.uk/CLC-Consumers/ABS-Register.aspx.

52. "Probate Register," Institute of Chartered Accountants in England and Wales, last modified on January 24, 2017, http://www.icaew.com/-/media/corporate/files/technical/legal-and-regulatory/probate-and-abs/probate-register-2017.ashx.

53. "The following entities are registered with IPReg as at 30 May 2017," IPReg, http://ipreg.org.uk/wp-content/files/2017/05/Registered-Bodies-List-170530.pdf; Bar Standards Board, "Entities, Including Alternative Business Structures," accessed June 19, 2017, https://www.barstandardsboard.org.uk/regulatory-requirements/entities,-including-alternative-business-structures/.

54. "Reserved Legal Activities," Legal Services Board, accessed on March 17, 2017, http://www.legalservicesboard.org.uk/can_we_help/faqs/Reserved_Legal_Activities.htm.

55. See generally, "Registered European Lawyers and Registered Foreign Lawyers," last modified on December, 2016, http://www.sra.org.uk/solicitors/registered-european-foreign-lawyers.page.

Chapter 5

Aftershocks on Their Way?

At the time this book went to press, there were about 430 ABSs listed on the SRA's registry, about 60 the CLC's, about 170 on the ICAEW's and about 40 on IPReg's. (The BSB had only just begun licensing ABSs). The shares of the large majority of these approximately 700 ABSs are privately held. The shares of approximately fifteen of them are held by the public not directly, but indirectly in that the ABS is owned, in whole or in part, by another company that is publicly held. For example, the joint venture Carole Nash Legal Services is owned in part by Carole Nash Insurance Consultants Ltd., which, in turn, is owned by Groupama SA, a French mutual company.

The shares of one UK-based ABS are listed directly on a stock exchange. That ABS is Gateley plc—its shares were first listed on AIM (Alternative Investment Market, a sub-market of the London Stock Exchange) in June 2015.

Is the number 700 large or small? The response depends upon who you ask. At least one person believes that this number will, or, at least that it should, grow significantly in the coming years: In October, 2015, Paul Philip, the Chief Executive of the SRA, stated that, in the future, there is no reason why solicitors setting up a new law firm should not do so as an ABS.[1] This is because, he elaborated, ABS creates a more flexible structure, with better opportunities for inward investment, such as IT. Further, ABSs offer better access to venture capital as well as better exit opportunities. In his opinion, England and Wales are moving to a world where lawyers will be "business people first and lawyers second."[2]

The implementation of the Legal Services Act has not been smooth. The new regulatory bodies learned their roles through some trial and error, and some would say this remains the case for the SRA. Different elements of the new framework have caused confusion and frustration: working through the long and complex ABS application process, securing professional indemnity insurance, understanding the exact roles and responsibilities of COLPs and COFAs and notably their reporting requirements[3] are just a few examples.

Nevertheless, many in England and Wales are enthusiastic about ABSs and about the regulatory reforms as a whole. For example, in its December 2014 Consumer Impact Report, the Legal Services Consumer Panel concluded that overall the reforms have been positive for consumers, who "are happier with the choice available to them," and are "more satisfied with value for money."[4]

On the other hand, some in England and Wales remain skeptical. One example is Jonathan Goldsmith, a former director of the Law Society:

> We know that we are entering a so-called paradise. Customer-friendly non-lawyers are offering low-price and easy-to-understand packages to rescue clients so misused by lawyers for so long.
>
> But is LegalZoom or Rocket Lawyer, EY, PWC Legal or KPMG going to go to the police station at midnight, or face abuse in parliament or the press, for taking on unpopular causes? Prophets of fashion tell us that legal services are going be revolutionised, and lawyers could disappear, with the onset of artificial intelligence, social networking, robotics, internet-based legal diagnostic tools, tele-lawyering, online dispute resolution, and virtual hearings.
>
> A flaw in such a future has always seemed to me that there is no place for the kind of work undertaken on behalf of the weakest and most abused, even more so the most unpopular.[5]

In this context, Goldsmith argues that the government and regulators need to take steps to assure the continuation of "awkward smaller firms"[6] that will undertake the kind of work that others shrink from, and notably the protection of human rights.

In the opinion of Sir Andrew Burns, the chairman of the BSB, for the time being, enough work has been done in England and Wales to break down barriers to competition, growth and innovation, and now "the supply side of the market needs time to take up the opportunities . . . on offer, including with appropriate assistance from their relevant front line regulators." In the meantime, he stated, the priority for the regulators today should be to address the impact of the reduction in government-funded legal aid by examining how the need for legal services can be met more effectively. In sum, he argues, regulators in England and Wales are prioritizing business users of the courts (property, probate and small business claims) ahead of the most vulnerable and disenfranchised, who need greater assistance in the areas of family, criminal and immigration.[7]

In contrast, others think that the changes in England and Wales have not gone far enough, and that continued evolution is not just needed, but needed urgently. For example, some argue that too many restrictions on in-house solicitors remain—that their employers, be they corporations or public authorities, should have more freedom for their in-house solicitors to be able to perform unreserved activities for outside clients without necessarily needing to acquire an ABS license.[8] (Under the current rules, authorized persons such as solicitors who work in-house may provide legal services, reserved or unreserved, to outside clients only if their employer is an ABS). The SRA has responded to this call for change, saying that it plans to implement consultations on the rules for in-house lawyers in the near future, with the expectation that it will lead to a new approach that will allow "much more freedom and flexibility for solicitors and businesses."[9] The LSB has expressed strong support for lifting certain restrictions, stating that while the risks must be balanced, "the removal of regulatory restrictions for in-house lawyers could provide greater access to justice for consumers," and that the SRA's review "will need to be far-reaching."[10]

Others who want to take the changes further include the Ministry of Justice and the Competition and Markets Authority (CMA), respectively:

In November, 2015, the Ministry of Justice announced that in 2016 it would launch a consultation on removing barriers to entry for alternative business models in legal services, and on establishing not just the operational but also the structural independence of legal service regulators from their representative bodies.[11] The SRA welcomed this announcement, in particular as regards the question of structural independence, issuing this official statement:

> In our view, a key requirement for the regulation of any profession or market in the public interest is the confidence of the public. If the regulator does not have public confidence, it cannot do its job. The key to public confidence is independence and public accountability.
>
> It is impossible to see how a regulator could have the confidence of the public if it is also the body that represents those who are regulated. The public deserves proper independent regulation, and the profession deserves proper representation. But the two functions must be, and must be seen to be, separate.
>
> Modern regulation has to be independent and fully accountable to the public. We welcome the Government's proposals and are looking forward to working with others as we explore the detail.[12]

On the other hand, the Law Society's reaction to the Ministry's announcement was less than welcoming. Seeking, some argue, to "roll back" the reforms of the Legal Services Act, the Law Society expressed opposition to the proposal for more complete independence, and also argued that certain power of the SRA should be returned to the Law Society, most notably the powers to set the standards and rules under which the legal profession operates, and with respect to legal education and training, "so that standards are led by the people who practice." In this manner, the Law Society argues, the

SRA's function should be to enforce the rules and standards set by the legal profession.[13]

For its part, over the course of 2016 the CMA conducted a study of the legal services sector for consumers and small businesses so as to examine "long-standing concerns" about affordability and standards of service as well as about the "complexity of the current regulatory framework."[14] The CMA explained that its motivations to conduct the study included, in part, the results of a recent Tracker Survey issued by the Legal Services Consumer Panel which found that one in ten consumers believed the service they received was "poor value for money."[15] In this context, the CMA focused its study on individuals and small businesses, on the assumption that large businesses have the resources to navigate the legal services sector with greater ease.

Released in December, 2016, the CMA's 518-page report makes a number of recommendations, including full independence for legal regulators, a move away from regulation by title to regulation based upon activity, and the adoption of regulatory requirements to increase price, quality and service transparency.[16] In a recommendation highly reminiscent of the 2001 report of the Office of Fair Trading (the report of the CMA's predecessor that lead to the 2007 Legal Services Act), the CMA's report includes the recommendation that the government launch "a review of the entire regulatory framework, with the aim of making the regulatory regime more flexible and risk-based in the long term."[17]

In other words, not only were the changes in England and Wales seismic, but also they are far from finished.

First-hand perspective

Alex Roy, Head of Development and Research, Legal Services Board (online): Roy explains why it is not just ABSs but the more generally open regulatory environment as a whole that allows firms to experiment with legal services and is the source of the competitive advantage of England and Wales.

NOTES

1. Nick Hilborne, "Philip: If It's a New Law Firm, It Should Be an ABS," *Legal Futures*, October 15, 2015, http://www.legalfutures.co.uk/latest-news/philip-if-its-a-new-law-firm-it-should-be-an-abs.
2. Ibid.
3. See, for example, Joan Loughrey and Sundeep Aulakh, "Framing Regulation and Compliance in Legal Services Firms: the Role of the Compliance

Officer for Legal Practice," (paper presented at Georgetown University Law Center, "Authorized Revolution: Regulatory Disruption of the Legal Services Market," Washington, D.C., April 24, 2015), http://www.law.georgetown.edu/continuing-legal-education/programs/academic-conferences/regulating-legal-services.cfm. See also Nick Hilborne, "COLPs Failing to Report Problems to SRA, Groundbreaking Study Finds," *Legal Futures*, March 3, 2016, http://www.legalfutures.co.uk/latest-news/colps-failing-to-report-problems-to-sra-groundbreaking-study-finds.

4. Legal Services Consumer Panel, "Consumer Impact Report 2014," December 5, 2014, 3, http://www.legalservicesconsumerpanel.org.uk/publications/research_and_reports/documents/Consumer%20Impact%20Report%203.pdf.

5. Jonathan Goldsmith, "Endangered Lawyers," *Law Society Gazette*, January 26, 2015, http://www.lawgazette.co.uk/analysis/comment%E2%80%94%20and%E2%80%94%20opinion/endangered%E2%80%94%20lawyers/5046285.article.

6. Ibid.

7. "LSB Underplaying Needs of 'Vulnerable' In Favour of Business, Warns Bar Regulator," *Legal Futures*, March 3, 2015, http://www.legalfutures.co.uk/latest-news/lsb-underplaying-needs-of-vulnerable-in-favour-of-business-warns-bar-regulator.

8. Nick Hilborne, "Rules Forcing Local Authorities to Set Up ABSs 'Risk Privatisation of Public Sector Legal Services,'" *Legal Futures*, August 3, 2015, http://www.legalfutures.co.uk/latest-news/rules-forcing-local-authorities-to-set-up-abss-risk-privatisation-of-public-sector-legal-services.

9. Nick Hilborne, "Business Services Giant Blames SRA Rules for Scuppering ABS Plans," *Legal Futures*, July 31, 2015, http://www.legalfutures.co.uk/latest-news/business-services-giant-blames-sra-rules-for-scuppering-abs-plans.

10. Neil Rose, "Reform of In-House Lawyer Regulation Could Improve Consumer Access to Justice, Says LSB," *Legal Futures*, July 30, 2015, http://www.legalfutures.co.uk/latest-news/reform-of-in-house-lawyer-regulation-could-improve-consumer-access-to-justice-says-lsb.

11. Nick Hilborne, "Government Promises to Clear Way for Supermarket and Estate Agent ABSs," *Legal Futures*, November 30, 2015, http://www.legalfutures.co.uk/latest-news/government-promises-to-clear-way-for-supermarket-and-estate-agent-abss.

12. "SRA Backs Call for Independent Legal Regulators," Solicitors Regulation Authority, December 2, 2015, http://www.sra.org.uk/sra/news/press/government-independence-plans-backed.page.

13. Neil Rose, "Profession Set on Collision Course with Government over Independent Regulation," *Legal Futures*, December 1, 2015, http://www.legalfutures.co.uk/latest-news/profession-set-on-collision-course-with-government-over-independent-regulation.

14. Nick Hilborne, "Competition and Markets Authority to Investigate Legal Services," *Legal Futures*, January 13, 2016, http://www.legalfutures.co.uk/latest-news/competition-and-markets-authority-to-investigate-legal-services. See "Competition and Markets Authority Case: Legal Services Market Study," last modified December 15, 2016, https://www.gov.uk/cma-cases/legal-services-market-study.

15. Hilborne, "Competition and Markets Authority to Investigate Legal Services."

16. "CMA Final Report: Demand for Better Price and Service Transparency from Law Firms, and Review of Legal Regulation," *Legal Futures*, December 15, 2016, http://www.legalfutures.co.uk/latest-news/cma-final-report-demand-better-price-service-transparency-law-firms-review-legal-regulation.

17. Competition & Markets Authority, "Legal Services Market Study: Final Report," December 15, 2016, 5, https://assets.publishing.service.gov.uk/media/58518dc1ed915d0aeb0000a4/legal-services-market-study-final-report.pdf.

Chapter 6

Assessment

To what extent has England and Wales implemented the OECD's six essential elements of an effective regulatory policy? For each element, the response lies upon a spectrum, from "yes," "for the most part," "sort of," "limited," "not really" and "no:"

Table 6.1 Assessment for England and Wales

1	Independent regulation	For the most part	The LSB is independent of the government as well as of members of the legal profession
2	Accountability and transparency	For the most part	The frontline regulators are accountable to the LSB; the LSB is accountable to Parliament, via the Lord Chancellor. Decisions taken and their enforcement are done in a manner that follows rules and regulations. Full information about the governing bodies of the LSB and SRA is available online. Each publishes annual reports, including annual accounts. The minutes of board meetings are posted online. However, only some—not all—board meetings are open to the public
3	Regulatory oversight bodies	Yes	The LSB is the regulatory oversight body for the frontline regulators of legal services. Parliament oversees the LSB, via the Lord Chancellor

(*Continued*)

Table 6.1 Assessment for England and Wales (Continued)

4	Public engagement	Yes	The LSCP is mandated to represent the interests of a variety of consumers of legal services
5	Regulatory impact assessments	Yes	The Clementi Report is arguably an archetypical example of an RIA. Further, the LSB, the SRA and the LSCP (and other regulators, including the CMA) conduct studies and issue reports on a continual basis
6	Risk-based approach	Yes	"Outcomes-focused regulation" is a risk-based approach

Part III

AUSTRALIA: DIVIDED YET UNITED

If the changes in England and Wales were sweeping and dramatic, then the changes in Australia were slow and progressive over a lengthy period of time. Or, at least they began that way. More recently, the Legal Profession Uniform Law has served, in many respects, to divide the country in two; it's unclear when or if the parts may be reunited. Whether they eventually reunite or not, however, they nevertheless remain united in this respect: in Australia, ILPs are today an accepted and uncontroversial part of the legal landscape.

Chapter 7

It's Easy to Forget that Australia Was First

Much ado has been made about the UK Legal Services Act of 2007. While the fuss is certainly warranted, it makes it easy to forget that the pioneers were not English, they were Australian. More specifically, it was New South Wales (NSW) who, in 2001, became the first common law jurisdiction to permit multidisciplinary practices and to open up ownership of law firms to nonlawyers.[1]

The legislation in NSW evolved in stages. Prior to 1990, the only organizational structures permitted for law practices were sole proprietorships or general partnerships. Beginning in the late 1970s, some professional associations began lobbying for a relaxation on these restrictions.[2]

A first response came in 1990, when the NSW legislature voted to allow lawyers to incorporate their practices. But this ability came with significant drawbacks—not only was shareholding restricted to lawyers, but it also imposed unlimited liability on the corporation. As a result, the structure was unattractive and little used.[3]

In 1994 new legislation was enacted to permit lawyers to form multidisciplinary practices and to share fees with nonlawyers. But this also came with significant restrictions, notably that lawyers had to retain the majority voting rights and at least 51% of the net income. Again, as a result the structure was little used.[4]

In 1998, the NSW Attorney General's Department undertook a general review of the rules governing legal practice structures. The resulting Final Report concluded that the rules were anti-competitive and should be repealed. More specifically, the Report found that partnership management and decision-making was "antiquated" by contemporary standards, particularly given the realities of a dispersed, multilocation practice, that the potential growth of partnerships was hamstrung by their inability to raise capital from the public, and that transparency could be increased through the introduction of corporate structures that were required by law to subject themselves to greater public scrutiny.[5]

The Law Society of NSW debated the issue of the liberalization of business structures, and in 1999, the Council for the Law Society adopted a resolution supporting both the "corporatization" of legal practices and the ability to raise capital from nonlawyers, subject to adequate safeguards to ensure the integrity of the practice.[6]

In 2000, the Attorney General of NSW introduced a bill to amend the Legal Profession Act to permit legal service providers to register as companies with the Australian Securities and Investments Commission, the agency responsible for assuring compliance with the corporation laws.[7] Under this amendment, any business in the state could offer legal services, as long as at least one director was a solicitor.[8]

While the Law Society of NSW supported the bill, few others in the legal community did.[9] Steve Mark, the Legal Services Commissioner for NSW, called the bill "an ethical minefield." Mark also expressed concerns that the legislation would not totally protect consumers, and that some of its regulatory provisions appeared to have been inadequately thought through, suspicions that it would be harder to extract information from incorporated legal practices and that it would be very easy for lawyers from incorporated practices to avoid complaints about their conduct and discomfort "philosophically" with the shift from profession to business because he did not believe it was possible for a profession to be businesslike.[10]

During the Parliamentary debates, Helen Sham-Ho cited opposition from the NSW Bar Association, the Law Institute of Victoria, and the NSW Legal Reform Group. She reported that the NSW Bar Association "is not persuaded that the Bill would result in any benefit to the public." This is because, she explained, lawyers should be the gatekeepers of the justice system and they must be responsible for the administration of justice. Further, it is very difficult for solicitor-directors to serve two masters: while shareholders want monetary returns from the company, this is opposed to fundamental principles of justice, ethics and professional responsibility.[11]

Another Member of Parliament stated that the bill will make it easier for solicitors to rip-off their clients through overcharging and fraud: "It will make justice more expensive and lawyers less accountable. It does nothing to improve the administration of justice; there is nothing in it for ordinary people."[12]

However, other Members of Parliament supported the bill. For example, Arthur Chesterfield-Evans acknowledged a conflict between business and ethics, but denied it was a problem exclusive to the legal profession. He further denied that the response to the problem was to prevent lawyers from having the business structures available to rest of the country. That, he argued, would be akin to seeking to solve traffic problems by putting people back in horses and carts.[13]

MP James Samios supported the bill for a number of reasons. To begin with, it would improve competition and allow Australia to become the legal hub for the provision of legal services in the Asia-Pacific region. Further, it would preserve both the safeguards already in place to protect clients and the ability of a solicitor to undertake pro bono work. Finally, he argued that the incorporation of legal practices could lead to more transparent management structures and enhance the accountability of individuals for the management of a practice.[14]

The NSW legislature adopted the bill with a vote of 28-9,[15] and everything changed. The restrictions that had made the prior structures so unattractive were lifted, permitting legal practices to freely incorporate, to create multidisciplinary practices without limits on ownership rights or income, to share fees with nonlawyers, and even to publicly list on the Australian Stock Exchange.[16]

Over time, all of the other states and territories of Australia except South Australia followed in the path of NSW. This was due for the most part to Australia's "Model Laws Project," which harmonized a number of laws and regulations on a national basis.[17]

However, today, Australia is essentially divided into two: on the one hand, the states of New South Wales and Victoria (which, together, account for approximately 80% of Australia's lawyers[18]), and, on the other hand, Queensland and the other states (except, again, South Australia). The reason for this is that as the other states of Australia have been catching up with the lead set by New South Wales, the regulatory framework of New South Wales has continued to evolve: In particular, under the Legal Profession Uniform Law, it has unified its framework for the regulation of legal services with the state of Victoria. This unification, which took effect from July 1, 2015, has led to some modifications to the way that incorporated legal practices (ILPs) are regulated in those two states. The two different resulting frameworks are described below.

NOTES

1. See generally, Steve Mark, Tahlia Gordon, Marlene Le Brun, and Gary Tamsitt, "Preserving the Ethics and Integrity of the Legal Profession in an Evolving Market: A Comparative Regulatory Response," undated, http://www.olsc.nsw.gov.au/Documents/preserving%20ethics%20integrity%20legal%20profession%20uk_paper.pdf. See also Devlin and Morison, "Access to Justice," 499–508.

2. Susan Fortney and Tahlia Gordon, "Adopting Law Firm Management Systems to Survive and Thrive: A Study of the Australian Approach to Management-Based Regulation," *University of St. Thomas Law Journal* 10 (2013): 156, http://ir.stthomas.edu/ustlj/vol10/iss1/4/.

3. Ibid., 157.

4. Ibid., 157–158.

5. Steven Mark and Tahlia Gordon, "Innovations in Regulation—Responding to a Changing Legal Services Market," *Georgetown Journal of Legal Ethics* 22 (2009): 503, http://www.olsc.nsw.gov.au/Documents/innovations_regulation_geo_journal.pdf.

6. Fortney and Gordon, "Adopting Law Firm Management Systems," 158.

7. Ibid.

8. Devlin and Morison, "Access to Justice," 502.

9. Ibid., 502–504.

10. Chris Merritt, "Incorporation could be 'Ethical Minefield,'" *The Australian Financial Review*, May 19, 2000.

11. New South Wales, Legislative Council, Official Report of Debates (Hansard), 52nd Parl, 2nd Sess., October 12, 2000 at 9152 (Helen Sham-Ho), https://www.parliament.nsw.gov.au/prod/parlment/hansart.nsf/V3Key/LC20001012006?open&refNavID=.

12. Ibid (Ian Cohen).

13. Ibid. (Arthur Chesterfield-Evans).

14. Ibid. (James Samios).

15. Ibid.

16. Fortney and Gordon, "Adopting Law Firm Management Systems," 158–159.

17. Christine Parker, "Peering Over the Ethical Precipice: Incorporation, Listing, and the Ethical Responsibilities of Law Firms," May 13, 2008, 7, http://dx.doi.org/10.2139/ssrn.1132926.

18. Steve Mark, "The Regulatory Framework in Australia," (paper presented at the ABA Center for Professional Responsibility 40th National Conference on Professional Responsibility, Long Beach, California, May 29, 2014), 11, http://www.americanbar.org/content/dam/aba/events/professional_responsibility/2014/05/40th-aba-national-conference-on-professional-responsibility/session1_02_mark_the_regulatory_framework_in_australia_final.authcheckdam.pdf.

Chapter 8

In This Corner

Queensland et al.

While this section will focus on the state of Queensland, the frameworks for certain other Australian states (Western Australia,[1] Northern Territory,[2] Tasmania,[3] and the Australian Capital Territory[4]) are comparable.

REGULATORY FRAMEWORK: ESSENTIAL COMPONENTS

The essential components of Queensland's regulatory framework are as follows:

Incorporated Legal Practice (ILP)

The creation and operation of an ILP is subject to these requirements:

Notification of Intention to Become ILP: Before a corporation starts to engage in legal practice in Queensland, it must give the Queensland Law Society (QLS) notice of its intention to do so. The Law Society, in turn, notifies the Queensland Legal Services Commission (the Law Society, a self-regulatory body, shares regulatory authority with the Legal Services Commission, an independent regulator).

This notification is done by the completion and submission of a document entitled "Notice of a Corporation's Intention to Engage in Legal Practice in Queensland" (Notification Form).[5]

In stark contrast to the SRA's 14- (and previously 30-) page form, the Notification Form is just two pages long. In addition, the form is one of simple notification not of application: in contrast to the authorization procedure with the SRA in England and Wales, neither the Law Society's nor the Legal Services Commission's prior approval is required for the ILP to begin operation.

Appointment of a Legal Practitioner Director: A prominent feature of the Notification Form is the place where the name of at least one "Legal Practitioner Director" (LPD) must be identified. Every ILP must appoint at least one LPD, who must hold a principal practicing certificate (that is, must be an admitted attorney) and be a validly appointed Director under the Corporations Act.[6] An ILP must have an LPD at all times—if it does not have one for a period exceeding seven days, it must stop providing legal services.[7]

An LPD bears three responsibilities. Firstly, in a general manner, the LPD must manage the legal services provided by the ILP. This responsibility is considered to be akin to the responsibility of a general partner in the context of a general partnership. Secondly, the LPD must implement and maintain "appropriate management systems" (AMS, discussed below) to enable the provision of legal services in accordance the professional obligations of legal practitioners. Finally, in the event of unsatisfactory professional conduct or professional misconduct by an employee of the ILP, the LPD must ensure that all reasonable action available is taken.[8]

Of these three requirements, the second regarding AMS is considered the most important. The failure to comply is considered professional misconduct, and it can lead to the LPD losing his/her practicing certificate (disbarment) as well as to liquidation of the ILP.[9]

Appropriate Management Systems: An ILP must have in place AMS;[10] as noted above, it is the LPD who has primary responsibility to assure this is the case.

The website of the Queensland Legal Services Commission describes AMS in this manner:

> Though the [Legal Profession Act] does not define "appropriate management systems" there are a number of key principles which law practices should consider when designing and implementing their management systems:
>
> - the regulatory purpose of AMS is for law practices to develop and maintain an ethical infrastructure that encourages ethical behaviour by its legal practitioner directors and employees.
> - the practical effect of AMS is to encourage law practices to "self-regulate" so as to prevent unethical behaviour and in the event that such conduct occurs, take remedial steps.
> - the legal practitioner director is the person responsible for both preventative and remedial steps to ensure compliance with the Act and professional rules. In the event of contravention . . . there are disciplinary outcomes for the legal practitioner director.
> - AMS evidences a move away from the traditional focus of professional discipline (which has been the individual) and to allow "practice-based

regulation." These provisions represent a recognition that the law practice as an entity has the power to prevent or encourage ethical behaviour.
- clearly a firm's management systems won't count as appropriate merely because they're intended to achieve that purpose—a firm's management systems hardly 'enable' the provision of legal services by the firm under the professional obligations of Australian legal practitioners if they're applied only sometimes and not others or are applied differently by different of its employees at different times or if the people 'down the line' don't know about them or understand them or worse still just don't care.

Obviously, what is "appropriate" for one practice will not be for another. As a result when assessing whether management systems are "appropriate" legal practitioner directors should have regard to:

- the size of the law practice;
- the experience and qualifications of their employees;
- the nature of the legal services provided;
- the nature of any business services provided in addition to legal services etc.

An appropriate management system, then, simply means a firms' formal and informal management policies, procedures and controls, work culture, and habits of interaction and practice that support and encourage ethical behaviour by all employees. In short, the intent of the Act is that the practice will develop and implement management systems and culture which enables them to detect, prevent and correct employee conduct which may result in contravention of their professional and legislative obligations.[11]

Self-Assessment: As the website of the Legal Services Commissioner notes, nothing in the Queensland legislative texts defines AMS. Indeed, nothing in the original New South Wales texts (the regime that Queensland adopted), defined the term either. In an effort to craft a definition, Steve Mark, (the Legal Services Commissioner for New South Wales who had called the amendment to the NSW Legal Profession Act that allowed for ILPs an "ethical mine-field"), organized and conducted a collaborative process with representatives of the Law Society of New South Wales, members of the legal profession, academics and representatives of the professional indemnity insurance body to determine collectively what objectives, if met, would ascertain whether an ILP has AMS in place.[12] The work-product of this process was a list of ten objectives. These objectives served as the foundation for the development of a self-assessment process for ILPs. In particular, the ten objectives were used to craft a self-assessment form for each ILP to complete and submit to the Legal Services Commissioner.[13] In this way, each ILP can assess for itself the extent to which it does or does not have AMS in place, and can take steps to remedy any deficiencies.

The 39-page self-assessment form in use in Queensland today addresses different objectives such as:

- Negligence (providing for competent work practices),
- Communication (providing for effective, timely and courteous communication),
- Delay (providing for timely review, delivery and follow up of legal services),
- Liens/file transfers (providing for timely resolution of document/file transfers),
- Cost disclosure/billing practices/termination of retainer (providing for shared understanding and appropriate documentation on commencement and termination of retainer along with appropriate billing practices during the retainer),
- Conflict of interests (providing for timely identification and resolution of conflict of interests, including when acting for both parties or acting against previous clients as well as potential conflicts which may arise in relationships with debt collectors and mercantile agencies, or conducting another business, referral fees and commissions etc),
- Records management (minimizing the likelihood of loss or destruction of correspondence and documents through appropriate document retention, filing, archiving, etc. and providing for compliance with requirements regarding registers of files, safe custody, financial interests),
- Undertakings (providing for undertakings to be given, monitoring of compliance and timely compliance with notices, orders, rulings, directions or other requirements of regulatory authorities such as the [Legal Services Commissioner], courts, costs assessors),
- Supervision of practice and staff (providing for compliance with statutory obligations covering license and practicing certificate conditions, employment of persons and providing for proper quality assurance of work outputs and performance of legal, paralegal and non-legal staff involved in the delivery of legal services),
- Trust account requirements (providing for compliance with applicable regulations and proper accounting procedures).

The full 39-page form is available online on the website of the Queensland Legal Services Commission.[14]

The LPD has principal responsibility for the completion of the self-assessment form, and the LPD must sign the form as the person with primary (but not sole) responsibility that the AMS are in place.

On its website, the Legal Services Commission explains that there is no expectation that LPDs rate the systems that their firm had in place when they first received the self-assessment form. Instead, the Commission will consider the form a success if it causes the firm to make improvements, which are then reflected in the completed self-assessment that is submitted. This is because, the website states, "The purpose of the exercise is not to catch anyone out but to help law firms develop and maintain management systems and workplace cultures that nurture and sustain best practice." Further, the Commission both hopes and expects that LPDs will "approach the exercise not as an administrative burden but as a positive opportunity to review their firm's systems and to take stock." In this manner, the Commission explains, LPDs can better engage with the exercise and candidly identify any gaps or shortcomings that require or might benefit from improvement.[15]

Finally, because nothing in Queensland's Legal Profession Act expressly establishes the Legal Services Commission's authority to require ILPs to conduct self-assessments, the Commission exercises the authority pursuant to a more general authority to conduct compliance audits of ILPs, described below.

Compliance Audit: No one could describe Queenlands's rules as overly formalized, and they favor a cooperative role between regulator and regulated, rather than a confrontational one. The rules do, however, have some teeth: the Legal Services Commission has the authority to audit any ILP in order to assure its conformity with the Legal Profession Act and other pertinent rules and regulations. This authority exists regardless of whether a complaint has been lodged with respect to the ILP or whether the Commission can otherwise demonstrate that it has any specific grounds to conduct the audit. In the event of non-compliance, the Legal Services Commission can apply to the Supreme Court to disqualify the ILP from providing legal services.[16] (The extent to which an ILP is subject to audit is in stark contrast to that of other legal practices that are not ILPs—in Queensland, legal practices that are not ILPs can be audited only with respect to client trust accounts, and the auditing responsibility lies with the Queensland Law Society, a professional body, rather than with the independent Legal Services Commission.)[17]

Multi-Disciplinary Partnership (MDP)

If a lawyer would like to provide services as a partner of an unincorporated MDP, the requirements are simpler:

Notification of Intention to Start Practice in Multi-Disciplinary Partnership: At the time a lawyer intends to join an MDP, he/she must notify the Queensland Law Society who, in turn, notifies the Legal Services Commission.

This notification is done by the completion and submission of a "Notice of Intention by Australian Legal Practitioner to Provide Legal Services as a Partner in a Multi-Disciplinary Partnership."[18]

This form is a very simple one—just two pages in length, beyond the obvious elements like contact information, it asks for little more than the names of the partners of the firm (both lawyers and nonlawyers) and the names of the lawyers (non-partners) who will be employed by the partnership.

Like the "Notice of a Corporation's Intention to Engage in Legal Practice in Queensland" that is filed upon the creation of an ILP, the notification form for an MDP is also one of simply notification not of application, and neither the Law Society's nor the Commissioner's prior approval is required for the lawyer to join the MDP or for the MDP to begin operation.

Responsibility for Management and Appropriate Management Systems: Each lawyer who is a partner in the MDP is responsible, generally, for the management of the provision of legal services by the MDP, and, more specifically, for ensuring that AMS are implemented and maintained.[19]

Vicarious Liability for Actions of Nonlawyers: The lawyer partners of the MDP assume responsibility for the actions of the nonlawyers in the firm, in so far as those actions pertain to the provision of legal services. Thus, in the event any conduct of a nonlawyer has an adverse effect on the provision of legal services by the MDP, the lawyer partners may be found to have engaged in professional misconduct.[20]

SIGNIFICANCE OF THE QUEENSLAND FRAMEWORK

As noted above, the regulatory framework in place in Queensland today was pioneered in New South Wales. Susan Fortney and Tahlia Gordon explain that at the time the self-assessment process was developed there, neither the process nor AMS more generally received nearly the attention accorded to the legislative changes that allowed for public ownership of law firms. Nevertheless, Fortney and Gordon describe AMS and the self-assessment process as a "watershed event in the regulation of law firms."[21] It is considered to be the "prototype" for "proactive, management based regulation," (PMBR, also referred to as compliance-based regulation) and the foundation of an "ethical infrastructure."[22] Later research supports their effectiveness: a study by Christine Parker, Tahlia Gordon and Steve Mark published in 2010 demonstrated both that (i) upon completion of a self-assessment, the complaints made against an ILP fell by two-thirds,[23] and (ii) in general, the rate of complaints against ILPs that had not yet performed the self-assessment was slightly lower than the rates of complaints against traditional firms, but that for ILPs that had performed the self-assessment, the complaint rate was two-thirds lower than the number of complaints received in relation to traditional firms (who are not required either to have AMS or to conduct self-assessments).[24] Fortney's own study, published in 2013, reported that a significantly large majority of LPDs

(62%)[25] described the self-assessment process as "a learning exercise that enabled [their] firm to improve client service," (in contrast, 12% described it as "meaningless box-ticking"),[26] and 71% said that as a result of the self-assessment process, their firm either had revised firm policies or procedures with respect to the delivery of legal services, or had gone further by adopting entirely new systems, policies or procedures.[27]

These highly compelling results have inspired a number of persons to call upon regulators in the United States (as well as other countries) to adopt PMBR (again, also referred to as compliance-based regulation), regardless of whether or not alternative structures are also permitted.

Those persons include Ted Schneyer, who questions the adequacy of the current approach in the US because it focuses nearly exclusively on individuals and is based upon reactive discipline.[28] More specifically, Schneyer argues that PMBR programs better protect clients from what is sometimes called "unsatisfactory professional conduct" as opposed to "serious professional misconduct." Further, they improve legal services by increasing compliance with lawyers' legal and ethical obligations. In addition, they help sole practitioners and small firms to improve their operations. The result should be, Schneyer argues, a reduction in the volume of complaints filed with disciplinary authorities, with a corresponding reduction in disciplinary costs.[29]

Susan Fortney argues that if PMBR were implemented in the United States and Canada it would lead to the same results as it did in Australia, namely a reduction in complaints and improved client service. The reduction in complaints would save regulators money and enable disciplinary counsel to focus more on those complaints that are filed. If that weren't enough, she continues, PMBR would enhance both client and lawyer satisfaction while raising ethical standards for attorney conduct.[30]

Finally, Russell G. Pearce and Eli Wald argue that the United States should return to a pre-Model Rules "relational approach"[31] to lawyer regulation, as opposed to the "individualist" or "autonomous"[32] approach that dominates today. Citing, among other examples, New South Wales's self-assessment process,[33] they argue that PMBR together with entity regulation offer an excellent foundation for a relational approach to regulation. This is because, they explain, these approaches "recognize that relationships within firms are essential to promoting ethical conduct and they create a reciprocal relationship between regulators and those they regulate."[34]

And it is not just US-based commentators who have identified the regulatory framework pioneered in New South Wales as an example to follow in their own jurisdictions: as discussed in detail below, regulators in Nova Scotia, Manitoba (together with the other Prairie provinces of Saskatchewan and Alberta), Ontario and British Columbia are doing the same. In all likelihood, they have been influenced at least in part by Amy Salyzyn's call upon Canadian regulators to become more active in promoting "effective ethical infrastructures" in Canadian law firms, notably, among other measures, by adopting a self-assessment process akin to the one pioneered in New South Wales.[35]

What if, just what if, in the meantime New South Wales turned its back, if not in whole then at least in part, on its so highly lauded regulatory framework?

First-hand perspective

Paul Clauson, Queensland Legal Services Commissioner and Scott McLean, Principal Legal Officer, Queensland Legal Services Commission (online): Clauson and McLean explain why, in their opinion, "the risks presented by the ILP structure have been overblown."

NOTES

1. Western Australia Legal Profession Act, September 6, 2014, 89–121, Sections 97–146,
2. Northern Territory of Australia Legal Profession Act, July 1, 2009, 82–110, Sections 117–166, http://lawsocietynt.asn.au/images/stories/LPA_2009.pdf.
3. Tasmania Legal Profession Act, August 15, 2007, Sections 110–159, http://www.austlii.edu.au/au/legis/tas/consol_act/lpa2007179/.
4. Australian Capital Territory Legal Profession Act, October 15, 2015, 83–121, Sections 101–149, http://www.legislation.act.gov.au/a/2006-25/current/pdf/2006-25.pdf.
5. A copy is available online: "Legal Profession Forms," Queensland Law Society, accessed March 20, 2017, http://www.qls.com.au/For_the_profession/Practice_support/Resources/Legal_profession_forms.
6. Queensland Legal Profession Act, December 1, 2014, 120–121, Section 110 and 133, https://www.legislation.qld.gov.au/legisltn/current/l/legalproa07.pdf.
7. Ibid., 120–121, Section 119.
8. "Obligations of LPDs," Queensland Legal Services Commission, last modified on November 11, 2013, https://www.lsc.qld.gov.au/compliance/incorporated-legal-practices/obligations-of-legal-practitioner-directors; See also Queensland Legal Profession Act, 118–120, Sections 117–118.
9. Ibid., 128–131, Sections 130–132. See also, generally, Queensland Law Society, "Information Kit: Incorporated Legal Practices ('ILPs')," Version 7.0, July 7, 2010.
10. Queensland Legal Profession Act, 118, Section 117.
11. "Appropriate Management Systems, Queensland Legal Services Commission, last modified on November 11, 2013, https://www.lsc.qld.gov.au/compliance/incorporated-legal-practices/appropriate-management-systems.

12. Steven Mark and Georgina Cowdroy, "Incorporated Legal Practices—A New Era in the Provision of Legal Services in the State of New South Wales," *Penn State International Law Review* 22 (2004): 689–690, http://ssrn.com/abstract=673021.

13. Queensland Legal Services Commission, "Incorporated Legal Practices Self-Assessment Audit," Version 4.0, June 1, 2012, https://www.lsc.qld.gov.au/__data/assets/pdf_file/0005/97781/ILP-Self-Assessment-Audit-Form-Version-4.pdf.

14. A copy is also available online: "Forms," Queensland Legal Services Commission, last modified on January 25, 2016, https://www.lsc.qld.gov.au/publications/forms.

15. "Self-Assessment Audits," Queensland Legal Services Commission, last modified on November 11, 2013, https://www.lsc.qld.gov.au/compliance/compliance-audits/self-assessment-audits. Amy Salyzyn refers to this regulatory approach as a "Coaching Model." Salyzyn, "From Colleague to Cop to Coach," 26–27.

16. Queensland Legal Profession Act, 129–131, Sections 130–132.

17. See "Compliance Audits," Queensland Legal Services Commission, last modified on November 11, 2013, https://www.lsc.qld.gov.au/compliance/compliance-audits.

18. "Notice of Intention by Australian Legal Practitioner to Provide Legal Services as a Partner in a Multi-Disciplinary Partnership," accessed March 17, 2017, http://www.qls.com.au/For_the_profession/Practice_support/Resources/Legal_profession_forms.

19. Queensland Law Society, "Information Kit for Multi-Disciplinary Partnerships (MDPs)," June 28, 2011, 5, http://www.qls.com.au/For_the_profession/Practice_support/Resources/Law_practice_structures/Multi-disciplinary_partnerships_MDPs.

20. Ibid.

21. Fortney and Gordon, "Adopting Law Firm Management Systems," 154.

22. Ibid. Ted Schneyer is credited with coining the term "proactive, management based regulation," in articles such as "The Case for Proactive Management-Based Self-Regulation to Improve Professional Self-Regulation for US Lawyers," *Hofstra Law Review* 42 (2013): 233–265, 235, http://www.hofstralawreview.org/wp-content/uploads/2014/02/BB.7.Schneyer.final2_.pdf. The concept is discussed in detail in Snyder, *Democratizing Legal Services*, 143–156.

23. Christine Parker, Tahlia Ruth Gordon, and Steve A. Mark, "Regulating Law Firm Ethics Management: An Empirical Assessment of the Regulation of Incorporated Legal Practices in NSW," *Journal of Law and Society*, 2010, 485, http://dx.doi.org/10.2139/ssrn.1527315.

24. Ibid., 487–488.

25. Fortney and Gordon, "Adopting Law Firm Management Systems," 175.

26. Ibid., 180.

27. Ibid., 172–173. See also Susan Saab Fortney, "The Role of Ethics Audits in Improving ManagementSystems and Practices: An Empirical Examination of Management-Based Regulation of Law Firms," *St. Mary's Journal on Legal Malpractice & Ethics* 4 (2014): 112–149, http://dx.doi.org/10.2139/ssrn.2660358.

28. Schneyer, "The Case for Proactive, Management-Based Regulation," 234.

29. Ibid., 235. Schneyer also argues that PMBR will bolster self-regulation of the legal profession by "heightening public perceptions [of its] efficacy." Ibid.

30. Susan Saab Fortney, "Promoting Public Protection through an 'Attorney Integrity' System: Lessons from the Australian Experience with Proactive Regulation of Lawyers," *The Professional Lawyer* 23 (2015): 7–8, http://www.americanbar.org/content/dam/aba/publications/professional_lawyer/volume_23_number_1/ABA_PLN_v023n01_001_promoting_public_protection_through_an_attorney_integrity_system_lessons_from_the_australian_experience_with_proactive_regulation_of_lawyers.authcheckdam.pdf. Fortney continues: "Given the resistance to ABS in the United States and the value of self-examination for all types of firms, regulators and other stakeholders should not await the advent of ABS. Rather a jurisdiction should implement a pilot program using management based principles. Ibid., 5.

31. Russell G. Pearce and Eli Wald, "Rethinking Lawyer Regulation: How a Relational Approach Would Improve Professional Rules and Roles," *Michigan State Law Review* 2012 (2012): 516, http://digitalcommons.law.msu.edu/cgi/viewcontent.cgi?article=1034&context=lr.

32. Ibid., 521–522.

33. Ibid., 532.

34. Ibid., 533–534.

35. Amy Salyzyn, "What If We Didn't Wait?: Canadian Law Societies and the Promotion of Effective Ethical Infrastructure in Law Practices," *Canadian Bar Review*, April, 2015, http://ssrn.com/abstract=2533229.

Chapter 9

And in this Corner

New South Wales and Victoria

Prior to July 1, 2015, the regulatory framework for both New South Wales and Victoria was highly comparable to that of Queensland. Indeed, as explained above, the regulatory frameworks of both Queensland and Victoria were modeled upon that of the pioneer, New South Wales. However, the Legal Profession Uniform Law (LPUL), to which New South Wales and Victoria have ascribed,[1] has brought some notable differences for those states, as follows:

Elimination of the role of "Legal Practitioner Director" for ILPs; Modification and shifting of corresponding responsibilities: The LPUL eliminates the position of LPD for ILPs. At the same time, it modifies the responsibilities of this role, and it shifts those responsibilities to fall upon a larger group of people.

More specifically, under the LPUL, each of the "principals" of each type of legal service provider (not just ILPs) is responsible for the firm's compliance with professional conduct and other rules.[2] As regards ILPs, "principals" are each of the lawyers of the ILP who are "validly appointed" directors under the Corporations Act.[3] As regards other types of structures, and notably partnerships, "principals" are each of the partners of the firm.[4]

The liability of each principal for the acts and omissions of the ILP is more nuanced than that of an LPD: a principal bears responsibility only if the principal "knowingly authorized or permitted" the act (or omission), or if the principal "was in or ought reasonably to have been in a position to influence"[5] the relevant conduct of the ILP.[6] In comparison, while the liability of an LPD might not go so far as to qualify as strict liability, nor is it limited by terms such as "knowingly" or "was in a position to influence."

"*Authorised Principal*": The LPUL requires ILPs have at least one lawyer to serve as an "authorised principal." This person must be authorized under his/her practicing certificate to supervise others. [7]

Unincorporated Legal Practices: Multi-disciplinary practices are no longer regulated separately but as part of a larger category of Unincorporated Legal Practices (ULPs). This structure allows an Australian lawyer to form a partnership not only with persons who are not lawyers, but also with persons who are lawyers in foreign countries (but not registered in Australia) and with foreign law firms and other legal entities. Like ILPs, ULPs must appoint at least one Australian lawyer to serve as an "authorised principal."[8]

Appropriate Management Systems: The LPUL does not contain a positive or proactive requirement for ILPs to have appropriate management systems in place. Instead, in the event of an audit by the regulator, the law allows for the regulator to require an ILP (as well as a ULP or any other kind of law practice) to implement and maintain appropriate management systems, and to provide periodic reports.[9]

Limited Right to Audit: The LPUL scales back the regulator's authority to audit. Instead of having the authority to audit for no reason and for any reason at all, the Commissioner has the authority to audit only when it considers "there are reasonable grounds to do so," based either upon the conduct of the ILP or of one of its lawyers or employees, or upon a complaint made against the ILP or one of its lawyers or employees (under the LPUL, this limited authority to audit also applies to other kinds of law practices).[10]

TAKING A STEP BACK

Considered as a whole, these differences with respect to ILPs that were ushered into New South Wales and Victoria under the LPUL take a step back from the pioneering regulatory framework first developed in New South Wales (the regulatory framework that is still in place in Queensland and the other Australian states). While they do not call into question the existence of ILPs or their right or ability to operate, they scale back significantly the regulator's ability to regulate them. They do this in four ways:

1. The LPUL eliminates the requirement to appoint at least one LPD, who, under the prior regime, had not only the responsibility to assure that the ILP implements appropriate management systems, but also a clearly and personally assigned liability in the event of unsatisfactory professional conduct or professional misconduct by the ILP. By eliminating this role, and spreading a lower level of responsibility (they must have knowingly authorized or permitted the act or omission or have been in or ought reasonably to have been in a position to influence it) among all of the ILP's

directors, it becomes much more difficult to identify precisely which individual(s) in an ILP has responsibility for what (mis)conduct, and it becomes more difficult to prosecute any one or more individuals for unsatisfactory or misconduct.

This change under the LPUL has been interpreted as a positive one, for the reason that it increases the number of persons responsible.[11] Commentators have predicted that it will be difficult for a principal—any individual principal—to escape liability because he/she would be forced to assert the "stupid lawyer" defense along the lines of "I was too busy" or "I was too naïve" to understand what was happening or do anything about it. On a superficial level, interpretations of this kind are difficult to argue with, at least in theory. But they fail to go beyond the theory to take into account the actual experience of the United States.

In fact, the language of the relevant sections of the LPUL is highly comparable to that of ABA Model Rules 5.1[12] and 5.3.[13] Taken together, these two rules require a law firm partner and lawyer(s) having managerial responsibility in a law firm to take "reasonable efforts" to ensure that the firm has in effect "measures" that give "reasonable assurance" that the other lawyers as well as nonlawyers in the firm act in conformity with the Rules. Under Model Rules 5.1(c) and 5.3(c), a lawyer is responsible for the conduct of another person—lawyer or nonlawyer—in the firm if either (i) the lawyer ordered the conduct or knowingly ratified the conduct, or (ii) the lawyer, in a partnership or managerial role, or with "a direct supervisory authority," knew of the conduct at a time when its consequences could have been avoided or mitigated but failed to take reasonable remedial action. These rules are little enforced in the United States in large part due to the way they both diffuse responsibility among a large group of persons and apply a "knowing" or "reasonable" threshold. Together, those elements of the rules make it difficult to identify precisely which individual(s) are responsible for precisely what offense(s).[14]

As late as 1991, Ted Schneyer described Model Rule 5.1(c) in particular as a disciplinary "dead letter."[15] He came to this conclusion in part because, as an evidentiary matter, in a group practice setting, courts may have difficulty in assigning blame to particular lawyers, each of whom has an incentive to shift responsibility onto others in the firm,[16] and in part because even if misconduct can be linked to one or more particular lawyers in a firm, courts and disciplinary agencies may be reluctant to sanction those lawyers for fear of making them scapegoats for others in the firm who would have taken the same actions to further the firm's interests.[17] It is certainly possible that Australian regulators will not be susceptible to these same difficulties or reluctance, but the US experience over a period of several decades suggests otherwise.[18]

2. The LPUL eliminates the generally applicable and proactive requirement that ILPs have appropriate management systems in place. Instead, the regulator can require they be put in place only reactively in the event of a compliance audit.[19]
3. The LPUL significantly restricts the regulator's authority to conduct a compliance audit—the regulator may do so only if "there are reasonable grounds" based upon specific conduct or a complaint made in relation to the ILP or one of its lawyers or employees.[20] (Of course, it remains to be seen how broadly the regulators, and perhaps subsequently also the courts, will interpret the term "conduct.")
4. By reason of the combination of (1) and (2), the LPUL eliminates the grounds upon which the regulator asserted its authority to require ILPs to perform self-assessments.[21]

   In sum, it could be argued that the LPUL took a proactive and progressive regulatory framework for ILPs and turned it into a reactive and regressive one. Stated more strongly, it could be argued that it took the jewel in Australia's regulatory crown—and Australia's regulatory gift to the world (based on Schneyer's and Fortney's high estimations)—and tossed it away.

WHY? HOW DID THIS HAPPEN? HOW COULD THIS HAPPEN?

In order to answer those questions, it is necessary to take a step back and look at the LPUL as a whole. Its principal purpose is much larger and more ambitious than the simple question of the regulation of ILPs: its principal purpose, as the name suggests, is to make uniform the regulatory framework for legal services across the country, in order to create "a common legal services market."[22] Taken as a whole, the regulations governing lawyers and legal services in Australia vary widely from state to state, with the result of imposing significant costs and administrative burdens on lawyers and legal practices that seek to operate across more than one state. The principal motivation of the LPUL is to reduce those costs and administrative burdens[23] (the expected extent to which was detailed in a lengthy Consultation Regulation Impact Statement[24]). In this context, the LPUL seeks to standardize the rules across the states with respect to, just to name some examples: practicing certificates (bar admission), cost and billing arrangements, client trust accounts, complaint handling processes, professional liability insurance, professional discipline and continuing professional education.[25] The resulting document is lengthy: the LPUL itself is over 360 pages,[26] and Victoria's version, as enacted, totals 575 pages.[27]

Indeed, most of the literature in the Australian press and issued by commentators and the competent regulatory bodies at the time the LPUL was adopted and then entered into effect in New South Wales and Victoria either does not refer to ILPs specifically,[28] or mentions them grouped together with other types of "law practices" (sole practitioners, law firms), without a specific focus on how or why the regulatory framework for ILPs has changed, or what the consequences of those particular changes may be.[29] To the extent the literature might focus on ILPs more specifically, it might mention that the position of LPD has been eliminated and that a general responsibility for the conduct of the ILPs has been spread across a larger group of persons (the directors), it might mention the elimination of the proactive requirement to have appropriate management systems in place, and it might mention the limitations on the regulator's authority to audit, but it does not mention the elimination of the requirement to conduct a self-assessment and it does not examine these changes in any depth.[30] Notably, beyond the overarching purpose of uniformity, there is little or no explanation or examination of the reasons for these changes as they relate to ILPs, or their expected consequences. Most of the available literature announcing the adoption of the LPUL and describing it gives the impression that either no one has thought about it, or, if someone has, they didn't think that, in the larger context of the LPUL as a whole, it was important enough to merit any particular focus.

Does this mean that the changes the LPUL brought with respect to ILPs were an accident? Does it mean that they were made not with any specific intention on the part of the decision-makers but simply as an unintended by-product of the process?

The response to that question is yes, and no. To understand, we have to go back even further, to the time of the development of the LPUL:

The draft bill that was ultimately adopted in New South Wales and Victoria as the LPUL was the work product of a special group established in April 2009 by the Council of Australian Governments (COAG) and called the National Legal Profession Reform Taskforce.[31] The five-member Taskforce was made up of two Attorneys General, a representative of the Law Council of Australia (a national representative body of the legal profession), and two representatives of the Department of Justice (of Victoria and the Australian Capital Territory, respectively).[32] At the same time, the COAG also established a Consultative Group for the purpose of advising and assisting the Taskforce. The 18-member Consultative Group included principally representatives of law societies (representative bodies that share regulatory authority with the independent Legal Services Commissions in the Australian states) and the legal profession, as well as one representative of an ILP (Andrew Grech of Slater & Gordon), a representative of a consumer action group, a small number of judges and academics, and one representative of a Legal Services Commission (John Briton, the Legal Services Commissioner for Queensland).[33] During a consultation period of just over one year, the Task

Force issued a number of consultation documents, with respect to which the members of the Consultative Group had the occasion to express their opinions to the Taskforce both orally during a series of meetings and in writing.[34]

The Taskforce's consultation documents included a paper issued in November, 2009 that addressed the topic of business structures specifically.[35] This document began with these words:

> The question of how different business models might impact on the responsibilities and liabilities of those who provide legal services has been a controversial issue in the past. For this reason, Incorporated Legal Practice and Multi-Disciplinary Partnerships are subject to their own regulatory regimes in the Model Bill. As there is now more confidence in different business structures, and in accordance with the Taskforce's desire to simplify the legislation, the Taskforce proposes a new system that applies consistent standards to law practices of all kinds, while seeking to ensure that legal service providers cannot hide behind the corporate veil.[36]

With these words, the Taskforce signaled that within the larger purpose of standardizing rules across the states, the Taskforce had another purpose of also standardizing the rules across business structures, and notably to modify the rules such that all business structures, ILP or not, would be subject to the same regulatory standards.

In this context, the consultation document proposed a number of regulatory objectives for the LPUL, including:

1. That the legal professional obligations for legal practitioners who are principals (partner of a traditional structure or director of an ILP or MDP) be the same for all principals, regardless of whether they practice in an ILP, an MDP or another (traditional) structure;
2. That each principal of a law practice be responsible for ensuring that all reasonable action is taken to ensure that: (i) all the legal practitioners within the law practice comply with their professional obligations and (ii) the legal services provided by the law practice are provided in accordance with the applicable professional obligations;
3. That if the regulator considers it necessary to do so, the regulator may conduct an audit of the compliance of a law practice with the professional rules, and the management of the provision of legal services by the law practice;
4. That if the regulator considers it necessary to do so, the regulator may require a law practice to: (i) ensure that an appropriate management system is implemented and maintained to enable the provision of legal services by the law practice in accordance with the professional rules and obligations of legal practitioners within the law practice, and (ii) provide periodic reports on its compliance with the appropriate management system.[37]

Briton warmly welcomed these proposals by the Taskforce, writing:

> I strongly support the central argument of the paper that the principals of all law firms should be subject to the same overarching professional obligations irrespective of the business structure of their firm.
>
> I have argued previously that the single most effective reform we could make to better protect consumers of legal services and to better promote, monitor and enforce high standards of conduct in the delivery of legal services would be to make all law firm principals subject to the same obligations as legal practitioner directors of incorporated legal practices and to make all law firms subject to the same regulatory oversight that now applies only to incorporated legal practices. The Taskforce's proposals would effectively achieve just that.[38]

In endorsing the Taskforce's proposals, Briton cited Parker's research, which both "found 'compelling evidence' that requiring incorporated legal practices to keep and implement appropriate management systems and to undertake self-assessment audits has achieved 'extraordinary cultural change,'" and resulted in a significantly reduced number of complaints.[39]

Briton did suggest a few modifications to the Taskforce's proposals, most notably that the regulator "must conduct an audit in such a way as to keep the compliance cost to a law practice subject to audit proportionate to the value of the information that is sought." Further, Briton pointed out that he would expect an oversight regulator to monitor the actions of the lower-level regulator to ensure there is not overreaching.[40]

For Briton, the regulator's unencumbered authority to audit a legal practice was particularly important because "we have [no] reason to believe that consumers identify and bring to attention more than a fraction of the conduct that might justify a complaint thereby enabling the appropriate action to be taken."[41] In fact, Briton's experiences as Legal Services Commissioner had convinced him that most unsatisfactory as well as unprofessional conduct was never the subject of a complaint. For that reason, in his opinion, the regulator could not effectively discharge its duties without an unencumbered authority to audit, and notably the authority to audit in the absence of a complaint.[42]

Andrew Grech of Slater & Gordon (an ILP and the first law firm in the world to list its shares on a publicly traded market), echoed Briton's endorsement:

> It has been our experience at Slater & Gordon that the need to be externally accountable for the implementation of AMS has tended to create a greater level of awareness of compliance issues and as a consequence has generally improved the quality of our legal services. The application of AMS across all legal practices, regardless of the ownership structure, should serve to improve

professional standards and, accordingly, ethical standards and client service should also improve.[43]

However, Grech's endorsement of the Taskforce's proposals differed from Briton's in two ways: The first difference was that Grech was concerned that "from a practical perspective the requirements may prove unnecessarily cumbersome" for sole practitioners or small firms, and thus he proposed "an arbitrary cut off point as a definition of small firm," for whom the implementation of AMS would not be required. The second difference is that while Grech did not express disagreement with the extension of a general responsibility to all principals of a law practice (the Taskforce's first proposal above), he advocated that all ILPs should also have at least one director who is an LPD.[44]

Finally, one more member of the Consultative Group also endorsed the Taskforce's proposal, and notably as it related to compliance audits. That member was Carolyn Bond, Co-Chief Executive Officer of the Consumer Action Law Centre of Victoria (again, this was the only consumer/public representation in the Consultative Group). Specifically as regards compliance audits, she stated that they were "an important part of the new system. A measure that has shown to prevent problems before they arise."[45]

As strong as these endorsements of the Taskforce's proposals were, the opposition by many other members of the Consultative Group was stronger, even vehement:

A first example is Robert Milliner, Chairman of the Large Law Firm Group Limited, an organization that represents Australia's largest law firms. Of the Taskforce's four proposals listed above, he objected to three of them.

As regards the second proposal, he opposed a general responsibility of a principal for the actions of other legal practitioners of the firm and for the services of the firm as a whole. Instead, he argued, "there should be no liability for acts which the principal could not reasonably have known of or could not influence or acts which they exercised appropriate diligence to prevent."[46] The reason for this, he explained is that "it is not realistic to expect that principals are in a position to control all behaviour that may give rise to a liability . . . especially in larger practices."[47]

As regards the Taskforce's third and fourth proposals, he stated:

> The power to give management system direction [AMS] is unacceptably paternalistic, draconian and intrusive. . . . The extension of the compliance auditing . . . powers to practices other than incorporated legal practices is unwarranted and highly intrusive. These powers should not be exercisable without cause. They should also remain exercisable only in relation to incorporated legal practices. No case has been made out to justify the expansion to unincorporated practices—there is no justification for allowing this intrusion into management of a business by principals who have unlimited liability for that business.[48]

A second example of the strong, if not vehement objections to the Taskforce's proposals came from a collective group of eight out of the eighteen members of the Consultative Group and consisting, for the most part, of leaders of various Australian Law Societies (again, representative bodies that share regulatory authority with the independent Legal Services Commissions).[49] Their objections were focused upon the Taskforce's third and fourth proposals, stating:

> The reason for the current regulatory obligations placed upon ILPs and MPDs . . . was to extend to the corporation, in its capacity as a separate legal entity, the "professional obligations" that already applied to Australian Legal Practitioners. The ILP was required to address these obligations in part by having in place "appropriate management systems," which, in turn were designed to balance the potential limitation on liability of the principals in a corporation. There is no demonstrated need to extend this requirement to partnerships, which do not enjoy the potential limitation on liability, and which have limitations on the persons who may be partners.
>
> To impose the additional obligations of [the third and fourth proposals] upon the many thousands of non incorporated law practices whose participants are required to observe their professional and other conduct obligations anyway is clearly unwarranted. . . . [A regulator's audit] has the potential to interfere at a micro level in the running of a business, and is fraught with difficulty. . . . This proposal is also seriously at odds with the expressed desire to reduce compliance costs. . . . We recognize that risk management, improved practice management and a sound understanding of applied ethics will support improved practice. However, we consider that this ought to be the primary work of the profession, through its member services organisations.[50]

The Taskforce was obviously swayed by these arguments as well as by Milliner's. At the end of the consultation process, the Taskforce issued an "Interim Report on Key Issues and Funding," in which it acknowledged that "concerns have been expressed that the Commissioner's power to conduct compliance audits is unnecessarily broad," notably because the Commissioner could conduct an audit simply because it considered it necessary to do so. The Taskforce explained that it had changed its position with respect to compliance audits, in favor of a compliance audit function that is "appropriately targeted."[51] More specifically, the Taskforce:

> now proposes a more clearly defined power. Under the proposal, the Commissioner may conduct an audit of the compliance of a law practice . . . if he or she considers there are reasonable grounds to do so, based on: (a) the conduct of the law practice or one or more of its associates; or (b) a complaint against the law practice or one or more of its associates. . . . In addition, the Commissioner may give a management system direction to a law practice if, after conducting a compliance audit, he or she considers it reasonable to do so.[52]

Indeed, as explained above, it is this proposal by the Taskforce that was ultimately reflected in the LPUL.

In sum, the LPUL rejects the world's "prototype" for proactive, management-based regulation, and the foundation of an "ethical infrastructure" as the result in part of an apparent oversight, and in part of an apparent miscalculation (or, if not a miscalculation, then an unfortunate ordering of priorities).

The apparent oversight concerns the elimination of the role of LPD. Nothing in the available documentation of the work of the Taskforce and the Consultative Group indicates that at any point either group or their individual members fully or directly addressed the fact that the LPUL would eliminate the role of LPD, what the reasons for this elimination were, or what its consequences might be. The only document that expressly mentions the role is Andrew Grech's submission on the topic of business structures, in which he argues that the role should be maintained. While it is not clear by any means, it appears that the generally accepted assumption by the members of the Taskforce and the other members of the Consultative Group (that is, save for Grech) was that by extending a general responsibility across all the principals of a law practice, the singular role of the LPD was no longer necessary. Other than Grech, it does not appear that anyone at any point questioned this assumption.

The apparent miscalculation (or unfortunate ordering of priorities) concerns the elimination of the proactive requirement that ILPs have in place AMS and to conduct self-assessments and the significant restrictions placed upon the regulator's authority to audit. At the beginning of the consultation process, the Taskforce fixed as an objective to make uniform the rules that governed not only the various states, but also the various types of business structures. At the beginning of the process, the Taskforce appeared optimistic that it could do so not by lowering standards to the lowest common denominator, but, instead, by raising them to the highest. This optimism is evidenced in Taskforce's November, 2009 consultation document, which proposed extending most if not all of the regulatory framework applicable to ILPs and MDPs to all types of structures. What the Taskforce appears not to have anticipated was the strong—vehement—opposition on the part of certain members of the Consultative Group. Nor, it appears, did the Taskforce anticipate that it would cede to that opposition yet at the same time maintain the objective to make uniform the rules governing the various types of business structures. The end result was that it was no longer an option to simply leave the higher standards applicable to ILPs and MDPs in place, without extending them to other types of structures. Instead, in order to meet the objective to make uniform the rules governing different business structures, those standards had to be lowered. It was in this way that Australia tossed away the jewel in its regulatory crown and negated its regulatory gift to the world.

John Briton has strongly criticized the LPUL for these reasons, stating:

> The LPUL extends the power to conduct a compliance audit to all law firms but at the same time narrows it in a way which robs it of its greatest strength as a regulatory tool, its capacity to be used proactively—and in a way which is entirely unnecessary to protect law firms from being subjected to an unjustified, additional regulatory burden. It shrinks the broad, unfettered discretion [the prior framework gave] the relevant regulatory authorities to conduct a compliance audit of an ILP, albeit only of an ILP, to a discretion which is properly exercised only in response to conduct which has or is alleged to have occurred in the past—and conduct which inevitably comes to attention only haphazardly, in ways which underreport conduct which ought attract regulatory scrutiny by many tens, if not hundreds of times.
>
> The consequences are all bad. The effect of the LPUL will be to prevent the relevant regulatory authorities using the compliance audit power imaginatively to 'identify the roots of potential problems in advance'—by requiring law firms to participate in on-line ethics checks, for example, and by inventing and deploying other like tools. Certainly it will prevent them even from continuing much less extending to all law firms the program of self-assessment audits that has proved so successful with ILPs.
>
> The LPUL was designed in this respect either in ignorance of or disregard for the evidence that self-assessment audits have achieved . . . 'extraordinary cultural change.' [There is] well-documented evidence that ILPs which have completed a self-assessment audit are two-thirds less likely to be subject to complaint than ILPs which have not, evidence which has been complemented more recently with similarly well documented evidence that the large majority of the directors of ILPs which have completed a self-assessment audit acknowledge that the process prompted their firm to deliver improved client service. So much for evidence based policy—and another sure sign that the profession has been more responsive to practitioners' concerns than those of the general public. And I note with some irony that while the LPUL takes Australia backwards in this respect there is forward momentum elsewhere, momentum premised in no small part on the Australian experience in conducting compliance audits and that very same evidence.[53]

Briton has not been alone in his criticisms. Tahlia Gordon (who from 1994 to 2013 worked with Steve Mark at the Legal Services Commission of New South Wales) together with industry commentator Paddy Oliver, observed:

> With the bar being this high to trigger a compliance audit (or an investigation or examination) it can be safely assumed that few compliance audits will be carried out with even fewer management systems directions being given.
>
> So, in an attempt to stop "over regulation" the leaders of the profession have, potentially, done many law firms and clients a disservice by ensuring that appropriate management systems will now not be considered as a positive addition

> rather something which must only be done after regulatory intervention. This is an absolute shame, particularly when many jurisdictions outside Australia are either in the process of, or thinking about, implementing AMS.[54]

Indeed, in part IV this book examines the Canadian provinces that are, as Briton, Gordon and Oliver have alluded, exploring the implementation of AMS (pioneered in but now rejected by New South Wales) in their own jurisdictions.

First-hand perspective

John Briton, former Legal Services Commissioner, Queensland and member of the Consultative Group to the National Legal Profession Reform Taskforce (Appendix and online): Briton explains why he, a nonlawyer, was appointed to head the Legal Services Commission and he compares the regulatory framework of Queensland to that of New South Wales and Victoria under the LPUL.

NOTES

1. For a general and brief history of the development and adoption of the LPUL, see, for example, "Professional Responsibility," Find Legal Answers, last modified December 21, 2015, http://www.legalanswers.sl.nsw.gov.au/guides/hot_topics/you_and_your_lawyer/professional_responsibility.html.
2. Legal Profession Uniform Law (New South Wales), 2014, Section 34, http://www5.austlii.edu.au/au/legis/nsw/consol_act/lpul333/s35.html; Legal Profession Uniform Law Application Act 2014 (Victoria), Section 34, http://www5.austlii.edu.au/au/legis/vic/consol_act/lpulaa2014406/sch1.html.
3. Legal Profession Uniform Law (New South Wales), 2014, Section 6, http://www5.austlii.edu.au/au/legis/nsw/consol_act/lpul333/s6.html; Legal Profession Uniform Law Application Act 2014 (Victoria), Section 6.
4. Ibid.
5. Legal Profession Uniform Law (New South Wales), 2014, Section 35(1), http://www5.austlii.edu.au/au/legis/nsw/consol_act/lpul333/s35.html.
6. Legal Profession Uniform Law (New South Wales), 2014, Section 35(1), http://www5.austlii.edu.au/au/legis/nsw/consol_act/lpul333/s35.html .
7. Law Institute of Victoria, "Legal Profession Uniform Law Guide," October 13, 2015, 7, http://fliphtml5.com/lxdj/eyqc/basic/.
8. Legal Profession Uniform Law (NSW) (2014 No 16a)," current as of November 2, 2016, 47, http://www.legislation.nsw.gov.au/inforce/dec0a7ed-40e0-430d-9970-9917cf457fb6/2014-16a.pdf.
9. Law Institute of Victoria, "Legal Profession Uniform Law Guide," October 13, 2015, 7, http://fliphtml5.com/lxdj/eyqc/basic/.

10. Legal Profession Uniform Law (New South Wales), 2014, Section 256, http://www.austlii.edu.au/cgi-bin/sinodisp/au/legis/nsw/consol_act/lpul333/s256.html?stem=0&synonyms=0&query=Audit.

11. Law Institute of Victoria, "Legal Profession Uniform Law Guide," October 13, 2015, 7, http://fliphtml5.com/lxdj/eyqc/basic/; see also John Briton, "National Legal Profession Reform and the Regulation of the Future," (paper presented at the St. Vincents' 48th Annual Queensland Law Society Symposium, Brisbane, Australia, March 27, 2010, 20–21, https://www.lsc.qld.gov.au/__data/assets/pdf_file/0015/106080/national-legal-profession-reform-and-the-regulation-of-the-future.pdf.

12. "Rule 5.1: Responsibilities of a Partner or Supervisory Lawyer," American Bar Association, accessed March 20, 2017, http://www.americanbar.org/groups/professional_responsibility/publications/model_rules_of_professional_conduct/rule_5_1_responsibilities_of_a_partner_or_supervisory_lawyer.html.

13. "Rule 5.3: Responsibilities Regarding Nonlawyer Assistance," American Bar Association, accessed on March 20, 2017, http://www.americanbar.org/groups/professional_responsibility/publications/model_rules_of_professional_conduct/rule_5_3_responsibilities_regarding_nonlawyer_assistant.html.

14. As regards the difficulty of enforcing these rules see, for example, Schneyer, "The Case for Proactive Management-Based Self-Regulation," 256–261. See also: Ted Schneyer, "Professional Discipline for Law Firms," *Cornell Law Review* 77 (1991): 18–20, http://scholarship.law.cornell.edu/cgi/viewcontent.cgi?article=3509&context=clr; Elizabeth Chambliss and David B. Wilkins, "A New Framework for Law Firm Discipline," *Georgetown Journal of Legal Ethics* 16 (2002): 336–341, http://heinonline.org/HOL/LandingPage?handle=hein.journals/geojlege16&div=18&id=&page=.

15. Schneyer, "Professional Discipline for Law Firms," 19.

16. Ibid., 8.

17. Ibid., 10.

18. On this topic, see also Julie R. O'Sullivan, "Professional Discipline for Law Firms? A Response to Professor Schneyer's Proposal," *Georgetown Journal of Legal Ethics* 16 (2002): 16–24, http://scholarship.law.georgetown.edu/cgi/viewcontent.cgi?article=1900&context=facpub. Sullivan argues that it is more difficult to identify responsible individuals in large firms as compared to small firms. For that reason, she suggests, the chances of enforcing Model Rules 5.1 and 5.3 are best in the context of a small firm. Ibid., 20. For a case study examining how Model Rule 5.1 provides little incentive to lawyers to report or take action regarding ethical violations committed by other lawyers in a firm, see Thomas A. Kuczajda, "Self Regulation, Socialization, and the Role of *Model Rule* 5.1," *Georgetown Journal of Legal Ethics* 12 (1998–1999): 119–149, http://heinonline.org/HOL/LandingPage?handle=hein.journals/geojlege12&div=13&id=&page=.

19. See, for example, Tahlia Gordon and Paddy Oliver, "The Demise of Appropriate Management Systems for Australian Law Firms," May 11, 2015, https://www.linkedin.com/pulse/demise-appropriate-management-systems-australian-law-firms-gordon.

20. Ibid.

21. Ibid.

22. "A New Framework for Practising Law in NSW," The Law Society of New South Wales, accessed on March 20, 2017, http://www.lawsociety.com.au/ForSolictors/professionalstandards/Ruleslegislation/nationalreform/. Although all of the Australian states were involved in the preparation of the LPUL, only two, New South Wales and Victoria, have adopted it to date. The other Australian states are "encouraged" to do so, and in principle it is possible for them to do so without the need for significant changes. Martin Pakula, "Uniform Law to Cut Red Tape and Protect Consumers," Premier of Victoria The Hon. Daniel Andrews MP, May 28, 2015, https://284532a540b00726ab7e-ff7c063c60e1f1cafc9413f00ac5293c.ssl.cf4.rackcdn.com/wp-content/uploads/2015/05/150528-Uniform-Law-To-Cut-Red-Tape-And-Protect-Consumers.pdf.

23. National Legal Profession Reform Taskforce, "National Legal Profession Reform Project – Consultation Regulation Impact Statement," May, 2010, 6–12, http://www.justice.nsw.gov.au/Documents/LPR_Documents/pdf/National+Legal+Profession+Reform+Project+-+Consultation+Regulation+Impact+Statement+(including+Attachments+A-C).pdf. See also, for example, "Uniform Law," Legal Services Council, accessed March 20, 2017, http://www.legalservicescouncil.org.au/Pages/uniform-framework/uniform-law.aspx; Leanne Mezrani, "Rules to Govern NSW and Vic Lawyers Locked In," *Lawyers Weekly*, May 28, 2015, http://www.lawyersweekly.com.au/news/16582-rules-to-govern-lawyers-in-nsw-and-victoria-locked-in.

24. National Legal Profession Reform Taskforce, "National Legal Profession Reform Project: Consultation Regulation Impact Statement."

25. Ibid.

26. "Legal Profession Uniform Law Application Act 2014: Authorised Version No. 003," April 22, 2015, 122–484, http://www.legislation.vic.gov.au/domino/Web_Notes/LDMS/LTObject_Store/ltobjst9.nsf/DDE300B846EED9C7CA257616000A3571/E737D364AFDF26E5CA257E2F00139C2B/$FILE/14-17aa003%20authorised.pdf.

27. Ibid., 1–575. The extra pages address constitutional and transitional issues.

28. See, for example, Mezrani, "Rules to Govern." See also, The Law Society of New South Wales, "Legal Profession Uniform Law," undated, http://www.lawsociety.com.au/cs/groups/public/documents/internetcontent/879344.pdf; Monika Holmwood, "The New Legal Profession Uniform Law Takes Effect from 1 July 2015. Be Prepared," Law Graduate in Pink, June 17, 2015, http://lawgradinpink.blogspot.fr/2015/06/the-new-legal-profession-uniform-law.html.

29. See, for example, Law Institute of Victoria, "Legal Profession Uniform Law Guide," October 13, 2015, http://fliphtml5.com/lxdj/eyqc/basic/.

30. See, for example: The Law Society of New South Wales, "Practising in NSW under the Uniform LawLaw Practices—Incorporated Legal Practice (ILP)," undated, http://www.lawsociety.com.au/cs/groups/public/documents/internetcontent/1021145.pdf; See also Paddy Oliver, "ILP Forum: Incorporated Legal Practices & Legal Profession Uniform Law," June 24, 2015, http://www.lexcel.com.au/wp-content/uploads/2015/07/Paddy-Oliver-ILP-Forum-Legal-Profession-Uniform-Law-Session-24-June-2015.pdf.

31. "National Legal Profession Reform—Background Information," New South Wales Department of Justice, accessed on March 20, 2017, http://www.

justice.nsw.gov.au/for-students-legal-profession/national-legal-profession-reform/background-information.

32. The members of the Taskforce were: Roger Wilkins AO, Secretary, Commonwealth Attorney-General's Department; Bill Grant, Secretary-General, Law Council of Australia; Laurie Glanfield AM, Director General, NSW Attorney-General's Department; Louise Glanville, Executive Director, Victorian Department of Justice; and Stephen Goggs, Deputy Chief Executive, ACT Department of Justice and Community Safety. Ibid.

33. Ibid.

34. A "document library" for the work of the Taskforce is available at this link: "National Legal Profession Reform: Document Library," New South Wales Department of Justice, accessed on March 17, 2017, http://www.justice.nsw.gov.au/for-students-legal-profession/national-legal-profession-reform/document-library#Consumerreport. Documentation relating specifically to the work of the Consultative Group is available at this link: "National Legal Profession Reform – Consultative Group Submissions," Australian Government Attorney-General's Department, accessed on March 17, 2016, http://web.archive.org/web/20110607011704/https://www.ag.gov.au/www/agd/agd.nsf/Page/Consultationsreformsandreviews_NationalLegalProfessionReform-TaskforcePapers-ConsultativeGroupSubmissions. A fuller list of public submissions is available at this link: "National Legal Profession Reform – Public Submissions," Australian Government Attorney-General's Department, accessed March 17, 2017, http://web.archive.org/web/20110604185916/http://www.ema.gov.au/www/agd/agd.nsf/AllDocs/9C0BF3BDCF90D8ECCA2576E2007E36FA?OpenDocument.

35. National Legal Profession Reform Taskforce, "National Legal Profession Reform—Consultative Group Paper: Business Structures—'Law Practices,'" November 25, 2009, http://www.justice.nsw.gov.au/Documents/LPR_Documents/pdf/NationalLegalProfessionReformTaskforcePaper-BusinessStructures-December2009.pdf.

36. Ibid., 1.

37. Ibid., 3–4.

38. John Briton, "A Response to the Business Structures Paper of 25 November 2009," December 15, 2009, 1, available at: http://web.archive.org/web/20110607011704/https://www.ag.gov.au/www/agd/agd.nsf/Page/Consultationsreformsandreviews_NationalLegalProfessionReform-TaskforcePapers-ConsultativeGroupSubmissions.

39. Ibid., 3

40. "Consultative Group—Summary of Key Issues," July 23, 2010, 34, http://web.archive.org/web/20110408032839/http://ag.gov.au/www/agd/rwpattach.nsf/VAP/(9A5D88DBA63D32A661E6369859739356)~CG+key+issue+summary+-+as+at+11+August+2010.PDF/$file/CG+key+issue+summary+-+as+at+11+August+2010.PDF.

41. John Briton, "National Legal Profession Reform and the Regulation of the Future," 24.

42. John Briton, "Between the Idea and the Reality Falls the Shadow" (paper presented at the fifth bi-annual Australian and New Zealand Legal Ethics Colloquium,

Melbourne, Australia, December 3–4, 2015), 6–10, http://www.monash.edu/__data/assets/pdf_file/0004/374872/Briton-Between-the-Idea-and-the-Reality-Falls-the-Shadow-1.pdf. See also John Briton, "Between The Idea And The Reality Falls The Shadow: A Case Study In Lawyer Regulation," October, 2015, 48–53, unpublished paper on file with author. For a brief discussion of "under-regulation as regulatory failure, see Salyzyn, "From Colleague to Cop to Coach," 31–32.

43. Andrew Grech, "Discussion Notes Prepared for the National Legal Profession Reform Consultative Group: Business Structures, December 15, 2009, 1, http://web.archive.org/web/20110607140709/https://www.ag.gov.au/www/agd/rwpattach.nsf/VAP/(8AB0BDE05570AAD0EF9C283AA8F533E3)~Grech,+Andrew+-+Business+Structures.PDF/$file/Grech,+Andrew+-+Business+Structures.PDF.

44. Ibid., 1–2.

45. "Consultative Group – Summary of Key Issues," 34. A group of nine academics from Australian law schools also submitted a statement in support of the regulator's power to conduct "proactive" compliance audits: Adrian Evans et. al., "Submission to National Legal Profession Reform Consultation on Proposed National Law," June 22, 2010, 10, http://web.archive.org/web/20110603165707/http://www.ema.gov.au/www/agd/rwpattach.nsf/VAP/(9A5D88DBA63D32A661E6369859739356)~134+Christine+Parker+Submission+to+NLP+Project+Consultation+22062010.pdf/$file/134+Christine+Parker+Submission+to+NLP+Project+Consultation+22062010.pdf.

46. Robert Milliner, "LLFG Limited Response," December 22, 2009, 6, http://web.archive.org/web/20110607140759/https://www.ag.gov.au/www/agd/rwpattach.nsf/VAP/(8AB0BDE05570AAD0EF9C283AA8F533E3)~Milliner,+Robert+(Chair+,+LLFG+Limited+(Large+Law+Firm+Group))+-+Business+Structures.PDF/$file/Milliner,+Robert+(Chair+,+LLFG+Limited+(Large+Law+Firm+Group))+-+Business+Structures.PDF.

47. "Consultative Group – Summary of Key Issues," 14.

48. Ibid., 34–35.

49. Tony Abbott et. al., "Response to Taskforce Discussion Paper on Business Structures 'Law Practices,'" undated, http://web.archive.org/web/20110607140350/https://www.ag.gov.au/www/agd/rwpattach.nsf/VAP/(8AB0BDE05570AAD0EF9C283AA8F533E3)~Abbott,+Tony;+Bradshaw,+Barbara;+Catanzariti,+Joe;+Cottee,+Harold;+L+Estrange,+Noela;+Hagan,+Martyn;+Selth,+Philip;+and+Stow,+Dudley+-+Business+Structures.PDF/$file/Abbott,+Tony;+Bradshaw,+Barbara;+Catanzariti,+Joe;+Cottee,+Harold;+L+Estrange,+Noela;+Hagan,+Martyn;+Selth,+Philip;+and+Stow,+Dudley+-+Business+Structures.PDF.

50. Ibid., 3–5.

51. National Legal Profession Reform Taskforce, "Interim Report on Key Issues and Funding," October, 2010, 5, http://www.justice.nsw.gov.au/Documents/LPR_Documents/pdf/Interim_Report_on_Key_Issues_and_Funding_PDF.pdf.

52. Ibid.

53. John Briton, "Between the Idea and the Reality Falls the Shadow" (paper presented at the fifth bi-annual Australian and New Zealand Legal Ethics Colloquium), 12.

54. Gordon and Oliver, "The Demise of Appropriate Management Systems."

Chapter 10

A Complex Regulatory Environment . . . Where ILPs Are Just Part of the Landscape

Chapter 7 describes the evolution of legal services regulation in Australia since 1990 with a focus on the development of ILPs. However, the evolution was not confined to that topic. It encompassed a number of other matters relating to legal services, including the identity and organization of regulatory bodies and their respective regulatory authority. The result is a complex regulatory structure allocating a variety of regulatory powers to a variety of bodies. Some of those bodies were created by statute and they are accountable to the state's attorney general; others are primarily representative bodies—accountable to their members—to whom certain regulatory powers have been delegated, in most cases in a "co-regulatory" arrangement with a statutory body. The structural complexity is even greater with respect to Victoria and New South Wales (the two states who have ascribed to the LPUL), as an additional regulatory body, the Commissioner for Uniform Legal Services Regulation is added to the mix.

With this complexity, it would be foolhardy to attempt to identify with precision all occurrences of regulatory oversight. At a minimum, what appears from Figure 10.1 is that the LPUL has formalized a web of oversight responsibilities: The Legal Services Council (LSC) and the Commissioner for Uniform Legal Services Regulation oversee the operation of the LPUL scheme. More specifically, the LSC sets the rules and policy to underpin the Uniform Law, ensuring it is applied consistently across participating States. The Commissioner oversees the dispute resolution and compliance functions. Finally, the LSC is overseen by a Standing Committee, which today comprises the Attorneys General of Victoria and New South Wales.[1]

With respect to accountability, Queensland's Legal Profession Act requires both the Legal Services Commissioner and the Law Society to issue reports to the Attorney General, either on an annual basis or upon request.[2] In Victoria

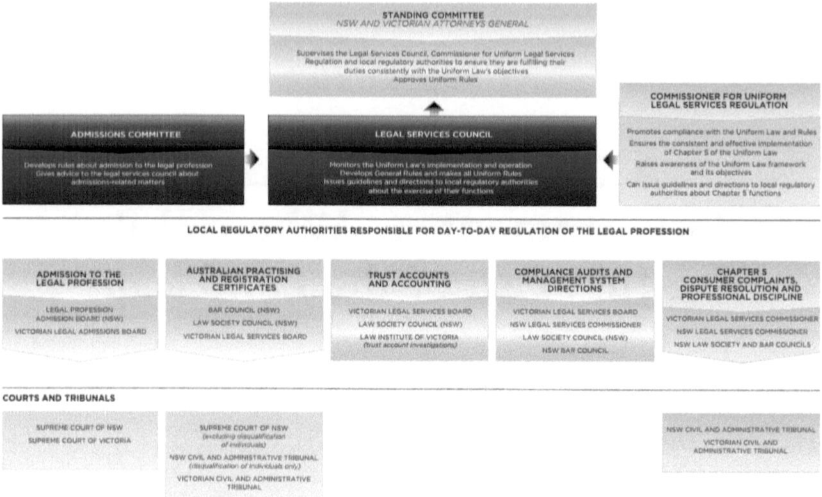

Figure 10.1 Role of bodies under the LPUL. *Source*: Website of Legal Services Council (http://www.legalservicescouncil.org.au/Documents/Web_accessible_Roles_of_bodies_under_the%20_Legal_Profession_Uniform_Law.pdf).

and New South Wales, the LPUL establishes a variety of reporting requirements, by "local regulatory authorities" to the LSC, and by the LSC to the Standing Committee.[3] Traditionally, these various authorities have made their annual as well as other reports available online.

Unlike England and Wales with respect to ABSs, in Australia there is no published registry for ILPs. Based upon the regulatory declarations that ILPs are obliged to file at the time they enter into operation, it is estimated that just over one-third of the legal practices in Australia today are ILPs (in 2014 that was about 1,700 firms).[4] Three ILPs are publicly listed: Slater & Gordon, Shine Lawyers (both of which are plaintiff/personal injury/consumer firms) and IPH Ltd. (an intellectual property firm). At the time this book went to press, a fourth, TST Partners Group (offering accounting, law and finances services), announced its plans to list its shares on the Australian Securities Exchange.[5] A fifth, Integrated Legal Holdings (ILH), publicly listed its shares shortly after Slater & Gordon in 2007, but in late 2014, after a string of financial difficulties, the company went into administration and its shares were delisted.[6] (At the time this book went to press, both Slater & Gordon and Shine were also experiencing significant financial difficulties).[7]

The LPUL has placed into question the role of the LPD, AMS and self-assessments. That is clear. There is something further that is equally clear, although perhaps overlooked. That is this: nothing in the LPUL places into question the existence of ILPs or their legitimacy as a choice of business structure. Indeed, going further, nothing in the commentary submitted to the Taskforce either by the members of the Consultative Group or by members of the public places into question the existence of ILPs or their legitimacy as a choice of business structure. Even the considerable and high-profile financial difficulties faced by Slater & Gordon and Shine, two of Australia's three publicly listed law firms, did not place into question the existence of ILPs or their legitimacy as a choice of business structure.[8]

Indeed, to take an example: Robert Milliner of the Large Law Firm Group—the one who had opposed so vehemently the extension of the obligations placed upon ILPs to other kinds of structures—went so far as to defend those who choose the form of ILP as "doing no more than seeking to take advantage of a business structure that is available to all other types of business."[9] And Milliner went even further than that—on several occasions during the consultancy period he complained to the Taskforce that the LPUL did nothing to address two fundamental problems in Australia with respect to business structures, one being the unavailability of the LLP (limited liability partnership) structure, and the other being "the most fundamental issue concerning alternative business structures, namely the tax and stamp duty issues that inhibit the adoption of alternative structures."[10] Milliner echoed these concerns in a 2011 article in the Australian Lawyer's Weekly, in which he stated that a major reason why existing large firms have not converted to ILPs is because the conversion would have significant tax and stamp duty implications—implications that are more complex the larger the firm is. This could be dissuasive for an existing law firm unless it had developed clear and strong motivations to make the conversion.[11]

However, as Milliner points out, these are concerns only for existing law firms, and acutely so for large ones—newly created law firms do not face the same stamp and tax duty obstacles. This most likely explains why John Briton describes ILP as the "business structure of choice of start-up law firms." (Briton also points out that very few of those who have selected the ILP structure have complained about the requirements of AMS and compliance audits, having seen the "positive impacts" it has had on their business).[12]

The LPUL can be criticized, and, indeed, strongly criticized for the way that it has addressed the questions of LPD, AMS, self-assessments and compliance audits. But that is not the only way to look at the LPUL. Another way to look at it is this: The LPUL shows us that the ILP structure is as much a part of the legal landscape in Australia as traditional structures are.[13] More than that, in Australia, the comfort level with ILPs is so high that most of the protective measures that were put in place at the time of their adoption have now been taken down, because they are no longer considered to be necessary.

First-hand perspective

Steve Mark, former Legal Services Commissioner for New South Wales and Tahlia Gordon, former Research & Projects Manager for the Office of the Legal Services Commissioner for New South Wales (online): Mark and Gordon describe what makes a good regulator and how ILPs in Australia have adjusted to the applicable regulatory requirements. They explain that there will always be resistance to change; what matters is how it is handled.

NOTES

1. Legal Services Council, "About Us," accessed on March 17, 2017, http://www.legalservicescouncil.org.au/Pages/about-us/about-us.aspx.

2. Queensland Legal Profession Act, 240, 369.

3. "Regulatory Arrangements in Victoria," Victoria Legal Services Board + Commissioner, last modified on December 21, 2016, http://lsbc.vic.gov.au/?page_id=21.

4. John Briton, "Between The Idea And The Reality Falls The Shadow: A Case Study In Lawyer Regulation," October, 2015, 40, unpublished paper on file with author.

5. Emma Ryan, "Multidisciplinary Legal Services Firm Announces ASX Listing," *Lawyers Weekly*, December 21, 2016, http://www.lawyersweekly.com.au/news/20275-multidisciplinary-legal-services-firm-announces-asx-listing?utm_source=lawyersweekly&utm_campaign=newsflash21_12_2016&utm_medium=email.

6. See, for example: Justin Whealing, "ILH's Future under a Cloud," *Lawyers Weekly*, December 19, 2014, http://www.lawyersweekly.com.au/news/15962-ILH-s-future-under-a-cloud; Chris Merritt, Integrated Legal Holdings Calls for Reprieve on $12.6m Loan Repayments," *The Australian*, September 12, 2014, http://www.theaustralian.com.au/business/legal-affairs/integrated-legal-holdings-calls-for-reprieve-on-126m-loan-repayments/story-e6frg97x-1227055657940; Sean Smith, "Administrators Called in to ILH," *West Australian*, December 18, 2014, https://au.news.yahoo.com/thewest/a/25810173/administrators-called-in-to-ilh/.

7. See, for example, Tony Boyd, "High Court Judge Warns of Conflicts Facing Listed Law Firms," *Australian Financial Review*, February 2, 2016, http://www.afr.com/brand/chanticleer/high-court-judge-warns-of-conflicts-facing-listed-law-firms-20160202-gmjues. See also Neil Rose, "The Sorry Tale of a Fallen Giant," *Legal Futures*, March 2, 2016, http://www.legalfutures.co.uk/blog/the-sorry-tale-of-a-fallen-giant; Mitch Kowalski, "Why One Scandal Shouldn't Doom a New Twist on Law Firm Ownership," *Financial Post*, August 17, 2015, http://business.financialpost.com/legal-post/why-one-scandal-shouldnt-doom-a-new-twist-on-law-firm-ownership.

8. See, for example, Boyd, "High Court Judge Warns," which describes concerns raised by a High Court judge about law firms being publicly held but not about the ILP structure itself.

9. Robert Milliner, "Regulatory Framework, Consumer Protection, Business Structures, Liability of Principals, Fidelity Cover and General Observations," December 22, 2009, 3, http://web.archive.org/web/20110607140747/https://www.ag.gov.au/www/agd/rwpattach.nsf/VAP/(8AB0BDE05570AAD0EF9C283AA8F533E3)~Milliner,+Robert+(Chair,+LLFG+Limited+(Large+~+Regulatory+Framework,+Consumer+Protection,+Business+Structures,+Liability+of+Principals,+Fidelity+Cover+and+General+Observations.PDF/$file/Milliner,+Robert+(Chair,+LLFG+Limited+(Large+~+Regulatory+Framework,+Consumer+Protection,+Business+Structures,+Liability+of+Principals,+Fidelity+Cover+and+General+Observations.PDF.

10. Ibid., 4. See also Robert Milliner, "LLFG Limited Response," 17–18; and "Consultative Group – Summary of Key Issues," 14.

11. "Incorporation: Why are Law Firms Reluctant to Move Away from the Partnership Model?" *Lawyers Weekly*, August 18, 2011, http://www.lawyersweekly.com.au/features/9018-incorporation-why-are-law-firms-reluctant-to-move.

12. John Briton, "Between the Idea and the Reality Falls the Shadow" (paper presented at the fifth bi-annual Australian and New Zealand Legal Ethics Colloquium), 23.

13. In Victoria, ILPs are often part of a tax-driven structure, notably in the context of a partnership of several ILPs, where the partner ILPs are corporate trustees of discretionary trusts. This has created regulatory issues that await a complete resolution. See, for example, "Partnerships of ILPs & the Legal Profession Uniform Law – Lexcel Consulting," The Profitable Lawyer Blog, March 21, 2016, http://www.lexcel.com.au/partnership-of-ilps-legal-profession-uniform-law/.

Chapter 11

Assessment

To what extent has Australia implemented the OECD's six essential elements of an effective regulatory policy? For each element, the response lies upon a spectrum, from "yes," "for the most part," "sort of," "limited," "not really" and "no:"

Table 11.1 Assessment for Australia

1	Independent regulation	Yes and No	The most populous Australian states have established "co-regulatory" systems in which a Legal Services Commissioner (or Legal Services Board) shares regulatory authority with the Law Society. The Commissioner is appointed by the state's Attorney General and is independent of the profession. The Law Societies are independent of the government, but represent the legal profession
2	Accountability and transparency	For the most part	Various regulatory bodies are required to issue reports, either in an annual basis or upon request by the Attorney General. These reports are usually posted online. On the other hand, only limited information about the governance of the regulatory bodies is available to the public

(*Continued*)

Table 11.1 Assessment for Australia (Continued)

3	Regulatory oversight bodies	For the most part	The LPUL establishes a complex web of oversight responsibility. On the other hand, the exercise of any other oversight authority, notably in the states that have not adopted the LPUL, is difficult to understand
4	Citizen engagement	No	Except for the one-off participation of one consumer action group on the Consultative Group for the National Legal Profession Reform Taskforce, there is no evidence of significant citizen engagement with respect to the regulation of legal services
5	Regulatory impact assessments	Yes	Australia does not appear to carry out RIAs with the frequency or scale of England and Wales, but RIAs are conducted, notably with respect to major legislation, such as the LPUL
6	Risk-based approach	For the most part	"Appropriate management systems" is a risk-based approach. In most states they are required and in Victoria and New South Wales they remain highly encouraged

Part IV

CANADA: "MERE" EVOLUTION OR STEALTH REVOLUTION?

Today, in the ten provinces and three territories of Canada, and save for limited exceptions, only licensed lawyers (and, in some jurisdictions, paralegals[1]) in sole practice or in firms owned and controlled by licensed legal professionals may provide legal services. Direct or indirect fee-sharing with persons who are not licensed legal professionals is also prohibited (some jurisdictions, such as Ontario, permit multi-disciplinary practices, but in those cases only in highly restricted forms).[2]

Cognizant of their restrictive regulatory frameworks, the Canadian provinces have not turned a blind eye to the changes in Australia and in England and Wales. To the contrary, a number of regulators and members of the bar have followed those changes closely, all the while considering what they could mean for their own legal services market.

The most notable actors in this regard are the Nova Scotia Barristers' Society, the Law Society of Manitoba, the Law Society of British Columbia, the Law Society of Upper Canada and the Canadian Bar Association.[3] As they go about their work without fanfare, Canada seems to be undergoing a stealth revolution in the regulation of legal services.

NOTES

1. With respect to Ontario, see "Paralegal Licensing Frequently Asked Questions," The Law Society of Upper Canada, accessed on March 17, 2017, http://www.lsuc.on.ca/licensingprocessparalegal.aspx?id=2147491230#s1q1; with respect to British Columbia, see "Paralegals," The Law Society of British Columbia, accessed on March 17, 2017, https://www.lawsociety.bc.ca/support-and-resources-for-lawyers/law-office-administration/paralegals/. See also "Paralegals in Canada, From Province

to Province," *Study Magazine*, July 19, 2013, http://studymagazine.com/2013/07/19/paralegals-in-canada-province-to-province/.

2. See "Multi-Discipline Practice and Multi-Discipline Partnership," The Law Society of Upper Canada, accessed March 20, 2017, http://www.lsuc.on.ca/For-Paralegals/Manage-Your-Practice/Practice-Arrangements/Multi-Discipline-Practice-and-Multi-Discipline-Partnership/. See also Edward M. Iacobucci and Michael J. Trebilcock, "An Economic Analysis of Alternative Business Structures for the Practice of Law," (paper presented at the Law Society of Upper Canada's symposium for the Alternative Business Structures, October 4, 2013), 23–25, http://www.lsuc.on.ca/uploadedFiles/ABS-report-Iacobucci-Trebilcock-september-2014.pdf.

3. For a short summary, see Salyzyn, "From Colleague to Cop to Coach," 40–41.

Chapter 12

Nova Scotia

The Road Is Made by Walking[1]

The Nova Scotia Barristers' Society (NSBS) is a regulatory body. It is governed by a Council, made up of three "Officers," thirteen elected lawyers, three appointed "public representatives," a representative of the Attorney General of Nova Scotia and the Dean of Schulich School of Law.[2] The Council includes both a president (a practicing lawyer) as well as an executive director, who is employed full-time by the NSBS. As regards the thirteen elected lawyers, the electorate is composed of all licensed lawyers from the relevant District.

The Council fixed two strategic priorities for 2013–16, and reaffirmed those priorities for 2016–19, at the same time adding a third: (i) transforming regulation and governance in the public interest, (ii) enhancing access to legal services and the justice system for all Nova Scotians, and (iii) promoting equity, diversity and inclusion in the legal profession. The Council has translated these priorities into nine strategic initiatives, including:

i. Implementing and adjusting as necessary legal services regulation,
ii. Promoting increased access to legal services through regulatory initiatives and monitor their impact,
iii. Implement a framework for enterprise risk management, and
iv. Implement regulatory objectives (discussed further below).[3]

In 2014, the NSBS announced its "Transforming Regulation and Governance Project" with this explanation:

> The legal profession is in the midst of a period of dramatic and profound change. For some it feels chaotic and destructive of traditional professional norms, while for others it is a time of great advancement and opportunity. It is clear that these changes are happening and will happen whether the [NSBS], as the regulator, leads or follows and whether lawyers embrace or try to avoid them.

Consider the following:

1. The impact of technology on the profession—access to legal information and products online, virtual law practices, nonlawyer provision of legal information and services;
2. Client empowerment arising from the unbundling of legal services, and demands for increased value from legal services at lower cost;
3. Changes in law firm structures and ownership around the world, such as multidisciplinary practices and alternate business structures;
4. Changes in the regulation of the legal profession around the world, which have shifted focus to risk-based, proactive and appropriate management system-based regimes rather than one-size-fits-all, rules-based models;
5. Increasing numbers of corporate and in-house counsel as an alternative to outsourcing legal work;
6. Globalization of the legal services market;
7. Legal process outsourcing such as document production to firms outside the country in order to reduce costs;
8. Significant focus on the crisis in access to justice and access to affordable legal services;
9. Changing demographics and an aging population, including lawyers; and
10. A likely change in legal education now made obvious by the decline in the number of law school applicants.

In the face of change all around us, we haven't really changed the way that we regulate lawyers. . . . In spite of much change in how and where lawyers practise and why people need lawyers, our method of regulation has not evolved on pace with the advancement of technology or of government, civil and commercial interactions. . . . Despite all these changes in the profession, we continue to regulate lawyers in essentially the same way as we have for many generations.[4]

In pursuing the project, the NSBS consulted extensively with the Australia-based consulting firm Creative Consequences. Not coincidentally, the two directors of this firm are Steve Mark and Tahlia Gordon, both formerly with the NSW Legal Services Commission and both considered to have been instrumental in the development of "ethical infrastructure" and self-assessments in that pioneering state.[5]

A significant step in Nova Scotia's journey has been the development of a 19-point Policy Framework, which the Council approved in November, 2015. Existing legislation having already granted to the NSBS a certain level of authority to regulate entities;[6] the Society is using that authority as a building block for the Framework. While the influence of Australia, and of Mark and Gordon, in particular, are evident throughout the Framework, their influence is especially evident in the Framework's call for regulation requiring firms to implement and maintain ethical management systems and to complete and report upon self-assessments. Additional and equally remarkable elements of the Framework include:

- The adoption of six regulatory objectives. The objectives include "protect those who use legal services," "promote the rule of law and the public interest in the justice system," "promote access to legal services and the justice system," and "establish required standards for professional responsibility and competence";[7]
- A focus on the anticipated risks associated with each area of regulated activity and, in assessing risk, the Society "will always give priority to the protection of the public";
- The regulation of the delivery of legal services by lawyers as well as by legal entities, "which include lawyers, law firms, law corporations, law departments and other similar entities";
- Each such law firm and other legal entity will be required to designate an individual who will be responsible for the entity's compliance with its regulatory requirements;
- Legal services may be delivered by legal entities in combination with other services, "so long as all delivered services are subject to the same ethical and professional standards as are required of the legal services";
- Regulation that requires "each law firm and legal entity" to designate an individual who will be responsible for the entity's compliance with its regulatory requirements, and to ensure that all persons associated with the entity who deliver or assist in the delivery of legal services comply with the applicable code of conduct;
- Amendments to the applicable code of conduct to eliminate barriers to fee sharing with nonlawyers; and
- A requirement that the Society develop the capacity to measure the impact of the regulatory changes on the public.[8]

From November, 2015 to January, 2016 the NSBS engaged in a consultation process with the members of the legal profession in Nova Scotia.[9] One of the outcomes of this process was the decision to implement a pilot project to test what the Society refers to as "Management Systems for Ethical Legal Practice" or "MSELP"[10] These terms that are highly reminiscent of Australia's "appropriate management systems" and "AMS," and, accordingly, the project is for a cross-section of Nova Scotia law firms and sole practitioners to test a proposed self-assessment form.[11] The self-assessment for the pilot project is composed of the following ten elements (which, predictably, are closely track the elements of the self-assessment form developed in New South Wales):

1. Developing competent practices;
2. Communicating in an effective, timely and civil manner;
3. Ensuring confidentiality;
4. Avoiding conflicts of interest;
5. Maintaining appropriate file and records management systems;
6. Ensuring effective management of the legal entity and staff;
7. Charging appropriate fees and disbursements;
8. Having appropriate systems in place to safeguard client trust money and property;
9. Sustaining effective and respectful relationships with clients, colleagues, courts, regulators and the community; and
10. Working to improve the administration of justice and access to legal services.[12]

Results of the pilot project were expected to be published in spring 2017.

Another outcome of the consultation process was the development of the legislative amendments that will be needed in order for the Society to be able to fully implement the Policy Framework. At the time this book went to press, several "packages" of proposed amendments had been submitted to the Department of Justice for review before submission to the Nova Scotia legislature, with the expectation that the amendments would be considered in the Fall 2017 legislative session.[13]

Conspicuously absent from the Policy Framework (as well as from the packages of legislative amendments) is any express reference to "alternative business structure" or the use of any comparable expression. This absence is not an oversight: it reflects an understanding on the part of the NSBS that the Policy Framework is the preliminary work that is necessary in order to allow alternative structures to operate. The elements necessary to regulate them include entity level regulation, ethical management systems and self-assessments, even multidisciplinary practices and fee-sharing with nonlawyers.

At the same time, however, the Policy Framework is an end in itself. In the words of the Society, once fully implemented, the Policy Framework will result in a new model of regulation that "is designed to be more responsive to a diverse and profoundly changing environment, to enhance the quality of legal services, to encourage ethical legal practice, to foster innovation in legal services and to increase access to justice."[14] This will be the case regardless of whether Nova Scotia adopts alternative structures at a later time.

One of the "packages" of proposed legislative amendments addressed a topic that the Policy Framework adopted in November 2015 did not mention.

That topic is the make-up of the NSBS's Council (again, its governing body): The amendment in question seeks to eliminate the representative of the Attorney General of Nova Scotia and the Dean of Schulich School of Law from the Council, and to replace them by two additional appointed members to the Council, bringing the total number of appointed (as opposed to elected) members to five. However (and oddly, for the reasons explained below), this package also seeks to clarify that the appointed members may be either public representatives or lawyers.[15]

The motivation for this additional change appears to be a draft policy document circulated by the Executive Council of the province of Nova Scotia. Entitled "Policy Respecting Self-Regulated Professions," this document contains a requirement that at least one-third of the members of the governing body of a self-regulated profession be "public representatives appointed by the government."[16] In explaining to the Council the need for the legislative amendment changing the make-up of the Council, the NSBS executive director, Darrel Pink, stated that such a change not only is called for by the (admittedly still draft) policy document, but also is "widely accepted as elements of good governance."[17]

While the draft policy document (and not the Policy Framework) does appear to be the motivating factor behind this additional proposed legislative amendment, certain questions nevertheless remain unanswered. For example, if the requirement of 33% public representation is a widely accepted element of good governance, then why not use the occasion of making legislative amendments to establish public representation on the Society's Council at 33% instead of just 25%? Further, and especially oddly, if the purpose of appointed representation under the draft policy is to assure representation of the public on the governing body of a self-regulated profession, then why seek to have the possibility for one or more of those positions to instead be filled by members of that profession? The possibility to do so appears to defeat the very purpose of this requirement in the draft policy—the purpose to assure adequate public representation. (If the goal is to create a Council whose lawyer membership is more diverse than would other result from elections alone, then a separate category of appointed lawyers could be created in addition to a category for appointed public representatives).

In fact, while Pink cited the draft policy document only in connection with public representation on the NSBS Council, the document has potentially much wider significance. This is because it seeks to establish a number of additional policies and procedures with respect to self-regulating professions in Nova Scotia (which includes the legal profession as well as, for example, engineers, surveyors, certain health and medical professions), and it does so in a way that clearly communicates skepticism if not outright suspicion of self-regulation.

In its first lines, the document states "It is the policy of the Nova Scotia government to establish self-regulated professions only when self-regulation is determined to be in the best interests of the public." To this end, the document continues, no legislative request to establish a new self-regulated profession may be submitted in the absence of a demonstration that: (i) the proposed self-regulation addresses risks that are real ("not remote") and cannot be better addressed through other means, and (ii) the members of the profession have the capacity to self-regulate, and notably that they have the necessary resources (financial and human), have demonstrated a commitment to democratic principles, and have demonstrated they are able to act collectively in the best interests of clients and the general public. As for professions which are already self-regulating, the document states that no request to amend legislation in their regard may be submitted in the absence of a demonstration that, among other items, that: (i) (echoing the above) the amendments are needed to address substantial risks which are real and cannot be better addressed through other means, (ii) the anticipated benefits of the amendments outweigh any negative impacts, and (iii) the responsible government department has concluded that a more comprehensive review of the existing statute is not needed at that time.[18]

Further, in the event both of establishing a new self-regulated profession and of amending legislation with respect to an existing one, the proposed legislation must comply with certain additional requirements. These include not only the minimum public representation on governing bodies mentioned above, but also the following:

- The legislation must clearly articulate that the primary duty of the profession is to regulate itself *in the public interest*. No mention is made of any other kind of interest, such as in the interest of the profession,
- The legislation creates appropriate mechanisms for assuring "accountability reporting" to the members of the profession, the responsible minister and the general public,
- Matters that are of interest to those outside the profession (government, the general public, potential members, clients, etc.) are to be dealt with in legislation or regulation subject to government approval rather than handled internally by the profession (such as in its 'by-laws").[19]

Given that the draft policy document was, at the time this book went to press, nothing more than a draft, it is not yet clear what its full import will be. That is, it is not clear if the document will eventually undergo formal adoption and implementation, and, if so, it is not clear how it might be modified in the meantime. Further, it is not clear to what extent provinces other than Nova Scotia are considering the adoption of comparable policies and procedures. In the meantime, this draft policy document from Nova Scotia appears to reflect an increased interest on the part of the Nova Scotia government in self-regulating bodies (such as the NSBS) and an intention to more closely scrutinize them.

First-hand perspective

Darrel Pink, Executive Director, Nova Scotia Barristers' Society (Appendix and online): Pink describes the Society's nearly two-decades-long journey toward a regulatory system that is "proactive, principled and proportionate." He explains why, in Nova Scotia, any debate around law firm ownership would be a false debate.

NOTES

1. Quoted from a paper by Victoria Rees and Gabriela Quintanilla, "Nova Scotia Barristers' Society: A Journey Towards a New Model of Regulation and Governance of Legal Services in the Public Interest," June 24, 2015, http://nsbs.org/sites/default/files/ftp/ERU_Newsletter/2015-06-24-IBATransformingRegulation.pdf.

2. "Council," Nova Scotia Barristers' Society, accessed on December 5, 2016, http://nsbs.org/about_us/council.

3. Nova Scotia Barristers' Society, "2016–2019 Strategic Framework," accessed March 20, 2017, http://cdn2.nsbs.org/sites/default/files/cms/menu-pdf/2016-2019_stratframework.pdf.

4. Nova Scotia Barristers' Society, "NSBS Seeks Your Assistance: Transforming Regulation – Consultation Document," 2014, http://nsbs.org/sites/default/files/ftp/InForumPDFs/2014-02-03_TransformingRegulation_Consultation.pdf. For an in-depth discussion, see Victoria Rees, "Transforming Regulation and Governance in the Public Interest," paper prepared for Council of the Nova Scotia Barristers' Society, October 15, 2013, https://nsbs.org/sites/default/files/cms/news/2013-10-30transformingregulation.pdf.

5. "Steve Mark," Creative Consequences, accessed on March 17, 2017, http://www.cc.lannix.com.au/about/steve/; "Tahlia Gordon," Creative Consequences, accessed March 17, 2017, http://www.cc.lannix.com.au/about/tahlia/. Over the course of 2014 Creative Consequences issued four reports in connection with its consultation. The reports, under the heading "NSBS consultants' reports," can be accessed at: "Reports & Resources," Nova Scotia Barristers' Society, accessed on March 17, 2016, http://nsbs.org/reports-resources.

6. Legal Profession Act. 2004, c. 28, as amended by S.N.S. 2010, c 56, http://nsbs.org/sites/default/files/cms/menu-pdf/legalprofessionact.pdf.

7. The Society adopted these objectives on November 14, 2014: "NSBS Regulatory Objectives," Nova Scotia Barristers' Society, November 14, 2014, http://nsbs.org/nsbs-regulatory-objectives. For a detailed discussion of on the topic of regulatory objectives, see Laurel S. Terry, Steve Mark, and Tahlia Gordon, "Adopting Regulatory

Objectives for the Legal Profession," *Fordham Law Review* 80 (2012): 2685–2760, http://ssrn.com/abstract=2085003.

8. "Legal Services Regulation: The Policy Framework," Nova Scotia Barristers' Society, accessed December 6, 2016, http://nsbs.org/legal-services-regulation-policy-framework.

9. "Consultations," Nova Scotia Barristers' Society, accessed on March 17, 2017, http://nsbs.org/consultations.

10. "Management Systems for Ethical Legal Practice (MSELP)," Nova Scotia Barristers' Society, accessed March 17, 2017, http://nsbs.org/management-systems-ethical-legal-practice-mselp.

11. "Pilot Project Update: Management Self-Assessment Tool," Nova Scotia Barristers' Society, accessed March 17, 2017, http://nsbs.org/pilot-project-update-management-system-self-assessment-tool.

12. The form can be accessed at this link: "Management System for Ethical Legal Practice," Nova Scotia Barristers' Society, accessed on March 17, 2017, http://cdn2.nsbs.org/sites/default/files/cms/page/mselpselfassessment_1.pdf.

13. Nova Scotia Barristers' Society, "Council Highlights," November 25, 2016, 1, http://nsbs.org/sites/default/files/ftp/CouncilMaterials/2016-11-25_CouncilHighlights.pdf. Amy Salyzyn explains that "although the Canadian legal profession is often described to be self-regulating, the law societies are still dependent on the approval of their respective legislatures if they wish to embark on significant regulatory reforms." Salyzyn, "From Colleague to Cop to Coach," 30.

14. "Legal Services Regulation," accessed March 17, 2017, http://nsbs.org/legal-services-regulation.

15. Nova Scotia Barristers' Society, Council Meeting Materials, November 25, 2016, 22–23, http://nsbs.org/sites/default/files/ftp/CouncilMaterials/2016-11-25_CouncilPkg.pdf.

16. Ibid., 28.

17. Ibid., 5, 22.

18. Ibid., 25–26.

19. Ibid., 28.

Chapter 13

Manitoba (and the other Prairie Provinces)

An Intimate Connection

Like the Nova Scotia Barristers' Society, the Law Society of Manitoba (LSM) is a regulatory body. It has a Board of Directors whose members are known as "benchers." The Board is composed of eight lawyers elected from Winnipeg, four lawyers elected from outside Winnipeg, four appointed lawyers, six appointed laypersons and several ex-officio members.[1] The LSM's full-time staff includes a CEO. As regards the elected lawyers, the electorate is composed of all licensed lawyers from the relevant District.

In the spring of 2014, the benchers held a "Revisioning Retreat," where they commenced a process to update the regulatory framework for Manitoba—a framework that then president of the LSM, Karen Clearwater, remarked "has been in place for over one hundred years." The culmination of this work included a recommendation by the LSM to the government of Manitoba that the Legal Profession Act be amended, among other changes: (i) to grant to the LSM the power to regulate law firms in addition to individual lawyers, (ii) to define law firm broadly enough to include any entity that provides legal services, regardless of whether or not it is owned or managed, in whole or in part, by nonlawyers, and (iii) to increase the number of lay (nonlawyer) benchers.[2]

In describing to the members of the Manitoba bar the work of the benchers, Clearwater wrote:

> Flowing out of the "Revisioning" exercise were four or five critical priorities designed to deal with current public needs and the fast pace of change in our profession. Some of these ideas were easy for us to wrap our heads around, like moving towards entity regulation [and] providing opportunities for Alternate Business Structures (ABS) to flourish while ensuring the public interest remains protected. . . . However, in addition to some of these less controversial changes

to our regulatory scheme, there was a call for us to think big, to think out of the box.[3]

Given the highly controversial nature of alternative structures in the United States, as well as in the United Kingdom (at one time) and in Ontario (as explored below), Clearwater's description of entity regulation and alternative business structures as "easy for us to wrap our heads around" and "less controversial" are remarkable.

In May 2015, the government of Manitoba complied with the LSM's recommendation, proposing to the Manitoba Legislative Assembly Bill 19, which, in part:

i. Expands the definition of "law firm" to include, in addition to traditional structures such as a sole proprietorship and a partnership, also "a law corporation or any other joint arrangement or legal entity that provides legal services."
ii. Grants to the LSM the power "to permit and regulate" not only law firms, but also "different types of arrangements to provide legal services, including arrangements between lawyers and between lawyers and nonlawyers."
iii. Increases the number of nonlawyer benchers from four to six.[4]

The Manitoba legislature responded to this proposal very quickly, enacting Bill 19 in November, 2015.[5]

The LSM is now engaging in a consulting process in order to propose specific changes to the rules of conduct in implementation of the new legislation. Rather than do this alone, it has joined forces with the Law Societies of the other "Prairie provinces" of Saskatchewan, and Alberta.

The law societies of the three provinces began their work with a November, 2015 jointly issued discussion paper called "Innovating Regulation: A Collaboration of the Prairie Law Societies," in which they describe a linked approach to the three "components" of "entity regulation, compliance-based regulation and ABS." The paper explains that for the three law societies, the three components are "intimately connected." More specifically, the paper states:

> The work of the Prairie provinces began with a focus on alternative business structures (ABS). Looking at what was happening around the world, and at the actual changes in the way legal services are delivered led to the conclusion that limitations we as regulators currently impose on lawyers are likely outdated. In particular, given the pressures lawyers face to run their practices as businesses, regulatory restrictions around fee sharing, referral fees, and other limitations may no longer be appropriate. Further, a move towards allowing ABS has the potential to open the door to innovations, which may assist in addressing unmet legal needs.

These factors, and others, led the Prairie law societies to an initial focus on ABS. However, as discussions evolved, it became clear that it was largely impractical to look at ABS alone. How would we regulate an ABS? What are the appropriate tools? In order to create opportunities for ABSs, we could regulate not only individual lawyers but also their organizations as a whole. In other words, we would have to regulate entities.

Further, as we began to investigate the possibility of entity regulation, it became clear that while paving the way for ABS was one motivation, even more important were the proactive regulatory possibilities that entity regulation presented. We know that most lawyers organize themselves into firms. In practice, it is the infrastructure of the firm that dictates how ethical issues such as conflicts are managed. The opportunity to influence everything from the way files are managed to the culture of the profession also resides at the firm level. If law societies were able to ensure that the appropriate infrastructures exist within a firm to avoid complaints, this would truly be a proactive and preventative approach to protecting the public. This took us back to the beginning and the recognition that three components—entity regulation, compliance-based regulation and ABS—are all intimately connected.

In brief, entity regulation would represent a move from largely regulating only individual lawyers to also regulating the organizations in which they work. A possible mechanism for entity regulation is compliance-based regulation, which would set out a series of objectives and require lawyers and their organizations to demonstrate how they are meeting those objectives within their organizations. Finally, ABSs would be a type of entity regulated through a compliance-based regime. There are many possible forms of ABS but they might include provisions for nonlawyer investment in law firms, multi-disciplinary practices or a variety of other arrangements.[6]

Over the course of May and June, 2016, the three law societies launched a consultation process. To facilitate the consultation the three law societies created a website *lawsocietylistens.ca*, billed as a "consultation hub."[7] In addition to a series of in-person meetings and webinars, the consultation process also included a three-set questionnaire—two sets regarding compliance-based entity regulation and one set regarding entity regulation. The law societies made a point of explaining that the consultation process did not encompass alternative business structures because the law societies were only "at the very early stages of exploring ABS."[8]

The Prairie law societies published a 22-page "Consultation Report" in September, 2016. The report contains a summary of the results of the consultation, prefaced with the observation that the number of lawyers that participated in the consultation was too small to be considered statistically representative (further, the number of registered users on the site describing themselves as nonlawyers was quite small: just two out of a total of 309).[9]

In spite of the small number of participants, the responses the law societies received were varied. In sum, some supported the concepts of compliance-based entity regulation and entity regulation, some wanted more information and continued dialog before expressing an opinion, and some opposed. Nine participants went beyond the questionnaire itself, submitting additional written comments. Some of these written comments were published in an Appendix to the Consultation Report.[10] Three of those comments do what the law societies' questionnaire deliberately did not do, which was address the topic of alternative business structures. Those three comments, submitted by the Alberta Civil Trial Lawyers Association (ACTLA), the Saskatchewan Trial Lawyers Association and the law firm Shores Jardine LLP, express greater or lesser support of the law societies taking a more "proactive approach"[11] toward regulation (that is, they express greater or lesser support for compliance-based regulation). At the same time, however, they also express objections to entity regulation on the grounds that it is "unnecessary"[12] and "may justify the introduction of new models of legal services delivery—including legal services being provided by large accounting firms—without this being made explicit in the consultation process."[13] Going further, the ACTLA recalls how the three law societies in their November, 2015 discussion paper directly link compliance-based regulation, entity regulation and alternative business structures. It is clear, the ACTLA states, that the authors of the discussion paper are in favor of alternative business structures, and it is equally clear that the law societies' real motivation in seeking regulatory jurisdiction over law firms is to "open the door" to alternative business structures.[14]

At the time this book went to press, this consultation process was ongoing, with the three law societies stating on the lawsocietylistens.ca website that further consultations may be conducted on the topics of compliance-based regulation, entity regulation and also possibly alternative business structures.

In sum, in contrast to the Nova Scotia Barristers' Society, the Prairie Law Societies have not shied away from an open discussion, as well as an open consideration, of alternative structures.[15] However, like the Nova Scotia Barristers' Society, the Prairie Law Societies also see the implementation of entity regulation together with the implementation of proactive, management-based regulation as necessary in order to lay the foundation for the regulation of alternative structures in their provinces. In other words, they see entity regulation together with proactive, management-based regulation as the way to be able both to update and improve their regulatory frameworks, as well to regulate alternative structures. Of course, whether or not the Prairie Law Societies achieve any of these objectives remains to be seen. The comments submitted by the ACTLA and the Saskatchewan Trial Lawyers Association, in particular, suggest that the road may not be an easy one.

First-hand perspective

Kristin Dangerfield, CEO, Law Society of Manitoba (online): Dangerfield explains that the mandate of the LSM is to regulate legal services in the public interest. For her, this means assuring that the public has the legal services they need to meet their issues and challenges. Now, she states, Manitoba has a legislative framework that will permit the province to move forward, notably by regulating entities, which, in turn, will allow for the regulation of alternative structures.

NOTES

1. "Benchers," Law Society of Manitoba, accessed March 17, 2017, http://www.lawsociety.mb.ca/for-lawyers/benchers.

2. Karen Clearwater, "President's Report: The Map Followed . . . ," *The Law Society of Manitoba Communiqué 2.0*, May, 2015, 1–2, http://www.lawsociety.mb.ca/publications/communique/May%202015.pdf.

3. Ibid., 1.

4. 40th Legislature of Manitoba, Government Bill 19, "The Legal Profession Amendment Act," 2015, 1–4, https://web2.gov.mb.ca/bills/40-4/pdf/b019.pdf.

5. "Fourth Session, Fortieth Legislature," The Legislative Assembly of Manitoba, accessed March 20, 2017, https://web2.gov.mb.ca/bills/40-4/index.php.

6. Prairie Law Societies, "Innovating Regulation: A Collaboration of the Prairie Law Societies," November, 2015, 2, http://www.lawsociety.sk.ca/media/127107/INNOVATINGREGULATION.pdf.

7. Prairie Law Societies, "Consultation Report," September, 2016, 1, available at http://www.lawsocietylistens.ca/ (hereinafter "Prairie Law Societies Consultation Report").

8. "FAQs," Law Society Listens, accessed March 17, 2017, http://www.lawsocietylistens.ca/start-dialogue/faqs.

9. Prairie Law Societies Consultation Report, 3.

10. Prairie Law Societies, "Consultation Report: Appendix – Paper Responses," September, 2016, available at http://www.lawsocietylistens.ca/.

11. Ibid., 2.

12. Ibid., 3.

13. Ibid., 19.

14. Ibid., 6–9.

15. Clearwater, "President's Report.' See also Prairie Law Societies, "Innovating Regulation;" Mitch Kowalski, "What if the Western Provinces Saved the Profession?" Slaw, February 7, 2013, http://www.slaw.ca/2013/02/07/what-if-the-western-provinces-saved-the-profession/.

Chapter 14

British Columbia

ABS? Who Said ABS?

The Law Society of British Columbia (LSBC) is also a regulatory body, and it is governed by a Board of Directors whose members, like the other Canadian law societies, are known as "benchers." The LSBC's Board is composed of twenty-five lawyers who are elected by other lawyers in nine regions across BC, and up to an additional six nonlawyers who are selected by the provincial Cabinet "to represent the public interest."[1]

In 2012, following the LSBC's request, the British Columbia Legislative Assembly amended the province's Legal Profession Act to provide the LSBC with specific authority to make rules governing law firms and to provide that such rules would be binding on law firms.[2] In order to "make law firm regulation a reality," the LSBC included in its Strategic Plan for 2015–17, the initiatives of "consider whether to permit Alternate Business Structures and, if so, to propose a framework for their regulation," and of "continue . . . the work currently underway to develop a framework for the regulation of law firms."[3]

In 2014, in order to make progress toward at least the second of these goals, the LSBC established a Law Firm Regulation Task Force. In October, 2015, the Task Force issued a "Law Firm Regulation Consultation Brief." The Brief explained that its purpose was:

> to bring the subject of law firm regulation to the attention of lawyers and law firms throughout British Columbia, to inform them that some version of law firm regulation is coming and will touch their professional lives in the future, and to encourage and enable consultation so that individual lawyers and law firms can provide their views and potentially their concerns for consideration by the Task Force.[4]

"Law firm regulation," the Consultation Brief makes clear, refers not only to "a limited form of entity regulation," but also to "proactive," or "principle-based, compliance-based" regulation.[5] With this terminology, the Consultation Brief obviously evokes, if indirectly, the regulatory framework pioneered in New South Wales. However, the relatively short (just thirteen pages) Consultation Brief makes only one direct reference to New South Wales (or Australia more generally), to England and Wales and even to Nova Scotia and Ontario—the purpose of the reference to clarify that while there may be similarities with systems of other jurisdictions, that "the intention of the Task Force is not to simply recreate those systems." Instead, the Task Force intends to "create a framework that will fit well with the existing regulatory system in the British Columbia context."[6]

The Consultation Brief makes a point of separating "law firm regulation" from alternative structures. A question and answer section at the end of the Paper reads as follows:

Does law firm regulation imply ABSs?

> Not necessarily and certainly not initially. The ABS question (whether to allow non-lawyer controlling ownership of legal services providers) is a separate matter from law firm regulation. The Task Force's recommendations on law firm regulation will focus on what components of regulation law firm regulation should cover, what kind of regulatory framework is most suitable for law firm regulation, and what kind of support and resources may be required in support of law firm regulation. At least initially, these aspects of law firm regulation can be addressed independently of questions such as whether law firm ownership restrictions should be changed or whether the Law Society should be engaged in the regulation of other kinds of entities.[7]

Indeed, given the discomforting way the Consultation Brief describes "ABS" it is not surprising that it shies away from them: ABS "would allow the separation of the ownership and control of the business of a law firm from those lawyers who have the professional and ethical obligations that go along with handling the firm's files and advising and representing the clients."[8]

In late 2015 and early 2016, the Task Force carried out a consultation process with lawyers in the province. The consultation included in-person meetings as well as an online survey. At the end of the process, the Task Force issued a 2-page summary of the results of the survey, in which it described that a majority of the over one hundred respondents expressed support for a proactive approach to regulation. That being said, some expressed reservations, such as a fear that shifting responsibility from the individual to the firm could increase the risk of unethical behavior, and a concern of overly burdensome amounts of regulation.[9]

In October, 2016, the Task Force issued an interim report. The Task Force began the report with two observations. The first was that law firms exercise a significant amount of power in the legal profession and have considerable impact on and influence over the professional values and conduct of their lawyers. The second was "there has been a steady expansion" in the number of regulators engaging in the regulation of law firms.[10]

Next, recalling its mandate to recommend a framework for regulating law firms in Canada, the Task Force listed and explained its first ten recommendations. The recommendations include:

1. The development of regulatory objectives is not necessary at this time (but this decision could be reconsidered later);
2. A "proactive, outcomes-based regulatory approach" should be emphasized;
3. "Professional infrastructure elements" should be adopted (the specific elements the Task Force proposes closely track the elements found in the self-assessment forms of New South Wales and Nova Scotia, such as ensuring confidentiality, avoiding conflicts of interest, maintaining appropriate file and records management systems, and charging appropriate fees and disbursements);
4. Firms should be required to have adequate policies and procedures in place to address each of the infrastructure elements;
5. Firms should be required to register (but not to complete an authorization process);
6. Firms should be required to nominate one or more of their lawyers as a designated contact person (while the precise role of the designated contact person remains to be clarified, the role should be more like the "less onerous" one exemplified in Australia rather than the more onerous one exemplified in England and Wales);
7. Firms should be required to conduct self-assessments (the precise mode and frequency to be decided later); and
8. Consider if the Law Society should be empowered to conduct "compliance reviews"—essentially audits—of firms to monitor compliance with the new regulatory framework.[11]

In the report, the Task Force recognizes that the development and implementation of this new regulatory framework will require resources, both financial and human. In the beginning, resources will be needed, in particular, in order to develop model policies, self-assessment tools and rules, to conduct consultations and communicate with the profession, to design specially tailored education and training, and to increase the regulatory functions of the law society. Once the new framework has been implemented, resources will then be required in order to investigate complaints against firms (that is, in addition to the investigation of complaints against individual lawyers) and to conduct compliance reviews (assuming the Law Society is empowered to conduct them). However, the Task Force states, over the longer term "the regulatory program will strive to become cost-neutral," under the assumption that regulatory efficiencies will increase at the same time that complaints decrease.[12]

The Task Force announced that its next step will be to conduct additional consultation with the profession. This consultation will seek input from across the province, as well as from specific "focus groups" designed to elicit feedback from specific types of practice structures (sole practitioners, space-sharing lawyers, etc.). The Task Force will also conduct internal consultations with the relevant departments of the law society. Upon the completion of those consultations, the Task Force will issue a final report to the benchers.[13]

In the interim report the Task Force clarifies that it expects that the new regulatory framework will be implemented in two phases. The first will be a "soft" implementation, where firms will be required to register and appoint a contact person, but where the law society would not yet require compliance or engage in enforcement. In this manner, firms would be given time to understand the new requirements and implement the necessary policies and procedures prior to enforcement. The second phase would, then, bring the compliance and enforcement elements into effect.[14]

Finally, as it did its previous papers, in its interim report the Task Force again takes pains to avoid the controversy of alternative structures, by seeking to clearly place them outside the scope of its work: "the question of whether to allow non-lawyer controlling ownership of legal service providers is a distinct issue from the matter of firm regulation." Consequently, the Task Force "will not address whether the Law Society should be engaged in the regulation of other kinds of entities."[15]

Of course, even if the Task Force does not address them, the work it is doing is laying groundwork for their implementation.

First-hand perspective

Herman Van Ommen, Chair, Law Firm Regulation Task Force, Law Society of British Columbia (online): Van Ommen explains that the Law Society sees law firm regulation as "housekeeping": law firms are responsible for much of the behavior of lawyers, and, for that reason, "it is time" to regulate law firms in addition to lawyers. He explains that the Task Force is working free of the political pollution of ABS.

NOTES

1. See "Benchers," The Law Society of British Columbia, accessed March 17, 2017, https://www.lawsociety.bc.ca/about-us/benchers/.

2. Law Firm Regulation Task Force, "Law Firm Regulation Consultation Brief," October 26, 2015, 3, https://www.lawsociety.bc.ca/docs/newsroom/highlights/Firm-Regulation-brief.pdf.

3. The Law Society of British Columbia, "2015–2017 Strategic Plan," 5, https://www.lawsociety.bc.ca/docs/about/StrategicPlan_2015-17.pdf.

4. Law Firm Regulation Task Force, "Law Firm Regulation Consultation Brief," 4.

5. Ibid., 3.

6. Ibid., 11.

7. Ibid., 12.

8. Ibid.

9. Law Firm Regulation Task Force, "Law Firm Regulation Survey Report," undated, https://www.lawsociety.bc.ca/docs/publications/survey/LawFirmRegulation.pdf.

10. Law Firm Regulation Task Force, "Interim Report of the Law Firm Regulation Task Force," October 3, 2016, 3, https://www.lawsociety.bc.ca/docs/publications/reports/LawFirmRegulation-2016.pdf.

11. Ibid., 6–26.

12. Ibid., 29.

13. Ibid., 30–31.

14. Ibid., 31.

15. Ibid., 12.

Chapter 15

Ontario

A False Start, but on its Way

Like the law societies described above, the Law Society of Upper Canada (LSUC) is also a regulatory body. The LSUC is governed by a Board of Directors whose members are also known as "benchers." The LSUC's Board is composed of twenty lawyers elected from inside Toronto, twenty lawyers elected from outside Toronto, eight appointed laypersons, and several ex-officio members.[1] As regards the elected lawyers, the electorate is composed of all licensed lawyers from the relevant region.

A FALSE START

In September 2012, the LSUC established an "Alternative Business Structures Working Group." For a period of three years, this group examined a possible change to the Ontario regulations in order to permit alternative structures. Their work involved extensive research including meetings with lawyers and paralegals, consulting with "experts" and reviewing research and related literature.[2]

In February, 2014 the Working Group issued a report that opened by describing the extensive work it had done.[3] On the basis of that work, the Working Group made these conclusions and recommendations:

i. Alternative Business Structures: The Working Group concluded that "there are negative consequences inherent in current regulatory limitations on the delivery of legal services in Ontario that could be addressed with the thoughtful liberalization of business structures and the related liberalization of what non-legal services can be provided by entities providing legal services." The Working Group identified four structural and services models as options for consideration as permissible regulatory frameworks, and recommended that those four models be the subject of a formal consultation with interested groups and individuals.

ii. Firm or entity-based regulation: The Working Group concluded that firm or entity-based regulation is a necessary element of effective ABS regulation, and also that it is advisable regardless of whether any form of ABS is ultimately adopted. While the Law Society already has some rights to regulate entities, the Working Group recommended that the Law Society seek statutory amendment that would grant it full and express authority to do so.

iii. Compliance-based regulation: The Working Group observed that while there were many differences in regulatory changes introduced in Australia and England and Wales, that there were certain commonalities, including the introduction of firm or entity based regulation together with "compliance based regulation." For the Working Group, compliance-based regulation means moving away from a complaints-driven, proscriptive and rules-based approach toward an objectives-based approach, where firms have flexibility as to how they meet those objectives. In this context, the Working Group recommended that the LSUC consider compliance-based regulation to supplement the existing rules-based regulation.[4]

In September 2014, the LSUC issued a discussion paper seeking input "on alternative business structures (ABS) as a means for delivering legal services in Ontario."

The Discussion Paper begins by outlining what business structures are currently available in Ontario, and by describing what an ABS is.

The Discussion Paper then explains that the LSUC is considering the ABS model "in light of several factors, including apparent gaps in the provision of legal services, the increasing globalization of the legal profession, and advances in technology and developments abroad, that significantly affect how legal services can be delivered."[5] In addressing potential challenges to the ABS model, the Discussion Paper describes professional and ethical considerations such as potential conflicts of interest and confidentiality, as well as implementation issues, such as the extent of regulatory supervision.[6]

Finally, the Discussion Paper describes developments in this area inside as well as outside Canada, and notably in Nova Scotia, British Columbia, Australia and England and Wales.

The Discussion Paper proposes four ABS models for feedback:

Model #1: Business entities providing *legal services only* in which individuals and entities who are not licensed by the Law Society can have up to 49% ownership.

Model #2: Business entities providing *legal services only* with no restrictions on ownership by individuals and entities who are not licensed by the Law Society.

Model #3: Business entities providing *both legal and non-legal services* (except those identified as posing a regulatory risk) in which individuals and entities who are not licensed by the Law Society would be permitted up to 49% ownership.

Model #4: Business entities providing *both legal and non-legal services* (except those identified as posing a regulatory risk) in which individuals and entities who are not licensed by the Law Society would be permitted unlimited ownership.[7]

The LSUC requested input on the Discussion Paper from "the public, the legal community and other interested parties."[8]

In a notable contrast to the Working Group's February, 2014 report, the September, 2014 Discussion Paper mentioned entity regulation and compliance-based regulation (PMBR) very briefly in passing, without explaining or developing either topic.

The September 2014 Discussion Paper triggered an avalanche. To begin, the Working Group received forty-one written submissions in response, of which twenty-one expressed opposition,[9] and, in many cases, very strong opposition to the introduction of alternative structures in Ontario (ten expressed support[10] and ten either expressed no position or their position was not clear[11]). Further, the Discussion Paper also spurred an intensified discussion of alternative structures in the legal press and on social media, one example being a December 2014 post on Slaw ("Canada's online legal magazine") by the commentator Mitch Kowalski entitled "Anti-ABS Arguments Continue to Be Based on Emotion—Not Fact."[12] Over a 29-day period from December 2014 to January 2015 his post generated just under 100 comments, many of them extraordinarily lengthy (well over 3000 words), and, especially, many of them impassioned. Just a few examples of the statements made include:

> "There is nothing that is claimed for ABS that cannot be achieved without ABS. We would be far better off if we put our talents and resources into achieving those benefits without resorting to the bottomless hell-hole of profit-motivated, bean-counter remote ownership of the legal profession. . . . Every real benefit foolishly attributed to the ersatz panacea of ABS can be achieved . . . without resorting to the myopic and irreversible blunder of selling the ownership of the legal profession to mostly remote bean-counters."[13]
>
> "We stumble around like drunks attacking the modest cost of wills and work assiduously at being bootlicks to big business by offering to sell them our profession. . . . Are we completely daft? Are we that blindly and brainlessly cavalier?"[14]
>
> "[ABS] is poison. It is immeasurably harmful. It is like communism once was—a superficially appealing philosophy that garnered a number of adherents even in the West, but which, as history has proven, engenders and spreads harm like an ebola virus sneezed into a classroom. You may not appreciate it but I am trying to prevent you and the other misguided sponsors of this evil from later garnering for yourselves the scorn of history."[15]

> "ABS is an irreversible blunder of stunning proportions that will do nothing for the public except to harm them. . . . It should be seen for what it truly is—the worst idea to hit the profession in centuries . . . [ABS] assuredly will prove to be, the most colossal, short-sighted, cynical, profiteering at the expense of the public, and unnecessary blunder in the history of the legal profession dating back 800 years."[16]

This impassioned argumentation exposes how controversial the topic of ABS became in Ontario. Understood in this context, the decision of the Working Group in late September 2015 to not further examine "any majority or controlling non-licensee ownership models for traditional law firms in Ontario" (that is, Models #2 and #4) is not a surprise. Nor was its explanation that "such non-licensee ownership levels do not appear to be warranted based on current information when the potential benefits to such external ownership levels are weighed against the regulatory risks and regulatory proportionality."[17]

The Working Group cited the following "concerns and risks" the submissions raised in relation to nonlawyer majority ownership: external ownership emphasizes profits over professionalism, it would be difficult to preserve client confidentiality and solicitor-client privilege due to pressure by non-licensee owners to learn about the firm's cases, there would be increased risks of conflicts, and it would result in market consolidation thereby limiting the choice of the public to counsel in certain areas.[18]

In issuing its decision, the Working Group concluded that it had fulfilled much of its mandate, and explained that its next steps would be limited to: (i) staying informed on developments elsewhere in Canada and in other countries, (ii) considering the level, "if any," and nature of any nonlawyer minority ownership that should be permitted, (iii) considering if any "franchise" arrangements should be permitted, (iv) considering if "civil society organizations, such as charities, not-for-profits, and trade unions," should become owners of entities "in order to facilitate access to legal services" and (v) considering when ABSs could be permitted "in areas not generally being served by lawyers and paralegals."[19]

At the time this book went to press, there was no publicly available evidence that the Working Group had undertaken any significant further activities since issuing the September 2015 decision.

THE UGLY HEAD OF SELF-REGULATION

In April, 2015—seven months after the Working Group issued its Discussion Paper and during the Working Group's consultation period—a bencher election was held in Ontario. In the run-up to the election, the Ontario Trial Lawyers Association (OTLA), a strident opponent to alternative structures, posted on its website a "Voting Guide for OTLA Members." The guide explained:

> Alternative Business Structures (ABS) has been presented by its supporters as a solution to access to justice in Ontario. After extensive research, the Ontario Trial Lawyers Association has determined that there is no empirical evidence to support this claim. In fact, evidence suggests that the implementation of ABS and Non-Lawyer Ownership of law firms will introduce unnecessary conflicts regarding professionalism and ethics, in addition to myriad regulatory issues.
>
> As a result, it is the position of the Ontario Trial Lawyers Association that it would be unwise to implement ABS.
>
> The timing of this discussion and the potential for a massive impact on members of the legal profession have catapulted the dialogue into a key Law Society Bencher Election issue.[20]

The guide then listed and endorsed sixty-five (out of ninety-seven) bencher candidates "that have signaled their opposition and that they would not vote in favour of the ABS examples as set out in the Law Society discussion paper."[21]

The OLTA was criticized for this approach to the bencher election. Criticisms included that the OLTA's approach was "hysterical" and threatened "to hijack Ontario's bencher elections to the detriment of the profession and the public interest."[22]

After the election, there was debate about the extent to which the OLTA's campaign made a difference to the outcome, with some suggesting it made a significant difference[23] and others suggesting that if it did make a difference, it was limited.[24]

Others argued that regardless of the difference the OLTA's campaign actually made to the election results, the campaign created "some risks and concerns about the viability of our current regulatory model" by raising the question can "elected lawyers be trusted to regulate in the public interest?"[25] This commentator, Alice Woolley, made a number of additional remarks regarding the OLTA's campaign that merit being quoted at length:

> The focus on ABS highlights starkly the disjunct that can exist between the electoral interests of the legal profession and the public in whose interests law societies must regulate. . . . A lawyer voting in a bencher election, or running as a bencher, is likely to be influenced as much by lawyer concerns as by those of the public interest. This is not an indictment of those lawyers. Human beings are always influenced by our own interests; even when we try not to be, our cognitive biases and weaknesses make true abandonment of self-interest impossible.

. . . A lawyer voting or running may also use the public interest concerns simply for effective advocacy in relation to lawyer-focused concerns. And—worst of all—it will be impossible to know whether a lawyer voting or running for bencher is in fact motivated by lawyer-based concerns or public-based ones. That may mean that even a largely public-interest focused candidate or voter will appear as lawyer-interested.

Not all regulatory issues raise this concern. On questions of, for example, the maintenance of solicitor-client privilege, to a great extent the public interest and lawyer interests will be aligned. But with ABS the distinction between public interests and lawyer interests is significant, and making this the focus of the election, and encouraging people to vote on the basis of prospective bencher's position on ABS, focuses attention on the difference between the interests of the regulators and those on whose behalf they are supposed to act. It has the potential to make the whole election as driven towards protection of lawyer concerns, rather than as attentive to who will do the best job of regulating in the public interest . . .

[T]he people whose interests benchers serve are not the same as those who elect them. Which makes a bencher having a closed mind problematic both legally and ethically. Because the bencher's closed mind could result from a commitment to the interests of lawyers supported by an electoral outcome, not from a commitment to the interests of the public supported by an electoral outcome.

ABS isn't decided based on a person's values and beliefs. It's something that may or may not be a desirable regulatory change based on available evidence and regulatory mechanisms for successfully implementing that change. Elected benchers need to assess it on that basis, and forcing them to declare a position prior to election—and the actual consideration of the issue as a regulator—is to ensure that the public interest will not be properly assessed, whatever the outcome.

An "OTLA List" election may also inhibit regulatory courage. With this precedent as a backdrop will an elected bencher be willing to take a stand unpopular with lawyers in an effort to protect the public interest? Or will she decline to do so because fully aware that such a stand will make her a target next time around.[26]

BACK TO THE DRAWING BOARD

In meantime—in June, 2015—the LSUC established a second group, the Compliance-Based Entity Regulation Task Force.[27] In early December, 2015—just over two months after the ABS Working Group issued its decision—the Task Force announced that it would conduct a consultation process with respect to compliance-based entity regulation.[28] Accordingly, in January, 2016, the Task Force issued a 24-page Consultation Paper in which it described its conception of entity regulation as well as compliance-based regulation and explained why the LSUC had taken an interest in it.

The Consultation Paper describes the LSUC's initiative as follows:

> The Law Society regulates lawyers and paralegals to achieve appropriate professional conduct by setting rules and by-laws which are applicable to individual practitioners. . . . [Further,] the regulatory process is primarily reactive, responding to conduct that has already occurred. It does not formally recognize the influence of practice arrangements on the way that legal services are being provided, and is based on proscriptive rules that must be followed by all individual lawyers and paralegals.
>
> These limitations have led the Law Society to look for a new approach, one that includes not only lawyers and paralegals, but also the entities through which they provide legal services. Compliance-based regulation supports individuals and entities to achieve best practices in a manner best suited to their environment. Rather than reacting to misconduct after it occurs, it would be much better for both the public and for practitioners if the problem never occurred in the first place.[29]

The Consultation Paper points out that of 4,781 complaints referred to the Law Society's Professional Regulation Division in 2014, more than half of these complaints—52%—involved client services and other issues relating to practice management infrastructure. The Consultation Paper explains that this 52% includes a variety of issues, such as "a lack of effective communication by the practitioner with the client."[30]

Interestingly, the Consultation Paper draws directly upon the "Innovating Regulation" paper issued by the Prairie Law Societies of Manitoba, Saskatchewan and Alberta (described above). It does so, for example, in listing no fewer than six ways that "proactive regulation through a compliance-based approach could benefit legal practices." The list includes the reduction of complaints, the ability for firms to develop with flexibility and autonomy the internal systems appropriate to their size and activities, and the ability for the regulator to respond to new issues as they arise without having to create new rules.[31]

The Consultation Paper briefly describes the relevant regulations in England and Wales and Australia—notably that both have implemented entity regulation as well as outcomes-focused (England and Wales) and proactive (Australia) regulation. In its description, the Consultation Paper makes one passing reference to the ILP structure in Australia.[32] However, the Consultation Paper seems to go out of its way to not use the expression "alternative business structure" or "ABS" or any variation of those terms, not only in its specific discussion of England and Wales, but, indeed, anywhere in the document's twenty-four pages. Given how highly controversial that subject proved to be in relation to the work of the ABS Working Group, the absence of any discussion or indeed any reference to them in this Consultation Paper was surely intentional.

The Consultation Paper concludes with a series of questions calling for input from "practitioners and the public." The questions are grouped into five categories relating to: (i) the key components, or principles, for compliance and entity regulation, (ii) the types of "practice arrangements" to which compliance-based entity regulation may apply, notably based upon size (small, medium and/or large firms), (iii) the roles and responsibilities of a "designated practitioner," (iv) whether entities should be required to be registered, and (v) the anticipated benefits, drawbacks and challenges with compliance-based entity regulation.[33] The Task Force also posed the questions via an online questionnaire.

In support of the Consultation Paper, on February 12, 2016, the Chair of the Task Force, Ross Earnshaw, guest authored a blog post on Slaw.[34] In the post, he explained the Law Society's reasons for considering compliance-based entity regulation and the work of the Task Force, and he urged readers to read the consultation paper and submit comments. In stark contrast to Kowalski's December, 2014 post on Slaw regarding alternative structures and the numerous, lengthy and impassioned comments that it generated, not a single comment was posted in response to Earnshaw's post.[35]

In its May 26, 2016 Report to Convocation, the Task Force reported that it had received ninety-seven responses to its call for input, of which seventy-seven came from individuals and the remainder from organizations.[36] A summary of the most pertinent responses includes:

- Generally speaking, the respondents expressed support for entity regulation and for compliance-based regulation. In this context, however, some expressed reservations about additional regulatory burdens that may result. Others opined that the law society should not become involved in management issues because to do so would undermine the principles of a "free economy and normal market drivers."
- With respect to the appointment of a "designated practitioner," there were a number of comments on the potential range of responsibilities, and notably statements that the person in this role should not bear personal responsibility for firm violations.
- Most respondents agreed that entities should be required to register with the Law Society (but not undergo a licensing process), some adding that the requirements should be different for sole practitioners in order to not unduly increase their regulatory burdens.
- Several respondents expressed concern that entity regulation could lead to a reduction in the professional responsibility of lawyers as individuals.

- Some respondents expressed concern on the relationship between entity regulation and alternative structures, stating, for example, that entity regulation should not become a "back door" for alternative structures.[37]

In its May, 2016, Report to Convocation, the Task Force made two recommendations: (i) that the Law Society seek to amend the Law Society Act to permit the Law Society to regulate the entities through which legal services are provided and (ii) that Convocation approve the development of a regulatory framework based upon the principles of compliance-based regulation.[38]

In explaining its first recommendation, the Task Force stated that "In 2016, it is not realistic to treat law or paralegal firms as mere collections of autonomous individual practitioners who happen to share a firm name. . . . Entity regulation recognizes that many professional decisions that were once made by an individual practitioner are increasingly determined by firm policies and procedures and firm decision-making processes." For the Task Force, entity regulation has three main benefits: that it enhances the efficiency and effectiveness of professional regulation, harmonizes Ontario's legislation with that of other provinces, and (cryptically) positions the Law Society "to respond more effectively to innovations in legal services delivery that may be required in the public interest."[39]

With respect to the second recommendation, the Task Force explained that it would develop or more options for a regulatory framework, which would be the subject of "focused consultation" with the professions (lawyers and paralegals) to obtain feedback on their potential feedback.[40]

At its meeting on May 26, 2016, Convocation approved the two recommendations. While it would be wrong to say that the approval went unnoticed, it certainly received little fanfare.[41] The *Financial Post* did run a short article about it, but the entire purpose of the article was to explain to a presumably otherwise uninterested audience why the Convocation decisions mattered. The article's author, Drew Hasselback, understood well why it mattered: because, as he wrote, "a journey of a thousand miles begins with a single step."[42]

First-hand perspective

Ross Earnshaw, Chair, Task Force on Compliance-Based Entity Regulation and Margaret Drent, Policy Counsel, Law Society of Upper Canada (online): Earnshaw and Drent explain that compliance-based entity regulation has a great number of potential benefits that have nothing to do with ABS. With the appointment of our Task Force, compliance-based entity regulation has been moved to be front and center, out of the shadow of the more controversial topic of alternative structures. [43]

NOTES

1. "Benchers," Law Society of Upper Canada, accessed March 17, 2017, http://www.lsuc.on.ca/with.aspx?id=1136.

2. "Alternative Business Structures," Law Society of Upper Canada, accessed March 17, 2017, http://www.lsuc.on.ca/ABS/.

3. Law Society of Upper Canada Professional Regulations Committee, "First Report to Convocation," February 27, 2014, 1443, http://www.lsuc.on.ca/uploadedFiles/ABS-report-to-Convocation-feb-2014.pdf.

4. Ibid., 1443–1445.

5. Alternative Business Structures Working Group, "Alternative Business Structures and the Legal Profession in Ontario: A Discussion Paper," September, 2014, 4, http://www.lsuc.on.ca/uploadedFiles/abs-discussion-paper.pdf.

6. Ibid., 17, 20–21.

7. Ibid., 22–26.

8. Ibid., 4.

9. The submissions can be consulted at this link (accessed on March 17, 2017): http://www.lsuc.on.ca/ABS/. The twenty-one submissions that can be characterized as more or less clearly in opposition are those of: The Advocates' Society, Barrie Real Estate Lawyers Association, Blair Botsford, Brendt, Lorne and group, Ken Chasse, The County District Lawyers Presidents' Association, County of Carleton Law Association, Janis Criger, Criminal Lawyers Association, Essex Law Association, Nicholas Gehl, Gordon Harris, McLeish Orlando, Ontario Bar Association, Ontario Trial Lawyers Association, Southwest Region Women's Law Association, Stewart Title, Murray Teitel, Thunder Bay Law Association, Waterloo Region Law Association and Women's Paralegal Association of Ontario.

10. The ten submissions that can be characterized as more or less clearly in support are those of: Julie Audet, Julie Audet and Nathalie Picard, Centre for International Governance Innovation, Cognition LLP, Conduit Law, Joseph Granton, Mitch Kowalski, Devon LaBuik, Liam Ledgerwood, and Baruch Lipinski.

11. The ten submissions that can be characterized either as expressing no position or their position was not clear are those of: Lee Akazaki, James Ball, Canadian Defense Lawyers, Equity Advisory Working Group on ABS, Federation of Asian Canadian Lawyers, John Hollander, Law Students' Society of Ontario, LawPRO, Ontario College of Social Workers and Social Service Workers, and David Wiseman.

12. Mitch Kowalski, "Anti-ABS Arguments Continue to Be Based on Emotion—Not Fact," *Slaw*, December 30, 2014, http://www.slaw.ca/2014/12/30/anti-abs-arguments-continue-to-be-based-on-emotion-not-fact/.

13. Bradley Wright, December 30, 2014 (6:28 pm), comment on Mitch Kowalski, "Anti-ABS Arguments Continue to Be Based on Emotion—Not Fact," *Slaw*, December 30, 2014, http://www.slaw.ca/2014/12/30/anti-abs-arguments-continue-to-be-based-on-emotion-not-fact/comment-page-1/#comments.

14. Bradley Wright, January 2, 2015 (1:43 pm), comment on Mitch Kowalski, "Anti-ABS Arguments Continue to Be Based on Emotion—Not Fact," *Slaw*, December 30, 2014, http://www.slaw.ca/2014/12/30/anti-abs-arguments-continue-to-be-based-on-emotion-not-fact/comment-page-1/#comments.

15. Bradley Wright, January 7, 2015 (10:31 am), comment on Mitch Kowalski, "Anti-ABS Arguments Continue to Be Based on Emotion—Not Fact," *Slaw*, December 30, 2014, http://www.slaw.ca/2014/12/30/anti-abs-arguments-continue-to-be-based-on-emotion-not-fact/comment-page-1/#comments.

16. Bradley Wright, January 23, 2015 (5:38 pm), comment on Mitch Kowalski, "Anti-ABS Arguments Continue to Be Based on Emotion—Not Fact," *Slaw*, December 30, 2014, http://www.slaw.ca/2014/12/30/anti-abs-arguments-continue-to-be-based-on-emotion-not-fact/#comments.

17. Law Society of Upper Canada Professional Regulation Committee, "Report to Convocation," September 24, 2015, 111, http://www.lsuc.on.ca/uploadedFiles/For_the_Public/About_the_Law_Society/Convocation_Decisions/2015/convocation-september-2015-prc.pdf.

18. Ibid., 116–117.

19. Ibid., 111–112, 130.

20. "2015 LSUC Bencher Election Voting Guide For OTLA Members," Ontario Trial Lawyers Association, accessed March 17, 2017, https://www.otla.com/index.cfm?pg=Bencher-Election-Voting-Guide.

21. Ibid.

22. Cristin Schmitz, "ABS Issue Dominating Bencher Vote," *The Lawyers Weekly*, April 17, 2015, http://www.lawyersweekly.ca/articles/2362.

23. EM, May 5, 2015 (11:33 am), comment on Alice Woolley, "Bencher Elections – The Challenge to Self-Regulations Legitimacy," *Slaw*, April 30, 2015, http://www.slaw.ca/2015/04/30/bencher-elections-the-challenge-to-self-regulations-legitimacy/.

24. Malcolm Mercer, May 18, 2015 (10:15 am), comment on Woolley, "Bencher Elections."

25. Woolley, "Bencher Elections."

26. Ibid.

27. Law Society of Upper Canada, "Report to Convocation: Treasurer's Report," June 25, 2015, 8–13, https://www.lsuc.on.ca/uploadedFiles/For_the_Public/About_the_Law_Society/Convocation_Decisions/2015/convocation-june-2015-treasurer.pdf.

28. Law Society of Upper Canada Compliance-Based Entity Regulation Task Force, "Report to Convocation," December 4, 2015, https://www.lsuc.on.ca/uploadedFiles/For_the_Public/About_the_Law_Society/Convocation_Decisions/2015/convocation%20december%202015%20compliance.pdf.

29. Compliance-Based Entity Regulation Task Force, "Call for Input Consultation Paper: 'Promoting Better Legal Practices,'" January 2016, 4, https://www.lsuc.on.ca/uploadedFiles/compliance-based-entity-regulation-consultation-paper.pdf.

30. Ibid., 6.

31. Ibid., 7 and Notes 10 and 12–14, Ibid. 21–22.

32. Ibid., 8–10, 17–18.

33. Ibid., 13–20.

34. Ross Earnshaw, "Promoting Better Practices—a Proactive Approach to Lawyer and Paralegal Regulation," *Slaw*, February 1, 2016, http://www.slaw.ca/2016/02/12/promoting-better-practices-a-proactive-approach-to-lawyer-and-paralegal-regulation/.

35. Ibid. A comparable blog post on Slaw by Herman Van Ommen, chair of British Columbia's Law Firm Regulation Task Force, also did not generate any comments in response. Herman Van Ommen, "Law Firm Regulation," *Slaw*, February 16, 2016, http://www.slaw.ca/2016/02/16/law-firm-regulation/.

36. Compliance-Based Entity Regulation Task Force, "Report to Convocation," May 26, 2016, 50, http://www.lsuc.on.ca/uploadedFiles/For_the_Public/About_the_Law_Society/Convocation_Decisions/2016/convocation_may_2016_cber.pdf.

37. Ibid., 52–56.

38. Ibid., 3.

39. Ibid., 3,6.

40. Ibid., 24.

41. See, for example, Amy Salyzyn, "Law Society of Upper Canada to Move Forward with Proactive Entity Regulation," Canadian Association for Legal Ethics, May 28, 2016, https://ethicsincanada.com/2016/05/28/law-society-of-upper-canada-to-move-forward-with-proactive-entity-regulation/.

42. Drew Hasselback, "Why the Law Society of Upper Canada's Move Toward 'Entity Regulation' Matters," *Financial Post*, May 31, 2016, http://business.financialpost.com/legal-post/drew-hasselback-why-the-law-society-of-upper-canadas-move-toward-entity-regulation-matters.

Chapter 16

Canadian Bar Association

Creating the Future

In contrast to the law societies profiled above, the Canadian Bar Association (CBA) is an entirely representative rather than a regulatory body. Further, it is national, rather than provincial: it represents the approximately 36,000 lawyers in Canada and reports that approximately two-thirds of practicing lawyers in Canada are members.[1]

In August 2011, the Governor General of Canada issued a challenge to the CBA: to craft a new definition of the lawyer as professional. He identified as key elements of that challenge access to justice and innovation in the delivery of legal services and the practice of law.[2]

In February 2012 the CBA Board of Directors voted unanimously to launch the CBA Legal Futures Initiative, to examine the future legal marketplace and the work of lawyers in the next decades. A steering committee began work in autumn 2012, with Richard Susskind (author of *The End of Lawyers? Rethinking the Nature of Legal Services*[3]) acting as Special Advisor.

To inform its work, the Futures Initiative commissioned seven research studies to examine general trends, demographics, economics, innovation and client needs and expectations. Further, over a period of eight months from June 2013 to January 2014, members of the Futures Initiative undertook a consultation of stake holders across Canada and abroad. Personal invitations to comment were extended to over 300 institutions and organizations. In addition, in-person presentations and meetings were held around Canada with local CBA representatives, new lawyers, lawyers with small, mid-sized and large law firms, public sector and in-house lawyers, "legal innovators," judges, law professors and law students. The consultation also included substantive written submissions and twitterchats. The consultation covered a wide range of topics, including law school education, new lawyer training, changing client expectations, how technology is changing the practice of law, unbundling, entity regulation, alternative structures, access to justice, diversity in the profession and the very conception of what it is to be a lawyer.[4]

In August 2014, the Futures Initiative issued its report, "Futures: Transforming the Delivery of Legal Services in Canada." The 102-page Report contains 22 recommendations, based upon seven "key findings."

While the recommendations and findings cover a number of topics, the majority are focused on two topics in particular: education and training of new lawyers on the one hand, and delivery models and their regulation, on the other. With respect to the latter, the Report found that lawyers need to be freed to work differently through new structures and in conjunction with other professionals, including alternative business structures.[5] This includes, the Report continues, allowing lawyers to practice in business structures whose owners, managers or investors may be nonlawyers. It also includes multi-disciplinary practices and fee-sharing with non-lawyers. However, the Report emphasizes, all of these proposed changes must be carried out "under the oversight of an enhanced regulatory framework," which includes entity regulation as well as compliance-based regulation.[6]

When the Report was issued, one commentator compared it in importance to the Clementi Report. He hailed the report as a "watershed moment for the legal market in Canada," if not North America, and said that it had the potential "to help usher in a new era in legal services on this side of the Atlantic, and to utterly remake the Canadian legal market."[7]

In contrast, another commentator was not nearly as impressed, stating that it was merely "noteworthy" that the CBA "recognized what has been happening in the Canadian legal landscape for years."[8]

The law societies of Canada have not rushed to implement all or even most of the Report's recommendations (and, as discussed above, in 2015 Ontario rejected some of them outright). This does not mean, however, that the report has not been influential. Notably, in their Discussion Paper "Innovating Regulation: A Collaboration of the Prairie Law Societies," the Law Societies of Manitoba, of Alberta and of Saskatchewan expressly cite the Report several times, with an emphasis on its recommendations with respect to compliance-based entity regulation.[9] The Report signals to the law societies that there is an awareness of the issues at stake as well as a desire for reform among at least certain (if not a significant number) of the members of the legal profession in Canada.

First-hand perspective

Fred Headon, Chair of the CBA Legal Futures Initiative, Canadian Bar Association (online): Headon explains that the objective of the CBA Legal Futures Initiative is to enable the legal profession to invent its future rather than have it thrust upon it.

NOTES

1. "About Us," Canadian Bar Association, accessed on March 17, 2017, http://www.cba.org/Who-We-Are/About-us.

2. CBA Legal Futures Initiative, "Futures: Transforming the Delivery of Legal Services in Canada," August, 2014, 29, http://www.cba.org/CBAMediaLibrary/cba_na/PDFs/CBA%20Legal%20Futures%20PDFS/Futures-Final-eng.pdf.

3. Richard Susskind, *The End of Lawyers? Rethinking the Nature of Legal Services* (Oxford: Oxford University Press, 2010).

4. CBA Legal Futures Initiative, "Futures," 84.

5. Ibid., 11, 29, 42.

6. Ibid., 6–7, 11, 42.

7. Jordan Furlong, "Watershed: The CBA Futures Report," Law21, August 14, 2014, http://www.law21.ca/2014/08/watershed-cba-futures-report/.

8. Ivan Mitchell Merrow, "In Futuro: What the CBA's Legal Futures Report Means for You," *Juris Diction*, November 18, 2014, http://juris-diction.ca/in-futuro-what-the-cbas-legal-futures-report-means-for-you/.

9. Prairie Law Societies, "Innovating Regulation," 1, 24, 30, 46, 52.

Chapter 17

The Continuing Path of Revolution

As the above discussion demonstrates, much is happening in Canada, and no doubt much will continue to happen in the future. The work of the CBA Legal Futures Initiative aside, most activity is occurring on a provincial rather than national basis. While certainly there is extensive communication among the provinces, and notably among the provincial law societies,[1] for the time being the provinces are acting independently of each other (save for the three Prairie states of Manitoba, Saskatchewan and Alberta, which as mentioned above are closely coordinating their work).

In light of this independence of activity, it is not surprising that there are differences, and, in some respects, significant differences, in their approaches and it can be expected that there will also be significant differences in the outcomes. That being said, there are a certain number of important commonalities:

1. There is a steady movement toward the development and implementation of some form of entity regulation combined with some form of compliance-based regulation (in Canada the term that seems to be most generally used is "compliance-based regulation," in favor of the alternatives of "proactive, management-based regulation" or "outcomes-focused regulation").
2. The fact that the Australian states of New South Wales and Victoria have taken a step back from compliance-based regulation does not appear to make a significant difference for the Canadian regulators. It appears that for the Canadian regulators, the step back in Australia was not a reflection on the value of self-assessments or of compliance-based regulation more generally.[2] That being said, both Nova Scotia and British Columbia[3] have made a point of distancing the frameworks they seek to develop from the framework pioneered in New South Wales.

3. While it would surely be incorrect to state that the movement toward compliance-based entity regulation has not raised any objections or controversy, any such objections or controversy has been limited—indeed, it is difficult to find and could arguably be characterized as insignificant in comparison to the objections and controversy raised in relation to alternative structures.
4. One explanation for the lack of controversy may be that alternative structures are not (or, with respect to Ontario, are no longer) the focus of the work of the Canadian regulators. At least, they are not the focus in any direct and obvious way. That being said, the approach of each province is different: Manitoba expressly embraces a move toward alternative structures as an element of its work, because they have "the potential to open the door to innovations, which may assist in addressing unmet legal needs."[4] On the other hand, British Columbia expressly rejects that "law firm regulation impl[ies] ABS," at least, "not necessarily and certainly not initially."[5] Nova Scotia barely mentions them and the radio silence of Ontario's Task Force on Compliance-Based Entity Regulation is deafening. Presumably the reluctance to more expressly and directly link compliance-based entity regulation with alternative structures is a result, at least in part, of desire to avoid a repetition of the highly contentious and ultimately unproductive debate that occurred in Ontario.
5. This does not mean that alternative structures are not on the map. The work the provinces are doing now is the groundwork that needs to be laid in order for Canada to permit alternative structures. While it is too early to predict with certainty whether the country ultimately will permit them, the work they are doing now makes it significantly more likely.
6. It appears unlikely that one or even a small number of provinces will adopt alternative structures independently or significantly in advance of the rest of the country. This is because of the issues it could pose with respect to mobility: the mobility of the legal profession across the territory of Canada is a high priority for the provincial law societies,[6] as well as for the national Federation of Law Societies.[7] The implementation of any regulation that had the effect of preventing lawyers (and also, presumably, law firms and other entities) practicing in one province from also easily practicing in another is likely to be rejected, or, at a minimum, postponed until a solution was available. In this light, if and when Canada does finally adopt alternative structures, it is likely that the entire country will do so more or less simultaneously.[8]

As much activity as there is in Canada, the outcome is not guaranteed: At least one commentator is guarded, if not skeptical, that any real change will happen in Canada. In his article "Legal Services Regulation in Canada:

Plus Ça Change?" Noel Semple observes that that the regulatory changes in England and Wales and Australia were initiated and championed by elected leaders, competition authorities and consumer groups. In contrast, in Canada, discussions of possible regulatory change are occurring only among lawyers in the legal services regulatory and academic communities[9] (that is, it's not just that the discussion is occurring only among only lawyers, it's also that the discussion is occurring only among a small subset of lawyers). In addition, Semple points out, even if the law societies in Canada are established by provincial legislation, the legislation provides the law societies with "ample" power and discretion, and the legislation is amended most typically in the ways specifically requested by the law societies, without any challenge by the government to the law societies' "hegemony." To the extent law societies are criticized, notably in the media, the criticism does not call for outside (such as government) intervention, but for the law societies themselves to lead change. In sum, if the law societies in Canada are considering regulatory change, they are doing so with little outside pressure. For this reason, Semple predicts, the regulators' steps will be "tentative compromises" rather than big bangs, and the resulting reform will be "evolutionary in nature rather than revolutionary."[10]

It is difficult to disagree with Semple's insight. And yet—one could be forgiven for wondering if there is a sign of change in the horizon, if not in all provinces then at least in Nova Scotia. The sign would be in the form of the "Policy Respecting Self-Regulated Professions" issued by the Executive Council of Nova Scotia and included in the materials for the November 25, 2016 meeting of the Council of the Nova Scotia Barristers' Society. As discussed above, this document, still in draft form, seeks to establish additional policies and procedures with respect to self-regulated professions in Nova Scotia, both for existing self-regulated professions and for those which seek to become self-regulated. If the bulk of the policies and procedures described in the draft are eventually implemented, it will mean (or, at least theoretically it should mean) that neither the Nova Scotia Department of Justice nor the legislature will continue to simply rubber stamp the NSBS's requests for amended legislation in the manner Semple describes. Instead, they will first seek to ascertain, among other things, whether the amendments are needed to address a substantial risk (and a risk that cannot be better addressed through other means), whether the anticipated benefit of the amendments outweigh any negative impact, and whether, in fact, a more comprehensive review of the regulatory framework is needed instead. If policies and procedures of this kind are, in fact, adopted in any one or more province, it could open the door to greater scrutiny of the law societies, and as a result place greater pressure on them to pursue revolutionary rather than merely evolutionary reform.

NOTES

1. See, for example, "Regulation Reform: A Cross-Canada Checkup," Nova Scotia Barristers' Society, accessed on March 20, 2017, http://nsbs.org/regulation-reform-cross-canada-checkup.

2. Compliance-Based Entity Regulation Task Force, "Call for Input Consultation Paper: 'Promoting Better Legal Practices,'" January 2016, 9–10, https://www.lsuc.on.ca/uploadedFiles/compliance-based-entity-regulation-consultation-paper.pdf.

3. Law Firm Regulation Task Force, "Law Firm Regulation Consultation Brief," 11.

4. Prairie Law Societies, "Innovating Regulation," 2.

5. Law Firm Regulation Task Force, "Law Firm Regulation Consultation Brief," 12.

6. See, for example, Prairie Law Societies, "Innovating Regulation," 2.

7. "National Mobility of the Legal Profession," Federation of Law Societies of Canada, accessed March 17, 2017, http://flsc.ca/national-initiatives/national-mobility-of-the-legal-profession/.

8. The importance of mobility has also been raised in the context of compliance-based entity regulation. See, for example, Law Society of Upper Canada, video "Promoting Better Legal Practices," February 8, 2016, 1:21:13, https://www.youtube.com/watch?v=Wz2lPSyfqbI. At least one regulator in Canada has reflected in this manner on the importance of a province making incremental regulatory changes: "So we don't get so far out in front that we are mistaken for the enemy." Ibid., 1:23:14. See also Karen Dyck, "Innovating Regulation on the Prairies," *Slaw*, January 20, 2016, http://www.slaw.ca/2016/01/20/innovating-regulation-on-the-prairies/.

9. Semple, "Legal Services Regulation in Canada," 3, 20. Semple cites Devlin and Morison's description of the discussion as a "monologue." Devlin and Morison, "Access to Justice," 539.

10. Semple, "Legal Services Regulation in Canada," 3, 5, 7, 20. See also Amy Salyzyn's general discussion of accountability and transparency of Canadian Law Societies. Salyzyn, "From Colleague to Cop to Coach," 32–36.

Chapter 18

Assessment

To what extent has Canada implemented the OECD's six essential elements of an effective regulatory policy? For each element, the response lies upon a spectrum, from "yes," "for the most part," "sort of," "limited," "not really" and "no:"

Table 18.1 Assessment for Canada

1	Independent regulation	Limited	The members of the governing bodies of the law societies are members of the profession who are elected by members of the profession. On the other hand, in most provinces the law societies are required to govern in the "public interest" rather than in the interest of the profession. Further, the law societies of certain provinces (most especially Nova Scotia) are led by professional regulators (full-time members of staff) who have asserted at least some independence from the profession
2	Accountability and transparency	Sort of	Most law societies have (or appear to have) accountability of some type to the province's Department of Justice However, the exact nature of the Department's role is unclear. Some law societies (most especially Nova Scotia) make available on their website significant amounts of information and documentation

(*Continued*)

Table 18.1 Assessment for Canada (Continued)

3	Regulatory oversight bodies	Limited	The Department of Justice in each province appears to exercise a limited form of regulatory oversight, notably with respect to requests for amended legislation. Other than that, no formal or informal system for regulatory oversight appears to be in place
4	Citizen engagement	Limited	The governing body of most law societies includes a minimum number of positions for appointed public representatives. (Oddly, in Nova Scotia, under requested legislative amendments, it will be possible to appoint lawyers rather than nonlawyers to these positions). Other than these positions, there is no evidence of significant citizen engagement with respect to the regulation of legal services
5	Regulatory impact assessments	Not really	There is no evidence that regulatory impact assessments with respect to legal services are made in a manner comparable to England and Wales or Australia. In Nova Scotia, this may change upon implementation of the Policy Framework (which calls for the NSBS to develop the capacity to measure the impact or regulatory changes) and the implementation of the Executive Council's Policy Respecting Self-Regulated Professions (which calls for certain assessments to be made prior to the submission of any request for amended legislation)
6	Risk-based approach	Limited	The NSBS's Policy Framework enshrines a risk-based approach. The Prairie provinces, British Columbia and Ontario are moving toward a risk-based approach

Part V

UNITED STATES: PRACTICE OF LAW AS "PERSONAL RIGHT"

The American Bar Association (ABA) is a voluntary, national association of lawyers and law students. It counts about 400,000 members out of the total of 1.2 million lawyers in the United States. It is governed by a body called the House of Delegates—most of its 560 members are selected or, in a few cases elected, by state and local bar associations.[1] The ABA does not make a listing of the members of the House of Delegates available to the public.[2]

The ABA is a private (non-governmental) organization that, officially, does not have any regulatory authority at all. However, in practice the ABA's regulatory power is immense, or, as two Canadian commentators describe it, "hegemonic."[3] It is the ABA that developed the Model Rules of Professional Conduct, a set of rules that, as the ABA explains on its website, has its origins in an 1836 list of "Fifty Resolutions" in book entitled "A Course of Legal Study."[4] The most current form of the rules, under its current name, was adopted by the ABA House of Delegates in 1983. While officially the Model Rules are only the recommendations of an unelected private organization, the reality is that forty-nine states as well as the District of Columbia and the US Virgin Islands have adopted the Model Rules, if not in their entirety then in very large part, including Model Rule 5.4. Model Rule 5.4 is important for our purposes: together with laws governing the unauthorized practice of law, it is the rule that operates to prohibit alternative structures. (California has not adopted the ABA Model Rules in the manner that the other states have. However, the California rules prohibit alternative structures in the same manner as Model Rule 5.4).[5]

From time to time, the ABA House of Delegates adopts amendments to the Rules. Those amendments are, in most cases, subsequently reviewed by each state's bar association(s), and then, perhaps with minor modifications, proposed to the state's Supreme Courts for adoption. While there is no legal provision that prevents a state Supreme Court from adopting rules that do not conform to the ABA's Model Rules as proposed by the state bar association, in reality this rarely occurs, and the greater the opposition of the ABA and/or the state bar association(s) to the amendment in question, the less likely it is to occur. This fact was recently underscored by Stephen Younger, an attorney who chaired a 2012 review of Model Rule 5.4 by the New York State Bar Association (a review that recommended the Rule not be changed): "Most chief judges who are responsible for the ethics rules in our states don't want to get too far ahead of the bar."[6]

The result of all this is that the Model Rules carry a de facto or "quasi-"[7] regulatory authority and they (combined with other legal texts, notably, as mentioned above, those relating to the unauthorized practice of law) have operated to limit the evolution of how legal services may be provided in the United States. They have served this purpose so well that a lawyer from the early 20th century would easily recognize both the service model and the law firm structure of the 21st century. In essence, legal services may be provided by lawyers only, acting as individuals only.

Even so, the United States has not always actively restricted the ability to provide legal services in this manner. The restrictions came into place progressively during the first half of the 20th century—a time period marked, in particular, by the growth of the modern business corporation, by the consolidation and growth of state bar associations and the ABA, and by the Great Depression. As will be seen below, the restrictions have been challenged on more than one occasion, but each time without success. The result is a regulatory framework that—in stark contrast to the regulatory frameworks of England and Wales and of Australia—severely limits not only who can provide legal services but also how they can do so. In this manner, in the United States, legal services are perceived through the narrow prism of the practice of law as a "personal right limited to a few good persons," rather than through a much larger context of the public's need to understand their obligations and to protect their rights.

NOTES

1. "House of Delegates—General Information," American Bar Association, accessed March 17, 2017, http://www.americanbar.org/groups/leadership/delegates.html.

2. Access to the webpage "Welcome to the House of Delegates Member Directory" is reserved for ABA members. Accessed on March 17, 2017, http://www.americanbar.org/directories/people_directories/hod_people_directory_members/people_directory_members.html.

3. Devlin and Morison, "Access to Justice," 526.

4. American Bar Association. "Model Rules of Professional Conduct: Preface," accessed on March 17, 2017, http://www.americanbar.org/groups/professional_responsibility/publications/model_rules_of_professional_conduct/model_rules_of_professional_conduct_preface.html.

5. Rules 1–310 and 1–320 of the California Rules of Professional Conduct: http://rules.calbar.ca.gov/Rules/RulesofProfessionalConduct/CurrentRules/Rule1310.aspx and http://rules.calbar.ca.gov/Rules/RulesofProfessionalConduct/CurrentRules/Rule1320.aspx.

6. Lance Duroni, "US Law Firms Still Flirting With Going Public," *Law 360*, July 15, 2015, http://www.law360.com/articles/671281/us-law-firms-still-flirting-with-going-public.

7. Laurel Terry describes the ABA as a "quasi-regulator." See Laurel S. Terry, "Globalization and the ABA Commission on Ethics 20/20: Reflections on Missed Opportunities and the Road Not Taken," *Hofstra Law Review* 43 (2014): 117, http://www.hofstralawreview.org/wp-content/uploads/2015/01/BB.3.Terry_.final2_.pdf.

Chapter 19

There Was a Time before Model Rule 5.4

In the United States, the first significant attempts to restrict the corporate practice of law (where lawyers employed by a company perform legal services for third parties) date back to the early 1900s—a time which coincides with the growth of the modern business corporation. One commentator observed that the modern business corporation posed a threat to lawyers both because the corporations developed legal needs that lawyers seemed to not yet be able to meet and because modern corporations had or could develop the capacity to compete effectively with lawyers in providing traditional kinds of legal services.[1]

During this period, in some respects the rules and courts were ambivalent, if not contradictory, in their approach to the corporate practice of law. For example, trust companies were held to be practicing law illegally when they offered will drafting services, and collection agencies were held to be unlawfully practicing law when they also offered collection services by lawsuits or free legal advice. On the other hand, lawyers employed by a trade association were allowed to represent members of the association in a lawsuit against a union, and, in some states, title companies were allowed to draft bills of sale and other instruments.[2]

THE CO-OPERATIVE LAW COMPANY

The situation of The Co-operative Law Company merits particular attention. A New York company formed in 1901, its stated object was "to furnish to its subscribers legal advice and service; to operate in connection with the above a department of law and collections for the use and benefit of the subscribers of the company only, and to accomplish these objects said company proposes to employ and maintain a staff of competent attorneys and counsellors at law to give such advice; and to prosecute or defend, through such counsel, any claim or suit entrusted to its care by subscribers." The areas of law in which the company acted for its subscribers were "general law business, including the prosecution and defense of suits; incorporation of business enterprises; drawing of contracts, leases and agreements, drawing and probating of wills, management of estates, etc."[3]

In 1909—eight years after the formation of The Co-operative Law Company—New York adopted a criminal statute that imposed a general ban on the practice of law by corporations, but allowed for certain exceptions, notably for title insurers, for companies to employ their own in-house counsel, and for "organizations organized for benevolent or charitable purposes, or for the purpose of assisting persons without means in the pursuit of any civil remedy," on the condition that such an organization obtained the approval of the competent court.[4]

Upon the adoption of this statute, The Co-operative Law Company applied to the competent court seeking approval for its continued existence and operation. In June, 1909, the court granted approval. However, in November 1909, an application to vacate the order and deny approval was filed before the same court by a Charles J. McDermott, Esq., "a member of the Kings county bar and the chairman of the committee on grievances of the Brooklyn Bar Association." After a hearing, the court vacated its prior order and denied the application for approval. The court's sole motivation for reversing its approval was that the company "is not a corporation whose existence, organization and incorporation this court has the power to approve under [the 1909 criminal statute]."[5] The Co-operative Law Company appealed that decision to the appellate court. In 1910, the appellate court upheld the lower court's decision to deny approval.

By the 1920s, courts in many states were in agreement that the corporate practice of law should not be permitted. The reasoning of the New York appellate court in relation to The Co-operative Law Company probably best summarizes the approach not only of that New York appellate court but also of a number of courts across the country and it merits quotation at length:[6]

> [T]he vital question is whether, prior to the [adoption of the 1909 criminal statute], a corporation could be lawfully organized to practice law. . . . The practice of law is not a business open to all, but a personal right, limited to a few persons of good moral character, with special qualifications ascertained and certified after a long course of study, both general and professional, and a thorough examination by a state board appointed for the purpose. The right to practice law is in the nature of a franchise from the state conferred only for merit. It cannot be assigned or inherited but must be earned by hard study and good conduct. It is attested by a certificate of the Supreme Court, and is protected by registration.

No one can practice law unless he has taken an oath of office and become an officer of the court, subject to its discipline, liable to punishment for contempt in violating his duties as such, and to suspension or removal. It is not a lawful business except for members of the bar who have complied with all the conditions required by statute and the rules of the courts. As these conditions cannot be performed by a corporation, it follows that the practice of law is not a lawful business for a corporation to engage in. As it cannot practice law directly, it cannot indirectly by employing competent lawyers to practice for it, as that would be an evasion which the law will not tolerate.

The relation of attorney and client is that of master and servant in a limited and dignified sense, and it involves the highest trust and confidence. It cannot be delegated without consent, and it cannot exist between an attorney employed by a corporation to practice law for it, and a client of the corporation, for he would be subject to the directions of the corporation, and not to the directions of the client. There would be neither contract nor privity between him and the client, and he would not owe even the duty of counsel to the actual litigant. The corporation would control the litigation, the money earned would belong to the corporation, and the attorney would be responsible to the corporation only. His master would not be the client but the corporation, conducted it may be wholly by laymen, organized simply to make money and not to aid in the administration of justice which is the highest function of an attorney and counselor at law. The corporation might not have a lawyer among its stockholders, directors, or officers. Its members might be without character, learning or standing. There would be no remedy by attachment or disbarment to protect the public from imposition or fraud, no stimulus to good conduct from the traditions of an ancient and honorable profession, and no guide except the sordid purpose to earn money for stockholders. The bar, which is an institution of the highest usefulness and standing, would be degraded if even its humblest member became subject to the orders of a moneymaking corporation engaged not in conducting litigation for itself, but in the business of conducting litigation for others. The degradation of the bar is an injury to the state.

A corporation can neither practice law nor hire lawyers to carry on the business of practicing law for it any more than it can practice medicine or dentistry by hiring doctors or dentists to act for it. . . . The legislature in authorizing the formation of corporations to carry on "any lawful business" did not intend to include the work of the learned professions. Such an innovation with the evil results that might follow would require the use of specific language clearly indicating the intention.[7]

The decision of the appellate court is interesting for what it says. But it is equally if not more interesting for what it does not say: The decision acknowledges and approves the 1909 statute's exception that allows for title guarantee companies, stating that "the searching of titles is open to all."[8] Nevertheless, the decision essentially declares that all forms of corporate practice of law are repugnant. In doing so, it pointedly ignores an additional exception found in the 1909 statute—the one that expressly allowed for the corporate practice of law in order to assist persons who otherwise would not have the means to pursue civil remedies. The court never considers whether The Co-operative Law Company may or may not have qualified under that exception and never states that the lower court should have made that consideration. Instead, the appellate court states that the company had not been lawfully formed and had never been in lawful existence—not for reasons connected to the 1909 criminal statute but because the state's general laws allowing for the formation of companies could not have included companies whose purpose was to provide legal services. Those general laws, the court states, related only to businesses "lawful to all who wish to engage in it." But the practice of law, the court explains, is not such a business—the practice of law is "a personal right, limited to a few good persons," it is "a franchise from the state conferred only for merit," and it is "not a lawful business for a corporation to engage in."[9]

Further, the decision lists at length the many dangers that the corporate practice of law may present. However, it lists these dangers in a purely theoretical manner—nothing in the decision evidences or even suggests that at any point during its eight years of operation that The Co-operative Law Company actually manifested any of those theoretical dangers. Indeed, nothing in the public record suggests that at any point during its eight years of operation any issue was raised with the manner by which The Co-operative Law Company was operated, nor does anything in the public record describe any specific ethical or other problem that the company's operation posed, or even that the company failed to adequately serve its members. Indeed, if any of those problems had been present, they presumably would have given pause to the lower court, and it would not have granted its approval the first time it was requested, or, at a minimum, the lower court would have mentioned the problems when it withdrew its approval, rather than issuing an essentially unmotivated decision.

This decision of the New York appellate court typifies the approach taken by courts at that time, and it is the approach that ultimately was codified in the ABA Canons in the late 1920s. (The Canons, in turn, were transposed first into the 1961 ABA Formal Opinion, then into the 1969 Model Code, and from there, in 1983, into the ABA Model Rules and notably Model Rule 5.4.).

Interestingly, in spite of a number of court decisions like *In re Co-operative Law Co*, the organized bar in the United States did not take a widespread interest in the unauthorized practice of law, and notably by corporations, until the 1930s. In his 1950 book *The Growth of American Law: The Law Makers*, James Willard Hurst, a professor at the University of Wisconsin Law School, explained that the ABA "gave no vigorous attention to the problem until it appointed a committee in 1930." By 1940, he continued, over 400 bar association committees had been appointed to consider the unauthorized practice of law.[10] Professor Hurst explained this intensified interest in the topic as follows:

> The depression of the 1930's stimulated the first really widespread and organized concern of the bar with its lay competition. This coincidence of events ill fitted claims that this activity was moved simply by regard for protecting the public against the incompetent or unscrupulous. The speedy development of the drive against "unauthorized practice," set against the circumstances of the time, suggested that the movement was born more of an emotional desire to do something in the face of social catastrophe, than out of any deeply reasoned analysis. Evidence of this was found in the almost complete lack of any scientific fact gathering out of all the sudden bustling of committees and associations.[11]

THE PROVISION OF LEGAL SERVICES BY SOCIAL SERVICE ORGANIZATIONS

Prior to the Great Depression, corporations were not the only organizations that sought to provide legal services. In her 2015 book *Women and Justice for the Poor: A History of Legal Aid, 1863–1945*, Felice Batlan unveils an otherwise unknown but exceptionally rich history of how free legal assistance was provided to poor and disadvantaged persons, and, in particular, to poor and disadvantaged women in the United States, over a period of decades. This assistance was not provided by traditional law firms, by the organized bar, or by legal aid organizations in the manner we know legal aid today. Instead, it was provided by a number of women's social services organizations, the most active of which included the Protective Agency for Women and Children in Chicago[12] and the Women's Educational and Industrial Union in Boston.[13]

As Batlan explains, while some of these organizations saw themselves primarily as providing legal aid, many of them performed a wide range of reform work as well as providing services to poor women. In that manner, legal assistance was integrated on a continuum with other types of assistance, such as to help to find employment, housing or clothing, to address domestic or family issues, and to enrich the cultural and spiritual lives of their communities.[14] (In today's parlance, we might describe it as "multidisciplinary").

The organizations that offered these services were not owned, controlled or managed by lawyers. They were charitable or not-for-profit organizations that were founded and run by, for the most part, middle- or upper-class women. Further, the women who provided legal assistance were, for the most part, not professional lawyers in that they did not have a formal legal education and were not admitted to the bar. This does not mean, however, that they did not have legal knowledge or experience. To the contrary, as Batlan explains, many of these "lay lawyers" acquired extensive knowledge and experience, and were accepted and even respected by professional lawyers and judges. Going further, Batlan states "there is no evidence that, historically, the work of nonlawyers was inferior to that of lawyers."[15]

Batlan has estimated that in a given year, one of these organizations would have handled anywhere from a couple of hundred to a couple of thousand cases or more.[16] That being said, as Batlan has explained, because precise records were not always kept, it is not possible to know exactly how many of these organizations existed.[17]

By the 1930s, these organizations ceased to exist. While several factors contributed to their demise, Batlan explains that the principal factor was the professionalization of legal aid, on the one hand, and of social work, on the other. With respect to legal aid, professional lawyers, in nearly all cases men, created legal aid societies which worked to progressively take over the legal work done by the women's social services organizations. These men believed both that only professional lawyers could provide the relevant services and that only men should be professional lawyers. At the same time, social work was undergoing a professionalization process of its own, creating a profession in which one would attend school, and learn the new discipline of social work. As a result of these dual processes, women "lay lawyers" working in social services organizations lost their place. They became sandwiched between professional lawyers, who were nearly exclusively men, and professional social workers, who were nearly exclusively women.[18]

In addition to losing their place, these women were written out of the history of legal aid. Batlan explains how this happened: Our principal source of knowledge about the history of legal aid comes principally from the 1919 book *Justice and the Poor*, by Reginald Heber Smith.[19] At the time Smith was doing research for his book, he visited fourteen cities and met with many people, including a limited number of women lay lawyers. To his shock, Batlan explains, he discovered that these women knew what they were doing: they knew the law, they followed cases through and their work was effective. The problem was that their model was radically different from the model that matched his vision for legal aid. For him, legal aid needed to look like any other law firm, which meant that legal services could be provided only by professional, male lawyers. He and his colleagues saw no role for women to play, believing that their mere presence would diminish the prestige of legal aid. For these reasons, in writing his book, Smith deliberately deleted references to them.[20]

Indeed, in his 1950 book, Hurst mentioned Smith's work[21] but made no allusion to any of the women's social services organizations profiled in Batlan's book. Instead, on the topic of unmet need for legal services, Hurst wrote that the record of the bar was "one of long inertia." Not only did the organized bar not originate the legal aid movement, Hurst explained that it was also slow to give it even limited support: "The bar became concerned with lay competition, largely under the spur of lawyers' economic distress; it then busied itself with attempts to suppress its lay competitors, and did little self-searching, to find out wherein lawyers were so inadequately serving people that they should turn to other advisers."[22]

In sum, before the organized bar took action in the Great Depression to have them prohibited, alternative structures were part of the legal landscape in many parts of the United States.

NOTES

1. Barlow F. Christensen, "The Unauthorized Practice of Law: Do Good Fences Really Make Good Neighbors—or Even Good Sense?" *American Bar Foundation Research Journal* 5 (Spring, 1980): 178.

2. Ibid., 182–183.

3. In re Co-operative Law Co., 198 NY 479 (1910) 481, https://casetext.com/case/matter-of-co-operative-law-co.

4. Ibid., 482.

5. Ibid., 482–483.

6. Christensen, 185–186.

7. In re Co-operative Law Co, 483–484.

8. Ibid., 485.

9. Ibid., 483.

10. James Willard Hurst, *The Growth of American Law: The Law Makers* (Boston: Little, Brown and Company, 1950), 323.

11. Ibid.

12. Felice Batlan, *Women and Justice for the Poor: A History of Legal Aid, 1863–1945* (New York: Cambridge University Press, 2015), 49–81.

13. Ibid., 36–46.

14. Ibid., 47–84.

15. Ibid., 4–5, 14.

16. Felice Batlan, interview with author, November, 2015, available at http://notjustforlawyers.com/felice-batlan/.

17. Ibid. Her research focused on organizations founded by white, Christian women in the Midwest and Northeast of the United States. She exhorts others to pick up the mantle of her research, in order to gain a better understanding of comparable organizations in other parts of the country as well as of comparable organizations founded by others, and notably by African-Americans and by immigrants. Batlan, *Women and Justice for the Poor*, 11.

18. Batlan, *Women and Justice for the Poor*, 123–153.

19. Reginald Heber Smith, *Justice and the Poor* (New York: Carnegie Foundation, 1919).

20. Batlan, *Women and Justice for the Poor*, 140–148.

21. Hurst, *The Growth of American Law*, 153.

22. Ibid., 328.

Chapter 20

Indestructible Model Rule 5.4

After the Great Depression and World War II, the first significant challenge to the restrictions on who may own and control organizations that provide legal services came in 1982, by the Commission on Evaluation of Professional Standards (the "Kutak Commission," which revamped the Model Code to develop the Model Rules). In that year, the Kutak Commission proposed a draft of Model Rule 5.4 permitting nonlawyer ownership of law firms as well as multidisciplinary practices, provided that certain safeguards were in place, and notably that "there is no interference with the lawyer's independence of professional judgment or with the client-lawyer relationship."[1]

When this proposal was debated in the House of Delegates, the question was asked: "Does this mean Sears can open a law firm?" "Yes," responded Geoffrey Hazard, the reporter for the Commission. With that response, the proposal was swiftly and decisively voted down, in favor of the more restrictive Model Rule 5.4 that remains in place today.[2] (Actually, that remains in place today in all jurisdictions in the United States except one: the District of Columbia. After the Kutak Commission the D.C. bar took its own path, ultimately adopting a revised version of the draft proposed by the Kutak Commission—the Rule adopted in D.C. is more restrictive than the Kutak proposal, but still permits a form of nonlawyer ownership, in contrast to the rest of the United States. The rule in place in D.C. is further discussed below).

The next challenge occurred in the late 1990s. In reaction to the extent to which consulting firms had become associated with large accounting firms, an ABA Commission on Multidisciplinary Practices was appointed to study this association and to recommend any modifications to the ethical rules "that would serve the public interest."[3]

In 1999, this Commission recommended to the House of Delegates that the Model Rules be amended to permit multidisciplinary practices , but again with safeguards in place, such as written undertakings to assure the independence of judgment of the lawyers.[4] The House of Delegates responded to this recommendation by adopting a resolution that no change will be made "unless and until additional study demonstrates that such changes will further the public interest without sacrificing or compromising lawyer independence and the legal profession's tradition of loyalty to clients."[5]

The Commission undertook additional study, after which, in 2000, it changed its recommendation to the House of Delegates: while still advocating for multidisciplinary practices, it suggested tighter restrictions, notably that such practices should be lawyer-controlled.[6]

In response, the House of Delegates adopted a resolution categorically refusing to amend the Model Rules to permit multidisciplinary practices in any form. The resolution stated, in part:

> The sharing of legal fees with nonlawyers and the ownership and control of the practice of law by nonlawyers are inconsistent with the core values of the legal profession.
>
> The law governing lawyers, that prohibits lawyers from sharing legal fees with nonlawyers and from directly or indirectly transferring to nonlawyers ownership or control over entities practicing law, should not be revised.[7]

The next challenge to Model Rule 5.4 began nine years later, in 2009.

COMMISSION ON ETHICS 20/20: THE CASE HAD NOT BEEN MADE

Cognizant of the reforms in England and Wales and Australia, in 2009 the President of the ABA created a new commission—the Commission on Ethics 20/20. This Commission was tasked to perform a review not only of alternative business structures and multidisciplinary practices, but of all the Model Rules "in the context of advances in technology and global legal practice developments."[8]

The 17-member Commission was composed of practicing lawyers, judges and law school professors.[9] One of the first orders of business for the Commission in February 2010 was to appoint working groups, one of which was referred to as "Law Firm Regulation/Alternative Business Structures."[10] This 7-member group was co-chaired by University of Arizona Professor Ted Schneyer and Sidley & Austin partner George Jones.[11]

According to the minutes of the Commission's meeting held on April 29, 2010, Schneyer announced that the Working Group would "focus first on issues relating to law firm/entity regulation." At the same time, the Working

Group would "also move forward contemporaneously with its study and analysis of developments relating to alternative business structures." According to the minutes, Schneyer described "developments" in the UK and Australia, and notably how those countries had moved from "law firm discipline" to proactive, compliance-based regulation. Schneyer apparently further explained that Australia stresses "systemic controls designed to foster development of an ethical culture" in law firms, accompanied by a self-assessment, audit and compliance mechanism that is technology driven. In contrast, the minutes point out, the United States "remains complaint based."[12]

It seems, however, that over the course of the following months Schneyer was not convincing because the minutes of the Commission's February 10, 2011 meeting state that the Commission decided that there was "insufficient evidence to proceed further" with consideration of a proposal for "New South Wales' style proactive practice management regulation." If either the Working Group or the Commission offered or discussed reasons for eliminating this option from further consideration, they are not reflected in the meeting minutes. As an alternative to pursuing this option, the Commission recommended that the Working Group and the ABA Standing Committee on Professional Discipline undertake further study "to help lawyers and law firms think more systematically about how to better serve clients."[13] (The Commission's documentation after this meeting accordingly reflects that the name of the Working Group was changed to "Alternative Business Structures.")

The minutes of the same February 10, 2011, meeting also state that the Working Group recommended that the Commission not submit to the House of Delegates a proposal that would allow "passive equity investment in law firms or the public trading in shares of law firms." The Commission agreed with this recommendation. If either the Working Group or the Commission offered or discussed reasons for eliminating these possibilities from further consideration, they are not reflected in the meeting minutes except for the statement that "these subjects are better suited for a White Paper commending these issues to individual jurisdictions for further study."[14]

On April 5, 2011, the Commission issued a paper "For Comment: Issues Paper Concerning Alternative Business Structures." The 20-page paper first warns that the ABA has undertaken several previous efforts to examine alternative structures, and that "the Working Group's efforts are necessarily informed by them." That being said, the paper continues, even if since 2000 few jurisdictions in the United States have considered alternative structures, other countries have implemented a wide range of approaches. The paper continues, "The economic challenges of the intervening period also invite reconsideration of whether ABS might serve to enhance access to legal services for those unable to afford them, and to provide new and varied opportunities for lawyers and firms domestically to better serve their clients."[15]

The paper then describes with certain detail the development of ILPs in Australia and ABSs in England and Wales and of multidisciplinary practices in Australia and Canada,[16] before touching briefly on related but significantly more limited developments in Scotland, Germany, Netherlands, Belgium and New Zealand.[17] The paper explains that in the opinion of the Working Group, the level of detail provided "will facilitate informed decision and comments about these issues."[18] In spite of the detail, however, glaringly absent from the discussion paper is any direct reference to, let alone express discussion of, the concepts of either entity regulation (or law firm regulation) or proactive regulation (what Ted Schneyer would, in his law review article published two years later, call "proactive-management based regulation"[19]). To the extent the discussion paper addresses either concept, it does so only indirectly, in mentioning Australia's ILPs and self-assessment process.

Prefaced with the explanation that the Commission had already excluded from consideration passive equity investment in law firms and public trading of shares of law firms,[20] the paper describes the three options the Working Group was evaluating, as follows:

In essence, the options were either (1) limited lawyer/nonlawyer partnerships with a cap on nonlawyer ownership and the nonlawyers would be subject to a "fit to own" test, (2) lawyer/nonlawyer partnerships with no cap on nonlawyer ownership but the firm could provide legal services only (no multidisciplinary services) and the nonlawyer partner(s) would be required to perform services for the firm (they could not be passive investors; as discussed further below, this option was considered to be the "D.C. approach"), or (3) the same as Option (2) except the firm could offer multidisciplinary services.[21]

The paper concludes by asking for input, with a deadline of June 1, 2011.[22]

The Commission held a meeting on 15–16 April, 2011—just days after the April 5, 2011 Discussion Paper was issued. At that meeting, Paul Paton, one of the Commission's Reporters, stated that while no decision had yet been made, already "it appears that, based on the information collected thus far, the choice will be between Options 2 and 3."[23] It is remarkable that such an observation would be made so quickly after the Issues Paper had been issued and so well in advance of the due date for the submission of comments.

The Commission received just six written submissions in response to its April 5, 2011 call for comments.[24] In brief, three submissions expressed opposition to alternative structures (those of the New York State Bar Association Standing Committee on Standards of Attorney Conduct, the US Chamber Institute for Legal Reform and the German Federal Bar), two took no position on the subject (those of the ABA Standing Committee on Client Protection and the Legal Services Board of England and Wales) and one submission, that of Responsive Law, expressed strong support.

The minutes of the Commission's June 13, 2011 meeting report on an "outreach" to other ABA groups, notably the General Practice, Solo and Small Firm Division and the Young Lawyers Division. The minutes describe the outcome of this process in an oddly contradictory manner. On the one hand, the minutes state that "there is no surprise that a number of lawyers are opposed to any changes to Model Rule 5.4." On the other hand, these groups "showed an interest in having more tools to allow lawyers to innovate in how they ethically provide legal services to clients in the 21st Century. This is also a willingness to learn more about alternative business structures (ABS) and how they can help lawyers and clients."[25] The minutes do not make an attempt to address this contradiction—however, assuming the willingness to learn more about ABS was genuine, any decision made at that point to oppose them would be premature.

It is notable that other than releasing the Issues Paper, there is no evidence that the Commission or the Working Group took any steps to seek or obtain input from outside the legal profession (indeed, even from outside the ABA and state bar associations). It is particularly notable that there is no evidence that the Commission or the Working Group sought input from persons who have experience and expertise in areas such as economic policy, human rights, competition or consumer affairs.

The next public document issued by the Commission on the topic of "Alternative Law Practice Structures" is dated December 2, 2011. In this document, the Commission states that it has "conducted research to understand the questions presented by changing technologies and the increasingly borderless practice of law," and that it has "engaged in extensive outreach and received helpful input."[26]

In this document, the forms of nonlawyer ownership that the Commission had ruled out grew in number from two to four: to the previously excluded passive nonlawyer investment in law firms and the public trading of shares of law firms, the Commission added multidisciplinary practices and the D.C. approach of ABS.[27]

(As discussed below, D.C. permits nonlawyers to have an ownership interest in a law firm, on the condition that the firm provides legal services only—it is not an multidisciplinary practice— and that the nonlawyer provides services that assist the firm in providing legal services (no passive ownership). The D.C. approach does not place a cap on nonlawyer ownership (although, as seen below, regulators in D.C. esteem that a cap applies nonetheless), nor does it impose a "fit to own" test on nonlawyers).

The Commission did not offer any explanation as to why it had decided to rule out the option of multidisciplinary practices since it had proposed it in its April 5, 2011 Issues Paper, beyond a mention that "the ABA had considered whether to permit MDPs in 1999–2000 and had strongly rejected the idea."[28]

The Commission ruled out the D.C. approach in favor of a "narrower," more restrictive approach, which was to require not only that the firm be engaged in legal practice only (not in combination with non-legal services) and that the nonlawyer provide services to assist the firm in providing legal services (again, no passive investment), but also imposing (i) a cap on nonlawyer ownership and (ii) a fit to own test on the nonlawyers.[29]

The Commission's explanation for rejecting the D.C. approach in favor of a more restrictive approach was that the more restrictive approach is the "most modest" and it "would provide comparable opportunities for innovation and increased access to justice while offering stronger protections consonant with the core professional values of the broader US legal community."[30]

In sum, in its December 2, 2011 paper, the Commission proposed this singular model for comment:

> Rule 5.4 Professional Independence of a Lawyer
> (a) A lawyer or law firm shall not share legal fees with a nonlawyer, except that:
> [. . .]
> (4) a lawyer or law firm may do so pursuant to paragraph (b)
> [. . .]
> (b) A lawyer may practice law in a law firm in which individual nonlawyers in that firm hold a financial interest, but only if:
>
> (1) the firm's sole purpose is providing legal services to clients;
> (2) the nonlawyers provide services that assist the lawyer or law firm in providing legal services to clients;
> (3) the nonlawyers state in writing that they have read and understand the Rules of Professional Conduct and agree in writing to undertake to conform their conduct to the Rules;
> (4) the lawyer partners in the law firm are responsible for these nonlawyers to the same extent as if the nonlawyers were lawyers under Rule 5.1;
> (5) the nonlawyers have no power to direct or control the professional judgment of a lawyer, and the financial and voting interests in the firm of any nonlawyer are less than the financial and voting interest of the individual lawyer or lawyers holding the greatest financial and voting interests in the firm, the aggregate financial and voting interests of the nonlawyers does not exceed [25%] of the firm total, and the aggregate of the financial and voting interests of all lawyers in the firm is equal to or greater than the percentage of voting interests required to take any action or for any approval;
> (6) the lawyer partners in the firm make reasonable efforts to establish that each nonlawyer with a financial interest in the firm is of good character, supported by evidence of the nonlawyer's integrity and professionalism in the practice of his or her profession, trade or occupation, and maintain records of such inquiry and its results; and
> (7) compliance with the foregoing conditions is set forth in writing.

> (c) A lawyer shall not permit a person who recommends, employs, or pays the lawyer to render legal services for another to direct or regulate the lawyer's professional judgment in rendering such legal services. [31]

In proposing this model, the Commission asked for comments, and received twenty-four written submissions in response.[32] Of these, fifteen expressed opposition to the Commission's proposal,[33] one commentator was partially opposed and partially in favor,[34] one submission expressed "no objection,"[35] and four submissions expressed favor or strong favor[36] (of those, two said the proposal did not go far enough[37]). Of the remaining three, two sought clarification on the status of lawyers who practice in association with firms based in jurisdictions that permit alternative structures,[38] and the position expressed in the final submission is unclear.[39]

As was the case with the prior (April 5, 2011) Issues Paper, there is no evidence that the Commission or the Working Group took any steps to seek or obtain input from outside the legal profession (indeed, even from outside the ABA and state bar associations). It is, again, particularly notable that there is no evidence that the Commission or the Working Group sought input from persons who have experience and expertise in areas such as economic policy, human rights, competition or consumer affairs.

On April 16, 2012, the Commission issued a one-page paper stating that:

> At its meeting on April 12–13, 2012,[40] the [Commission] decided not to propose changes to the ABA policy prohibiting nonlawyer ownership of law firms. . . . The Commission considered the pros and cons, including thoughtful comments that the changes recommended in the [December 2, 2011 paper] were both too modest and too expansive, and concluded that the case had not been made for proceeding with even a form of nonlawyer ownership that is more limited than the D.C. model.[41]

The Commission would, it explained, continue to consider how to provide practical guidance in relation to choice of law problems that arise because D.C. and a growing number of jurisdictions outside the US permit nonlawyer ownership of law firms.[42] (Later, on August 19, 2013, the ABA Standing Committee on Ethics and Professional Responsibility issued Formal Opinion 464, which clarifies that a lawyer subject to Model Rule 5.4 may share fees with a law firm practicing in a jurisdiction that permits nonlawyer ownership, even if those fees might be distributed to a nonlawyer, provided that there is no interference with the lawyer's independent professional judgment.)[43]

Andrew Perlman acted as the Chief Reporter of the Commission, and in that role he had a front-row seat to the Commission's activities. In his 2015 article "Towards the Law of Legal Services," Perlman writes: "History offers a useful guide as to why the ABA House of Delegates was highly likely to reject any changes proposed by the Commission in this area. Since the Model Rules were adopted more than thirty years ago, the House of Delegates has repeatedly indicated its strong opposition to the idea of ABSs."[44]

Perlman explains that for the ABA House of Delegates, and for the Ethics 20/20 Commission in particular, the entire proposal of alternative structures was a "nonstarter" and that any proposal to allow them "would likely have failed." He offered several reasons for this, including the "lack of empirical support for the idea that ABSs would benefit the public." However, and much more persuasive than that, he explains, was the "significant political effort" on the part of state bar associations to oppose them, and, especially because "some members of the House of Delegates were opposed to change as a matter of principle," even if there had been evidence that change "would benefit the public without attendant harm."[45] These words on the part of Perlman—again, someone who had a front-row seat to the activities of the Commission—are highly remarkable. They stop just short of describing the Commission's activities as a sham, if not in whole than at least with respect to its consideration of alternative structures. Perlman makes it clear that a decision to not change Model Rule 5.4 had been made in advance, giving the impression that the activities of the ABS Working Group were little more than a show performed to divert criticism of the ABA's inaction on the topic.

COMMISSION ON THE FUTURE OF LEGAL SERVICES: SOMEONE SHOULD COLLECT DATA

In August 2014, the new ABA president, William C. Hubbard, appointed a new Commission—the Commission on the Future of Legal Services. Declaring that this Commission will be a priority for the ABA, Hubbard further stated:

> The commission will evaluate how we can help bridge the justice gap in this country, make better use of technology, and develop new, innovative platforms for access to justice and new opportunities to meet client needs.
>
> For too long, we've tried to do things the same way in the legal system. We are tradition bound, and sometimes rightly so. But we're at a point where our clients and the public are looking to the legal profession to be more accessible, more efficient, and more user-friendly.
>
> Other industries have transformed themselves. For example, no one banks the way we once banked. We don't shop the way we used to shop. So we also need to look at different ways we can deliver legal services. If we can take advantage of technology and innovative approaches to the delivery of legal services, we

could potentially significantly close the justice gap in our country and better meet the needs of our clients.

About 80 percent of the poor in our country do not have adequate access to legal services. Increasingly, people of moderate means are not using lawyers. They're going it alone. We see that particularly among small business owners. We need to be more accessible to the poor and to those of moderate means. We need to evolve as a profession by taking advantage of developing technologies and innovation to close the justice gap. The result will be a justice system that is more efficient and more accessible for everyone.

It's important to understand that in 2012, $66 million was invested in legal technology startups. A year later that number jumped to $458 million. These investments were not made in law firms, but in technology companies.[46]

Like the Commission on Ethics 20/20, the 28-member Commission was composed of practicing lawyers, judges and law school professors[47] (with one exception, Stephen Cone, who was the Chief Revenue Officer of the ABA).

On November 3, 2014, the Commission released an "Issues Paper on the Future of Legal Services" in which it explained that it is conducting a "comprehensive examination of the issues relating to the delivery of, and the public's access to," legal services in the United States. By way of background, the Commission echoed Hubbard's prior statements: many persons who need legal services do not obtain them, because either they cannot afford them or they opt for less expensive alternatives. At the same time, "technology, globalization, economic and other forces" transform how legal services are accessed and delivered, with new, untraditional, providers emerging online and offline to offer services in very different ways.[48]

In this context, the Commission created six working groups to study these developments and draft recommendations for the Commission's consideration. The six working groups included: (i) Data on Legal Services Delivery, (ii) Dispute Resolution, (iii) Preventive Law, Transactions and Other Law-Related Counseling; (iv) Access Solutions of the Underserved, (v) Regulatory Opportunities and (vi) Blue Sky. More specifically, the Issues Paper describes that the group "Regulatory Opportunities" is charged with studying existing regulatory innovations, such as ABSs and the CBA's Legal Futures Initiative Report, and then recommending "regulatory innovations that improve the delivery of, and the public's access to, competent and affordable legal services."[49]

The Issues Paper then listed just over two pages of questions—about thirty-five in total—upon which the Commission sought comment.[50] The questions ranged from how, generally, clients and potential clients can be better served, to whether access to legal services can be improved by authorizing persons without a full law school education and law license to provide them, to what insights can be gained from innovations in other professions and industries. The questions included, notably:

- Can access to legal services be improved if the pool of available providers is expanded to include people without a J.D. and full law license?
- To what extent should those who are not licensed to practice law be permitted to have an ownership in law firms?
- What other kinds of regulatory innovations in the US or other countries could help to improve the delivery of legal services (e.g., entity regulation and proactive risk-based management/compliance programs, such as those in Australia that have helped foster ethical infrastructures and reduced complains against regulated firms?).[51]

The Commission received over sixty written submissions in response to the Issues Paper.[52] Those submissions addressed, in whole or in part, the gamut of the thirty-five questions posed in the Issues Paper. Just eleven of the submissions made an express reference to alternative structures (of those, a few also made reference to entity regulation). Of those eleven, two expressed opposition to them,[53] three were (more or less) neutral[54] and six were in favor.[55]

Nothing in the November 2014 Issues paper mentioned regulatory objectives, let alone proposed them as a topic for consideration. Accordingly, none of the written submissions in response addressed the topic in any meaningful way. Nevertheless, the next step the Commission took was to prepare and circulate for comments a draft Report to the House of Delegates with respect to proposed Model Regulatory Objectives.[56]

While the public record is unclear in this respect, it appears that the Commission circulated one or more drafts of the Report at first among selected groups within the ABA, and then later, in late September, 2015, among "all ABA entities, state and local bar associations, and affiliated entities."[57] There is no public record of the Commission having reached out to a wider range of organizations or individuals. Notably, there is no record that the Commission posted a draft Report on its website for public consultation.[58]

The content and wording of the Report underwent modification during its restricted consultation process, but in essence the Report contained a proposed resolution for adoption by the House of Delegates containing ten model regulatory objectives, together with an explanation of the development of the proposed model regulatory objectives, the purpose of the objectives and the reasons why, in the Commission's opinion, the House of Delegates should adopt the proposed resolution.

The ten model objectives include, among others, "protection of the public," "advancement of the administration of justice and the rule of law," "meaningful access to justice and information about the law," "independence of professional judgment" and "diversity and inclusion among legal services providers and freedom from discrimination for those receiving legal services and in the justice system."[59]

The proposal, as it appears in the Report, included an additional resolution urging that "each state's highest court, and those of each territory and tribe, be guided by the ABA Model Regulatory Objectives for the Provision of Legal Services when they assess the court's existing regulatory framework and any other regulations they may choose to develop concerning non-traditional legal service providers."[60]

The Report asserts that "U.S. jurisdictions" are considering the adoption of regulatory objectives to serve as a framework for the development of standards in response to a changing legal profession and legal services landscape," and the Report recalls that "numerous countries" already have adopted their own regulatory objectives. In this context, the Report explains that, for the Commission, the development of regulatory objectives is a "useful initial step" to guide supreme courts and bar authorities in assessing their regulatory framework and in considering any new regulations they may choose to develop concerning non-traditional legal service providers. "Given that supreme courts in the U.S. are beginning to consider the adoption of regulatory objectives and given that providers of legal assistance other than lawyers are already actively serving the American public, it is especially timely and important for the ABA to offer guidance in this area."[61]

Citing an article by Laurel Terry, Steve Mark and Tahlia Gordon, "Adopting Regulatory Objectives for the Legal Profession," the Report lists five benefits of the adoption of regulatory objectives, including that they serve as a guide to assist those regulating the legal profession and those being regulated, and they assist in ensuring that the function and purpose of the particular regulation is transparent.[62]

One additional benefit, the Report states, is that model regulatory objectives will be useful to guide the regulation of "an increasingly wide array of already existing and possible future legal services providers."[63] The Report, again echoing Hubbard, continues:

> The legal landscape is changing at an unprecedented rate. In 2012, investors put $66 million dollars into legal service technology companies. By 2013, that figure was $458 million. One source indicates that there are well over a thousand legal tech startup companies currently in existence. Given that these services are already being offered to the public, the Model Regulatory Objectives for the Provision of Legal Services will serve as a useful tool for state supreme courts as they consider how to respond to these changes.[64]

This language is remarkable, if not extraordinary. In perhaps the most open and direct manner than any ABA body has ever done before, it acknowledges the existence of, if not implicitly approves of (albeit after the fact), legal service providers that are not lawyers. In light of the fact that these structures are, today, unregulated, this language suggests, if not directs, state supreme courts to consider whether and, if so, how, to regulate such providers. Indeed, a primary purpose of the model regulatory objectives is to establish guidelines for their regulation.

But after making these remarkable statements, the Report then pulls back (or, perhaps, tries to reassure):

> From the outset, the Commission has been transparent about the broad array of issues it is studying and evaluating, including those legal services developments that are viewed by some as controversial, threatening, or undesirable (e.g., alternative business structures). The adoption of this Resolution, however, does not predetermine or even imply a position on those issues by the ABA. If and when any other issues come to the floor of the House of Delegates, the Association can and should have a full and informed debate about them.[65]

The Commission posted on its website sixteen of the written comments it received in relation to the Report and the proposed resolutions. Of those sixteen submissions, eight were from "ABA entities" (other commissions, committees, sections and divisions), three were from state or local bar associations and four were from individuals—of which one was a practicing lawyer, one a law student and one a law school professor.[66] Most of those submissions (about eleven of them[67]) voiced support for the adoption of model regulatory objectives, either as they appeared in the Report, or with certain more or less minor modifications. For example, the ABA Commission on Lawyer Assistance Programs, citing research indicating disproportionately high levels of substance abuse and rates of depression and anxiety among lawyers, wrote twice in order to recommend that the Commission enumerate an objective "that would lead to regulatory innovations addressing the needs of legal service providers to confront impairments in the most effective manners for individuals and our legal system."[68] As another example, the ABA Solo Small Firm and General Practice Division wrote that the comments to the regulatory objectives should "expressly state that it is not encouraging non-attorney legal providers."[69]

Just two of the written submissions clearly expressed strong opposition. The New Jersey State Bar Association (NJSBA) wrote that the proposal "is contrary to our profession's core values, and promotes a tiered system of justice that will imperil those most vulnerable in our society." The NJSBA objected that the resolution assumes that nonlawyers should be permitted to provide legal services and that it implicitly endorses ABSs, in contradiction to "the core principle of our legal system that lawyers are singularly and uniquely qualified to provide legal counsel." Further, the NJSBA was not impressed by arguments that large sums of money had already been invested or that a "vast array of non-lawyer service providers" were already offering their services online. For the NJSBA, this did not mean that their continued existence was inevitable, nor was it a reason for the ABA "to endorse their continued existence." In this manner, the NJSBA argued that the ABA was failing to fulfill its unique role of protecting "the public and the justice system from unethical and illegal infringement by non-lawyers into the justice system."[70]

The second objector was Lawrence J. Fox, a partner with the Philadelphia-based firm Drinker Biddle. He stated that the proposal should be rejected out of hand, in part because the Commission had taken an "intellectually dishonest approach, hoping we would not notice the real purpose of the Regulatory Objectives is to be a stalking horse for non-lawyers practicing law, non-lawyers owning law firms and multi-disciplinary practices." For Fox, the situation was dire: if the House of Delegates were to adopt the objectives "it will be the end of our profession as we know it.[71]

The Report was the subject of a heated debate by the House of Delegates at its Midyear Meeting in February, 2016. The American Lawyer called it "one of the most controversial issues before the ABA in years."[72] The more vocal opponents at the debate included David Miranda, president of the New York State Bar Association (and a partner with the Albany firm Heslin Rothenberg Farley & Mesiti), Miles Winder III, president of the NJSBA (and a solo practitioner based in Bernardsville), and Marjorie O'Connell, representing the National Conference of Women's Bar Associations (and a practitioner based in Washington D.C.). Miranda reportedly stated that the resolution could "open the doors to entrepreneurs trying to make money off backs of lawyers who are starving for work." Winder "expressed concern that the resolution could lead to a two-tier system where nonlawyers serve the poor, while the rich use lawyers."[73] O'Connell reportedly stated that her members were "mad as anything" at the prospect of handing legitimacy to poorly trained practitioners, particularly since so many female lawyers have struggled to be taken seriously: "We have no patience with the idea of a big corporation coming in and saying, 'We can for $5 get you a lawyer and get you an answer.' . . . It's not informed by an education, by adherence to professional standards."[74]

Supporters of the Report included William Johnston, a partner with the Wilmington, Delaware firm Young Conaway & Stargatt & Taylor, chairman-elect of the ABA's Business Law Section, and a past president of the Delaware State Bar Association. He challenged the notion that the resolutions would harm the profession, stating "I would submit that this is an invalid premise—that this is a zero sum game and that nonlawyers will be taking food out the mouth of lawyers. . . . There are substantial unmet legal needs that are not being met by members of the organized bar."[75]

Ultimately, the House of Delegates voted in favor of the Resolution, but only after adding this additional clause:

> FURTHER RESOLVED, That nothing contained in this Resolution abrogates in any manner existing ABA policy prohibiting non lawyer ownership of law firms or the core values adopted by the House of Delegates.[76]

Taken as a whole, what exactly does the Resolution mean? What is its significance?

Prior to the adoption of this Resolution, the manner that most bar associations, the ABA included, have typically addressed the topic of "non-traditional legal service providers" has been either to criticize the quality or utility of their services and/or to argue that they engage in the unauthorized practice of law.[77] Like the Commission's statements in the Report, the fact of the House of Delegates' adoption of the Resolution is remarkable in that it breaks away from this much more typical approach in order, if not to implicitly approve of their existence, then at least to acknowledge it. And this acknowledgement extends not only to the fact that they exist today, but also to the fact that it is highly likely that they will also exist tomorrow, quite possibly in even greater numbers. With the Resolution, the ABA seems to finally accept this state of affairs and, in doing so, says that if "non-traditional legal service providers" are to exist, then there should be at least some guiding principles for their regulation—principles that should apply to the regulation of traditional legal service providers as well.

What neither the Resolution nor the Report does is define "non-traditional legal service providers." Does it encompass only the types of providers that exist today? That is, more particularly, does it only encompass: (i) individuals (as opposed to companies or other organizations) who are not lawyers but who provide legal services in a limited and strictly defined context, such as Washington State's Limited Licensed Legal Technicians[78] and New York State's Court Navigators,[79] and/or (ii) companies that are owned by nonlawyers but that provide legal services, such as LegalZoom and RocketLawyer, Modria and Axiom?

Or, does the term "non-traditional legal service providers" go further than that? Does it—could it—also encompass structures, be they companies or other types of organizations, that are owned in whole or in part by nonlawyers, and that provide legal services outside the limited contexts of existing companies like the ones listed above, but in a "nontraditional" manner such that it could be difficult to describe the structure as a traditional "law firm"?

Let's look again at the additional clause added by the House of Delegates. It states "nothing contained in this Resolution abrogates in any manner existing ABA policy prohibiting non lawyer ownership of *law firms*." What is a "law firm?" At what point does an organization that provides legal services cross the line into to constituting a "law firm," and vice-versa? Does the choice of wording for this clause imply that it is fine for nonlawyers (together or not with lawyers) to own legal service providers—regardless of how wide the range of services they provide—as long as those providers are operated as companies or not-for-profit organizations and instead of as traditional "law firms?"

The questions are very interesting ones, without a doubt. But in large part they are academic. Nothing in the Resolution expressly changes Model Rule 5.4 and its restrictions remain in place.

The Commission's next steps appeared to be a whirlwind of more or less focused activity just before the Commission's mandate expired in August, 2016. More specifically, between October, 2015 and April, 2016, the Commission released four "Issues Papers," three of which concerned the following topics, respectively, "New Categories of Legal Services Providers," "Unregulated LSP Entities" and "Alternative Business Structures."

In the first of these three Issues Papers ("New Categories of Legal Services Providers"[80]), the Commission sought feedback on whether persons (individuals, not companies or other organizations), referred to as "LSPs" should be allowed, via judicial authorization and regulation, "to perform discreet and limited legal tasks with the goal of improving access to legal services." The Commission explains that it is inspired by certain US states, such as New York and Washington State, which already have experience with them. Such persons can potentially serve, the Commission argues, to address an "escalating access to justice crisis"[81] in the United States. The Commission states that it is seeking feedback on whether "more supreme courts should be encouraged to authorize and regulate these kinds of LSPs." In this context, the Commission takes pains to clarify that its proposal regarding LSPs "is consistent with the long-standing ABA policy in support of state-based judicial regulation of the legal profession and the practice of law by licensed lawyers."

The Commission posted on its website a total of twenty-four responses to this Issues Paper.[82] Of those twenty-four, fifteen expressed opposition (and, in many cases, strong opposition) to the creation of new categories of LSPs,[83] five expressed support for them,[84] and four either expressed no opinion, or their opinion was unclear.[85]

Interestingly, the state of New Jersey was particularly represented among the opponents, as not only did the NJSBA submit a response in strong opposition but so did the county bar associations of each of eight[86] (out of a total of twenty-one) New Jersey counties. Their comments included:

> "The [NJSBA] is strongly opposed to allowing non-lawyers to provide any kind of legal services, even in a limited fashion. We do not agree with the premise

that the public will be better served by creating categories of legal service providers. On the contrary, we believe such action will create a tiered system of justice that will imperil those most vulnerable in our society,"[87] and

"The ABA's proposal would expose the public to substantially inferior advice on significant matters. A better solution would be (1) a public education campaign informing people that there are organizations to help them find a lawyer, and (2) the creation of one or more mechanisms to match lawyers willing to provide representation at reduced rates with clients having this need."[88]

The opposition expressed by another state bar association, this time that of New York, was particularly forceful:

> [T]he ultimate responsibility for the provision of legal services [should] remain with lawyers. . . . [L]egal licensed technicians was developed and instituted by the judiciary in the State of Washington over the strong objections of the state bar association of that state. We have strong concerns about any proposal that may diminish the independence of the legal profession, or that modifies rules of ethics to permit nonlawyers to offer legal services to the public.[89]

The opposition expressed by the ABA Solo, Small Firm and General Practice Division is also noteworthy:

> [T]he ABA should be at the forefront at protecting the American Public and its membership and should be advocating and educating the public as to why one should retain a lawyer and not advocating or endorsing non-lawyers offering legal services which will directly compete with the solo and small firm lawyer.[90]

The five responses that expressed support for the creation of new categories of LSPs included that of Responsive Law, a Washington D.C.-based, tax-exempt organization that describes itself as "the consumer's voice in the legal system." In its submission, Responsive Law states that LSP programs are essential as a means to "close the justice gap."[91] Responsive Law then goes further, to question two fundamental presumptions that the Paper explicitly refused to question: that legal services are best regulated by, and should continue to only be regulated by, state supreme courts, and that only licensed lawyers should be allowed to engage in the practice of law. To the contrary, Responsive Law argues that "the legal industry is just that—an industry." It should be governed by state legislative and executive branches, not by potentially self-interested lawyers, if new, innovative solutions are going to occur. Further, Responsive Law continued, the definition of what it is to practice law also needs to change and unauthorized practice of law regulations need to be modified so that greater access to legal help from multiple sources, not just lawyers, is available to the public. "The justice gap in America is so big and the country is so dependent on the rule of law that without making these changes its citizens' right to due process will be fundamentally impaired."[92]

In the second of these three Issues Papers ("Unregulated LSP Entities"), the Commission observes there has been a "proliferation" of non-traditional unregulated LSP entities (as opposed to individuals) that deliver legal or law-related services. The Commission explains that this has occurred "due to the fast pace of technological advancements and growing consumer demand for easy access to legal services."[93] The Commission further explains that for these entities, the governing law is simple: Either they are prohibited from providing services because the services constitute the practice of law, or they are free to offer their services, often without the kinds of regulations that apply to lawyers. This approach is problematic, the Commission continues, for two reasons. Firstly, it is notoriously difficult to define the practice of law, and thus to determine whether any such entity is engaged in it. Secondly, regardless of whether it constitutes the practice of law or not, these entities may offer services that warrant regulation beyond that provided by generally applicable consumer protection laws. To this end, the Commission states, "the courts might usefully consider whether the creation of a regulatory structure for currently unregulated LSP entities is necessary to protect the public," and "one potential approach a court may undertake is entity regulation."[94] To this end, the Commission sought data and evidence about currently unregulated LSP entities, information concerning any efforts to regulate them, and input on whether state judicial authorities should be encouraged to regulate currently unregulated LSP entities and, if so, what form those regulations should take.[95]

The Commission posted twenty-four responses to this Issues Paper. Of those, five were from other ABA organizations (Standing Committees and one Division) and five were from state or local bar associations. Of the remainder, one was from an LSP (Avvo, Inc.), one was from an organization of LSPs (New England Litigation Technology Professionals), one was from an organization that advocates for the rights of disabled persons (Colorado Cross-Disability Coalition) and, one, again, was from Responsive Law (an organization that advocates for the interests of individuals in the legal system). The final ten were from individuals, all but two of which were lawyers (the two that were not, John Cosmides and Meng Weng Wong, were co-founders of their respective LSPs).[96]

The content of the responses was highly varied and difficult to summarize. Some respondents were opposed to the existence of LSPs and as a result they were opposed their regulation of LSPs as entities because doing so would legitimize them.[97] Some respondents were opposed to the existence of LSPs, but, more or less resigning themselves to their existence, advocated for their regulation.[98] Some respondents championed LSPs as important for meeting the access to justice gap, but argued against their regulation by state courts on the grounds either it is unnecessary (they are already regulated by consumer protection laws), that it would unnecessarily increase costs, or that regulation would only enable the state bars and courts to exercise their "protectionist instincts."[99] On the other hand, while other respondents also championed LSPs, they felt it's not possible to "responsibly advocate" for them without also advocating for their "meaningful regulation."[100] Other respondents simply weren't sure whether regulation was a good idea or not,[101] and one respondent told the Commission in no uncertain terms that both its Issues Paper and its work on the subject were insufficient, stating that "far more thought and analysis" was required with respect to the "notion of entity regulation if it is to be extended beyond the governance of law firms."[102]

In fact, whether it was done purposefully or not, this response (of the ABA Standing Committee on the Delivery of Legal Services) puts its finger on the essential problem with this Issues Paper issued by the Commission. In this Issues Paper, the Commission uses the expression "entity regulation" entirely divorced from the regulation of law firms as entities, and entirely divorced from proactive, management-based/compliance-based/outcomes-focused regulation. In this manner, the Issues Paper was confusing. Even though the Commission made a point of using the buzz words "entity regulation," the real focus of the paper was not so much on entity regulation as that term is typically understood as it was on the much different question of whether "non-traditional legal services providers" should be regulated by state courts at all.

In the third of these three Issues Papers ("Alternative Business Structures"), the Commission appeared to openly defy the House of Delegates. That is, even though just two months earlier the House of Delegates had adopted a resolution emphatically confirming "existing ABA policy prohibiting non lawyer ownership of law firms,"[103] the Commission nevertheless released this Issues Paper, explaining the document's purpose as (i) to describe recent developments with respect to ABS and (ii) to seek "broad feedback and additional factual information regarding ABS."[104] More specifically, the Commission explained, other jurisdictions, and most notably England and Wales and Australia, permit them. The Commission listed and discussed four "potential benefits" of ABS (increased access to justice, enhanced financial flexibility, enhanced operational flexibility and increased cost-effectiveness and quality of service) and four "potential risks" (threat to lawyers' core values, decreased pro bono work, threat to attorney-client privilege and failure to deliver identified benefits). In "analyzing the evidence regarding ABS," the Commission concludes: (i) there is no evidence that ABS caused harm, (ii) ABS has increased funding for innovation and (iii) jurisdictions have "stayed with ABS." In this context, the Commission called for comments on the "potential benefits and risks associated with ABS," as well as "evidence or other input" on the relative advantages and disadvantages of different types of ABS (for example, with limits on the percentage of nonlawyer ownership and/or multidisciplinary practices).[105]

The Commission got a lot of feedback—well over one hundred responses[106]—an overwhelming number relative to the responses to the other Issues Papers. Of those responses, ninety-four expressed opposition, and in many cases vehement opposition, to alternative structures as compared to just twelve responses expressing support (the remaining responses took no position, were unclear, or duplicated another response—one that expressed strong opposition).[107] Nearly all of the responses were from lawyers, speaking either individually as lawyers or on behalf of a group of lawyers, most notably bar associations but also some law firms. Predictably, some expressed surprise, if not outrage, that the Commission had put the issue back on the table so soon after the February 2016 resolution of the House of Delegates.[108] Others raised the objections to alternative structures that are commonly raised:[109] that they are a threat to the profession's core values,[110] that they will trigger irresolvable conflicts of interest,[111] that lawyers will lose their independence,[112] that there is no evidence that alternative structures have increased access to justice in Australia or England and Wales,[113] that law firms can attract employees by paying competitive salaries without the need to offer employee shareholding,[114] that the burden of proof lies with those who advocate for alternative structures,[115] that there is no way to regulate alternative structures,[116] that alternative structures will lead to a consolidated market for legal services,[117] that more research is required,[118] etc.

Some raised otherwise commonly raised objections, but with new twists:

- "Not only do England & Wales and Australia have different systems from ours, but their systems are flawed, and "they should be more like us and not us like them;"[119]
- Alternative structures are a "utopian ideal as cited by socialist societies in Italy, Great Britain, Germany, Spain and Australia . . . strong capitalistic countries like France, Switzerland and Brazil have not adopted such a system;"[120]
- "The nonlawyer investment ownership and management reforms adopted by our common law cousins were put into place many years ago. Given the quick pace of technological change those reforms . . . may simply no longer be applicable or appropriate for the current American experience."[121]

As colorful and interesting as these objections are, even more interesting are the many objections that do not even try to hide that the House of Delegates' priority must lie not with the best interests in the public, but with the best interests of the members of the profession—or more accurately, with the perceived best interests not of the members of the profession as a whole, but the members of the ABA. In fact, it's not just that those expressing these objections do not hide this priority for the House of Delegates, they go further—they openly and boldly flaunt it, as can be seen in these examples:

- "Goal 1 of the ABA's mission to service our members cannot be ignored or marginalized. [The Commission's Issues Paper regarding alternative business structures] seems to stray from the core of ABA Goal 1 and risks further alienation of our membership."[122]
- "The American Bar Association is an organization which should promote and preserve the professional essence of what it means to be a lawyer. I trust it will live true to its mission and reject the ABS proposal."[123]
- "The ABA is in the midst of a membership crisis . . . which is creating a severe financial strain . . . which will inevitably dictate cuts in service to our members which will cause us to continue to bleed members. I do not think that this particular proposal helps us in that regard. . . . While the stated goals might be laudable, I think the ABA continues to push dues paying members away with the executive decisions we make and the policies we adopt. Goal 1 of the Association is service to our members."[124]
- "It appears that ABA is choosing to disregard a core principle of its mission statement: serving as the national representative of the legal profession. The ABA's very existence is founded on representing a profession, not corporate sponsors. The ABA should not even consider serving as the agent for venture capitalists and non-lawyers that are seeking to profit from the public at any cost."[125]
- "The best thing that [a bar association] can do for its lawyer membership is to enhance the lawyer's ability to practice law, and to enhance the level of services that lawyers are able to provide their clients . . . enhancing opportunities for outsiders to own interests in law firms [does not] meet that objective."[126]
- "Please do not put the House of Delegates through another bruising battle. It will only result in the American Bar Association enduring yet another decline in membership as our profession views the ABA as having lost its way, losing the respect it once had when giants like Robert MacCrate[127] defended our eternal values and principles and lawyers proudly displayed their ABA membership certificate on their office walls."[128]
- "I am absolutely astounded that something this significant could be proposed by the ABA without a careful market survey of its constituents. . . . The ABA is losing touch with its constituents. The current political climate clearly demonstrates the voters' total dissatisfaction with leadership which has disconnected from constituents. . . . This type of proposal leads me to

believe that the ABA may be losing touch with its core values, its mission and the needs of its constituents—the lawyers in the profession."[129]

- "I urge the ABA to stand tall for the profession and the future of the profession. Reject any attempt to allow non-lawyers [to] own some or all of a law firm.[130]
- As a bar organization, how about proposing ideas that will help lawyers—not nonlawyers?"[131]

The comments below merit particular attention, because they were submitted by persons who identified themselves as members of the House of Delegates:

- "[T]he ABA is losing membership and money. From a purely self-preservation perspective, we are more likely to have members drop from adopting and seemingly promoting these ABS recommendations than gain constituents. You are making it harder for me to entice lawyers into joining the ABA than to disavow it. Lawyers want to be part of a professional association that lobbies for them, not against them."[132]
- "Goal 1 of the ABA is to serve its members and such changes would not."[133]

After all these comments were submitted, what happened next is . . . well, what happened next is nothing. That is, the Commission reportedly had a deadline of May 10, 2016 to submit proposals for consideration by the House of Delegates at its Annual Meeting in August. The deadline passed without the Commission submitting any proposals.[134] More than one commentator did not find this surprising, especially with respect to alternative structures, "given the overwhelming lack of support for ABS within the ABA."[135]

Instead, in August, 2016, the Commission issued its final report. Spanning 105 pages, as much could be said about what it does not contain as about what it does. For the purposes of this book, the following observations should suffice:

1. As regards the topics of two of the three Issues Papers described above, the Commission booted one to "courts" and a second to "states," without recommending any further action on the part of the ABA or "the legal profession." More specifically, with respect to New Categories of Legal Services, the report recommends that *courts* "should examine, and if they deem appropriate and beneficial to providing greater access to competent legal services, adopt rules and procedures"[136] in their regard. That being said, the report takes care to clarify, the Commission "does not endorse the authorization of any LSPs" in any particular situation or category. And with respect to Unregulated LSP Entities, the report recommends that

states should explore how they provide legal services "and then assess the benefits and risks to the public associated with those services."[137] Other responsibilities that the report assigns to courts include "making courts more accessible, user-centric and welcoming" and creating programs for training and mentoring prison inmates.[138]

2. However, as regards the topic of the third Issues Paper described above, Alternative Business Structures, the Commission takes a different tactic. Rather than boot this topic to "courts" or "states," instead the Commission keeps it yet longer for the ABA, stating that the ABA should "engage in an organized and centralized effort to collect ABS-related information and data." It should not do this entirely alone, however, as the Commission calls upon the jurisdictions that permit ABS to "seek to compile relevant data on this subject as well." The Commission explains: "By creating a centralized repository for this information and data, the ABA can continue to perform a vital and longstanding function: ensuring that deliberations on a subject of import to the profession are fact-based, thorough, and professional."[139]
3. The report contains additional recommendations, including "all members of the legal profession should keep abreast of relevant technologies," "individuals should have regular legal checkups" and "the legal profession should partner with other disciplines and the public for insights about innovating the delivery of legal services." In addition, the report recommends, the ABA should establish a "Center for Innovation." The Center would be responsible for "proactively and comprehensively encouraging, supporting and driving innovation in the legal profession and the justice system." The Center can do this, the report explains, in a variety of ways, such as by providing "materials and guidance" to commissions organized by state and other bar associations, by providing educational programming on how to improve the delivery of and access to legal services, and by maintaining a comprehensive inventory and evaluation of the innovation efforts taking place. Perhaps most notably, the Center can operate a program of "innovation fellowships" to provide "fellows in residence" with the opportunity to work with a range of other professionals (technologists, entrepreneurs and design professionals) "to create delivery models that enhance the justice system."[140]

Reception of the report was mixed. For example, one commentator said that the report left her "wishing for more" and that its recommendations were not sufficiently bold.[141] Other commentators reflected that in "passing the buck"[142] and taking the route of recommending further study, the report avoids the hardest issues.[143] Perhaps most colorfully, another commentator stated that the report's recommendations "could not be lamer," and that they read "like 150 people got together on it and nothing could be included in it unless at least 149 of them agreed to it."[144]

At the time this book went to press, the ABA had already followed up on one of its recommendations, having announced the creation of a Center for Innovation practically simultaneously with the publication of the Commission's final report. The first chair of the Center's governing council was Andrew Perlman, who had served as vice-chair of the Commission on the Future of Legal Services (and who had also served as reporter for the Commission on Ethics 20/20). The Center's first announced projects, as reported in the ABA Journal, were to assist the ABA Judicial Division in implementing a court-annexed online dispute resolution pilot program in New York, and to participate in the development of guidelines and standards to help lawyers and bar associations administer regular legal checkups for individuals.[145] On the other hand, at the time this book went to press, there was no evidence that the ABA had taken any steps to implement the report's Recommendation 2.4, namely that the ABA create a centralized repository for ABS-related information.

Positive or negative, whatever else may be said about the Commission and its work, it soundly confirmed the seemingly indestructible nature of Model Rule 5.4.

NOTES

1. John H. Matheson and Edward S. Adams, "Not 'If' but 'How:' Reflecting on the ABA Commission's Recommendations on Multidisciplinary Practice," *Minnesota Law Review* 84 (2000): 1280, http://scholarship.law.umn.edu/cgi/viewcontent.cgi?article=1098&context=faculty_articles.

2. James E. Moliterno, *The American Legal Profession in Crisis: Resistance and Responses to Change* (New York: Oxford University Press), 165.

3. "The Commission on Multidisciplinary Practices," American Bar Association, accessed on March 17, 2017, http://www.americanbar.org/groups/professional_responsibility/commission_multidisciplinary_practice/mdp_abt_commission.html.

4. ABA Commission on Multidisciplinary Practice, "General Information Form," accessed on March 17, 2017, http://www.americanbar.org/groups/professional_responsibility/commission_multidisciplinary_practice/mdpgeninfo.html.

5. Louise Lark Hill, "The Preclusion of Nonlawyer Ownership of Law Firms: Protecting the Interest of Clients or Protecting the Interest of Lawyers?" *Capital University Law Review* 42 (2014): 916, http://ssrn.com/abstract=2546886.

6. Ibid., 916–917.

7. "MDP Recommendation – Center for Professional Responsibility," American Bar Association, accessed on March 20, 2017, http://www.americanbar.org/groups/professional_responsibility/commission_multidisciplinary_practice/mdprecom10f.html.

8. "About Us," American Bar Association Commission on Ethics 20/20, accessed on March 17, 2017, http://www.americanbar.org/groups/professional_responsibility/aba_commission_on_ethics_20_20/about_us.html.

9. Ibid. The Commission was co-chaired by Michael Traynor, president emeritus and chair of the Council of the American Law Institute and a former president of the Bar Association of San Francisco, and Jamie S. Gorelick, a partner with the Washington D.C. firm WilmerHale. Gorelick was a controversial figure: She was dubbed the "Mistress of Disaster" in connection with the roles she played, for example, while serving as Deputy Attorney General from 1994 to 1997 and as vice chairman of the Federal National Mortgage Association (Fannie Mae) from 1997 to 2003. Also dubbed "swamp queen," Gorelick was considered a front-runner to be Hillary Clinton's Attorney General. At the time this book went to press, Gorelick was acting as ethics adviser to President Trump's daughter and son-in-law, Ivanka Trump and Jared Kushner. See Ted Krager, *Skullduggery: The True Causes of the Financial Crisis* (Bloomington, IN: Authorhouse, 2012), 228–230; see also Eric Lichtblau, "Jamie S. Gorelick," *New York Times*, November 9, 2008, http://www.nytimes.com/2008/11/08/us/politics/08gorelick.html; Todd Bishop, "Amazon Board Adds Jamie Gorelick, Former Fannie Mae and DOJ Official," *Geekwire*, February 10, 2012, http://www.geekwire.com/2012/amazon-board-adds-fannie-mae-doj-official-jamie-gorelick/; Jack Shafer, "Fannie Mae and the Vast Bipartisan Conspiracy: A List of Villains in Boldface," *Slate*, September 16, 2008, http://www.slate.com/articles/news_and_politics/press_box/2008/09/fannie_mae_and_the_vast_bipartisan_conspiracy.html. James Simpson, "Why is Swamp Queen Jamie Gorelick Advising Jared Kushner?" *Canada Free Press*, March 26, 2017, http://canadafreepress.com/article/why-is-swamp-queen-jamie-gorelick-advising-jared-kushner. Another member of the Commission was Kenneth W. Starr, known for his controversial role as independent counsel investigating alleged abuses in connection with President Bill Clinton and the Clinton Administration. See "Starr Report," Wikipedia, accessed on March 17, 2017, https://en.wikipedia.org/wiki/Starr_Report.

10. ABA Commission on Ethics 20/20, "Minutes," February 4, 2010, 9, http://www.americanbar.org/content/dam/aba/migrated/2011_build/ethics_2020/feb_2010_minutes.authcheckdam.pdf.

11. Ibid.

12. ABA Commission on Ethics 20/20, "Minutes," April 29, 2010, 7, http://www.americanbar.org/content/dam/aba/migrated/2011_build/ethics_2020/apr_2010_minutes.authcheckdam.pdf.

13. ABA Commission on Ethics 20/20, "Minutes," February 10, 2011, 6–7, http://www.americanbar.org/content/dam/aba/administrative/ethics_2020/20110328_ethics2020_minutes_february_10-11-2011-approved.authcheckdam.pdf.

14. Ibid., 6.

15. ABA Commission on Ethics 20/20 Working Group on Alternative Business Structures, "For Comment: Issues Paper Concerning Alternative Business Structures," April 5, 2011, 2, http://www.americanbar.org/content/dam/aba/administrative/ethics_2020/abs_issues_paper.authcheckdam.pdf.

16. Ibid., 7–15.

17. Ibid., 15–16.

18. Ibid., 2.

19. Schneyer, "The Case for Proactive Management-Based Self-Regulation," 233–265.

20. ABA Commission on Ethics 20/20 Working Group on Alternative Business Structures, "For Comment: Issues Paper Concerning Alternative Business Structures, April 5, 2011, 2, 19.

21. Ibid., 17–19.

22. Ibid., 20.

23. ABA Commission on Ethics 20/20, "Minutes," April 15–16, 2011, 9, http://www.americanbar.org/content/dam/aba/administrative/ethics_2020/20110812_ethics2020_minutes_april_15_16_2011_approved.authcheckdam.pdf.

24. The responses can be accessed on the ABA's website at this link (last updated on August 28, 2012): http://www.americanbar.org/content/dam/aba/administrative/ethics_2020/alps_working_group_comments_chart.authcheckdam.pdf.

25. ABA Commission on Ethics 20/20, "Minutes," June 13, 2011, 7, http://www.americanbar.org/content/dam/aba/administrative/ethics_2020/20110812_ethics2020_minutes_june_13_2011_approved.authcheckdam.pdf.

26. Jamie S. Gorelick and Michael Traynor, "For Comment: Discussion Paper on Alternative Law Practice Structures," December 2, 2011, 1, http://www.americanbar.org/content/dam/aba/administrative/ethics_2020/20111202-ethics2020-discussion_draft-alps.authcheckdam.pdf.

27. Ibid., 1–2.

28. ABA Commission on Ethics 20/20, "Discussion Draft for Comment: Alternative Law Practice Structures," December 2, 2011, 5, http://www.americanbar.org/content/dam/aba/administrative/ethics_2020/20111202-ethics2020-discussion_draft-alps.authcheckdam.pdf.

29. Ibid., 9.

30. Ibid., 5–6, 9.

31. Ibid., 14–15.

32. The responses can be accessed on the ABA's website at this link (accessed on March 17, 2017): http://www.americanbar.org/content/dam/aba/administrative/ethics_2020/alps_working_group_comments_chart.authcheckdam.pdf.

33. J. Leeds Barroll, David J. Carr, Nine General Counsel, Lawrence J. Fox, Illinois State Bar Association, Bruce Mann, Larry Murrell, New Jersey State Bar Association, Douglas R. Richmond, John Wm. Ringer, Charles Ruffin, Loretta A. Sheridan, State Bar of Arizona, Richard L. Thies, Alex Wulwick.

34. Jeffrey Antonelli.

35. ABA Section of Dispute Resolution.

36. ABA Commission on Law and Aging, Thomas D. Morgan, National Federation of Paralegals Associations, Responsive Law.

37. Thomas D. Morgan, Responsive Law.

38. ABA Section of International Law, New York City Bar Association.

39. Linda F. Marshak.

40. The author requested from the ABA the minutes of the April 12–13, 2012 meeting, but did not receive them. Given that the decision to not proceed had been made at that meeting, presumably the minutes would reflect the reason(s) for this decision.

41. ABA Commission on Ethics 20/20, "ABA Commission on Ethics 20/20 Will Not Propose Changes to ABA Policy Prohibiting Nonlawyer Ownership of Law Firms," April 16, 2012, http://www.americanbar.org/content/dam/aba/administrative/ethics_2020/20120416_news_release_re_nonlawyer_ownership_law_firms.authcheckdam.pdf.

42. Ibid.

43. ABA Standing Committee on Ethics and Professional Responsibility, "Formal Opinion 464: Division of Legal Fees With Other Lawyers Who May Lawfully Share Fees with Nonlawyers," August 19, 2013, http://www.americanbar.org/content/dam/aba/publications/YourABA/fo_464.authcheckdam.pdf.

44. Andrew M. Perlman, "Towards the Law of Legal Services," *Cardozo Law Review* 37 (2015): 75, http://ssrn.com/abstract=2561014.

45. Ibid., 75–79. Perlman's account is as interesting for what it says as it is for what it does not say. At no point does Perlman question either: (i) the process the ABA followed (for example, that no significant input was sought or received from persons outside the legal profession (such as experts in economic policy, competition, human rights and consumer affairs) or (ii) the legitimacy of the ABA's regulatory power in this regard.

46. "Welcoming The ABA's New President," *Metropolitan Corporate Counsel*, August 22, 2014, http://www.metrocorpcounsel.com/articles/29818/welcoming-aba%E2%80%99s-new-president.

47. "Commission Roster," American Bar Association, accessed on March 17, 2017, http://www.americanbar.org/groups/centers_commissions/commission-on-the-future-of-legal-services/CommissionRoster.html.

48. ABA Commission on the Future of Legal Services, "Issues Paper on the Future of Legal Services," November 3, 2014, 1–2, http://www.americanbar.org/content/dam/aba/images/office_president/issues_paper.pdf.

49. Ibid., 2.

50. Ibid., 3–5.

51. Ibid., 3.

52. The submissions can be accessed at this link: "Comments - Future of Legal Services Issues Paper" American Bar Association, accessed on March 17, 2017, http://www.americanbar.org/groups/centers_commissions/commission-on-the-future-of-legal-services/Comments.html.

53. Justice Earl Johnson, Jr., Pat Monks.

54. Standing Committee of the Delivery of Legal Services, ABA Standing Committee on Professional Discipline, Task Force on the Evolving Business Model of Law Firms.

55. Ashley Balls, Richard Granat, Sands McKinley, Chas Rampenthal and James Peters (both of LegalZoom), Responsive Law, Slater & Gordon. An additional seven responses that did not expressly mention alternative structures but did address issues related directly to them: Richard Zorza, ABA Commission on Homelessness and Poverty, ABA Law Student Division, ABA Standing Committee on Technology and Information Systems, Avvo, George Chandler, Nina Cornett (issues such as access to justice, limited licensure systems, more effective collaboration between lawyers and the technology industry, pro se representation, self-regulation of the legal profession).

56. ABA Commission on the Future of Legal Services et al., "Report to the House of Delegates (105)," November, 2015, http://www.americanbar.org/content/dam/aba/images/office_president/final_regulatory_objectives_resolution_november_2015.pdf (hereinafter, "Report 105").

57. Report 105, 12.

58. In its December 2015 Informational Report to the House of Delegates, the Commissions states that it solicited comments from the public. ABA Commission on the Future of Legal Services, "Informational Report to the House Of Delegates," December 2015, 3, http://www.americanbar.org/content/dam/aba/images/office_president/final_hod_informational_report_midyear.pdf. However, there is nothing in the public record to evidence that any consultation of "the public" occurred in any meaningful way. Further, in the Report to the House of Delegates containing the proposed model regulatory objectives, the Commission states that the Commission that it released the draft Report for comment only "to all ABA entities, state and local bar associations, and affiliated entities." Report 105, 12.

59. American Bar Association, "Resolution 105 Revised and Amended," February 2016, http://www.americanbar.org/content/dam/aba/images/abanews/2016mymres/105.pdf.

60. Report 105.

61. Ibid., 1.

62. Ibid., 1–2.

63. Ibid., 2.

64. Ibid.

65. Ibid., 3.

66. The fourth is difficult to understand. It is dated February 12, 2000. The writer, George Abbott, describes himself as a small business owner, and his statement appears to be testimony he provided before the ABA Commission that was contemplating multidisciplinary practices at that time.

67. Those of the ABA Standing Committee on Client Protection, ABA Commission on Lawyer Assistance Programs, ABA Standing Committee on Paralegals, ABA Standing Committee on Professional Discipline, ABA Standing Committee on Professionalism, ABA Section of Real Property, Trust & Estate Law, ABA Solo, Small Firm and General Practice Division, Indiana State Bar Association, The Bar Association of San Francisco, Laurel S. Terry. The Supreme Court of Colorado can also be included in this list, although its submission could be described as simply informing the ABA of the state's own recently adopted regulatory objectives, without expressing an opinion on the ABA's.

68. ABA Commission on Lawyer Assistance Programs, "Proposed Resolution Regarding Model Regulatory Objectives," October 28, 2015, http://www.americanbar.org/content/dam/aba/images/office_president/lawyer_assistance_programs.pdf; ABA Commission on Lawyer Assistance Programs, "Proposed Resolution Regarding Model Regulatory Objectives," January 11, 2016, http://www.americanbar.org/content/dam/aba/images/office_president/lawyer_assistance_programs_b%20.pdf.

69. Solo Small Firm and General Practice Division, Memo to ABA Commission on the Future of Legal Services, undated, http://www.americanbar.org/content/dam/aba/images/office_president/solo_small_firm.pdf.

70. New Jersey State Bar Association, Letter to ABA Commission on the Future of Legal Services, October 27, 2015, http://www.americanbar.org/content/dam/aba/images/office_president/new_jersey_state_bar_association.pdf.

71. Lawrence J. Fox, "Burying the Lede," 2015, 3–6, http://www.americanbar.org/content/dam/aba/images/office_president/larry_fox.pdf.

72. Susan Beck, "Divided ABA Adopts Resolution on Nonlawyer Legal Services," *The American Lawyer*, February 8, 2016, http://www.americanlawyer.com/id=1202749202171/Divided-ABA-Adopts-Resolution-on-Nonlawyer-Legal-Services#ixzz3zlhUQwOI.

73. Ibid.

74. Lorelei Laird, "ABA House Approves Model Regulatory Objectives for Nontraditional Legal Services," *ABA Journal*, February 8, 2016, http://www.abajournal.com/news/article/house_approves_proposed_model_regulatory_objectives_for_nontraditional_lega/.

75. Beck, "Divided ABA."

76. Resolution 105 Revised and Amended.

77. See, for example, Deborah L. Rhode and Lucy Buford Ricca, "Protecting the Profession or the Public? Rethinking Unauthorized-Practice Enforcement," *Fordham Law Review* 82 (2014): 2587–2610, http://fordhamlawreview.org/assets/pdfs/Vol_82/No_6/RhodeRicca_May.pdf; Laurel A. Rigertas, "The Legal Profession's Monopoly: Failing to Protect Consumers," *Fordham Law Review* 82 (2014): 2683–2703, http://fordhamlawreview.org/assets/pdfs/Vol_82/No_6/Rigertas_May.pdf; Benjamin H. Barton, "The Lawyer's Monopoly—What Goes and What Stays," *Fordham Law Review* 82 (2014): 3067–3090, http://ir.lawnet.fordham.edu/cgi/viewcontent.cgi?article=5008&context=flr; Pierce G. Hunter, "Constitutional Law—Unauthorized Practice of Law: Driving Legal Business Without a License, LegalZoom, Inc., and Campbell v. Asbury Automotive, Inc., 2011 Ark. 157, 381 S.W.3d 21.," *University of Arkansas at Little Rock Law Review* 36 (2014): 201–228, http://lawrepository.ualr.edu/lawreview/vol36/iss2/5; Gerard J. Clark, "Internet Wars: The Bar Against the Websites," *Journal of High Technology Law* XIII (2013): 247–296, https://www.suffolk.edu/documents/jhtl_publications/CLARKMACRO-FINAL-FINAL.pdf; George Leef, "Why The Legal Profession Says LegalZoom Is Illegal," *Forbes*, October 14, 2014, http://www.forbes.com/sites/georgeleef/2014/10/14/why-the-legal-profession-says-legalzoom-is-illegal/#580de4037664. These types of assertions date back a century if not more and significantly increased in intensity with the Great Depression. See, for example, Hurst, *The Growth of American Law*, 319–322; Quintin Johnstone, "Unauthorized Practice Controversy: A Struggle Among Power Groups," *Kansas Law Review* 4 (1955): 1–57, http://digitalcommons.law.yale.edu/fss_papers/1912.

78. Robert Ambrogi, "Washington State Moves Around UPL, Using Legal Technicians to Help Close the Justice Gap," *ABA Journal*, January 1, 2015, http://www.abajournal.com/magazine/article/washington_state_moves_around_upl_using_legal_technicians_to_help_close_the/; Gene Johnson, "Washington Experiments with More Affordable Legal Advice," *The Seattle Times*, September 27, 2015, http://www.seattletimes.com/seattle-news/washington-experiments-with-more-affordable-legal-advice/.

79. Zolan Kanno-Youngs, "Tenants in Maze of New York Courts Get a Helping Hand: The Court Navigator Program Guides People Who Don't Have An Attorney Through Their Civil Case," *The Wall Street Journal*, February 15, 2016, http://www.wsj.com/articles/tenants-in-maze-of-new-york-courts-get-a-helping-hand-1455591801.

80. ABA Commission on the Future of Legal Services, "Issues Paper Concerning New Categories of Legal Services Providers," October 16, 2015, http://www.americanbar.org/content/dam/aba/images/office_president/delivery_of_legal_services_completed_evaluation.pdf.

81. Ibid., 2.

82. ABA Commission on the Future of Legal Services, "Comments - Legal Services Providers Issues Paper," accessed on March 17, 2017, http://www.americanbar.org/groups/centers_commissions/commission-on-the-future-of-legal-services/Comments1.html.

83. ABA Standing Committee on the Delivery of Legal Services, ABA Standing Committee on Group & Prepaid Legal Services and Group Legal Services Association, ABA Solo, Small Firm and General Practice Division, NJSBA, New York State Bar Association, Essex County Bar Association, Gloucester County Bar Association, Hunterdon County Bar Association, Middlesex County Bar Association, Monmouth County Bar Association, Somerset County Bar Association, Union County Bar Association, New Jersey Association for Justice, Lawrence J. Fox.

84. ABA Business Law Section, ABA Standing Committee on Professionalism, Massachusetts Access to Justice Commission, New York Permanent Commission on Access to Justice, Responsive Law.

85. ABA Standing Committee on Ethics and Professional Responsibility, ABA Standing Committee on Paralegals, ABA Standing Committee on Professional Discipline, National Organization of Bar Counsel.

86. Bergen County Bar Association, Essex County Bar Association, Gloucester County Bar Association, Hunterdon County Bar Association, Middlesex County Bar Association, Monmouth Bar Association, Somerset County Bar Association, Union County Bar Association. See Comments – Legal Services Providers Issues Paper.

87. New Jersey State Bar Association, Letter to Katy Englehart, December 28, 2015, http://www.americanbar.org/content/dam/aba/images/office_president/lspcomments_new_jersey_state_bar_association.pdf.

88. Middlesex County Bar Association, Letter to Katy Englehart, December 3, 2015, http://www.americanbar.org/content/dam/aba/images/office_president/lspcomments_middlesex_county_bar_association.pdf.

89. New York State Bar Association, Letter to Katy Englehart, December 22, 2015, http://www.americanbar.org/content/dam/aba/images/office_president/lspcomments_new_york_state_bar_association.pdf.

90. ABA Solo, Small Firm and General Practice Division, Memo to ABA Commission on the Future of Legal Services, December 30, 2015, 4, http://www.americanbar.org/content/dam/aba/images/office_president/lspcomments_solo_small_firm_and_general_practice_division.pdf.

91. Responsive Law, "Comments on: Issues Paper Concerning New Categories of Legal Services Providers," January 8, 2016, 1, http://www.americanbar.org/content/dam/aba/images/office_president/lspcomments_responsive_law.pdf.

92. Ibid., 9.

93. ABA Commission on the Future of Legal Services, "Issues Paper Concerning Unregulated LSP Entities," March 31, 2016, 3, https://www.americanbar.org/content/dam/aba/images/office_president/final_unregulated_lsp_entities_issues_paper.pdf.

94. Ibid., 4–5.

95. Ibid., 8.

96. The comments are available online: "Comments - Unregulated LSP Entities Issues Paper," American Bar Association Commission on the Future of Legal Services, accessed March 20, 2017, https://www.americanbar.org/groups/centers_commissions/commission-on-the-future-of-legal-services/Comments3.html.

97. See, for example, Broome County Bar Association, "Issues Paper Concerning Unregulated LSP Entities," June 29, 2016, https://www.americanbar.org/content/dam/aba/images/office_president/broome_county_bar_association.pdf; New Jersey State Bar Association, "Comments on Issues Paper Unregulated LSP Entities," April 28, 2016, https://www.americanbar.org/content/dam/aba/images/office_president/new_jersey_state_bar_association_unregulated.pdf.

98. New York State Bar Association, "New York State Bar Association's Comments on the ABA Commission on the Future of Legal Services' Issues Papers On Legal Checkups, Unregulated LSP Entities and Alternative Business Structures," April 28, 2016, https://www.americanbar.org/content/dam/aba/images/office_president/new_york_state_bar.pdf.

99. Avvo, Inc., "Unregulated Legal Service Provider Entities," April 28, 2016, https://www.americanbar.org/content/dam/aba/images/office_president/avvo_unregulated.pdf; New England Litigation Technology Professionals, "For Comment: Issues Paper Concerning Unregulated LSP Entities," April 28, 2016, https://www.americanbar.org/content/dam/aba/images/office_president/new_england_litigation_technology_professionals_board_of_directors.pdf; Responsive Law, "Issues Paper Concerning Unregulated Legal Service Providers," April 28, 2016, https://www.americanbar.org/content/dam/aba/images/office_president/responsive_law_unregulated.pdf.

100. ABA Standing Committee on Professionalism, "Comment On Issues Paper Concerning Unregulated LSP Entities," April 28, 2016, 2, https://www.americanbar.org/content/dam/aba/images/office_president/professionalism_standing_committee_unregulated.pdf.

101. Colorado Cross-Disability Coalition, "Comments on Civil Legal Service Providers," April 24, 2016, https://www.americanbar.org/content/dam/aba/images/office_president/julie_reiskin.pdf; Richard Zorza, "Does the Concept of "Entity Regulation" Provide an Entry Point for Access Contribution Requrements [sic]", April 2, 2016, https://www.americanbar.org/content/dam/aba/images/office_president/richard_zorza_unregulated.pdf.

102. ABA Standing Committee on the Delivery of Legal Services, "Issues Paper on 'Unregulated Legal LSP Entities,'" May 2, 2016, 4, https://www.americanbar.org/content/dam/aba/images/office_president/delivery_of_legal_services_unregulated.pdf.

103. Resolution 105, American Bar Association, February, 2016, http://www.americanbar.org/content/dam/aba/images/abanews/2016mymres/105.pdf. See also Richard Zorza, "Good News from the ABA—Regulatory Objectives Adopted,"

Richard Zorza's Access to Justice Blog, February 9, 2016, http://accesstojustice.net/; Beck, "Divided ABA."

104. ABA Commission on the Future of Legal Services, "For Comment: Issues Paper Regarding Alternative Business Structures," April 8, 2016, 2, http://www.americanbar.org/content/dam/aba/images/office_president/alternative_business_issues_paper.pdf.

105. Ibid., 7–15.

106. The responses can be consulted at this link: "Comments - Alternative Business Structures Issues Paper," American Bar Association Commission on the Future of Legal Services, accessed on March 17, 2017, https://www.americanbar.org/groups/centers_commissions/commission-on-the-future-of-legal-services/Comments4.html.

107. More specifically, five respondents simply voiced their agreement with the response submitted by Texas Association of Defense Counsel, Texas Trial Lawyers Association and Texas Chapters of the American Board of Trial Advocates.

108. See, for example, D. Clark Smith, "Response to Commission's Issues Paper Regarding Alternative Business Structures dated April 8, 2016," April 29, 2016, https://www.americanbar.org/content/dam/aba/images/office_president/d_clark_smith_jr_abs.pdf.

109. Each of these objections is addressed in detail in Snyder, *Democratizing Legal Services*, 1–93.

110. See, for example, Jess C. Rickman, "ABS Survey–Rejection of the Proposal," April 27, 2016, http://www.americanbar.org/content/dam/aba/images/office_president/jess_c_rickman_abs.pdf.

111. See, for example, DRI – The Voice of the Defense Bar, "Issues Paper Regarding Alternative Business Structures," 4.

112. International Association of Defense Counsel, "ABA Commission on the Future of Legal Services – Alternative Business Structures," May 3, 2016, 1, http://www.americanbar.org/content/dam/aba/images/office_president/international_association_of_defense_counsel_abs.pdf.

113. Greg Curry and Thompson & Knight, LLP, n.t., n.d., https://www.americanbar.org/content/dam/aba/images/office_president/greg_curry_and_thompson_and_knight_abs.pdf.

114. Illinois State Bar Association, "Issues Paper Regarding Alternative Business Structures: Request for Comments," n.d., http://www.americanbar.org/content/dam/aba/images/office_president/illinois_state_bar_association_abs.pdf.

115. New York State Bar Association, "New York State Bar Association's Comments," 7.

116. Matthew Walko, "Comment on ABA's Issues Paper Regarding Alternative Business Structures dated April 8, 2016," April 25, 2016, http://www.americanbar.org/content/dam/aba/images/office_president/matthew_walko_abs.pdf.

117. J. Michael Weston, "ABA Commission on the Future of Legal Services – Alternative Business Structures," April 27, 2016, http://www.americanbar.org/content/dam/aba/images/office_president/lederer_weston_craig_abs.pdf.

118. Los Angeles County Bar Association, "Comment of the Los Angeles County Bar Association to the American Bar Association's Commission on the Future

of Legal Services Regarding Alternative Business Structures," April 29, 2016, 3, https://www.americanbar.org/content/dam/aba/images/office_president/los_angeles_county_bar_association_abs.pdf.

119. Laura Bellegie Sharp, "Comments Regarding the Alternative Business Solutions Issues Paper," April 28, 2016, 2, http://www.americanbar.org/content/dam/aba/images/office_president/laura_sharp_abs.pdf.

120. Terrence T. Snook, "Proposal to Allow ABS (Non Lawyer Ownership of Law Firms) and MDPs (Multi Disciplinary Programs)," April 28, 2016, https://www.americanbar.org/content/dam/aba/images/office_president/terry_snook_abs.pdf.

121. Illinois State Bar Association, "Issues Paper Regarding Alternative Business Structures," 4.

122. Tort Trial & Insurance Practice Section, "ABA Commission on the Future of Legal Services / Issue Paper Regarding Alternative Business Structures," May 6, 2016, 1, http://www.americanbar.org/content/dam/aba/images/office_president/tips_abs.pdf.

123. James T. Murphy, "Comment: Issues Paper Regarding Alternative Business Stuctures [sic]," April 26, 2016, http://www.americanbar.org/content/dam/aba/images/office_president/james_t_murphy_abs.pdf.

124. Forum on the Entertainment and Sports Law Industries, "ABA Commission on the Future of Legal Services—Issues Paper on Alternative Business Structures/Comments Requested," May 3, 2016, http://www.americanbar.org/content/dam/aba/images/office_president/entertainment_and_sports_abs.pdf.

125. Middlesex County Bar Association, "Issues Paper Regarding Alternative Business Structures," May 6, 2016, 3, http://www.americanbar.org/content/dam/aba/images/office_president/middlesex_county_bar_association_abs.pdf.

126. Michael J. Sullivan, "Alternative Business Structures," April 26, 2016, https://www.americanbar.org/content/dam/aba/images/office_president/michel_j_sullivan_abs.pdf.

127. Robert MacCrate, a former President of the ABA, is credited as the driving force behind the resolution that the ABA House of Delegates adopted in 2000 stating: "The sharing of legal fees with nonlawyers and the ownership and control of the practice of law by nonlawyers are inconsistent with the core values of the legal profession. The law governing lawyers, that prohibits lawyers from sharing legal fees with nonlawyers and from directly or indirectly transferring to nonlawyers ownership or control over entities practicing law, should not be revised." See John Gibeaut, "'It's a Done Deal': House of Delegates Vote Crushes Chances for MDP," *ABA Journal* 9 (2000): 92–93, http://www.jstor.org/stable/27841689; Paul D. Paton, "Multidisciplinary Practice Redux: Globalization, Core Values, and Reviving the MDP Debate in America," *Fordham Law Review* 78 (2010): 2209, http://ir.lawnet.fordham.edu/cgi/viewcontent.cgi?article=4527&context=flr.

128. Lawrence J. Fox, "What Would Bob MacCrate Think?", n.d., http://www.americanbar.org/content/dam/aba/images/office_president/lawrence_j_fox_abs.pdf.

129. Henry Mills Gallivan, "ABA Proposal in Alternative Business Structures," April 28, 2016, http://www.americanbar.org/content/dam/aba/images/office_president/henry_mills_gallivan_abs.pdf.

130. Benjamin H. Hill, III, "Non-Lawyer Ownership of Law Firms," April 25, 2016, http://www.americanbar.org/content/dam/aba/images/office_president/benjamin_j_hill_abs.pdf.

131. Christopher G. Betke, "Proposal for ABS," April 28, 2016, http://www.americanbar.org/content/dam/aba/images/office_president/christopher_g_betke_abs.pdf.

132. Laura Bellegie Sharp, "Comments Regarding the Alternative Business Solutions Issues Paper," 2.

133. Paula Hudson Holderman, "Commentary on the Report from the ABA's Commission on the Future of Legal Services," April 27, 2016, http://www.americanbar.org/content/dam/aba/images/office_president/paula_hudson_holderman_abs.pdf.

134. Blake Edwards, "The Debate Over Non-Lawyer Firm Ownership Is Officially Closed, For Now," *Bloomberg Law*, May 17, 2016, https://bol.bna.com/the-debate-over-non-lawyer-firm-ownership-is-officially-closed-for-now/.

135. Mark Behrens and Christopher Appel, "Controversial ABA Alternative Business Structures Proposal Stalls . . . Again," IADC Committee Newsletter, June, 2016, 7.

136. ABA Commission on the Future of Legal Services, "Report on the Future of Legal Services in the United States," August, 2016, 6, http://abafuturesreport.com/#1 ("Futures Commission Final Report").

137. Ibid., 41.

138. Ibid., 6, 45–47.

139. Ibid., 43.

140. Ibid., 6, 48.

141. Jayne Reardon, "ABA Commission's Future of Legal Services Report: A Clarion Call for Action," *2Civility*, August 11, 2016, https://www.2civility.org/aba-commissions-future-of-legal-services-report-a-clarion-call-for-action/.

142. Robert Ambrogi, "ABA Future Panel Calls for Broad Changes in Legal Services," Above the Law, August 8, 2016, http://abovethelaw.com/2016/08/this-week-in-legal-tech-aba-future-panel-calls-for-broad-changes-in-legal-services/.

143. Alberto Bernabe, "ABA Commission on Future of Legal Services issues Its Final Report; I Am Not Particularly Impressed – UPDATED," *Professional Responsibility Blog*, August 11, 2016, http://bernabepr.blogspot.fr/2016/08/aba-commission-on-future-of-legal.html.

144. Dan Harris, comment on Renee Knake, "ABA Commission on Future of Legal Services Responds," *Lexblog*, August 24, 2016, http://kevin.lexblog.com/2016/08/24/aba-future-delivery-legal-services-responds/.

145. Victor Li, "ABA's New Center for Innovation Will Drive Efforts for New Methods of Delivering Legal Services," *ABA Journal*, November 1, 2016, http://www.abajournal.com/magazine/article/aba_center_for_innovation.

Chapter 21

The Two Commissions

Different or the Same?

There is no question that the work of the Futures Commission was prolific. In addition to releasing issues papers and reports, it also organized or fostered the organization of a "National Summit on Innovation in Legal Services"[1] and local "grassroots meetings."[2] While the topics of those meetings varied, their principal focus was to discuss the obstacles that individuals and businesses face in obtaining legal services and to share ideas and experiences with respect to existing and proposed innovations in the delivery of legal services and in legal education (for example, the use of technology to streamline court processes and/or assist unrepresented litigants,[3] prepaid legal service plans,[4] limited scope legal services,[5] inclusion of technology-focused courses in a law school curriculum,[6] and a single point of entry into the justice system[7]). The Commission also organized webinars on comparable topics, including one that juxtaposed Gillian Hadfield, one of the most prominent advocates of alternative structures, with Lawrence Fox, one of the most prominent opponents.[8] The Commission's website contains the webinars as well as videos of a number of presentations—considered as a whole, they contain a wealth of information and insight. While the 20/20 Commission could not be described as inactive, the extent and the scope of its meetings and other activities pale in comparison to those of the Futures Commission.

Further, the Resolution proposed by the Futures Commission and adopted by the House of Delegates is remarkable. As noted above, it expressly recognizes the existence of "non-traditional legal service providers." Instead of criticizing the quality or utility of the services of non-traditional legal services providers and/or contending that they engage in the unauthorized practice of law, the ABA has done an about-face and expressly accepts them. And it goes further: it provides guidelines to state courts with respect to how to regulate them and, in doing so, provides the ABA's implicit permission for state courts to regulate them. In contrast, while the 20/20 Commission did make a number of recommendations to the House of Delegates,[9] all of which were accepted, none of them could be or, indeed, have been described as "remarkable." (To the contrary, Laurel Terry argues that the 20/20 Commission missed an opportunity because it failed to ask the "big picture" question of "whether, and how, lawyer regulation and the ABA should adapt in light of global developments."[10])

But as remarkable as the Resolution proposed by the Futures Commission and adopted by the House of Delegates is, it is hardly groundbreaking. It doesn't create a path for the creation of non-traditional legal service providers, as they have already been created (albeit in highly limited forms given the restrictions of Model Rule 5.4, which, again, remain in place). It doesn't alter the quality or the usefulness of the services of non-traditional legal service providers, nor does it have any bearing on the extent to which their activities may or may not constitute the unauthorized practice of law (although the Resolution may very well dampen enthusiasm for future lawsuits by state and local bar associations in that regard). While certainly state courts will find the ABA's suggested guidelines on how to regulate non-traditional legal service providers to be interesting and quite likely also useful, the state courts did not need such guidelines from the ABA; indeed, the Supreme Court of Colorado did not wait for them in order to develop its own.[11] Finally, at no point has any state supreme court required the ABA's permission, implicit or not, to regulate anything. At least, on paper none has.

In fact, as remarkable as the work of the Futures Commission was, and as different it was from that of the 20/20 Commission, the two Commissions shared a number of fundamental commonalities. Those commonalties served to severely compromise the effectiveness as well as the integrity of the work of each Commission, especially (but not only) when considered in the context of alternative structures. Those fundamental commonalties most notably included these five:

1) Little, if any, consideration of entity regulation or compliance-based regulation: As discussed in detail above, in neither England and Wales nor Australia were alternative structures adopted in isolation of other regulatory considerations. To the contrary, in both places, they were adopted in the context of significant modifications to, if not a transformation of, the larger regulatory framework. While such modifications (or transformations) comprised a number of elements, two of the most essential were: (i) the adoption of a scheme to regulate entities in addition to individual lawyers and (ii) a move away from proscriptive, rules-based regulation in favor of compliance-based regulation (also termed "proactive, management based regulation," or, in England and Wales, "outcomes focused regulation").

In the United States as well as in Canada, a number of objections to alternative structures have been raised. While the objections vary in nature, many of them are in essence driven by a concern as to how alternative structures can be regulated, and, in particular (but not only), how they can be regulated to ensure compliance with ethical standards. Compliance-based entity regulation responds directly to that concern.

While the experiences of the Canadian provinces are not yet conclusive, they strongly indicate that the adoption of alternative structures in isolation of other regulatory modifications, and notably of these two essential ones, is nearly if not entirely impossible. In Ontario, alternative structures, as an isolated proposal, was simply too contentious and proved impossible to debate without provoking a myriad of strong emotions. In contrast, the (albeit as yet unfinished) experience of Manitoba and the other Prairie provinces demonstrates that when the discussion of alternative structures expressly recognizes that they are "intimately connected" with both entity regulation and compliance-based regulation, the resulting discussion can be productive rather than fruitlessly contentious and emotional. Finally, as the (also as yet unfinished) experiences of Nova Scotia and British Columbia demonstrate, the elements of entity regulation and compliance-based regulation can, in a first step, be discussed and adopted in a manner that is entirely divorced from alternative structures, and in isolation from them. In this manner, should either province decide at a later date to address the topic of alternative structures, much of the preliminary work needed to adopt them will already be done, and, especially, the concern as to how they will be regulated will already be addressed.

When the 20/20 Commission created Working Groups in February, 2010, it initially called one of them "Law Firm Regulation/Alternative Business Structures Working Group,"[12] or, alternatively, "Entity Regulation/Alternative Business Structures Working Group."[13] At a meeting held in April, 2010, that Working Group reported back to the Commission that it had "initially decided to focus first on issues relating to law firm/entity regulation. It will also move forward contemporaneously with its study and analysis of developments relating to alternative business structures."[14] However, the minutes of the Commission's meetings (at least, the minutes that are available to the public) make no further mention of either law firm or entity regulation until a meeting held in February, 2011. The minutes of that meeting simply state that the Commission agreed with the Entity Regulation Subcommittee that "there was insufficient evidence" to proceed further with the development of a proposal regarding proactive, management-based regulation. Instead, the Commission recommends that the Entity Regulation/Alternative Business Structures Working Group develop a White Paper on how to "help lawyers and law firms think more systematically about how to better serve clients."[15]

There is nothing in the public record that sheds light on exactly what evidence the Commission considered in order to draw such a conclusion. Further, there is nothing in the public record suggesting that the recommended follow-up work was performed. In the minutes subsequent to this February, 2011 meeting, the relevant Working Group is referred to simply as the "Alternative Business Structures Working Group."[16]

In its first (2014) Issues Paper, the Futures Commission included a single mention of "entity regulation and proactive risk-based management/compliance programs"[17] in its two-page list of about thirty-five questions. Of the more than sixty submissions that the Commission received in response, only three mentioned entity and/or compliance-based regulation in any meaningful way, two to briefly express support for each of them,[18] and one to remind the Commission that they can be adopted independently of alternative structures.[19]

After that, the Futures Commission itself did not mention compliance-based regulation again in any of its publicly available documents. It mentioned entity regulation just once more—in its December, 2015 Informational Report to the House of Delegates, in a list of the Commission's ongoing work, it included a reference to "Ongoing discussion and study of additional regulatory opportunities, including but not limited to alternative business structures and entity regulation."[20] (As discussed above, its Issues Paper Concerning Unregulated LSP Entities, the Commission uses the expression "entity regulation," but it does so entirely divorced from the concept of the regulation of law firms as entities as well as from compliance-based regulation.)

Based upon the publicly available documentation, it is clear that neither the 20/20 Commission nor the Futures Commission considered either entity or compliance-based regulation to be topics worthy of their focus. What is less clear is the extent to which they understood the importance of these topics in relation to alternative structures, as demonstrated first by the examples of England and Wales and Australia, and, later, by the examples of the various provinces of Canada. Either way, for each Commission, its failure to focus on these prerequisite topics guaranteed that it would be unable to address the topic of alternative structures in any productive manner.

2) Continued abdication by those who hold de jure power to regulate legal services (state supreme courts) in favor of the de facto (or quasi[21]) regulatory power exercised by the ABA.[22] Very generally speaking, it is the state supreme courts that hold the de jure authority (that is, the authority accorded by law) to regulate the legal profession, if not the legal services market as a whole (in many states, the supreme court shares that authority with a unified or integrated bar association).[23] From time to time the ABA reasserts that the authority to regulate lawyers, if not the legal services market as a whole, not only lies with state supreme courts or the judicial branch of government, but also that it should lie there.[24] The two Commissions repeated these assertions:

The 20/20 Commission's "Preliminary Issues Outline" opened with the words "In the United States, the highest court of each state and the District of Columbia has the authority to regulate lawyers within its borders."[25] And in its Issues Paper Concerning New Categories of Legal Services Providers, the Futures Commission made a point of explaining that the paper's concept of authorizing and regulating nonlawyer legal service providers "is consistent with the longstanding ABA policy in support of state-based judicial regulation of the legal profession."[26]

However, while the pertinent legal texts might place this regulatory power in the hands of the state supreme courts (and while the ABA might from time to time repeat the mantra that it does), the reality of how the power is exercised is entirely different. As discussed in part I, state supreme courts are highly deferential to the positions taken by the organized bar, and, in particular, to the positions taken by the ABA House of Delegates.[27] It is rare for a state supreme court to adopt a regulatory measure that was not proposed to it, if not directly by the national organization of the ABA, then indirectly through a state or local bar association, acting at the state level on the behest of the ABA. It is equally rare for a state supreme court to not adopt the regulatory measures that such bar associations do propose to it. In this manner, state supreme courts effectively abdicate their regulatory power to the ABA and to the state and local bar associations (again, for the most part acting at the ABA's behest).[28]

Specifically in relation to the work of the 20/20 and the Futures Commissions, some documents evidence this abdication of regulatory power:

- In a written submission dated July 5, 2010, Sally Evans Lockwood, director of Admissions for the Office of Bar Admissions of the Supreme Court of the State of Georgia, wrote to the 20/20 Commission to acknowledge that she was aware that the Commission was considering certain proposals on the topic of foreign lawyers practicing in the United States, and to assure the Commission that the State Bar of Georgia and well as the Georgia Supreme Court not only had already adopted prior ABA proposals in this regard, but also had already set in motion the procedure required to adopt the anticipated new ones.[29]
- In a written submission dated October 4, 2012, Stephanie S. Libhart, assistant director of the Pennsylvania Interest on Lawyers Trust Account (IOLTA) Board of the Supreme Court of Pennsylvania wrote to the 20/20 Commission to "encourage" it to clarify the wording of a particular proposal under consideration by the Commission in order to assure that the proposal did not, presumably unintentionally, "interfere" with some of the state's existing practices—practices that, questions of wording aside, Libhart made a point of explaining already complied with the spirit and

intention of the proposals in question. (The proposal related to the attribution of the fees paid by out-of-state lawyers requesting temporary permission to appear on behalf of a client in that state, a procedure known as "Pro Hac Vice Admission.")[30]

- In a written submission dated December 21, 2015, Paul Burgoyne, president of the National Organization of Bar Counsel (NOBC, whose website describes it as an organization "*whose members work in the regulation of the practice of law.*"[31]), wrote to the Futures Commission to state that it "takes no position" with respect to the question of new categories of legal services providers that was under consideration by the Commission. Instead, he wrote "it is appropriate for the ABA to play a leadership role in evaluating and guiding the manner in which the delivery of legal services will be regulated so that all US jurisdictions can make informed decisions." In that context, he was writing to offer up the NOBC's members as an "invaluable resource" for the Commission, as "eager to assist in all aspects of the ABA's work to improve judicial regulation of the practice of law."[32] (This comment is particularly ironic given that in its August, 2016 Final Report, the Futures Commission kicked responsibility for this issue to the courts.)[33]
- At its Midyear Meeting on February 3, 2016 (just a few days before the ABA House of Delegates adopted the Futures Commission's proposal with respect to regulatory objectives), the Conference of Chief Justices (CCJ) adopted "Resolution 9: Recommending Consideration of ABA Model Regulatory Objectives for the Provision of Legal Services." (By way of reminder, the CCJ brings together the highest judicial officer in each state, typically the Chief Justice. The Chief Justice presides over the state's supreme court). In this Resolution of its own, the CCJ begins by explaining that the Futures Commission "concluded that the development of regulatory objectives is a useful step to guide state supreme courts and bar authorities as they assess the existing regulatory framework and identify and implement regulations related to legal services beyond the traditional regulation of the legal profession." The Resolution then repeats the list of Model Regulatory Objectives that had been developed and proposed by the Futures Commission, and recommends that the members of the CCJ (that is, state supreme court justices) consider the objectives in the manner intended by the Commission (i.e., "as a means to help assess the state's existing regulatory framework and to help identify and implement regulations related to legal services beyond the traditional regulation of the legal profession"[34]).

In the documents described above, state judicial authorities, acting either individually (in these specific cases, the Supreme Courts of Georgia and of

Pennsylvania), or collectively through the NOBC and the CCJ, demonstrate in an unequivocal manner their failure to exercise their regulatory powers, instead deferring to the processes and the "policy" decisions of the ABA. The Supreme Court of Georgia wrote for no other reason than to affirm its past and future compliance with ABA dictates, without questioning those dictates in any manner, or even appearing to contemplate that they might question them. The Supreme Court of Pennsylvania "encouraged" the ABA to amend its proposed text in order to not cause confusion with existing Pennsylvania practices—such an "encouragement" would be unnecessary if the Supreme Court of Pennsylvania considered itself to be free to amend, or, indeed, to not adopt at all, ABA dictates. The NOBC all but bowed before the ABA, in stating that it "takes no position" but that, instead, "it is appropriate for the ABA to play a leadership role." Finally, the CCJ, in recommending state supreme courts to consider the ABA's regulatory objectives, underscored the fact that it failed to develop any of its own (as did each of the other state supreme courts other than that of Colorado).

These documents (among others) evidence that, regardless of what the applicable legal texts may state and that the ABA may claim to the contrary, much of the real power to regulate the legal profession as well as legal services in the United States lies principally with the ABA. While state supreme courts and other state judicial authorities have the de jure power, for the most part they fail, for whatever reason(s), to exercise it, leaving a regulatory vacuum open for the ABA to fill. However, in filling the vacuum, the ABA hides behind assertions that the power lies with state judicial authorities. In doing so, the ABA is able to deflect any argument that it should conduct itself as a true and effective regulatory authority—one that acts in a fully transparent manner and is accountable not to its members or to state and local bar associations, but to the public as a whole.[35] This abdication on the part of state judicial authorities combined with this duplicity on the part of the ABA have a number of consequences, two of which are discussed immediately below.

(The 20/20 Commission was open about this duplicity: Even if its Preliminary Issues Outline opened with the words "In the United States, the highest court of each state and the District of Columbia has the authority to regulate lawyers within its borders," the 20/20 Commission went on to repeat on multiple occasions that in its work it adhered to three "guiding principles," one of which was "maintaining a strong, independent, and *self-regulating* legal profession."[36])

3) <u>Lack of transparency</u>. The 20/20 Commission reported that, at its first meeting in September, 2009, "the Commission agreed that transparency . . . would be crucial."[37] On several later occasions the 20/20 Commission repeated an intention to act with transparency.[38] However, in practice, the 20/20 Commission barely made a pretense of transparency. A prime example

is the Commission's decision-making process with respect to alternative structures. As described in detail above, the Commission made a series of decisions in their regard without ever explaining its decision-making criteria and without providing any explanation of its decisions beyond statements such as "these subjects are better suited for a White Paper,"[39] "there was insufficient evidence to proceed further,"[40] and "the case had not been made."[41] While the Commission released minutes for some of its meetings, it failed to do so for a number of others, and the ABA even refused to provide them in response to a specific request.

Kenneth Grady, CEO of SeyfarthLean Consulting, described the ABA in general, and the work of the 20/20 Commission in particular, in this manner:

> I have trouble concluding the ABA is following [a transparent, fact-based and unbiased] process. The materials I have read do not include standards for analyzing the issue, data about the performance of schemes with or without ABS, or descriptions of the data needed to decide the issue. Nevertheless, the position of the ABA is that "the case for making changes has not been made."[42] . . . Put simply, the public cannot understand what would permit the ABA to permit ABS arrangements. This opaque process makes it difficult to build public trust and supports the perception that a decision on the issue will be made behind closed doors to a politics and emotion process.[43]

It is tempting to argue that the Futures Commission acted in a more transparent manner. Evidence of this could be found, for example, in the large amount of materials posted on the Commission's website (videotaped presentations, webinar, written submissions) and the Commission's efforts to facilitate a large number of what it termed "grassroots meetings," which the Commission described as "local conversations [to] create new avenues for access to justice for all and open doors to new career opportunities for current and future lawyers."[44]

However, a closer examination reveals that the Futures Commission was hardly more transparent than the 20/20 Commission. Examples of this include the Futures Commission's failure to explain its reasons for deciding to propose regulatory objectives as opposed to any other proposal it could have made, especially given that its 2014 Issues Paper did not even mention them. Further, the limited information on the Commission's website makes it impossible to fully understand the consultation process that the Commission followed with respect to the topic of regulatory objectives—based upon the information that is provided, it appears that only a small number of groups and individuals, namely ABA entities, state and local bar associations and a law school professor, were asked or even put in a position to be able to provide comments before the Commission submitted its Report to the House of Delegates. Another example of the Futures Commission's lack of transparency is that its prominently publicized May, 2015 "National Summit" was organized (with Stanford Law School) on an "invitation only" basis. At no point did the Commission publicly explain its criteria for selecting the persons who were invited to speak or to attend, nor was a list of attendees ever made public. Finally, and perhaps especially, none of the minutes of the Commission's meetings has been made available to the public. Without them, it is impossible to have any insight into the processes the Commission followed or the decision-making criteria it applied. Especially it is impossible to critique them.

If the ABA were, as its website describes, nothing more than a "voluntary professional association" with a primary goal of "serving our members," it would be difficult for anyone except the ABA's members to criticize this lack of transparency. However, the ABA is much more than that—rightly or wrongly, it is our country's de facto regulator of the legal profession and of legal services. For this reason, its lack of transparency can and must be severely criticized. As discussed in detail in part I, transparency is an essential component under any definition of "good governance." Further, the lack of transparency of this "quasi-regulator" flies in the face of the international commitments that the United States has made and notably its commitment under the United Nations 2030 Agenda for Sustainable Development to develop "effective, accountable and transparent institutions at all levels."[45]

4) Lack of empirical or evidence-based research: The lack of any empirical or evidenced-based research was noted in comments submitted comments to both Commissions. For example, Douglas Richmond stated that the 20/20 Commission "has gathered absolutely no evidence that non-lawyer ownership in firms . . . is desired by any material percentage of United States lawyers . . . multiple anecdotes are not evidence."[46] Richard Thies stated that the 20/20 Commission did not have "any evidence that there is a necessity for these changes other than the competition of the marketplace."[47] A few years later, the Los Angeles County Bar Association asserted that the Futures Commission "must frame a data-driven proof of concept that meets the Commission's stated ABS goals."[48] The Defense Research Institute argued "there is no empirical evidence that greater access to justice has been achieved in jurisdictions that allow [for alternative structures]."[49]

The 20/20 Commission did not expressly acknowledge the calls for additional evidence and research, nor did it otherwise address the topic. In contrast, the Futures Commission did acknowledge it, stating that "ongoing, systematic research is an essential component of improving the quality and availability of legal services."[50] At the same time, the Futures Commission lamented that "systematic research on the current delivery of legal services—especially services for 'ordinary individuals'—is strikingly limited"[51] and that "limited data has impeded efforts to identify and assess the most effective innovations in legal services delivery."[52] However, the Futures Commission did not recommend that the ABA itself or other bar associations take steps to fill this gap, in whole or in part, by conducting its own research, because "it would be impossible" for them "to explore every potential innovation. Instead, the Commission recommended that the ABA's role be confined to the collection, organization and centralization of ABS-related information and data.[53] As for who should actually conduct the research, the Futures Commission observed that "fortunately, academic and federal governmental interest in 'access to justice' research is increasing." As a general matter, the Commission stated, it "strongly supports 'evidence-based' assessment of both new and existing forms of legal services delivery."[54] In particular, "where ABS is allowed, evidence and data regarding the risks and benefits associated with these entities should be developed and assessed."[55]

5) Treatment of certain questions—and one in particular—as taboo: During the course of their work, both the 20/20 and the Futures Commissions posed a large number of questions. The questions were by no means limited to the topic of alternative structures, but also addressed many other topics. For example, the 20/20 Commission asked questions about the conditions under which foreign lawyers should be allowed to practice in the United States, whether virtual law firms are adequately regulated, the rules that should govern a lawyer's involvement with alternative litigation financing, the ethical issues that arise from lawyers' use of internet-based client development tools, and the extent to which lawyers require guidance in their use of technology, notably to assure the confidentiality of client information. Examples of the questions the Futures Commission asked include how the legal profession can better serve clients and potential clients, what are the most important problems in the delivery of legal services and how can those problems be addressed, whether certain persons who do not have a JD and are not fully licensed lawyers should be permitted to provide limited legal services, and how can the legal profession address diversity and inclusion in the recruitment and retention of practicing lawyers.

Having posed those questions, each of the Commissions engaged in a consultation process in order to seek and discuss responses. The 20/20 Commission's process was relatively closed, in that it consulted nearly exclusively with members of the legal profession: other ABA entities, state and local bar associations, judges, law school professors and individual lawyers. In comparison, the Futures Commission was slightly more open in that it also invited persons it deemed to be "innovators"[56] to make presentations and make written submissions—that group, again, was composed principally of lawyers but also included a small number of nonlawyers (Colin Rule, Co-Founder and COO of Modria,[57] John Suh, CEO of LegalZoom,[58] Richard Barton, Co-founder and Executive Chairman of Zillow[59] and Mark Britton, CEO of Avvo[60]).

Could the consultation process conducted by either Commission be described as "extensive?" That could be debated, both in regard to the questions each Commission posed and the persons and organizations it involved in its search for responses. Regardless of the outcome of that debate, there is at least one fundamental question that neither Commission dared to pose, and certain persons and organizations that neither dared to involve in the consultation process—persons who in all likelihood would have raised that question as well as offered their responses to it.

That question is this: To what extent does the role the ABA and state and local bar associations play in excluding nonlawyers, be they individuals or nonlawyer-owned organizations, from the legal services market violate unfair competition and antitrust laws and policies?

Concerns about the anti-competitive or antitrust nature of certain actions and policies of the ABA and of state and local bar associations had been raised well before the 20/20 Commission was convened in 2009. Examples include:

- The Federal Trade Commission (FTC) and the Department of Justice, who, on a large number of occasions over a period of decades,[61] have opined that practice rules proposed by bar organizations, notably proposed rules that define the practice of law, "unduly restrain competition" with the result of "forc[ing] consumers to pay increased prices."[62]
- The American Antitrust Institute (AAI), who, as far back as 2000, argued that the ABA's repeated refusal to lift its ban on multidisciplinary practices "raise[s] serious issues of our national policy favoring competition and consumer choice, rising even to the level of a possible violation of the antitrust laws."[63]
- In 2003 (six years before he was appointed Chief Reporter for the 20/20 Commission and eleven years before he was appointed Vice Chair of the Futures Commission), Andrew Perlman wrote that "the ABA's structural rules—the rules that have the most to do with the business aspects of the profession—have emphasized self-protection and public image at the expense of more appropriate emphases."[64] In a second article published in 2004, Perlman recounts a history, notably since the Great Depression, of bar associations engaging in economic protectionism, in that case specifically with respect to admission rules for out-of-state lawyers.[65]

In February, 2015, just a few months after the Futures Commission began its work, these already repeatedly raised concerns were raised again, this time by no less than the US Supreme Court, in its decision *North Carolina Board of Dental Examiners v. FTC*. In this case, the North Carolina dental board, consisting mostly of practicing dentists, took certain actions to keep non-dentists from offering teeth-whitening services in North Carolina. The FTC sued the dental board under federal antitrust laws, claiming anticompetitive conduct. However, the issue before the Supreme Court was not if the actions of the dental board were anticompetitive. Instead, the issue was whether the dental board was acting under a doctrine that would give it, as a "state actor," immunity from claims of anti-competitive conduct in violation of federal antitrust law. The dental board claimed that is was a state actor and thus was eligible for such immunity, on the grounds that an act of the North Carolina legislature appointed the dental board as the "agency of the State for the regulation of the practice of dentistry."[66] The Court, however, disagreed, stating that "active market participants cannot be allowed to regulate their own markets free from antitrust accountability" and that "prohibitions against anticompetitive self-regulation by active market participants are an axiom of federal antitrust policy." Additionally, the Supreme Court stated "The question is not whether the challenged conduct is efficient, well-functioning, or wise . . . [t]he question is whether the State's review mechanisms provide 'realistic assurance' that a [private party]'s anticompetitive conduct 'promotes state policy, rather than merely the party's individual interests.'"[67]

While this case involved the dental rather than the legal profession, the decision of the court is highly pertinent for the legal profession, and for legal services more generally. It places anti-competitive actions by any group of "active market participants"—such as bar associations—under intensified scrutiny.[68] Its relevance has not gone unnoticed by the ABA, which created a page on its website devoted exclusively to the case and the issues it raises with respect to legal services.[69] This page contains links to articles opining on those very issues. For example, acting as a guest columnist in Forbes magazine, Ken Friedman, vice president of Legal and Government Affairs for LegalZoom, wrote:

> The Court's ruling recognizes that letting professionals enforce their own monopolies creates a "real danger" that they will act to further their "own interests," rather than the public interest. These practices increase prices to the detriment of consumers while decreasing consumer choice. The Court recognized that the problem is far worse when the boundaries of the state-granted monopoly are not "clearly articulated and affirmatively expressed as state policy," and the professionals are given the power to decide what is the "unauthorized practice" of their profession . . .
>
> Bar associations across the country use their power to limit competition. For example, states prohibit law firms from including non-lawyer partners or accepting investment from non-attorneys. Bars justify these rules arguing they are necessary to maintain independence and lawyer loyalty to clients, but they cannot point to evidence of harm should a lawyer partner with an accountant,

> engineer, or outside investor. In the United Kingdom and Australia, where those rules have been relaxed, there have not been reports of such harm.
>
> What this really boils down to is reversing actions by state bars that have blocked people from getting the legal help they need.[70]

A May, 2015 article appearing in the ABA Journal quoted Professor Deborah Rhode of Stanford Law School as follows:

> [I]t is hard to characterize this decision as narrow. . . . I think it signals the willingness of the court to look behind the facade of state-action doctrine to determine whether there is real anticompetitive activity benefiting the members [of the regulated group]. . . . I think the legal profession needs to take a hard look at its own activities in the area of the unauthorized practice of law. . . . It would be a good thing if it did so.[71]

In *North Carolina Board of Dental Examiners v. FTC*, the Supreme Court stated that "[t]he question is whether the State's review mechanisms provide 'realistic assurance' that a [private party]'s anticompetitive conduct 'promotes state policy, rather than merely the party's individual interests.'"[72] The documents described in (2) above issued by the Supreme Courts of Pennsylvania and of Georgia and by the NOBC and CCJ evidence that, with respect to the regulation of legal services, it would be impossible for a state's review mechanism to provide any kind of "realistic assurance" because, in fact, there is no state review mechanism to speak of—the regulators have abdicated their regulatory responsibilities to persons who can only be described as "active market participants."

Of course, it is possible to disagree with these observations. For example, a counterargument might be asserted that it is state supreme courts that have the de jure right to regulate legal services, and at any moment they could simply choose to exercise greater oversight over the work of the ABA and state and local bar associations.

The question of whether or not, in the end, any one or more actions or policies of the ABA or any state or local bar association effectively do, in any final analysis, violate unfair competition or antitrust laws or policies, is an important one. But it's not the focus of this discussion. The focus of this discussion is that both Commissions failed to raise the question. They failed to do so even though Judy Martinez, the chair of the Futures Commission, stated that "nothing is off the table," even ideas that seemed too radical.[73] They failed to do so even though, over a period of many years, a number of persons and organizations, including Andrew Perlman (the chief reporter of the 20/20 Commission and the vice-chair of the Futures Commission) and the US Supreme Court, had put the question on the table. Those persons and organizations had put the question on the table in a repeated manner and for legitimate and justified reasons. Yet, in the plethora of questions that both the 20/20 and the Futures Commissions posed, not one acknowledged this fundamental issue or attempted to initiate a discussion in its regard. Further, there is nothing in the public record demonstrating that in the course of their respective consultation processes either Commission sought the input of, for example, experts in antitrust and unfair competition from the FTC, the US Department of Justice,[74] or the AAI. They, presumably, would not have hesitated to put the question on the table, or to provide their responses to it.

To the contrary, on the home page of its website, the Futures Commission affirms that "The American Bar Association (ABA) is well-positioned to lead the effort to improve the delivery of, and access to, legal services in the United States."[75] In December, 2015, ten months after the *North Carolina* decision, the Futures Commission repeated this assertion in its Informational Report to the House of Delegates,[76] and in August, 2016 it again repeated it in its Final Report.[77]

It is easy to understand why both Commissions chose to ignore the question. Indeed, back in 2004, Clementi predicted this choice, when he stated it is "particularly difficult for professional bodies that combine both regulatory and representative roles to deal with competition issues."[78] Raising the question would have invited criticism of the organization itself. It might have placed into question the very legitimacy of the Commissions, and it could have led to a loss of some or all of the ABA's de facto or quasi-regulatory power. Very few organizations have the necessary courage to voluntarily initiate such discussions.[79] At the same time, however, the fact that the ABA fails to raise much less to address a question that is highly central to the debate of how to better deliver legal services demonstrates the incongruity, if not the absurdity, of entrusting the debate to the ABA. As long as there are highly relevant questions that the ABA regards as taboo, and as long as there are persons and organizations the ABA is not willing to involve in its consultation processes, out of fear that they might raise (and respond to) those taboo questions, both the effectiveness and the integrity of the debate are necessarily compromised.

NOTES

1. ABA Commission on the Future of Legal Services, "National Summit on Innovation in Legal Services," accessed on March 20, 2017, http://www.americanbar.org/groups/centers_commissions/commission-on-the-future-of-legal-services/national_summit.html.

2. ABA Commission on the Future of Legal Services, "Upcoming & Past Events," accessed March 17, 2017, http://www.americanbar.org/groups/centers_commissions/commission-on-the-future-of-legal-services/events-new.html.

3. Charles Harrington, "Customer Service and the Courts," slides at: http://www.americanbar.org/content/dam/aba/images/office_president/charles_harringon_focus_on_the_client_slides.pdf and video presentation at: http://bcove.me/p38g7l0m.

4. Keith McLennan, ABA Standing Committee on Group & Prepaid Legal Services and Group Legal Services Association, video presentation: http://bcove.me/ki6oyi77.

5. Stephen R. Crossland, "Limited License Legal Technician Program," slides at http://www.americanbar.org/content/dam/aba/images/office_president/stephen_crossland_programs_to_bridge_the_gap_slide.pdf and video presentation at: http://bcove.me/6wa30tz8.

6. Andrew Perlman, "Innovation in Legal Education," slides at: http://www.americanbar.org/content/dam/aba/images/office_president/andy_perlman_programs_to_bridge_the_gap_slides.pdf and video presentation at: http://bcove.me/ygsgfnp4.

7. Alex R. Gulotta, video presentation at: http://bcove.me/kjkazo82.

8. Gillian Hadfield and Larry Fox, "Regulating the Future Delivery of Legal Services," webinar, http://bcove.me/la7z1w1b.

9. See ABA Commission on Ethics 20/20, "House of Delegates Filings," http://www.americanbar.org/groups/professional_responsibility/aba_commission_on_ethics_20_20/house_of_delegates_filings.html.

10. Terry, "Globalization and the ABA Commission on Ethics 20/20," 113.

11. "[Draft] Regulatory Objectives of the Supreme Court of Colorado," November 12, 2015, http://www.americanbar.org/content/dam/aba/images/office_president/supreme_court_of_colorado.pdf;

12. ABA Commission on Ethics 20/20, "Minutes," February 4, 2010, 9.

13. ABA Commission on Ethics 20/20, "Minutes," April 29, 2010, 7.

14. Ibid.

15. ABA Commission on Ethics 20/20, "Minutes," February 10, 2011, 6–7.

16. ABA Commission on Ethics 20/20, "Minutes," April 15–16, 2011, 8–9; ABA Commission on Ethics 20/20, "Minutes," June 13, 2011, 7.

17. ABA Commission on the Future of Legal Services, "Issues Paper on the Future of Legal Services," 3.

18. Chas Rampenthal and James Peters (LegalZoom). Task Force on the Evolving Business Model of Law Firms.

19. ABA Standing Committee on Professional Discipline.

20. ABA Commission on the Future of Legal Services, "Informational Report to the House of Delegates," 3.

21. Laurel Terry describes the ABA as a "quasi-regulator." Terry, "Globalization and the ABA Commission on Ethics 20/20," 95.

22. For a detailed discussion of the abdication of regulatory power by state supreme courts in favor of the ABA and other bar associations, see Snyder, *Democratizing Legal Services*, 199–206.

23. See, for example, Judith L. Maute, "Global Continental Shifts in a New Governance Paradigm," 30.

24. See, for example, American Bar Association, "Lawyer Regulation for A New Century," accessed on March 20, 2017, http://www.americanbar.org/groups/professional_responsibility/resources/report_archive/mckay_report.html.

25. ABA Commission on Ethics 20/20, "Preliminary Issues Outline," November 19, 2009, 1, http://www.americanbar.org/content/dam/aba/migrated/ethics2020/outline.authcheckdam.pdf.

26. ABA Commission on the Future of Legal Services, "Issues Paper Concerning New Categories of Legal Services Providers," 1.

27. See, for example, Barton, "The Lawyer's Monopoly," 3080–3081.

28. Benjamin Barton provides a detailed and interesting analysis of the extent to which state supreme courts abdicate their regulatory power and the multiple motivations they have to do so: Benjamin H. Barton, "An Institutional Analysis of Lawyer Regulation: Who Should Control Lawyer Regulation-Courts, Legislatures, or the Market?" *Georgia Law Review* 37 (2003): 1167–1250.

29. Sally Evans Lockwood, Letter to ABA Commission on Ethics 20/20 Working Group on Inbound Foreign Lawyers, July 5, 2010, http://www.americanbar.org/content/dam/aba/administrative/ethics_2020/ethics_20_20_comments/supremecourtofgeorgiaofficeofbaradmissions_inboundforeignlawyersmemorandaandtemplate.authcheckdam.pdf.

30. Stephanie S. Libhart, Letter to ABA Commission on Ethics 20/20, October 4, 2012, http://www.americanbar.org/content/dam/aba/administrative/ethics_2020/ethics_20_20_comments/pa_iolta_board_of_the_supreme_court_comments_pro_hac_vice_admission.authcheckdam.pdf.

31. "Mission Statement," National Organization of Bar Counsel, accessed March 20, 2017, http://www.nobc.org/index.php/about-us/mission-statement.

32. National Organization of Bar Counsel, "Comments to 'Issues Paper Concerning New Categories of Legal Services Providers,'" December 21, 2015, http://www.americanbar.org/content/dam/aba/images/office_president/lspcomments_national_organization_of_bar_counsel.pdf.

33. Futures Commission Final Report, 6.

34. Conference of Chief Justices, "Resolution 9: Recommending Consideration of ABA Model Regulatory Objectives for the Provision of Legal Services," February 3, 2016, https://richardzorza.files.wordpress.com/2016/02/ccj-2016-res-9.pdf.

35. Barton discusses the lack of public accountability by judges who regulate legal profession in his article "An Institutional Analysis of Lawyer Regulation," 1200–1204. For a detailed discussion of the ABA's lack of public accountability, see Snyder, *Democratizing Legal Services*, 212–213.

36. See, for example: American Bar Association, "Message from the Co-Chairs: Message from Commission on Ethics 20/20 Co-Chairs Jamie S. Gorelick and Michael Traynor," accessed on March 20, 2017, http://www.americanbar.org/groups/professional_responsibility/aba_commission_on_ethics_20_20/about_us/message_from_the_co_chairs.html; ABA Commission on Ethics 20/20," Informational Report to the House of Delegates, February, 2010 and February, 2011, both available at: http://www.americanbar.org/groups/professional_responsibility/aba_commission_on_ethics_20_20/house_of_delegates_filings.html; ABA Commission on Ethics 20/20 Working Group on Alternative Business Structures, "For Comment: Issues Paper Concerning Alternative Business Structures, April 5, 2011, http://www.americanbar.org/content/dam/aba/administrative/ethics_2020/abs_issues_paper.authcheckdam.pdf; Jamie S. Gorelick and Michael Traynor, "For Comment: Discussion Paper on

Alternative Law Practice Structures," December 2, 2011, http://www.americanbar.org/content/dam/aba/administrative/ethics_2020/20111202-ethics2020-discussion_draft-alps.authcheckdam.pdf. See also a manifestation of this duplicity in this paragraph contained in the Preamble to the Model Rules:

> The legal profession is largely self-governing. Although other professions also have been granted powers of self-government, the legal profession is unique in this respect because of the close relationship between the profession and the processes of government and law enforcement. This connection is manifested in the fact that ultimate authority over the legal profession is vested largely in the courts. . . . To the extent that lawyers meet the obligations of their professional calling, the occasion for government regulation is obviated.
>
> http://www.americanbar.org/groups/professional_responsibility/publications/model_rules_of_professional_conduct/model_rules_of_professional_conduct_preamble_scope.html.

37. ABA Commission on Ethics 20/20, "Outreach," accessed on March 20, 2017, http://www.americanbar.org/groups/professional_responsibility/aba_commission_on_ethics_20_20/outreach.html.

38. ABA Commission on Ethics 20/20, "Preliminary Issues Outline," 2; American Bar Association, "Message from the Co-Chairs: Message from Commission on Ethics 20/20 Co-Chairs Jamie S. Gorelick and Michael Traynor," accessed on March 20, 2017, http://www.americanbar.org/groups/professional_responsibility/aba_commission_on_ethics_20_20/about_us/message_from_the_co_chairs.html; ABA Commission on Ethics 20/20, "Report to the House of Delegates: Resolution 105A," August, 2012, 10, http://www.americanbar.org/content/dam/aba/administrative/ethics_2020/2012_hod_annual_meeting_105a_filed_may_2012.authcheckdam.pdf.

39. ABA Commission on Ethics 20/20, "Minutes," February 10, 2011, 6.

40. Ibid.

41. ABA Commission on Ethics 20/20, "ABA Commission on Ethics 20/20 Will Not Propose Changes."

42. Kenneth Grady, Video Testimony to the ABA Commission on the Future of Legal Services, 1:15 to 1:54, February, 2015, http://bcove.me/x9hwfqsq.

43. Ibid., 3:22 to 3:38.

44. ABA Commission on the Future of Legal Services, "Legal Services Grass Roots Resources," accessed March 17, 2017, http://www.americanbar.org/groups/centers_commissions/commission-on-the-future-of-legal-services/legal-services-grass-roots-resources.html.

45. Agenda for Sustainable Development," 25.

46. Douglas R. Richmond, "Discussion Paper on Alternative Law Practice Structures," January 6, 2012, 1–2, http://www.americanbar.org/content/dam/aba/administrative/ethics_2020/ethics_20_20_comments/richmond_alpsdiscussiondraft.authcheckdam.pdf.

47. Thies, Letter to the ABA Commission on Ethics 20/20, 3.

48. Los Angeles County Bar Association, "Comment of the Los Angeles County Bar Association," 3.

49. DRI – The Voice of the Defense Bar, "Issues Paper Regarding Alternative Business Structures," 2.

50. Futures Commission Final Report, 18.
51. Ibid., 5.
52. Ibid., 18.
53. Ibid., 43.
54. Ibid., 18
55. Ibid., 6.
56. ABA Commission on the Future of Legal Services, "Informational Report to the House of Delegates," 1–2, 6.
57. Colin Rule, "Online Dispute Resolution: Expanding Access to Justice" (presentation to 2015 National Summit on Innovation in Legal Services, Stanford, California, May 3, 2015) http://www.americanbar.org/content/dam/aba/images/office_president/colin_rule_programs_to_bridge_the_gap_slides.pdf; video of presentation at: http://bcove.me/aysp906c.
58. John Suh, "Democratizing Law" (presentation to 2015 National Summit on Innovation in Legal Services, Stanford, California, May 4, 2015), http://www.americanbar.org/content/dam/aba/images/office_president/john_suh_slides.pdf.
59. Richard Barton, May 4, 2015 video of presentation available at: http://bcove.me/k5xf2812.
60. Mark Britton, "Avvo: National Summit on Innovation in Legal Services" (presentation to 2015 National Summit on Innovation in Legal Services, Stanford, California, May 3, 2015) http://www.americanbar.org/content/dam/aba/images/office_president/mark_britton_challenges_to_innovation_slides.pdf; video of presentation at http://bcove.me/vz01uvx2.
61. A list of links to such opinions is accessible at ABA Center for Professional Responsibility, "FTC Letter Opinions on the Unlicensed Practice of Law," accessed on March 20, 2017, http://www.americanbar.org/groups/professional_responsibility/resources/client_protection/ftc.html. See also, for example, Thomas R. Andrews, "Nonlawyers in the Business of Law: Does the One Who Has the Gold Really Make the Rules?" *The Hastings Law Journal* 40 (1989): 617–621.
62. Federal Trade Commission and US Department of Justice, Letter to Kansas Bar Association, February 4, 2005, 1–2, https://www.ftc.gov/sites/default/files/documents/advocacy_documents/ftc-and-department-justice-comment-kansas-bar-association-concerning-proposed-definition-practice/v050002.pdf.
63. American Antitrust Institute, "AAI Says Legal Profession's Recommendations on Multidisciplinary Practices May Violate Antitrust Laws," February 8, 2000, http://www.antitrustinstitute.org/content/aai-says-legal-professions-recommendations-multidisciplinary-practices-may-violate-antitrust.
64. Andrew M. Perlman, "Toward a Unified Theory of Professional Regulation," *Florida Law Review* 55 (2003): 999, http://dx.doi.org/10.2139/ssrn.449200.
65. Andrew M. Perlman, "A Bar Against Competition: The Unconstitutionality of Admission Rules for Out-of-State Lawyers," *Georgetown Journal of Legal Ethics* 18 (2004): 148–150, http://ssrn.com/abstract=664194.
66. North Carolina State Board of Dental Examiners v. Federal Trade Commission, February 25, 2015, 6, http://www.supremecourt.gov/opinions/14pdf/13-534_19m2.pdf.

67. Ibid., 2, 8–9.

68. See, for example, Hadfield and Rhode, "How to Regulate Legal Services," 1194–1195, 1214–1215. See also Ken Friedman, "Could Dental-Board Decision Unlock Lawyer Control of State Bar Regulations?" *Forbes*, March 4, 2016, http://www.forbes.com/sites/danielfisher/2015/03/04/dental-board-decision-could-unlock-lawyer-control/#75de2e7b68cf.; and Tamara Tabo, "What Lawyers Must Learn From Dentists About The Unauthorized Practice Of Law," *Above the Law*, March 2, 2015, http://abovethelaw.com/2015/03/what-lawyers-must-learn-from-dentists-about-the-unauthorized-practice-of-law/?rf=1.

69. ABA Center for Professional Responsibility, "North Carolina Board of Dental Examiners Decision Resources," accessed on March 17, 2017, http://www.americanbar.org/groups/professional_responsibility/resources/client_protection/north-carolina-board-of-dental-examiners-decision-resources.html.

70. Friedman, "Could Dental-Board Decision Unlock Lawyer Control of State Bar Regulations?"

71. Mark Walsh, "Dental Board Ruling May Drill into State Bar Associations' Immunity," *ABA Journal*, May 1, 2015, http://www.abajournal.com/magazine/article/dental_board_ruling_may_drill_into_state_bar_associations_immunity.

72. North Carolina State Board of Dental Examiners v. Federal Trade Commission, 9.

73. Marilyn Cavicchia, "Which Way Forward?: National Conference of Bar Presidents Discusses Possible Futures for the Profession and for Bar Associations," *Bar Leader* 39 (March-April 2015) http://www.americanbar.org/publications/bar_leader/2014-15/march-april/which-way-forward-national-conference-bar-presidents-discusses-possible-futures-profession-bar-associations.html.

74. Lisa Foster, director of the Office for Access to Justice of the US Department of Justice, reportedly met with representatives of the Futures Commission on at least one occasion. She does not have expertise in antitrust or unfair competition law. It appears that she did not raise issues of antitrust or unfair competition but instead "called for each state to develop its own legal help portal, where users could post a legal problem or question and get directed to potential answers." "Highlights from the ABA's National Summit on Innovation in Legal Services," 3 Geeks and a Law Blog, June 4, 2015, http://www.geeklawblog.com/2015/06/highlights-from-abas-national-summit-on.html. See also James Podgers, "Lots of Ideas, But No Single Theme at Commission on the Future of Legal Services' Public Hearing," *ABA Journal*, February 7, 2015, http://www.abajournal.com/news/article/lots_of_ideas_but_no_single_theme_at_commission_on_the_future_of_legal_serv; "Lisa Foster: Director, Office for Access to Justice, U.S. Department of Justice," accessed on March 18, 2016, http://www.americanbar.org/content/dam/aba/images/office_president/foster_short_bio.pdf.

75. Commission on the Future of Legal Services, "Background," accessed March 20, 2017, http://www.americanbar.org/groups/centers_commissions/commission-on-the-future-of-legal-services.html.

76. ABA Commission on the Future of Legal Services, "Informational Report to the House of Delegates," 1.

77. Futures Commission Final Report, 9.

78. Clementi Report, 29.

79. That being said, and in stark contrast to the ABA, the Legal Services Board of England and Wales has expressly placed on its agenda "our proposal for how the LSB and other regulators can be phased out over time." Legal Services Board, "LSB Publishes Annual Report for 2013/14," June 10, 2014, http://www.legalservicesboard.org.uk/news_publications/LSB_news/PDF/2014/20140610_LSB_Annual_Report_Published.htm.

Chapter 22

The Outliers

Washington DC, Colorado and Illinois

As great, even as hegemonic,[1] as the ABA's regulatory power is, it is not omnipotent. This is evidenced by the unique paths that first Washington D.C. and, very recently, Colorado and Illinois, have chosen to take.

WASHINGTON D.C.

As mentioned above, in 1986, after the Kutak Commission, the District of Columbia took its own path. Mark Lynch, a member of the D.C. Bar Ethics Committee, later explained: "The committee perceived a market demand for one-stop shopping—for collaborative services of lawyers with such other professionals as accountants, lobbyists, social workers and economists."[2]

As a result, Lynch advocated for a rule that would permit lawyers to partner with nonlawyers to provide legal services, and a rule very similar to the draft rule of the Kutak Commission was proposed to the D.C. Board of Governors.[3]

The Board raised several concerns about the proposed rule: did it adequately address conflicts of interest, would it adequately protect attorney-client privilege, did it adequately assure that nonlawyers would not commit acts that, if committed by a lawyer, would violate ethical rules? As a result of these concerns, the version of the rule that the Board submitted for the approval of the D.C. Court of Appeals in 1986 was modified to limit the activities of the partnership to the practice of law. (Interestingly, a member of the D.C. Board of Governors who raised many of these concerns later served as co-chair of the ABA Commission on Ethics 20/20: Jamie Gorelick, a partner with Wilmer Hale).[4]

The Court of Appeals had its own concerns, notably the same one of the Kutak Commission itself—the "fear of Sears." Those concerns led to additional modification of the rule—to require that a nonlawyer may be a partner only if the nonlawyer performs professional services that assist the firm in providing legal services.[5]

The rule that D.C. ultimately adopted in 1990 reads as follows:

> Rule 5.4—Professional Independence of a Lawyer
> (a) A lawyer or law firm shall not share legal fees with a nonlawyer, except that: . . . .
> (4) Sharing of fees is permitted in a partnership or other form of organization which meets the requirements of paragraph (b) . . .
> (b) A lawyer may practice law in a partnership or other form of organization in which a financial interest is held or managerial authority is exercised by an individual nonlawyer who performs professional services which assist the organization in providing legal services to clients, but only if:
> (1) The partnership or organization has as its sole purpose providing legal services to clients;
> (2) All persons having such managerial authority or holding a financial interest undertake to abide by these Rules of Professional Conduct;
> (3) The lawyers who have a financial interest or managerial authority in the partnership or organization undertake to be responsible for the nonlawyer participants to the same extent as if nonlawyer participants were lawyers under Rule 5.1;
> (4) The foregoing conditions are set forth in writing.
> (c) A lawyer shall not permit a person who recommends, employs, or pays the lawyer to render legal services for another to direct or regulate the lawyer's professional judgment in rendering such legal services.[6]

While no statistics are kept on the number of firms that have taken advantage of D.C.'s Rule 5.4, it is generally believed that few firms have done so. Hope Todd, Assistant Director for Legal Ethics, Regulation Counsel of the District of Columbia Bar explains that in her opinion, this is for two reasons: the first is that the Rule is very restrictive. It both limits the services the structure may provide to legal services only (MDPs are not permitted), and, by requiring nonlawyer shareholders to provide professional services to the structure, excludes passive investment. The second reason is because most of the lawyers admitted in D.C. are also admitted to the bar in one or more US states, and none of those states have a comparable rule. As a result, those lawyers may be afraid to take advantage of D.C.'s Rule 5.4 because in doing so they may be found to be in violation of the rules of another jurisdiction.[7]

First-hand perspectives

Hope C. Todd, Assistant Director for Legal Ethics, Regulation Counsel, District of Columbia Bar (online): Todd explains why, in her opinion,

Washington D.C.'s experience with its Rule 5.4 has been disappointing in its ability to serve as a pilot or model for other states.

Saul Singer, Senior Legal Ethics Counsel, District of Columbia Bar (online): Singer explains why any firms seeking to take advantage of Washington D.C.'s Rule 5.4 can do so only with great care.

Wallace E. "Gene" Shipp, Jr., Bar Counsel and Lawrence Bloom, Senior Staff Attorney, DC Office of Bar Counsel (online): Shipp and Bloom explain that DC's Office of Bar Counsel has never been presented with any complaint, and the Office has never investigated any firm, in connection with nonlawyer ownership of a law firm.

COLORADO

As compared to Washington D.C., Colorado's status as an outlier is much more recent, and the changes in Colorado are still a work in progress. As the changes take shape, they appear to be inspired most directly by the Canadian province of Nova Scotia:

In 2015, the Colorado Supreme Court formed a Proactive Management-Based Regulation (PMBR) Subcommittee. The Supreme Court's website describes the membership of the Subcommittee as including a large variety of persons such as members of the Supreme Court Advisory Committee, Colorado Bar Association leadership and staff members, sole practitioners and other private practice lawyers, a law firm administrator, a Better Business Bureau representative, an Office of the Presiding Disciplinary Judge staff attorney, the executive director of the Colorado Lawyers Assistance Program, Attorney Regulation Counsel and staff members.[8]

The Subcommittee's first order of business was the development of Regulatory Objectives for approval by the Colorado Supreme Court. The Subcommittee developed nine objectives, including:

- Enhancing client protection and promoting consumer confidence through [. . .], the regulation of non-lawyers engaged in providing legal services, and other proactive programs;
- Assisting providers of legal services in maintaining competence and professionalism through [. . .] proactive programs;
- Helping legal service providers throughout the stages of their careers successfully navigate the practice of law and thus better serve their clients, through [. . .] proactive programs and
- Promoting access to justice and consumer choice in the availability and affordability of competent legal services.[9]

Based upon a superficial reading, these objectives may not appear remarkable. However, a closer reading reveals the contrary. They are remarkable for a number of reasons:

They do not refer to the regulation of lawyers at all. Instead, they refer to the regulation of "non-lawyers engaged in providing legal services" and "providers of legal services." In this manner, the Colorado Supreme Court states very clearly its intentions both to allow for non-lawyers to provide legal services and to regulate them.

They refer to "proactive programs" not once, not twice, but three times. Clearly, the development and implementation of "proactive programs" is a priority for the Colorado Supreme Court.

The reference to the promotion of consumer choice is slightly more ambiguous, but, when considered along with the references to "providers of legal services," it could be interpreted as openness to new kinds of business models, such as alternative structures. Certainly, in contrast to the ABA's regulatory objectives, Colorado's regulatory objectives leave the door to alternative structures open.

Another reason why Colorado's regulatory objectives are remarkable is found in its preamble, which includes the sentence "Legal service providers must be regulated in the public interest." No other regulator of lawyers or of legal services in the United States, be it de jure or de facto, has ever made a statement of this kind, much less posed it as the guiding principal behind its regulatory activities. The ABA's regulatory objectives make reference to "protection of the public," but this is not the same thing. To begin, the expression "protection of the public" is ambiguous—exactly what does it mean? Further, it could be argued that "less" protection of the public (for example, in the form of a non-fully qualified lawyer providing legal services) could sometimes be in the public interest. In contrast, the statement "legal service providers must be regulated in the public interest" is not ambiguous. It makes clear that in regulating legal services, the Colorado Supreme Court will (or at least should) prioritize the interests of the public over the interests of the legal profession.

The Subcommittee's second order of business was the development of "a Proactive Management-Based Regulation program." The goal of this program is "to assist lawyers in implementing and maintaining effective management systems for ethical law practice." The program includes "ten common principles, or elements, that are encouraged for any law firm's ethical infrastructure." At the time this book went to press, the Subcommittee was in the late stages of developing a self-evaluation tool for those ten categories, "so law firms have effective management systems in place to address these common risks."[10] In looking at the tool, it is clear that it was heavily inspired by comparable tools developed by the Nova Scotia Barrister's Society and the Canadian Bar Association as well as the Colorado Supreme Court's own "Self-Audit Checklist."[11] At the time this book went to press, the Subcommittee was still considering how the tool would be rolled out and used. The Subcommittee appeared to prefer that its use by members of the Colorado bar would be "incentive-based and voluntary, not mandatory." Proposals for how to incentivize its use included offering a cost/benefit analysis, continuing legal education credit and/or public recognition through certification.[12]

Nothing in the Colorado Supreme Court's explanation of its work mentions alternative structures. Nevertheless, the work that Court is undertaking, if successful, will begin to lay a regulatory groundwork for them.

First-hand perspective

James Coyle, Attorney Regulation Counsel, Colorado Supreme Court (online): Coyle explains that Colorado is taking "baby steps." It is doing this by examining the systems of England and Wales, Australia and the various provinces of Canada, selecting the most desired parts of those systems, and adapting them to Colorado.

ILLINOIS

On January 25, 2017 the Illinois Supreme Court adopted an amended Rule 756(e), for entry into effect in 2018. Under the amended rule, Illinois lawyers in private practice who do not have malpractice insurance will be required, every other year, to complete an online self-assessment regarding professional responsibility requirements for the operation of a law firm. In what appears to be attempt to be sure it is not merely a "check the box" exercise, the Rule expressly states that "the self-assessment shall require that the lawyer demonstrate an engagement in learning about those requirements." Further, the lawyer must assess his or her law firm's operation based upon the requirements. While the Rule makes it clear that completing the form is not optional, it offers something back to the lawyer: four hours of continuing legal education credit. Finally, presumably in order to encourage lawyers to complete the self-assessment honestly and in good faith, the Rule explains that while aggregated data from completed self-assessments may be made public, the information that an individual lawyer provides shall remain confidential. Most notably, it may not be offered as evidence in any disciplinary proceeding.[13]

In its press release announcing the Rule, the Supreme Court took pride in being the first state in the nation to adopt PRBR. The Court explained that the change is intended to "help minimize" the risks that lawyers face in the private practice of law, and to help them to avoid disciplinary problems before they occur. The Court further explained that the change was based upon a multiyear study of PMBR initiatives in other countries and the United States, and that the change was adopted after consultation with "key Illinois stakeholders," which the court seemed to define as "bar association and lawyer groups." In spite of that narrow definition of stakeholders, the press release asserted that "PMBR promises a new level of protection for the public."[14]

Chief Justice Lloyd Karmeier is quoted in the press release stating that the Court is optimistic that PMBR will be "embraced" by practicing attorneys with enthusiasm.[15] While "embrace" might not be entirely accurate, "accepted" might be, in that, at the time this book went to press in early 2017, the amended Rule seemed to have attracted little attention much less objection by Illinois lawyers.[16]

In an interview with the author of this book, James Grogan, Deputy Administrator and Chief Counsel of the Illinois Attorney Registration and Disciplinary Commission (ARDC, the administrative agency of the Illinois Supreme Court charged with licensing, regulating and disciplining Illinois lawyers),[17] explained the Court's—and the ARDC's—work on the amended Rule as follows: As regulators gain more experience as well as professionalism, it is "natural" that regulators seek to regulate "better," and seek to be more proactive rather than reactive. That being said, Grogan clarified that the regulatory changes that are adopted in Illinois will be directed to lawyers as individuals, and not to law firms or other entities. This is in part, Grogan stated, because the ARDC does not have the authority to regulate entities. Further, the ARDC does not intend to seek any such authority because, in the opinion of the ARDC, "given how often lawyers move among firms, entity regulation would be a moving target." Further, Grogan asserted, "we can get to an entity via its individuals, on the grounds that a partner was not properly managing his or her office."

Grogan underlined that for the ARDC, PMBR is not connected to alternative structures, or, at least, that it does not need to be. For the ARDC, the principal or at least the most immediate purpose of PMBR is to help lawyers, and sole practitioners in particular, to avoid regulators to provide "optimum service" to their clients. That being said, Grogan stated, even if the ARDC's current focus is on PMBR, "everything is on the table for review."

First-hand perspective

James Grogan, Deputy Administrator and Chief Counsel, Illinois Attorney Registration and Disciplinary Commission (online): Grogan explains that for the ARDC, the principal purpose of PMBR is to help lawyers, and sole practitioners in particular, to have successful careers.

NOTES

1. Devlin and Morison, "Access to Justice," 526.

2. Roberta S. Karmel, "Will Law Firms Go Public?" *University of Pennsylvania Journal of International Law* 35 (2014): 500, http://scholarship.law.upenn.edu/jil/vol35/iss2/4.

3. Ibid., 500.

4. Ibid., 500–501; "People: Jamie Gorelick," Wilmer Hale, accessed March 20, 2017, https://www.wilmerhale.com/jamie_gorelick/.

5. Karmel, "Will Law Firms Go Public?" 501–502.

6. "Rules of Professional Conduct: Rule 5.4--Professional Independence of a Lawyer," DC Bar, accessed March 20, 2017, http://www.dcbar.org/bar-resources/legal-ethics/amended-rules/rule5-04.cfm.

7. Interview with author, December, 2014, available at http://notjustforlawyers.com/hope-todd/.

8. Jim Coyle, "Subcommittee Turns to Proactive Regulation," Colorado Supreme Court, Winter 2016, http://www.coloradosupremecourt.com/newsletters/winter2016/Subcommittee%20turns%20to%20proactive%20regulation.htm.

9. Colorado Supreme Court, "Rule Change 2016(06): Chapters 18 to 20 Rules Governing the Practice of Law," April 7, 2016, http://www.coloradosupremecourt.com/PDF/AboutUs/2016(06)%20clean%20-%20PREAMBLE%20(regulatory%20objectives)%20ADOPTED%2004-07-16.pdf.

10. Coyle, "Subcommittee Turns to Proactive Regulation."

11. Ibid, referencing Nova Scotia Barristers' Society, A Management System for Ethical Legal Practice," March 2016), http://nsbs.org/sites/default/files/cms/page/2016-03-29_revisedmselpselfassessment.pdf; The Canadian Bar Association, "CBA Ethical Practices Self-Evaluation Tool," http://www.coloradosupremecourt.com/Newsletters/Winter2016/Canadian%20Bar%20Association's%20Ethical%20Practices%20Self-Evaluation%20Tool.pdf; Colorado Supreme Court, "Self-Audit Checklist," http://www.coloradosupremecourt.com/pdfs/Regulation/SELF-AUDIT%20CHECKLIST.pdf.

12. Colorado Supreme Court Attorney Regulation Advisory Committee Subcommittee on Proactive Management-Based Program, "Meeting Minutes," October 19, 2016, http://www.coloradosupremecourt.com/PDF/AboutUs/PMBR/PMBP%20Subcommittee%20Minutes%2010-19-16.pdf; see also Colorado Supreme Court Attorney Regulation Advisory Committee Subcommittee on Proactive Management-Based Program, "Meeting Minutes," January 18, 2017, http://www.coloradosupremecourt.us/PDF/AboutUs/PMBR/PMBP%20Subcommittee%20Minutes%201-18-17.pdf.

13. M.R. 3140 In the Supreme Court of the State Of Illinois: Amended Rule 756, January 25, 2017, 5, http://www.illinoiscourts.gov/SupremeCourt/Rules/Amend/2017/012517_756.pdf.

14. Supreme Court of Illinois, "Illinois Becomes First State to Adopt Proactive Management Based Regulation," January 25, 2017, http://www.illinoiscourts.gov/Media/PressRel/2017/012417.pdf.

15. Ibid., 1.

16. See, for example, Andrew Strickler, "Ill. Likely Set Trend for New Professional Conduct Training," *Law360*, January 27, 2017, https://www.law360.com/articles/885424/ill-likely-set-trend-for-new-professional-conduct-training; see also Mark Mathewson, "Illinois Supreme Court Adopts 'Proactive Management-Based Regulation,'" *Illinois Lawyer Now*, January 27, 2017, https://iln.isba.org/blog/2017/01/25/illinois-supreme-court-adopts-proactive-management-based-regulation.

17. The full interview is available at http://notjustforlawyers.com/james-j-grogan/.

Chapter 23

Effect of Model Rule 5.4 and the Current Regulatory Framework

The current regulatory framework severely restricts who may provide legal services and in what manner they may do so. However, even in the absence of changes to the regulatory framework, certain elements of the legal services market in the United States are being reengineered. During the past few years, many companies have identified gaps in legal services not filled by traditional law firms, and have created new services and new business models to fill them. These companies include the technology companies that ABA President Hubbard mentioned at the time he appointed the Commission on the Future of Legal Services—the companies that received $458 million in investment in 2013.[1]

But in filling those gaps, these companies need to negotiate their way around a highly restrictive regulatory framework, and this has forced them to take one of two paths.

The less risky path has been to craft and market services for law firms themselves or for other companies, and notably for large companies with their own in-house legal departments. This is the path that companies like Axiom Law (legal placement and outsourcing), Lex Machina (legal data analytics), kCura (web-based e-discovery) and Anaqua (intellectual property asset management), to name a few examples, have followed.[2]

In essence, the framework allows for more exceptions if the players are limited to licensed lawyers, and notably if it is in-house lawyers who are making the legal purchasing decisions. These companies have built their business models around those exceptions.[3]

The other path, the one taken by companies that develop and market their services for individual consumers and small businesses, is significantly riskier. RocketLawyer and Shake are two examples of companies whose shareholders and senior management include nonlawyers. Because they sell directly to individuals and small businesses without the intermediary of a licensed lawyer as the purchaser, they must carefully restrict their offerings to avoid running afoul of the Model Rules. For example, RocketLawyer can sell document templates, but it cannot offer the services of its lawyers in direct client support for using those templates. The most it can do is offer an attorney referral service with the option of a limited prepaid legal plan.[4]

In other words, while there certainly are changes taking place in the legal services market, the changes remain limited. Business models have to be tailored to fit within a highly restrictive regulatory framework, and this fact significantly limits what can be done.

The consequences of these limitations are not theoretical. In 2014, when the ABA Commission on the Future of Legal Services was appointed, the World Justice Project Rule of Law Index ranked the United States ranked an already very low 65th out of 99 countries with respect to affordable and accessible civil justice.[5] In 2016, when the Commission finished its work, the United States had fallen to 94th out of 113 countries. Countries like Albania, Belarus, China, Iran, Kazakhstan, Myanmar, Russia, and Zimbabwe provide more affordable and accessible civil justice than the United States does.

NOTES

1. "Welcoming The ABA's New President," *Metropolitan Corporate Counsel.*
2. Snyder, "Does the UK Know Something We Don't."
3. Ibid. This is underscored by Axiom's purchase of only a division of Canada-based Cognition LLP. Axiom purchased the division that serves companies with in-house legal departments, leaving behind the division that serves companies that do not have in-house counsel. See, for example, Mitch Kowalski, "Axiom Gobbles Up Canadian Market Share in Fascinating Deal with Cognition," *Financial Post*, January 20, 2016, http://business.financialpost.com/legal-post/mitch-kowalski-axiom-gobbles-up-canadian-market-share-in-fascinating-deal-with-cognition.
4. Snyder, "Does the UK Know Something We Don't."
5. Danny Foster, "World Justice Project Describes the Failure of America's Legal Services Marketplace," *Responsive Law Blog*, March 14, 2014, http://responsivelaw.org/index.php/blog/item/100-world-justice-project-report?highlight=WyJ3b3JsZCIsIndvcmxkJ3MiLCJqdXN0aWNlIiwiJ2p1c3RpY2UiLCJwcm9qZWN0IiwicHJvam-VjdCdzIiwicnVsZSIsIm9mIiwibGF3IiwibGF3J3MiLCJpbmRleCIsIndvcmxkIG-p1c3RpY2UiLCJ3b3JsZCBqdXN0aWNlIHByb2plY3QiLCJqdXN0aWNlIHByb-2plY3QiLCJydWxlIG9mIiwicnVsZSBvZiBsYXciLCJvZiBsYXciLCJvZiBsYXc-gaW5kZXgiLCJsYXcgaW5kZXgiXQ.

Chapter 24

Assessment

To what extent has the United States implemented the OECD's six essential elements of an effective regulatory policy? For each element, the response lies upon a spectrum, from "yes," "for the most part," "sort of," "limited," "not really" and "no:"

Table 24.1 Assessment for the United States

1	Independent regulation	No	The ABA as de facto regulator holds enormous if not hegemonic power. The ABA is controlled by members of the legal profession. The ABA's first goal is not of public interest but to "serve our members," and its second goal is to "improve our profession"
2	Accountability and transparency	No	Neither the ABA (who holds de facto regulatory power) nor state supreme courts (who hold de jure regulatory authority) are accountable in any formal or informal manner to anyone except state and local bar associations. The exercise of de facto regulatory power by definition lacks transparency. Further, the ABA carries out its regulatory activities in an opaque manner
3	Regulatory oversight bodies	No	No oversight body oversees the regulatory activities of either the ABA or the state supreme courts
4	Citizen engagement	No	There is no significant citizen engagement to speak of

(*Continued*)

Table 24.1 Assessment for the United States (Continued)

5	Regulatory impact assessments	No	ABA does not conduct regulatory impact assessments and it denies any responsibility to do so. To the extent any state supreme courts do, it is rare if not one-off
6	Risk-based approach	Not really	Illinois is the only state to have adopted a risk-based approach, and it is a highly limited form (Colorado is taking steps in this direction)

Part VI

WHAT'S NEXT?

Now that we've conducted an in-depth examination of each of the four countries, what is the final assessment? Further, now that the ABA's Commission on the Future of Legal Services has wrapped up its work, what is next for the United States? Can the United States modernize its regulatory environment for legal services? If not, will the United States (and other countries) be left behind?

Chapter 25

Final Assessment

Table 25.1 brings together the assessment for each country:

The table reflects four different regulatory environments: one that has fully embraced these six elements of good governance, one that has accepted them in large part, one that is cautiously experimenting with them, and one that rejects them entirely. The consequences of these differences are clear to see:

While England and Wales is by no means perfect, it has a robust and productive—even prolific—regulatory environment. The legal professions have a voice in how legal services are regulated, but their voices do not control, nor does any one of the large variety of other voices that are also heard. Debate about how legal services should be regulated is constant, open and (usually) frank. Multiple actors conduct empirical research and publish it in open access. Regulatory decisions are made only after conducting that research and taking into account the perspectives of most if not all stakeholders (most notably citizens/the public).

In Australia, the variety of authorities and actors that play roles is not as large. Most notably, citizen engagement is practically nonexistent and the legal profession still plays an overly dominant role in regulation: these factors likely explain why the LPUL failed to extend the regulatory framework for ILPs to all legal service providers. Nevertheless, the other elements of good governance are more or less closely embraced, with the result of a regulatory environment that is also robust and productive, and where regulatory decisions are also made, for the most part, only after conducting empirical research.

Canada has been described as the "last bastion of unfettered self-regulation" in the common law world. Nevertheless, Canada has implemented the six elements in limited ways, and it appears to be moving, however cautiously, toward broader implementation. In certain provinces professional

Table 25.1

	England and Wales	*Australia*	*Canada*	*United States*
World Justice Project Rule of Law Index: Score for accessible and affordable civil justice*†	.56 (UK)	.57	.56	.41
Rank of 113 countries	46th	42nd	48th	94th
Independent regulation	For the most part	Yes and no	Limited	No
Accountability and transparency	For the most part	For the most part	Sort of	No
Regulatory oversight bodies	Yes	For the most part	Limited	No
Citizen engagement	Yes	No	Limited	No
Regulatory impact assessments	Yes	Yes	Not really	No
Risk-based approach	Yes	For the most part	Limited	Not really

*Factor 7.1. Data are normalized on a scale of 0 to 1, where 0 is the lowest and 1 is the highest.
†The World Justice Project, *Rule of Law Index 2016*, 15, 37.

regulators serving on staff of the law societies (rather than the "benchers" who are elected from among practicing members of the profession) appear to be the driving force behind a movement towards a risk-based approach. While the words "robust" and "productive" may not be the most accurate to describe Canada's regulatory environment, increased openness and exploration are.

The United States could not be more different. It has not embraced, or even partially implemented any of the six elements, not even in a limited manner (save for Illinois, which has partially implemented one element in a highly limited manner). The result is a regulatory environment that is paralyzed and unproductive, if not moribund.

This analysis raises the question: Why are there such differences among these four countries? While no doubt there is more than one response to that question, an important if not crucial one is this: the more actively the country's legislative and executive branches participate in the regulation of legal services, the more modern—the better—the regulatory environment. In England and Wales it was the executive that instigated the countries' metamorphosis and the legislature that brought it to fruition, over the objections of some (but by no means all) of the members of the countries' legal professions. In Australia, it was primarily the legislature, and especially the Parliament of New South Wales, that brought ILPs into being, with minimal input from the legal profession. It is not a coincidence that later when the legal profession was given greater power in the decision-making process, and notably when the National Legal Profession Reform Taskforce (made up principally of representatives of the executive) and the state legislatures deferred to the Consultative Group (made up principally of members of the legal profession) that the regulatory environment in New South Wales and Victoria took a step backward. In Canada, the legislature and the executive play minor roles as compared to the outsized role of the profession in its own regulation: this no doubt explains on the one hand why Canada's progress is relatively slow and incremental, but also, on the other hand, why it is able to make any progress at all.

In very stark contrast, in the United States, on the federal as well as state level, the executive and legislative branches play virtually no role in the regulation of legal services. Further, as discussed in chapter 2 and again in chapter 21, while the judicial branch of each state holds *de jure* power to regulate the legal profession, it has for the most part abdicated in the exercise of this power, leaving a vacuum for the profession, and notably for the ABA, to fill. For so long as the three branches of government: executive, legislative and judicial all fail to assert regulatory power over the legal profession and, by extension, over legal services, it will be virtually impossible for the country's regulatory environment to improve.

This analysis also demonstrates that in the United States, a debate that focuses exclusively on whether not the legal profession is, or should be, self-regulating is a false and ultimately futile debate. Instead, the real (and constructive) debate is: How do we create a regulatory environment that embraces the OECD's elements of good governance, in order improve regulation of the legal profession as well as of legal services as a whole? What are the changes that we need to make in order to breathe life into—to modernize—our regulatory environment—to make it as robust and productive as that of England and Wales?

Chapter 26

How to Modernize a Regulatory Environment

Modernizing a state's regulatory environment for legal services will not, and cannot, be easy, nor will it be quick. It will likely need to take place in stages, with certain changes being implemented and entering into the norm before more, arguably more radical, changes are made. The examples of England and Wales, Australia and Canada demonstrate that there will be fierce opposition and setbacks. Different branches of government—executive, legislative and judicial—will have to work together. They will need to obtain input and expertise from within the legal profession, of course, but also, and especially, from outside the legal profession: from members of the public as well as from persons with expertise in consumer services, human rights, competition, economics and regulation itself, to name a few.

The priority should be to establish a regulatory environment that, at a minimum, embraces the six elements of good governance that are described in this book. There is not just one way to do that—there are many ways—England and Wales and Australia (and to a more limited extent, Canada) each provide their own examples.

Let's again look at each of the elements, in turn:

INDEPENDENT REGULATION

As discussed in part I, independence means acting and making decisions in a manner that is disinterested and without regard for personal gain. Independence also means freedom not only from undue influence of public authorities (the executive as well as the legislature) but also from the regulated industry and from consumer groups and other special interest organizations. As the OECD documentation explains, regulators should regulate in the public interest, and undue influence from any of these actors makes regulation in the public interest very difficult, if not impossible.

With respect to independence from public authorities, the OECD states that in certain situations there is a need for the regulatory agency to be seen as independent in order to maintain public confidence.[1] In those situations, regulators should have sufficient autonomy to conduct their functions without interference from the executive or legislature.[2] Few would argue that the regulation of legal services is not such a situation.

It is in this context that a state should establish a regulatory board (Board). The relevant text creating the Board should stipulate that at least half of its members may not be lawyers, nor may the Board's Chair. Instead, those members should be required to bring other knowledge and expertise to the table, most notably consumer affairs, complaints handling, competition matters and the regulation of professions (that is, professions other than legal). In this manner, the Board can benefit from a wide range of expertise, including that of lawyers, without being dominated by them.

A selection committee for Board members should also be established. This committee can be composed, for example, of the state's attorney general, members of legislative committees (such as human services, commerce and judiciary), and members of the state's supreme court. Selected by such a committee, the Board should have sufficient autonomy to carry out its functions without interference from the executive or legislature. At the same time, however, it should allow for the Board's long-term strategy and policy goals to be in line with broad strategic state priorities. Further, selection in this manner should also shield the board from undue influence from the legal profession, and most notably from the organized bar.

The Board should have access to the financial and human resources it needs to effectively regulate in the public interest, and should have autonomy in managing them. Notably, the Board should be supported by a staff of full-time, professional regulators.

The members of the Board should be subject to clear policies as regards conflicts of interest. Notably, such policies should contain clear descriptions of what can lead to a conflict of interest situation: the financial or pecuniary interests of a Board member, related-party business undertakings, affiliations with for-profit or non-profit organizations or with political or professional organizations (such as bar associations), personal relationships and potentially relevant non-financial personal interests.[3] The policies should also explain what should occur in the event of a conflict of interest, such as disposal of the private interests that present a conflict, recusal from one or more relevant decisions, or disclosure of the conflict.[4]

Clear policies should also be in place with respect to the Board's staff. Rules for attracting, motivating and retaining staff should all be established to safeguard regulatory independence.[5] The rules should be particularly sensitive to the problem of the "revolving door:" the movement of people back and forth between key regulatory positions and the private sector. In this case, this would mean that candidates from, for example, private legal practice and/or the governance or staff of a bar association should be subject to special scrutiny.[6] Further, as the OECD cautions, secondments (where private sector personnel are seconded into regulatory agencies for a period while remaining employees in the private sector) and advisory appointments (where personnel take on the role of 'special advisors' or sit on advisory committees, while continuing to be employed by their 'pre-regulatory' employer) should be avoided because of the special risks to conflicts of interest that they raise.[7]

It is important to note that rules such as these do not mean that lawyers (persons with legal knowledge and expertise) cannot serve on the Board or staff of such a regulatory body. It does not mean that such a regulatory body cannot benefit from the knowledge and expertise of lawyers. It simply means that those lawyers must be free of conflicts of interest, and, to the extent that is not possible, the conflicts must be disclosed.

ACCOUNTABILITY AND TRANSPARENCY

As explained in part I, for the OECD accountability and transparency comprise a number of components, such as requiring the regulator to regularly and publicly report upon defined issues (subject to penalty for failure to report), and the openness of process to external scrutiny. It means that decisions are made in a manner that follows rules and regulations, and all relevant information is freely available and directly accessible to those who will be affected by such decisions. Further, significant delegated decisions should be subject to a published, arm's length process for review, and all major decisions (delegated or not) should be accompanied by publicly stated reasons.

On this basis, a state that is modernizing its regulatory environment for legal services should adopt rules to assure regulatory accountability and transparency as follows:

- Requiring that full information about the members of the Board be made available online;
- Requiring the Board's meetings to be open to the public and that meeting minutes are made available online;
- Requiring that any significant delegated decisions be subject to an arm's length review, and establishing a process for that review;
- Requiring that all significant decisions (delegated or not) be publicly motivated;

- Requiring the Board to make available to the public a written annual report of its activities and accounts;
- Requiring the Board to publish the findings of the research it conducts;
- Granting to the state's attorney general (for example) and/or judicial committee of its legislature the right to ask the Board at any time for an account of its activities.

REGULATORY OVERSIGHT BODIES

As explained in part I, a regulatory oversight body (a "regulator of regulators") commonly serves one or more four core functions: coordination and supervision; training, advice and technical support; advocacy; and challenge and scrutiny. As also explained in part I, the fourth function, challenge and scrutiny, is the most resented and controversial, yet also the most essential for high-quality regulations.[8]

Further, an oversight body must be properly "located" among other public authorities. Especially, it should be at the "center of government" such that it can exercise its functions in a manner that is coherent with other regulatory policies.[9]

Finally, as warned in part I, the establishment of a regulatory body will likely be met with resistance: the regulator may perceive it as reducing its autonomy and discretion, and the persons subject to regulation may perceive it as threatening to their "cozy" relationship with the regulator.

With this in mind, a state seeking to modernize its regulatory environment for legal services should establish (or identify an existing) authority charged with overseeing the decisions and actions of the Board. For example, the selection committee for Board members could also function as an oversight authority. Alternatively, an existing authority, such as the state's attorney general, could assume principal oversight authority. In this case, certain decisions and actions by the oversight authority could require the advice and consent of another existing authority, such as a legislative judicial committee and/or a member of the state's supreme court. Of course, whatever authority is established/identified, it, too, should operate free of conflicts of interest.

Regardless of the authority that is established/identified, the modernizing state should be prepared to proceed in the face of criticism and resistance. It is difficult to imagine that the ABA as well as many other bar associations, law firms and individual lawyers would not object, and object strongly, to what they will certainly perceive as encroachment on their own regulatory power.

Further, in establishing the oversight authority, its principal purposes and priorities should be clearly delineated. Especially its purpose to challenge and scrutinize the decisions and actions of the regulator should be clarified.

CITIZEN ENGAGEMENT

As discussed in part I, in order for citizen engagement to succeed it must include as wide a variety of citizen's voices as possible. This means going beyond industry and other special interest groups to include all the stakeholders as well as those who have specific knowledge or expertise with respect to the subject at hand. In order to include them, it is necessary to make extra efforts to reach out to them—merely creating a "level playing field" which allows for passive access to participation is not enough.

There is debate over what models are and are not effective for citizen engagement. The most commonly used model is what has been termed the "consultation model." With this model, a government panel of some kind invites the public to express their views, which they typically can do in a number of ways (online, town-hall meeting, etc.). Once the allotted time period for submissions has passed, the panel reviews them, deliberates, reaches conclusions and makes recommendations to government, which then decides how it will respond.[10]

This model has been criticized as doing more to divide the public rather than contribute to good decision-making. This is because its pits different interest groups against each other, who then seek to create a sense of urgency and bring competing claims into disrepute. It encourages participants to adopt uncompromising positions that they are not willing to modify in the face of conflicting evidence, and it discourages them from engaging in genuine debate or discussion. As a result, when the panel reviews the positions and decides upon its recommendations, it necessarily results in at least some participants perceiving they have "lost," and that their demands have been ignored. It also causes the panel to become secretive about its rationale and defensive about its choices which, in turn, makes the public even more suspicious of the process and the advocates more strident in their criticism.[11]

Drawing from his experience with insurance regulation, Daniel Schwarcz suggests two alternative (or cumulative) models if not of direct public engagement than of a means to assure that the public interest is taken into account in regulatory decision-making. He describes the models as "consumer empowerment programs," and he offers them as a solution to the "collective action problem that citizens and consumers face in advocating for their preferred outcomes." In particular, Schwarcz suggests them as a means to counteract the undue influence of industry in regulation (that is, of regulatory capture). He explains that the models offer both a means to overcome any barriers (real or perceived) to participation that the public may have because of lack of expertise and a formal mechanism for public influence in regulation.[12]

The models are, on the one hand, "proxy advocacy," and, on the other hand, "tripartism:"

Under the proxy advocacy model, an independent governmental entity is tasked with representing the public interest in designated regulatory proceedings. The entity can take various forms, including: (i) an independent organization, (ii) a designated division within an attorney general's office, or (iii) specialized staff housed within a regulator. Regardless of the form it takes, such entities are typically assigned specific procedural rights or duties in the regulatory process (such as to participate in hearings), and they "wield their influence" primarily by providing information and a consumer perspective to the regulator.[13]

Under the tripartism model, independent (non-governmental) public interest groups hold a formal role in a regulatory proceeding. In order to exercise that role, they are fully informed regarding regulatory issues, allowed to participate in the negotiation of regulatory outcomes, and permitted to challenge industry behavior through the same mechanisms as the regulator. The formalization of the role of the group includes a means to compensate them in some manner. This compensation may take different forms, for example a participating group can be reimbursed some amount if they make "a substantial contribution" to the proceeding in question. Alternatively, they can be reimbursed for their expenses.[14]

These alternative models can work only if the proxy advocates/public interest groups are assigned specific procedural rights in the regulatory process. Further, public interest groups have limited resources, and this is especially the case if they are not compensated for their time. For this reason, they often focus their efforts on certain issues, to the expense of others. For all their imperfections, however, these alternative models offer a viable means to enhance the regulatory influence of the public, especially as compared to the more passive consultation model. These alternative models can be particularly useful with respect to the regulation of legal services, in that legal services are regulated on a state (rather than federal) level, the subject matter can be regarded as technical, and legal services concern powerful entrenched interests (that of the professional bar).[15]

Taking the above into account, for a state seeking to modernize its regulatory environment for legal services, two possibilities to assure citizen participation and engagement in the regulatory process are:

1) The establishment of a panel comparable to England and Wales's Legal Services Consumer Panel. The panel should be made up exclusively of persons who are not lawyers; instead, they should have expertise in the areas of consumer services and consumer welfare. The panel should have the mandate and the resources to conduct research with respect to the use of legal services. The panel should have a formal, defined role in the Board's decision-making procedures. Finally, while the Board should not be obliged to follow the panel's advice (if it were, the regulation would no longer be independent), it

should obliged to take it into account. This could be evidenced, for example, by requiring the Board to provide a written explanation when it rejects the panel's advice; or

2) Public interest groups could be granted a formal role in regulatory procedures. That is, they would be fully informed with respect to regulatory issues and proceedings, they would play a full and meaningful role in the proceedings (most notably participate in the negotiation of outcomes), and they would have standing to challenge industry actions and behavior in the same manner as the Board. In order to support these activities, the public interest groups would be compensated in some manner, and, at a minimum, they would be reimbursed for their expenses. There is at least one public interest group ready today to fill this role: Responsive Law, a Washington DC-based not-for-profit organization that "work[s] to make the legal system more affordable, accessible, and accountable to the people it is meant to serve."[16]

There are obstacles to public engagement, and both resources and careful planning are required. Even so, the success of any specific project or program is not guaranteed. A project or program could be perceived as mere tokenism or simply to be badly organized. A process could be distorted, even abused, and thus generate the wrong outcome.[17] The project or program could fail as a result, both undermining the legitimacy of citizen engagement and wasting precious resources.[18] Nevertheless, the obstacles to successful citizen engagement must be overcome both in order to build open and democratic institutions and as a condition to effective governance. The fact that any given project or program may fail is not a reason to try, and try again, if need be.

REGULATORY IMPACT ASSESSMENTS

The Board as well as any consumer panel that is established should have both the mandate and the resources to conduct extensive empirical research in the area of legal services (including the commissioning of research to other organizations). But they should not be alone: other authorities, such as competition authorities, should also conduct relevant research in the area of legal services. All research should be published in open access. The results of all research should be fully utilized in order to critically and continually assess and re-assess existing regulations as well as to develop new regulations and non-regulatory alternatives.

A state seeking to modernize its regulatory environment for legal services should establish both conditions under which the performance of an RIA is mandatory and the analysis it must contain. Such conditions could include, for example, any proposal to adopt, amend or repeal any "major regulation." "Major regulation" could be defined, for example, as expected to have an impact on consumer access to legal services, or an expected impact defined in financial terms, such as greater than $X. Required analysis could include most notably the expected effects on consumer access to legal services, as well as the expected effects on the creation of jobs; on the competitiveness of businesses in the state; on investment in the state; on incentives for innovation in services, products, materials or processes; and on the health, safety and welfare of the state's residents.

RISK-BASED APPROACH

As discussed in part I, a risk-based approach is the use of systematized frameworks of supervision or inspection which are primarily designed to manage regulatory or institutional risk, and notably risks to the regulatory agency itself that it will not achieve its objectives. Importantly, risk-based regulation is *not* focused on the potential risks that individuals or firms may present to their customers, to the public, or to the economy. Instead, risk-based regulation is focused on the risks the regulator faces in failing to achieve its objectives. One particular kind of risk-based regulation is management-based regulation. Its underlying concept is to deploy regulatory authority in a way that leverages the private sector's knowledge about its particular circumstances and engages firms in developing their own internal procedures and monitoring practices that respond to risks.[19]

Upon the establishment of the Board, one of its first orders of business should be to develop regulatory objectives. Those objectives can then be used for the Board to determine what risks it faces in not meeting those objectives. Those risks can then guide the Board in its regulatory decisions.

The Board will also need to determine its risk appetite. That is, the Board will need to decide if it will adopt a "zero-failure" or "notional zero-failure" policy, or a "non-zero failure policy." In the case of a state seeking to modernize its regulatory framework, the adoption of a "zero-failure" or "notional zero-failure" policy would not make sense. That is because, unlike other types of regulation (like of food additives or pesticide residues), with respect to the regulation of legal services it would be unworkable for the regulator to seek to prevent any failure from occurring. That is, it simply wouldn't be possible for the regulator to prevent every "negative event," such as every incidence of financial failure of a firm and every incidence of non-compliance.[20] And if the regulator tried to do so, it could have other (highly) undesirable and also risky consequences, such as to discourage innovation.[21]

The Board will also need to determine "the risk indicators." Risk indicators are those activities or events that are likely to result in the risk crystallizing; Risk crystallization occurs when the adverse event that the regulator was trying to prevent in fact happens—that there is, for example, a discharge, accident, food contamination or financial failure.[22] In the case of legal services, the Board may, for example, identify that certain types of firm structures, certain internal processes (or lack thereof), or certain types of substantive areas of legal work present certain risks that other types of firm structures, internal processes or other practice areas do not.

Finally, since knowledge about risks changes over time, often slowly but sometimes rapidly, the Board will be required to make wise decisions in a dynamic context where flexibility is needed to account for new information.[23] Risk-based regulation will require the Board to take risks, and, in all likelihood, to make mistakes. Neither are reasons to not implement a risk-based approach.

NOTES

1. OECD Supporting the Public Interest, 84.
2. OECD Being an Independent, 41.
3. OECD Managing Conflict of Interest, 16–17.
4. OECD Managing Conflict of Interest, 25–26; OECD Revolving Doors, 10–11.
5. OECD Being an Independent, 4.
6. OECD Revolving Doors, 9.
7. OECD Revolving Doors, 13–14.
8. Ibid., 9–12.
9. Ibid., 21,38–39, 49.
10. Lenihan, "Public Engagement Is a Must," 208.
11. Ibid., 208–209.
12. Daniel Schwarcz, "Preventing Capture Through Consumer Empowerment Programs: Some Evidence from Insurance Regulation," in *Preventing Regulatory Capture: Special Interest Influence and How to Limit It*, ed. Daniel Carpenter and David A. Moss (New York: Cambridge University Press, 2014), 365–368. Nolan McCarty adds an interesting twist to these observations. He states that when the regulator relies upon the expertise of a public interest group, it "forces" special interest groups to make policy concessions that are more favorable to the public interest. In other words, the expertise that a public interest group can provide to a regulator reduces at least in part the regulator's need for the expertise of special interest groups. Nolan McCarty, "Complexity, Capacity and Capture," in *Preventing Regulatory Capture: Special Interest Influence and How to Limit It*, ed. Daniel Carpenter and David A. Moss (New York: Cambridge University Press, 2014), 119–120.
13. Schwarcz, "Preventing Capture," 366–369.
14. Ibid., 369, 384.
15. Ibid., 386–387, 391.
16. Responsive Law, "Mission Statement," accessed March 20, 2017, http://www.responsivelaw.org/index.php/about-us.

17. See, for example, Edward T. Walker, Michael McQuarrie and Caroline W. Lee, "Rising Participation and Declining Democracy," in *Democratizing Inequalities: Dilemmas of the New Public Participation*, ed. Caroline W. Lee, Michael McQuarrie, and Edward T. Walker (New York: New York University Press, 2015), 3–23.

18. OECD Studies on Public Engagement, 15; Andersson and Wilson, "Globalised Democracy," 302.

19. Coglianese, "Management-Based Regulation," 159, http://dx.doi.org/10.1787/9789264082939-en.

20. Black, "Risk-Based Regulation," 193.

21. D. John Graham, "Why Governments Need Guidelines for Risk Assessment and Management," in *Risk and Regulatory Policy: Improving the Governance of Risk*, OECD (Paris: OECD Publishing, 2010), 239, http://dx.doi.org/10.1787/9789264082939-en.

22. Black, "Risk-Based Regulation," 195–196.

23. Graham, "Why Governments Need Guidelines," 238.

Chapter 27

Rules for a Flat World (or Regulatory Dystopia)

As discussed in part II, the complex regulatory framework for legal services in England and Wales, which has its origins in the fragmentation of the legal services market of those countries, has led to a seemingly novel result: regulatory competition or competitive regulation. In essence, legal service providers in England and Wales are not necessarily required to work with one regulator—in some contexts, they can select one from a panel of approved regulators.

As novel as the framework in England and Wales may appear, the phenomena of regulatory competition by no means originated there. Corporate law in the United States, and notably the choices available to companies as regards state of incorporation, is an obvious example. More specifically, in the United States, a company is not required to incorporate in the state where its principal place of business is located. In this context, corporations can "shop" for the state that offers the rules of corporate governance that they find most amenable for them.

In her book *Rules for a Flat World: Why Humans Invented Law and How to Reinvent It For a Complex Global Economy*, Gillian Hadfield provides additional examples, both historical and current, such as the international markets of medieval Europe which competed for merchants based upon the quality of their rules and mechanisms for resolving commercial disputes, and the Dubai International Financial Center, which Hadfield describes as the world's first modern "competitive law zone" created to attract international financial services to Dubai.[1]

On the topic of alternative structures, Hadfield has published a number of groundbreaking and highly compelling pieces. They are essential reading for anyone interested in the topic. As just a brief sampling, in "The Cost of Law: Promoting Access to Justice through the (Un)Corporate Practice of

Law"[2] and "Life in the Law-Thick World: The Legal Resource Landscape for Ordinary Americans"[3] (with Jaime Heine), Hadfield uses empirical evidence to demonstrate that there can never be enough pro bono (free) legal work or enough money for legal aid that could even come close to satisfying the huge unmet need for legal services in the United States. In doing so, she powerfully brings home the importance as well as the urgency of ending the lawyer monopoly on legal services so that others can try to fill at least some of the unmet need. In "Legal Barriers to Innovation: The Growing Economic Cost of Professional Control Over Corporate Legal Markets,"[4] Hadfield explains how much of legal work is economic activity. As such, she makes clear the importance of the regulation of legal services for the effective functioning of a market economy. In "Legal Infrastructure and the New Economy,"[5] Hadfield provides fascinating and valuable insight on the challenges that companies like Google, Mozilla and Cisco Systems face in obtaining legal services. In doing so, she resoundingly disproves the commonly held assumption that large, well-resourced companies are able to easily meet their needs for legal services.

A GIANT LEAP

In *Rules for a Flat World*, Hadfield also discusses alternative structures[6] but most of the book addresses a different topic. She extolls the virtues of regulatory competition. In doing so, she takes a step beyond regulation as we know it. She not just applauds competition among public (or governmental or state) regulators, but also encourages competition among *private* regulators in a *privatized market* of regulatory services.

In a nutshell, Hadfield's explanation is as follows: mass digitalization has changed how we interact with the world, particularly changing our economic interactions. No longer are they embedded in physical objects or fixed locations: instead, they are disembodied and exist everywhere and nowhere at the same time. Powerful computers can analyze information at very high speed; virtual reality devices allow us to immerse ourselves in places many miles away; the internet of things connects us all in ways of which we are barely aware. This "massive leap" in the complexity of the economy has had an enormous impact on the demand for law, and our "legal infrastructure" is not able to catch up.[7]

There are three different "lenses" Hadfield presents through which we can observe that our existing systems are "bursting at the seams." The first lens is that of complexity: contracts for seemingly the simplest things, like buying a song or installing a software update, are multiple thousands of densely worded documents that are nearly incomprehensible. Statutes, and the regulations they generate, are often hopelessly complicated. Hadfield cites the example of the Dodd-Frank law, which generated ten thousand pages of regulations, including 46 rules involving four different regulators governing just one type of financial transaction. For Hadfield, the "most dramatic evidence" of complexity lies in the 2008 financial collapse: subprime mortgage agreements and the "fancy financial instruments" created by slicing them up were incomprehensible not only to ordinary people but also to sophisticated investors like Warren Buffet.[8]

The second lens is that of cost: lawyers and legal processes often cost far more than the benefit they offer. Further, even if it might be worth it, many people simply don't have enough money to pay. As a result, in many cases people try to resolve their legal problems without lawyers, or simply give up and forgo their rights.[9]

The third and perhaps, for Hadfield, most important lens is that of quality. She uses this term not only in its traditional sense of how "good" a lawyer's work is, but also—and especially—in a much broader sense. "Quality" encompasses the growing needs for highly specialized lawyers, for a greater range of types of legal help available on the market (not everyone can afford or wants high-end "BMW" legal services); for lawyers who better understand both the needs of businesses in general and those of global businesses; for lawyers who better understand "how to think about risk;" and for lawyers who know how to calibrate the amount of time and effort they devote to a piece of work to the value the client places on work for the client ("lawyers insist on serving up fine china when a paper cup would do"). Additionally, Hadfield explains that businesses that work across borders are forced to meet their legal needs in a fragmented and often incoherent manner. This is because on an international level, our legal systems don't offer solutions for those types of businesses.[10]

In sum, the legal system that lawyers built over the past few hundred years has served us immensely well in that it has grounded the "spectacular growth" the advanced world has enjoyed since 1800. Hadfield, however, argues that today it is not enough. The system has too many limits, and it needs to be reinvented to meet the needs of today's highly complex society.[11]

Why hasn't our legal system been able to reinvent itself, Hadfield asks: "Why hasn't our legal infrastructure responded better to the changes in the global economy?"[12] For Hadfield, the reason is that "we rely too much on central planning and not enough on markets" to build the components of our legal infrastructure. Hadfield explains that in the 20th century virtually all industrialized countries—ranging from the far left Soviet Union to far right fascist countries like Germany and Italy and including democratic societies like Britain and the United States—were drawn to central planning as the best way to assure that resources were put to the best use. However, by the end of the 20th century, the complexities of the economy placed far too great a burden on anyone who tried to "sit atop the pile and direct from on high." At this point Hadfield cites the economist F.A. Hayek, considered by many to be a founder of neoliberalism.[13] Hayek argues that the more complex an economy becomes, the less amenable it is to centralized planning. After pointing this out, Hadfield then quickly asserts: "the reason is nonideological and has nothing to do with liberal democracy and the proper role of government in promoting human well-being. It is supremely practical."[14]

Following Hayek's "deep insight," Hadfield argues that "markets," and not government, are the solution to this problem. This is for three reasons: First, through decentralization markets allow us to give greater discretion in how to solve a problem to those across the globe who are at the "bottom of the pyramid:" They are the ones who are most likely to have the specialized information and expertise required to solve that problem. Second, markets create economic incentives for those people to do their work: to discover and apply information. Third, markets help to manage the "information burdens" of a complex economy because they systematically transmit the information they have: when a competitor in the market succeeds, others learn from them and use it in their own businesses. For these reasons, Hadfield urges, we should "create competitive markets for the production of legal infrastructure." In doing so, we can harness the power of markets to drive investment and innovation in legal infrastructure research and design. We can also build up specialization in the knowledge of how legal infrastructure works and how it can be made to work better and we can get that information transmitted widely and systematically. No number of expert panels and no number of international agency reports can do that: "If we want smart ideas for how to deliver a stable, productive platform on which to build the more complex relationships of the global economy, we should be finding ways to get markets into the mix."[15]

For Hadfield, markets are clearly the answer, and just as clearly, governments are not. Governments cannot be "fixed" because the "production" of rules by governments is hamstrung by our "political, bureaucratic and judicial rule production methods." Those methods promote, as well as thrive, on greater complexity in rule making. However, these "rule-making machines" don't experience the cost of the complexity they produce. Further, most government agencies don't face competition. They have little motivation to change how they do things because they won't go out of business if they don't. So, the bottom line is that we need the "iPhone for law," something that hits the sweet spot between increased complexity costs and increased benefits. And the only way to get it is to figure out how to "get more markets into the legal infrastructure business."[16]

It is at this point that Hadfield takes a giant leap past mere regulatory competition. As the examples described at the beginning of this chapter evidence, there is nothing particularly new about regulatory competition, per se. It has occurred in different contexts, both historically and presently. In most cases, however, the competitors are not private actors, they are public ones. The most salient example is corporate law in the United States. While US companies can chose among the corporate laws of all fifty states as well as the District of Columbia and US territories, in each case the "competitor" for the company's regulatory "business" is the *government* of that state/district/territory. That is, it's a *public* agency or body of some kind.

Hadfield contends that not only are public rule-making and regulatory bodies hamstrung by their propensity for high levels of complexity resulting in high costs for businesses, but also, and perhaps worse, they lack resources. They do not have the financial, technical or human resources to develop the completely new "legal infrastructure" that is required to adequately regulate today's hypercomplex and hyperconnected global economy. Hadfield points in particular to artificial intelligence: "Regulating AIs, almost surely, will require almost as much if not more AI than the AI targets of regulation themselves." For Hadfield, "our conventional approaches to producing regulation, exclusively through governments and public officials, are increasingly unable to cope with the levels of complexity and scale of some of our new technologies."[17]

Who does have those resources? Who is able to "cope" with such levels of complexity and scale? Self-regulation is not a better option than the government, Hadfield quickly confirms. Instead, for her, the answer is obvious: it's the "garage guys." Reincarnations of Google's Sergey Brin and Larry Page, who have the technical skills, access to private capital, high appetite for risk, and ability to fail, are required. *Private* regulators, operating in a "market" for regulation, who are overseen "as necessary" by public regulators are what is needed.[18]

An important element of this proposition, Hadfield emphasizes, is the prospect of profit (or, for the "philanthropically minded," the prospect of social impact).[19] She explains:

> The key to a market-based approach to regulation is to create the potential for innovation and incentives to invest in smarter, more effective, and less expensive systems for meeting regulatory objectives. Private regulators that secure a larger market share and *higher profits* (or better returns on non-profit goals—the motive animating many nonprofit organizations such as private universities and hospitals) by offering a better regulatory service have powerful incentives to figure out how to achieve regulatory objectives more effectively at lower costs.[20] [Emphasis added]

In the privatized regulatory world that Hadfield paints, private regulators would receive payment from the users of their private regulatory systems. That is, rather than a government subcontracting regulatory services to a private subcontractor (in the manner of private prisons, for example), instead a government would grant to a private regulator the right to offer private regulatory services, subject to defined rules and objectives. The users—the customers—of those services would pay the private regulator directly in order to have access to them.[21]

ENGLAND & WALES: PRIVATIZED OR INDEPENDENT?

Hadfield offers as an example of regulatory competition among private regulators the regulatory framework for legal services in England & Wales. (This framework is described in detail in chapter 4 of this book). She offers the nine approved regulators as "private nonprofit organizations." Hadfield explains that each "private" regulator must demonstrate to the LSB (the oversight regulator) that it (the "private" regulator) meets the regulatory objectives set out in the Legal Services Act, and that the LSB monitors the performance of each "private" regulator as well as the legal system as a whole. Hadfield further explains that the LSB can create rules that the "private" regulators must follow, such as setting the maximum penalties that can be imposed, requiring a minimum number of lay persons on their governing bodies and forbidding interference from professional representative bodies/trade associations.[22]

Hadfield lauds the regulatory framework for legal services in England & Wales as a "more intelligent approach to regulation, one focused on innovation, improving quality, and reducing costs." She states that it puts England & Wales in "a much better position to meet the challenges of building better legal infrastructure for an increasingly complex world." Most especially, she extols the framework of England & Wales as a "straightforward model for how other countries can keep up."[23] On these points, Hadfield is convincing.

However, upon reviewing the English/Welsh framework more carefully, the description of "private nonprofit" doesn't seem to fit. Of the nine approved regulators, five have Royal Charters (the Law Society, the Chartered Institute of Legal Executives, the Chartered Institute of Patent Attorneys, the Chartered Institute of Trade Mark Attorneys, and the Institute of Charted Accountants in England and Wales), one was established by statute (the Council for Licensed Conveyancers), and one is a functionary in the office of the Archbishop of Canterbury (the Master of the Faculties).[24]

The status of Royal Charter is principally reserved for professional institutions and charities that work in the public interest and that demonstrate "pre-eminence, stability and permanence" in their particular field. Organizations subject to Royal Charter may not freely amend their Charter or bylaws; the Charter may be amended only by the Queen in Council and certain amendments to the bylaws must be approved by the Privy Council (made up of all Cabinet Ministers and some junior ministries). In sum, chartered organizations surrender a significant amount of control over their internal affairs.[25]

Further, the Legal Services Act requires all approved regulators (chartered or not) to act in a manner that is "transparent, accountable, proportionate, consistent and targeted only at cases in which action is needed."[26] While this list of requirements clearly encompasses a large variety of practices and behaviors, what is most relevant for our purposes here is that it operates to require each approved regulator to publicly report on its activities, and notably to publish its annual accounts.

Finally, and perhaps most significantly, the governors of each of the approved regulators (with the possible exceptions of the Costs Lawyer Standards Board and the ecclesiastical Master of the Faculties) are required to act in accordance with "The 7 Principles of Public Life," issued by the Committee on Standards in Public Life.[27] Previously referred to as the "Nolan Principles," they apply to "anyone who works as a *public* office-holder." The four principles most significant for our purposes read as follows:

> Selflessness: *Holders of public office* should act solely in terms of the public interest;
>
> Integrity: *Holders of public office* . . . should not act or take decisions in order to gain financial or other material benefits for themselves, their family or their friends. They must declare and resolve any interests and relationships;
>
> Accountability: *Holders of public office* are accountable to the public for their decisions and actions and must submit themselves to the scrutiny necessary to ensure this.
>
> Openness: *Holders of public office* should act and take decisions in an open and transparent manner. Information should not be withheld from the public unless there are clear and lawful reasons for doing so.[28] [Emphasis added]

Taking all of the above into account, it appears that the approved regulators for legal services in England & Wales are not "private" as we commonly think of that term in the economic marketplace. They are perceived to be serving public functions. They are required to act in the interest of the public as a whole, to the exclusion of any private or personal interest.

It would be more accurate to describe each of these approved regulators as conforming to the OECD's description of an *independent* regulator, as explained in chapter 1 of this book. While these regulators have sufficient autonomy to conduct their functions without political interference from the executive or legislature, at the same time their structures facilitate the alignment of their long term strategy and policy goals with the broad strategic national priorities as set by elected representatives in the executive and legislature.[29]

In making the case for truly private regulation, Hadfield holds up the approved regulators of England & Wales as proof that her proposal can and does work. But the "garage guys" that Hadfield calls for in *Rules for a Flat World* would not be working "solely in terms of the public interest." How could they be if, as Hadfield recommends, the prospect of profit (or of philanthropic social impact) and other enticements such as the protection of intellectual property, would be "dangled"[30] in front of them? A number of public services have been privatized in the UK in recent years but the regulation of legal services is not one of them.[31]

THE US EXPERIENCE WITH THE PRIVATIZATION OF PUBLIC SERVICES

The US has also privatized a number of public services in recent years. Hadfield mentions one in her book, the operation of prisons. She mentions it in passing, stating only that the private contractors operating private prisons were not "effectively" regulated.[32] That leaves much unsaid about the US experience with the privatization of prisons:

The 1970s War on Drugs and harsher sentencing policies, including mandatory minimum sentences, fueled a rapid expansion in our nation's prison population. Prisons became so overcrowded that you could have said, and some did, that they were "bursting at the seams."[33] Beginning with the Reagan Administration in the 1980s and then again with the Clinton Administration in the 1990s, the solution for the Federal Bureau of Prisons as well as a number of states was to contract with private companies to provide prison services. From 1999 to 2010, nationwide, in both federal and state prisons, the population of private prisons increased by 80% as compared to just an 18% increase in the prison population overall (private and public).[34] The use of private prisons reached its peak in 2013, when approximately 15% of the federal prison population, or nearly 30,000 inmates, were in privately operated prisons.[35]

Proponents of private prisons argued that public prisons had become "outmoded and obsolete." Governments did not have the resources to renovate existing prisons or to build new ones to accommodate the burgeoning prison population. In addition, unlike public prisons, private prisons would not be "mired" in bureaucracy and red tape. Notably, unlike public agencies, private prison operators can hire and fire without the constraints of civil services, and they can discipline and reassign employees with far greater ease, especially if labor is not unionized. Further, proponents argued that private prisons would be more efficient. This was because public prisons have a monopoly, and as a result they have few incentives to develop more efficient methods or seek greater productivity. In contrast, because private prison operators compete in the private marketplace, they have every reason to seek greater efficiency, else lose money or go out of business. In sum, as regards public prisons, proponents argued that quality is low, prices are high, and supply has not kept up with demand: "Public sector corrections systems are in a state of chronic failure by any measure, and no other politically or economically feasible solution is on the table."[36]

What was the result of the US's nearly forty-year experiment with private prisons? In August, 2016, US Department of Justice Deputy Attorney General Sally Yates announced that the Federal Bureau of Prisons would begin to reduce, with the intention of ultimately ending, the use of privately operated prisons.[37] The Department made this decision on the basis of a report issued by the Office of the Inspector General that was highly critical of privately operated prisons.[38] The report found that, as compared to federal public prisons, private prisons do not provide the same level of correctional services, programs, or resources, do not save substantially on costs, and do not maintain the same level of safety and security. Further, Yates noted that private prisons have struggled to replicate the rehabilitative services that public prisons provide: services such as educational programs and job training that are considered essential for reducing recidivism and improving public safety.[39] (In February 2017 new Attorney General Jeff Sessions rescinded Yates's announcement at the same time that the Trump Administration began enforcing strict immigration policies, including mass detention of undocumented immigrants).[40]

The August 2016 report of the Office of the Inspector General was not by any means the first or the only report highly critical of privately operated prisons. For example, a 2012 report prepared for The Sentencing Project found that there is no evidence that privately operated prisons are more cost effective than publicly operated ones. Complicating cost comparisons, the report explained, was the fact that private prisons tend to cherry pick the less expensive prisoners (low or medium levels of security), leaving the more expensive ones (high security/ high risk) for public prisons. The report also found that there is high staff turnover in private prisons, which was attributed to lower salaries and shorter training periods as compared to public prisons.[41] The report observed that the rate of assaults in private prisons is significantly higher than in public prisons and attributed this fact, at least in part, to high staff turnover. In sum, public prisons were found to be safer as compared to private ones because "privately operated prisons appear to have systemic problems in maintaining secure facilities."[42] The report also found that many privately operated prisons fail to provide adequate medical care.[43]

The report explains that the operators of private prisons themselves do not hold out greater efficiency as a cornerstone to their business models. At least one private company has described that its potential for growth instead depends upon "factors we cannot control," such as "crime rates and sentencing patterns in various jurisdictions, . . . the relaxation of enforcement efforts, leniency in conviction or parole standards and sentencing practices or through the decriminalization of certain activities that are currently proscribed by our criminal laws." They see their growth—and their profits—as dependent in large part if not in whole upon a greater number of persons entering the incarceration system.[44]

Further, even if a private prison operator might suggest that the number of persons entering the incarceration system is something it cannot control, that hasn't stopped private operators from trying to influence it. As The Sentencing Project report explains, private prison operators spend heavily on lobbying as well as on campaign contributions to both state and federal candidates. Their efforts have gone toward not only promoting the use of private prisons, but also increasing the nation's prison population (such as through strict immigration laws), and seeking to block unfavorable bills, such as those that would put private prisons under the jurisdiction of the Freedom of Information Act.[45] Congresswoman Sheila Jackson Lee of Texas sought no fewer than six times to make private prisons subject to the same federal public records laws as public prisons. Private prison operators lobbied strongly against her bill each time. Those in the House of Representatives who opposed Lee argued that such a requirement would set a "dangerous precedent" of applying public record law to private companies, and would raise the cost of private contractors by increasing legal fees and record-keeping staff. Lee's bill failed each time, with the result that our information about how private prisons are run and what happens inside their walls is still limited.[46]

The problems in the private prisons demonstrate that they do not operate better than government operated ones do. They are not more efficient, and the possibility of profit has not enticed private operators to create better prisons, much less a better system of incarceration. Instead, private prison operators have a highly perverse incentive: to seek to increase the number of incarcerated persons in a country which already has the highest incarceration rate in the world.[47] Private prisons do not operate in the public interest and make no pretense of doing so. They operate exclusively in the interest of their shareholders, and they do so to the detriment of inmates and the public as a whole.[48]

The situation with respect to privatization of another public service, water, is not much different: During most of the 1800s, most of the US population (94%) was supplied primarily by private water companies. However, between 1880 and 1920 the majority of the country's large cities moved to public systems and the rest of the country followed; By the 1990s, just 15% of the market was supplied by private companies. The shift to public systems was prompted by a number of problems attributed to private companies: the outbreak of diseases due to contaminated water, the inability to fight fires due to low water pressure, and the failure on the part of private companies to supply low-income areas.[49]

Over the course of the 20th century, the country's mostly public water providers grew to provide potable water to more than 99% of the country. In doing so, however, they failed to adequately maintain their infrastructure, with the result of water main breakage and leakage being common place around the country. There are an estimated 240,000 breaks and an estimated 7 billion gallons in leakage, per year. Due to aging infrastructure, the pipes are literally bursting at the seams. And they are not only bursting, but in some places in the country they carry contaminated water that is poisoning local populations (prominent examples being Flint, Michigan and East Chicago, Indiana).[50] The reason for the failure to maintain the infrastructure is lack of resources. In particular, from 1977 to 2009, federal grants for water and sewer systems fell by 75% (after accounting for inflation). This left the financial burden, estimated to be between $655 billion and $1 trillion to restore the infrastructure nationwide, [51] on the shoulders of local water authorities. They have been reluctant to raise rates, in part for fear of political backlash, and also because, in low income areas, residents can ill-afford to pay.[52]

In some municipalities, the response was to privatize the water system. In the 1990s, many made the switch, including, for example, cities like Atlanta, Indianapolis, and Tampa Bay, and a number of municipalities in states like New Jersey, Pennsylvania, California and Illinois.[53] Proponents of privatization argued that private companies have easier access to capital markets for infrastructure investment and can borrow at better interest rates.[54] In addition, they offer measurable efficiency gains—as much as one-third more.[55] "Profitability dictates that a system be as efficient as possible so that it can be as profitable as possible."[56] Further, private companies are less bureaucratic and they are "demonstrably ahead of government owned utilities in terms of technology and state-of-the-art practices."[57] While such technologies may have a higher initial cost, they offer savings, too, it was argued, "which can be shared with customers while improving service and quality."[58]

What has been the result of the country's most recent experience with the privatization of water? Between 2002 and 2014, no fewer than 33 municipalities in the US chose to "remunicipalize" their water systems by taking them back under public control.[59] A number of reports explain the reasons for this: Privatization has resulted neither in increased infrastructure investment,[60] nor in increased private financing. Private water companies have instead preferred to use public investment finance (government loans and bonds), which are considered to be less costly than private finance. Further, in lobbying Congress for access to federal funding, private companies have made it more difficult for public systems to access federal funding.[61] Private water companies have not been shown to operate more efficiently than public ones.[62] Also, in many cases privatization has led to increased costs, as a result of profit requirements, dividends, income taxes, executive compensation, and the mere complexities involved in negotiating a privatization and then monitoring it once it's in place.[63]

Further, there is no evidence that privatization has led to better water quality: Not only do private water companies actively lobby Congress and the Environmental Protection Agency to refrain from adopting higher quality standards,[64] but there are a number of examples where privatized systems (including Atlanta's and Indianapolis's) have produced inferior if not contaminated water that has required boiling before use.[65] Additionally, private companies tend to cherry pick the localities they will service, avoiding economically depressed areas where household income is low, where water quality problems are significant, or where repair and maintenance of the infrastructure would be particularly expensive.[66] Finally, private water companies have successfully lobbied against bills that would require them to be more transparent in their operations, notably to require them to submit quarterly and annual reports, to alert users in the event of a request to increase rates, or to provide more information in the event of boil-alert notices.[67]

In sum, there is no evidence that the privatized water systems are superior to public ones and in a number of instances they have proven to be worse.

Let's look at one more example of the privatization of a public service in the United States: primary and secondary education. For many years, a number of people have argued that many of our country's public schools are in trouble: they don't have the resources they need to provide quality education;[68] without competition, they have no incentive to operate efficiently;[69] they aren't able to innovate (some are even "technologically backward"[70]); they are mired in bureaucracy;[71] their class sizes are too large and their facilities are so overcrowded, they are "bursting at the seams."[72] In sum, they argue, our public schools are failing.[73]

Several states have responded by creating a voucher system in which parents can use publicly-funded credits to send their children to the private school of their choice. In essence, it is the use of public money to finance private schools. The first modern voucher program was implemented in Milwaukee in 1990; since then approximately fifteen states plus the District of Columbia have adopted a school voucher program in some form.

Advocates of school voucher programs argue that they give parents choice about where they send their children to school, and notably they enable students from low-income families to escape "failing" schools.[74] They create needed competition among schools, forcing the "failing" public ones either to improve or close. They increase the quality of public schools as well as increasing the quality of schools available overall.[75] They enable more efficient spending of public money.[76] They enable schools to experiment with innovation.[77]

What is the result of the country's nearly three decade experiment with school vouchers? A number of studies come to the same conclusions: School voucher programs have limited to no effect on student achievement, and in a number of cases they have had a negative effect.[78] The level of regulatory oversight exercised over a private school did not seem to make a difference because if a school was sanctioned for poor academic performance, performance did not improve.[79] In some areas, student achievement did improve in *public* schools at the time a voucher program was implemented, but researchers ascribe most if not all of that improvement to increased public accountability measures that were put in place at the same time as the voucher program.[80] In addition, there is no evidence that school voucher programs have led to greater innovation: notably, the vouchers have benefitted many pre-existing religious schools (especially Catholic and also Islamic), some of which had seen dramatic drops in enrollment just prior to the implementation of the program.[81] There is no evidence that any private school, subsequent to entering a voucher program, has developed any curriculum or teaching method that could be described as "innovative" in any effective manner, and there is no convincing evidence that voucher programs have reduced racial segregation in schools.[82] Further, there is no evidence that vouchers have resulted in more "efficient" spending of public funds. There are, however, a number of examples of self-dealing, fraud and embezzlement of public funds by private schools participating in voucher programs.[83]

Finally, private schools that benefit from voucher programs have limited accountability and transparency. Notably, in most cases they are not obliged to disclose the subjects they teach, the experience or qualifications of their teachers, or their students' performance outcomes (besides the results of an annual standardized test).[84] Most especially, most such schools are not accountable for how they spend public funds, and, in many cases, nor are they required to disclose their accounting or have it subject to audit. Proponents of voucher programs actively lobby against greater accountability and transparency on the grounds that it would re-create the bureaucracy of public schools and restrict them from being "creative in the classroom and more open to trying different approaches." For them (proponents of voucher programs and other forms of privatization of public education, like charter schools), sole accountability should lie with parents: if they don't like a school, they can simply remove their child from it.[85]

In sum, there is no evidence that the privatization of public education has been beneficial for American children, and in many cases it has been detrimental.

There is a definite pattern in these examples of privatization of public services. Proponents of privatization in each case complained of the bureaucracy and inefficiency of the government. Because the government had a monopoly, it had no motivation to strive to improve its service. Further, proponents of privatization observed that demand was so great, the service was "bursting at the seams." Yet, also in each case, they asserted that government did not have the resources to meet the demand. On the other hand, private enterprises did. They had greater access to capital and to expertise. Privatization, it was argued, would result in greater innovation. Freed of bureaucracy and motivated by the possibility of profit, in each case private enterprises would develop innovative services that would better meet the needs of the public (themselves transformed into customers). Faced with competition, they would be forced to operate as efficiently as possible. The end result would—necessarily—be greater innovation and choice, better quality, and greater customer satisfaction.

Except that's not how it turned out. Not in any case. There is no convincing evidence that the privatization of these public services (prisons, water, schools) has resulted in greater innovation, higher quality, or increased efficiency. There is evidence of service failures. There is evidence of many unsatisfied customers. There is evidence of perverse incentives. There is evidence of fraud, conflicts of interest, and self-dealing. There is evidence not just of lack of accountability and transparency, but of active and strong resistance to both. In each case, there is scant to no evidence that the privatization of the public service has, on the whole, actually benefitted the public.

In *Rules for a Flat World*, Hadfield states that her proposal to privatize regulation is "not as crazy as it sounds." She continues, "In fact, there's a story to be told that this is just the natural next step in the evolution of human systems for managing complexity."[86] If you consider her proposal in the context of the privatization of other public services, notably of prisons, water and education, then she is right that the privatization of regulation is the "natural next step" in a story of progression towards the privatization of a greater number of public services in the US. But is it a step we want to take?

CLEARING UP CONFUSION AND CALLING OUT CONTRADICTIONS

It is important not to confuse regulatory competition with the privatization of regulation. As discussed above, regulatory competition has occurred historically and continues to occur today in a number of contexts, including the regulation of legal services in England & Wales. However, in most if not all cases, it occurs among public regulators, all under an obligation to act in the public interest. Hadfield recommends the greater use of regulatory competition, but she goes one giant step further: that such competition should be among *private* actors, motivated by profit (or, in the event of a nonprofit, by the ability to have a social impact).

It is also important not to confuse alternative structures (the focus of this book in your hands) with the privatization of regulation. Alternative structures, and the larger issue of ending the lawyer monopoly on legal services, relate to *private* actors already acting in an existing, already long privatized, market for legal services. The argument for alternative structures is an argument to open up that market—already serviced by private actors—to a greater variety of private actors. Alternative structures and ending the lawyer monopoly on legal services are fundamentally about access to justice and equal protection of the law. If lawyers are not able or willing to meet 100% of our country's needs for legal services, then they need to get out of the way—they need to stop blocking others who would like to step up and try meet some of those unmet needs.

In stark contrast (and with the exception of self-regulation), regulation today concerns nearly exclusively *public* actors, acting mostly in the absence of any kind of "market" (or, as advocates for the privatization of public services would put it, acting in a near-monopoly situation). Further, the proposal to privatize regulation concerns the regulation of not just legal services, but of potentially anything that is or could be regulated by public bodies today (The specific examples in *Rules for a Flat World* relate to contracts, business organizations, employment and consumer law[87]). Hadfield describes her book as bringing out "the critical question of how we build and implement the legal infrastructure we need for a new complex and more inclusive global economy."[88] Seen from this economy-focused perspective, the privatization of regulation is not fundamentally about access to justice or equal protection of the law, but about facilitating business transactions and maximizing profits.[89]

Hadfield correctly points out that today our public regulatory bodies do not have the resources they need to regulate effectively. But she appears to accept this lack of resources as an immutable fact that she does not question. It is as if their lack of resources has resulted from an act of god—not man, and certainly not from the policies of "small government" and minimal taxation adopted by our elected politicians—it is as if it were something we have no power to change.[90] That is simply not the case. With every election we have the power to change it.

Or, at least, in a democracy, we would. Today many argue that the United States is no longer a democracy. This is in large part, they argue, because of the inordinate power that private companies now have in our political and regulatory processes.[91] A 2014 study conducted by Martin Gilens and

Benjamin Page found that Americans do enjoy certain features central to democratic governance, such as regular elections, freedom of speech and association, and a widespread (if contested) franchise. However, on the basis of their empirical research, Gilens and Page conclude that these "features" today do not translate into political power for ordinary American citizens. To the contrary, they found that majorities of ordinary citizens have little influence over the policies that government adopts. Instead, the actual power to shape both political agendas (what issues are considered) as well as policy outcomes (the decisions made with respect to those issues) is nearly entirely controlled by "economic elites" and organized groups representing business interests. They further found that while occasionally the interests of majorities of American citizens and the interests of economic elites and business interests align, this is rarely the case. And when they do not align (which, again, is nearly always), the citizen majority loses.[92]

It is in this context that the proposal to privatize regulation can in fact be seen as a proposal to transfer *political processes along with government itself* directly to business interests, eliminating the need to bother with the "bureaucratic" (and only ostensibly democratic) institutions of legislatures, executives and courts. Proponents of the proposal would likely object to this depiction, and argue that there is nothing political in the privatization of regulation. But how can that be, when the proposal entails transferring to private business entities, operating for a profit, the power both to make and to enforce rules that govern our society?[93] What is politics and what is government, if not, at their very core, the making and the enforcement of rules that govern our society?[94]

Hadfield argues that "voters" would be protected from bad private regulators because they can (and should) expect governments to exercise sufficient regulatory oversight over private regulators. In fact, the argument goes, this would place voters in an even better position because while it is "demanding" to expect voters to actively evaluate how government regulators are regulating individual businesses, it is "less demanding" to expect voters to merely evaluate how government regulators are regulating how private regulators regulate individual businesses. However, this argument is undermined if not contradicted by other arguments, and notably by one stating that using the vote as means to get government regulators to pay attention to your needs as a voter "is a blunt instrument at best." It is much better, Hadfield argues, to be able to sue a private regulator when it fails to "fund [its] courts adequately and it takes a year to get a court date," or "it costs you millions in e-discovery costs to litigate your case."[95]

If the privatized "court" who is earning a profit from adjudicating your lawsuit isn't doing a good job, your "better" solution is to instigate a *second* lawsuit? This time you should sue in front of a public court which is already under-resourced and which will likely be even further starved of resources as a result of privatization?

There are additional contradictions. Hadfield frequently emphasizes the importance of a competitive regulatory market in order for private regulation to work.[96] She states that this will depend upon a "slew of laws:"[97] antitrust to protect against monopolies, financial regulation to assure access to capital, internet rules to assure access to communication infrastructures, etc. In this privatization scenario, it is extremely important for public regulators to oversee private regulators—to assure that private regulators are respecting those laws and are otherwise meeting the targets government has set for them.[98] Hadfield states "relying on market-based private regulators will be only as effective and attractive as the quality of the government oversight of the system. She also states that regulating private regulators will "almost certainly be a new and substantial challenge for governments."[99] However, governments already don't have the resources they need to regulate effectively, and this is presented as an immutable fact. Where will governments find the additional resources to effectively regulate private regulators? Hadfield offers scant assurance on this point, stating merely that "there are good reasons to think" that privatized regulation will place lower demands on governments, but only in "several settings," not all of them.[100] The failure to address this need for additional public oversight and how to fund it is highly troublesome.[101]

The proposal is troubling in another manner. Hadfield argues that in order to induce private companies to make investments in the development of better regulation, their ideas and inventions should be protected. This could be with a patent or copyright, or by allowing the private company to maintain secrecy, further protected by confidentiality agreements and trade secret laws.[102] This element, alone, turns the entire concept of regulation on its head. How can regulation fulfill its very reason of existence—to serve the public interest—if it can be kept secret? If it can be considered to be "private" property protected by intellectual property laws and accessible only to those able to pay the "market" rate to access it? If the owner of the "private" property could be permitted, at its discretion, to keep it secret, with the right to refuse to grant access to any one or more persons at any price? This element flies in the face of the United Nations 2030 Agenda for Sustainable Development, under which the United States has committed, among other things, "to develop effective, accountable and *transparent institutions at all levels*." [103]

Further, the privatization of regulation would represent a significant step backwards in a nation- and world-wide movement to establish free access to law and legal information. The Declaration on Free Access to Law affirms: that public legal information from all countries and international institutions is part of "the common heritage of humanity;" that maximizing access to this information promotes justice and the rule of law; that public legal information is "digital common property" and should be accessible to all on a non-profit basis and free of charge; and that organizations (such as legal information institutes) have the right to publish public legal information and the government bodies that create or control that information should provide access to it so that it can be published by other parties.[104] By operating to privatize what had previously been public legal information and by protecting that information with intellectual property and trade secret laws, we would reject outright these affirmations. We would destroy the "common heritage of humanity," and we would make law—and thereby justice itself—that much more difficult and expensive to access.

The proposal to privatize regulation has another troubling aspect. Hadfield explains how there is an "economic demand" for law because of the protection that it offers businesses.[105] As a hypothetical, she paints a picture for a business in a world with "lousy legal infrastructure." In this world, employees and other businesses have no reliable identification or addresses, there are no reliable credit-rating agencies, there are no courts (and notably no courts that can't be bribed by those richer and better connected), no one answers the 911 call when the business's computers are stolen, the business can't find an internet provider because its competitors have entered into exclusive contracts with all of them, and government representatives insist the business owes many thousands of dollars in back taxes that in fact were already paid.[106]

Having painted this picture, Hadfield rightfully explains that we need rules—that we need law. She rightfully points out that rather than objecting to rules, and seeking to avoid them, we should be happy for their existence and, especially, we should appreciate and be glad for how our "legal infrastructure" protects us.[107]

Indeed, the protection laws offer to us—to *each* of us, equally—is considered to be so important that it is enshrined in the Constitution. Specifically, the 14th Amendment, ratified in 1868 in the wake of the Civil War, forbids any state as well as local government from denying to any person within their jurisdiction the *equal* protection of its laws. The impetus for this amendment was to assure that states, including states of the former Confederacy, would act to protect the civil rights of all its citizens, including former slaves. It has since been applied on a much broader basis, and in particular it has been used to protect businesses from arbitrary or discriminatory state actions. The amendment applies only to state (government) actors; it does not apply to private actors.

There is irony in stressing the importance of the protections that law offers to us. This is because privatized regulation has the potential of significantly if not drastically reducing the application of the 14th Amendment by reducing the application of all our rules and processes to all citizens on an equal basis. Indeed, it would leave certain citizens—perhaps many—without the protection of any law or process, depending upon the "setting." This is because rules and processes previously adopted by public actors would instead be adopted and enforced by private actors. As private actors, they would be free to exclude persons from the application—protection—of their rules and processes. In particular, they would be free to exclude those unable to pay "market" price. If that occurs, those persons would have no choice but to fall back upon public rules and processes. But those would necessarily be inferior to the private ones, given that, as Hadfield points out, governments do not have the resources they need to effectively regulate. It is also quite possible that, as noted above, public regulators would be even further starved of resources on the assumption that they didn't need any since private regulators were on the scene. In that event, it is quite possible that, depending upon the "setting," there would no longer be any applicable public law or process, with the result that persons unable to pay the "market" rates for private regulation would lose all protection of the law.

In a "pay to play" scenario, Hadfield describes a situation when a hypothetical private, for profit regulator would need a ruling from a California court before the private regulator is able to continue with its own regulatory process, but where the California court might take a long time to issue such a ruling. Hadfield's recommendation for a "really smart" private regulator to get around this problem is that it "make arrangements" with the California courts to get quick rulings, and that it pay the courts for that fast-track service.[108] This suggestion ironically echoes Hadfield's description of a "lousy legal infrastructure" where courts can be bribed by those richer and better connected, and it exacerbates the failure of law to provide equal protection for all citizens.

Our country's experiences with the privatization of prisons, water and education show us that the privatization of a public service is unlikely to benefit the public. There is no reason to believe that the privatization of another, crucial, public service—regulation—would have better results. If Hadfield's proposal were to be adopted in the manner she proposes and function in the manner she predicts, it would result in a regulatory dystopia where: decisions that concern society as a whole that were formerly made by at least ostensibly democratic institutions would instead be made by private companies seeking to maximize profit and shareholder value; where rules and processes that concern society as a whole can be kept secret, or made available only upon payment of "market" price; and where at least some persons and possibly many lose their right to equal protection under the law. It would turn citizens of a democracy into mere customers of a corporate state.

Hadfield is wholly correct in her observation that we desperately need better regulation—not just for legal services (the focus of this book) but in many if not all other domains. However, if regulation is a public service—if it is something that we as a society need and value because it brings economic as well as social value to everyone—then it cannot be financed or developed privately. It must be financed publicly through equitable, progressive revenue sources, and it must be developed by public, democratic processes.[109] Are the processes messy? Certainly they are. But, to quote Colin Crouch, "we are enmeshed in needs for collective and public goods. To seek to wriggle out from the challenges that this presents is to wriggle out of being human."[110]

ASSESSMENT

In the spirit of the rest of this book, it makes sense to examine the extent to which the proposal to privatize regulation would, if implemented, correspond to the OECD's six essential elements of an effective regulatory policy. For each element, the response lies upon a spectrum, from "yes," "for the most part," "sort of," "limited," "not really," and "no:"

Table 27.1 Assessment for Privatized Regulation (as proposed in *Rules for a Flat World*)

1	Independent regulation	No	This element requires that regulators operate free of conflicts of interest, including without regard for personal gain, so that the regulator can regulate in the public interest. In allowing a private regulator to seek profit for itself and/or its shareholders (or in allowing a nonprofit private regulator to seek social impact for defined, targeted stakeholders), there is conflict with the interests of the public as a whole
2	Accountability and transparency	No	The proposal does not suggest that private regulators be required to conduct any of their activities in a manner that is open to the public or to government oversight regulators, nor does it suggest that private regulators be required to publish annual reports or accounts. It recommends that the ideas and inventions of private regulators be protected as intellectual property and/or as confidential information, protected by trade secret laws

3	Regulatory oversight bodies	Limited	The importance of government oversight of private regulators is emphasized, but the fact that governments do not have the resources to carry out regulation in an effective manner is also emphasized. The proposal does not contain a recommendation that government regulators be supplied with the necessary resources or explain in general how that could occur
4	Citizen engagement	No	The proposal does not anticipate or recommend citizen engagement of any kind. Unsatisfied customers of private regulators must sue in public courts
5	Regulatory impact assessments	Sort of	The proposal contains a recommendation for more research to improve knowledge about "legal infrastructure." However, it is not clear who should carry it out. One suggestion is that private companies should, because competitive markets "create an incentive to invest in information." Another suggestion is that governments and universities should. "Donors" are exhorted to provide resources, and governments are urged to spend "much more" for this purpose. The general basis of how to fund research through government that is already lacking resources is unclear
6	Risk-based approach	No	While the book mentions management-based regulation, nothing in the proposal specifically advocates in favor of a risk-based approach. It advocates more generally, in favor of private regulators engaging in "serious innovation" in order to develop better "legal infrastructure." This theoretically involves taking *market* risks, but that is different from the concept of risk-based regulation

NOTES

1. Hadfield, *Rules for a Flat World*, 48–54, 335–340.
2. Hadfield, "The Cost of Law."
3. Hadfield and Heine, "Life in the Law-Thick World."
4. Hadfield, "Legal Barriers to Innovation."
5. Hadfield, "Legal Infrastructure and the New Economy."
6. Hadfield, *Rules for a Flat World*, 219–245.
7. Ibid., 130.
8. Ibid., 169–175.
9. Ibid., 176–185. See also Hadfield and Heine, "Life in the Law-Thick World."
10. Hadfield, *Rules for a Flat World*, 185–194.
11. Ibid., 194–195.
12. Ibid., 199.
13. Daniel Stedman Jones, *Masters of the Universe: Hayek, Friedman, and the Birth of Neoliberal Politics* (Princeton, New Jersey: Princeton University Press, 2012); George Monbiot, "Neoliberalism—The Ideology at the Root of all Our Problems," *The Guardian*, April 15, 2016, https://www.theguardian.com/books/2016/apr/15/neoliberalism-ideology-problem-george-monbiot.
14. Hadfield, *Rules for a Flat World*, 199–205.
15. Ibid., 205–207.
16. Ibid., 207–212.
17. Ibid., 247.
18. Ibid., 228, 248.
19. Ibid., 248.
20. Ibid., 269.
21. Ibid., 250, 260–277.
22. Ibid., 245, 267.
23. Ibid., 245.
24. The Law Society, "Our Constitution," https://www.lawsociety.org.uk/About-us/our-constitution/; CILEx, "Royal Charter," https://www.cilex.org.uk/about_cilex/who_we_are/royal-charter; CIPA, "About Us," http://www.cipa.org.uk/about-us/about-us/; CITMA, "The Making of Our Royal Charter," https://www.citma.org.uk/about_citma/royal_charter/making_our_royal_charter; ICAEW, "Charter and Bye-laws," http://www.icaew.com/en/about-icaew/who-we-are/charter-and-bye-laws; Administration of Justice Act 1985, Art. 28, http://www.legislation.gov.uk/ukpga/1985/61/section/12; The Faculty Office, "About the Faculty Office & Our History," http://www.facultyoffice.org.uk/about-us/ (all accessed March 20, 2017).
25. See Privy Council: "Royal Charters," https://privycouncil.independent.gov.uk/royal-charters/; "Charted Bodies," https://privycouncil.independent.gov.uk/royal-charters/chartered-bodies/; "Privy Council Members," https://privycouncil.independent.gov.uk/privy-council/privy-council-members/ (all accessed March 20, 2017).
26. Legal Services Act of 2007, Art. 28, http://www.legislation.gov.uk/ukpga/2007/29/pdfs/ukpga_20070029_en.pdf.
27. See: (1) Solicitors Regulation Authority, SRA Governance Handbook, January, 2015, 44; (2) Constitution of the Bar Standards Board as amended 12

November 2011, 4, 10, 14–15; Standing Orders for the Bar Standards Board, January 26, 2017, 3, https://www.barstandardsboard.org.uk/media/1818467/bsb_standing_orders_2017__approved_january_2017_.pdf; (3) CILEx Regulation, "Code of Conduct for Board Members," last reviewed January 2015, http://www.cilexregulation.org.uk/~/media/pdf_documents/cilex-regulation/code-of-conduct/code-of-conduct-for-board-members.pdf?la=en; CILEx Regulation, "Applicants for Membership of the Disciplinary Tribunal and Panels: Application Pack," undated, 5–6, http://www.cilexregulation.org.uk/~/media/pdf_documents/cilex-regulation/vacancies/professional_conduct_panel_lay_member/panel-and-tribunal-pool-members-application-pack.pdf?la=en; (4) Council for Licensed Conveyancers, "Professional Member of the Council," undated, 5–6, http://www.conveyancer.org.uk/CLCSite/media/Current-Vacancies/Professional-Member-of-Council-Candidate-Pack.pdf; (5) IPReg, "Promotion of the Regulatory Objectives Policy Statement," undated, 9, http://ipreg.org.uk/wp-content/files/2012/09/Promotion-of-the-Regulatory-Objectives-Policy-Statement-LSB.pdf; The Patent Regulation Board and Trade Mark Regulation Board, "Minutes," November 27, 2014, 7, 9, http://ipreg.org.uk/wp-content/files/2012/09/Minutes_November_2014_Board_Meeting_and_supporting_papers-_website.pdf; (6) ICAEW, "Probate Committee Terms of Reference," undated, 2, https://www.icaew.com/-/media/corporate/files/members/regulations-standards-and-guidance/reserved-legal-services/20-terms-of-reference-for-the-probate-committee.ashx?la=en.

28. Committee on Standards in Public Life, "Striking the Balance: Upholding the Seven Principles of Public Life in Regulation," September, 2016, https://www.gov.uk/government/uploads/system/uploads/attachment_data/file/554817/Striking_the_Balance__web__-_v3_220916.pdf; see also Committee on Standards in Public Life, "The 7 Principles of Public Life," accessed March 1, 2017, https://www.gov.uk/government/publications/the-7-principles-of-public-life/the-7-principles-of-public-life—2.

29. OECD Being an Independent, 41.

30. Hadfield, *Rules for a Flat World*, 248.

31. For an interesting discussion of the privatization of public services in the UK, see Colin Crouch, *The Knowledge Corrupters: Hidden Consequences of the Financial Takeover of Public Life* (Cambridge, UK: Polity Press, 2016), 97–127.

32. Hadfield, *Rules for a Flat World*, 271, 277.

33. J.C. Oleson, "The Punitive Coma," *California Law Review* 90 (2002): 846, http://dx.doi.org/doi:10.15779/Z38HH7S; Sacramento Bee and Andy Furillo, "California's Prisons Bursting at Seams and Understaffed," *East Bay Times*, November 26, 2005, http://www.eastbaytimes.com/2005/11/26/californias-prisons-bursting-at-seams-and-understaffed/; Illinois Criminal Justice Information Authority, "Blueprint for the Future: Final Report of Trends & Issues for the 1990s," January, 1991, 38.

34. Cody Mason, "Too Good to Be True: Private Prisons in America," report prepared for The Sentencing Project, January, 2012, 1, http://sentencingproject.org/wp-content/uploads/2016/01/Too-Good-to-be-True-Private-Prisons-in-America.pdf.

35. Sally Q. Yates, "Phasing Out Our Use of Private Prisons," The United States Department of Justice, August 18, 2016, https://www.justice.gov/opa/blog/phasing-out-our-use-private-prisons.

36. Joseph Shannon Gregson, "Comparing Public and Private Prison Systems," Paper presented to the Public Administration Faculty at the University of

Michigan-Flint In Partial Fulfillment of the Requirements for the Master of Public Administration, Fall, 2000, iv, 2, 4, 16, https://deepblue.lib.umich.edu/bitstream/handle/2027.42/117712/Gregson.pdf?sequence=1&isAllowed=y.

37. Matt Zapotosky and Chico Harlan, "Justice Department Says It Will End Use of Private Prisons," *The Washington Post*, August 18, 2016, https://www.washingtonpost.com/news/post-nation/wp/2016/08/18/justice-department-says-it-will-end-use-of-private-prisons/?amp;tid=ss_tw&utm_term=.57f0149acafa&postshare=9221471534255226&utm_term=.0b4001c3b3f9.

38. Office of the Inspector General, US Department of Justice, "Review of the Federal Bureau of Prisons' Monitoring of Contract Prisons," August, 2016, https://oig.justice.gov/reports/2016/e1606.pdf#page=2.

39. Sally Q. Yates, "Memorandum for the Acting Director, Federal Bureau of Prisons," August 18, 2016, https://www.justice.gov/opa/file/886311/download.

40. See, for example, New York Times Editorial Board, "Under Mr. Trump, Private Prisons Thrive Again," *New York Times*, February 24, 2017, https://www.nytimes.com/2017/02/24/opinion/under-mr-trump-private-prisons-thrive-again.html?_r=0; Justin Carissimo, "Jeff Sessions Reverses Obama Order to Phase Out Private Prisons," *Independent*, February 23, 2017, http://www.independent.co.uk/news/world/americas/jeff-sessions-signals-support-for-private-prisons-a7596661.html.

41. Mason, "Too Good to Be True," 6–8, 10; see also In the Public Interest, "How Privatization Increases Inequality," September, 2016, 40–42, https://www.inthepublicinterest.org/wp-content/uploads/InthePublicInterest_InequalityReport_Sept2016.pdf.

42. Mason, "Too Good to Be True," 11, quoting Scott D. Camp and Gerald G. Gaes, "Growth and Quality of U.S. Private Prisons: Evidence from a National Survey," paper prepared for Federal Bureau of Prisons, Office of Research and Evaluation, September 21, 2001, 16, https://www.bop.gov/resources/research_projects/published_reports/pub_vs_priv/oreprres_note.pdf.

43. Mason, "Too Good to Be True," 11–12; See also, for example, Linda Greenhouse, "Outsourcing the Constitution," *New York Times*, March 1, 2017, https://www.nytimes.com/2017/03/01/opinion/outsourcing-the-constitution.html.

44. Mason, "Too Good to Be True," 12.

45. Ibid., 13–16.

46. Christie Thompson, "Everything You Ever Wanted to Know About Private Prisons . . . is None of your Damn Business," The Marshall Project, December 18, 2014, https://www.themarshallproject.org/2014/12/18/everything-you-ever-wanted-to-know-about-private-prisons#.nQOGdI8Gw; Mike Tartaglia, "Private Prisons, Private Records," *Boston University Law Review* 94 (2014): 1689–1744, http://www.bu.edu/bulawreview/files/2014/10/TARTAGLIA.pdf.

47. Michelle Ye Hee Lee, "Yes, U.S. Locks People Up at a Higher Rate than Any Other Country," *The Washington Post*, July 7, 2015, https://www.washingtonpost.com/news/fact-checker/wp/2015/07/07/yes-u-s-locks-people-up-at-a-higher-rate-than-any-other-country/?utm_term=.854bffd0aa07.

48. Clint Smith, "Why the U.S. Is Right to Move Away from Private Prisons," *The New Yorker*, August 24, 2016, http://www.newyorker.com/news/news-desk/why-the-u-s-is-right-to-move-away-from-private-prisons.

49. Committee on Privatization of Water Services in the United States, National Research Council, *Privatization of Water Services in the United States: An Assessment of Issues and Experience* (Washington, DC: National Academy Press, 2002), 30–32, https://doi.org/10.17226/10135; Center for International Environmental Law, "The Ebb and Flow of the Water Privatization Debate Briefing Paper for the Fourth World Water Forum," March 2006, 2, http://www.ciel.org/Publications/EbbFlow_Mar06.pdf; Food & Water Watch, "The State of Public Water in the United States," February, 2016, 3–4, http://www.foodandwaterwatch.org/sites/default/files/report_state_of_public_water.pdf.

50. "America's Neglected Water Systems Face a Reckoning," Knowledge@Wharton, June 10, 2015, http://knowledge.wharton.upenn.edu/article/americas-neglected-water-systems-face-a-reckoning/; Alana Semuels, "Aging Pipes Are Poisoning America's Tap Water," *The Atlantic*, July 29, 2015, https://www.theatlantic.com/business/archive/2015/07/dont-drink-the-water/399803/; Michael Hawthorne, "EPA Warns of Lead in Water in East Chicago," *Chicago Tribune*, March 2, 2017, http://www.chicagotribune.com/suburbs/ct-east-chicago-lead-water-20170302-story.html.

51. United States Government Accountability Office, "Water Infrastructure: Information on Selected Midsize and Large Cities with Declining Populations," Report to the Ranking Member, Subcommittee on Environment and the Economy, Committee on Energy and Commerce, House of Representatives, September, 2016, 2, http://gao.gov/assets/680/679783.pdf; American Water Works Association, "Buried No Longer: Confronting America's Water Infrastructure Challenge," February 27, 2012, 10, http://www.awwa.org/Portals/0/files/legreg/documents/BuriedNoLonger.pdf.

52. America's Neglected Water Systems Face a Reckoning," Knowledge@Wharton; Maude Barlow and Wenonah Hauter, "The Dangerous Return of Water Privatization," Utne Reader, January/February 2014, http://www.utne.com/politics/water-privatization-zm0z14jfzros?pageid=2#PageContent2.

53. Committee on Privatization of Water Services, *Privatization of Water Services*, 17, 20–21, 24; Shiney Varghese, "Privatizing U.S. Water," paper prepared by the Institute for Agriculture and Trade Policy Trade and Global Governance Program, July, 2007, 2–3, http://www.iatp.org/files/451_2_99838.pdf.

54. Edwin S. Rubenstein, "The Untapped Potential of Water Privatization," A Hudson Institute Report for American Water Works, Inc., October, 2000, http://www.esrresearch.com/Theprivatewaterindustry.htm.

55. "Are We Better Off Privatizing Water?" *Wall Street Journal*, October 8, 2012, https://www.wsj.com/articles/SB10000872396390443816804578002280926253750; Rubenstein, "The Untapped Potential of Water Privatization.

56. Crystal Lombardo, "Water Privatization Pros and Cons," Vision Launch, January 7, 2015, http://visionlaunch.com/water-privatization-pros-and-cons/#.

57. Rubenstein, "The Untapped Potential of Water Privatization."

58. "Are We Better Off Privatizing Water?" *Wall Street Journal.*

59. Emanuele Lobina with Corporate Accountability International, "Troubled Waters: Misleading Industry PR and the Case for Public Water," November, 2014, 18, https://www.stopcorporateabuse.org/sites/default/files/resources/troubledwaters_

webres.pdf; see also Food & Water Watch, "The State of Public Water in the United States," 5–6.

60. David Gordon, "An Analysis of the Privatization of Drinking Water Facilities in the United States," Masters project submitted in partial fulfillment of the requirements for the Masters of Environmental Management degree in the Nicholas School of the Environment of Duke University, May, 2011, 2, 40–49, http://dukespace.lib.duke.edu/dspace/bitstream/handle/10161/3708/Gordon_David_Final_MP.pdf;sequence=1; Lobina, "Troubled Waters," 16.

61. Lobina, "Troubled Waters," 16, 22–24; Food & Water Watch, "Water Privatization: Facts and Figures," August 31, 2015, http://www.foodandwaterwatch.org/insight/water-privatization-facts-and-figures; Public Citizen, "Top 10 Reasons to Oppose Water Privatization," undated, 2, https://www.citizen.org/documents/Top10-ReasonsToOpposeWaterPrivatization.pdf.

62. Craig Anthony Arnold, "Water Privatization Trends in the United States: Human Rights, National Security, and Public Stewardship," *William & Mary Environmental Law and Policy Review* 33 (2009): 803, http://scholarship.law.wm.edu/wmelpr/vol33/iss3/4/; see also Lobina, "Troubled Waters," 10–12.

63. Food & Water Watch, "The State of Public Water in the United States," 7; Food & Water Watch, "The Public Works How the Remunicipalization of Water Services Saves Money," December, 2010, http://www.foodandwaterwatch.org/sites/default/files/The%20Public%20Works%20FS%20Dec%202010.pdf.

64. Sara Ehrhardt and Maude Barlow, "A Debate on Water Privatization," Part Six, *Grist*, July 17, 2004, http://grist.org/article/barlow2/; Public Citizen, "Top 10 Reasons to Oppose Water Privatization," 2.

65. Jon R. Luoma, "Water for Profit," *Mother Jones*, November/December, 2002, http://www.motherjones.com/politics/2002/11/water-profit; Corporate Accountability International, "Public Water Works! The Case for Prioritizing our Most Essential Public Service," 2012, 19, https://www.stopcorporateabuse.org/sites/default/files/resources/public-water-works.pdf; George Potanovic, "Take Back Our Water: How Trump's Appetite for Privatization Threatens Your Drinking Water," *Salon*, January 23, 2017, http://www.salon.com/2017/01/23/take-back-our-water-how-trumps-appetite-for-privatization-threatens-your-drinking-water_partner/; Food & Water Watch, "Has Water Privatization Gone Too Far in New Jersey?" June, 2010, 6, https://www.inthepublicinterest.org/wp-content/uploads/FWW_PrivatizationInNewJersey.pdf.

66. Food & Water Watch, "The State of Public Water in the United States," 7–8; Lobina, "Troubled Waters," 32.

67. Lobina, "Troubled Waters," 24–25.

68. "Why America's Schools Have A Money Problem," *NPR*, April 18, 2016, http://www.npr.org/2016/04/18/474256366/why-americas-schools-have-a-money-problem; "More Than 40% of Low-Income Schools Don't Get a Fair Share of State and Local Funds, Department of Education Research Finds," US Department of Education, November 30, 2011, https://www.ed.gov/news/press-releases/more-40-low-income-schools-dont-get-fair-share-state-and-local-funds-department-; Meredith Broussard, "Why Poor Schools Can't Win at Standardized Testing," *The Atlantic*, July 15, 2014, https://www.theatlantic.com/education/archive/2014/07/why-poor-schools-cant-win-at-standardized-testing/374287/.

69. John Merrifield, *The School Choice Wars* (Lanham, Maryland: Scarecrow Press, 2001), 10; Nathan J. Robinson, "Why Is 'The Decimation of Public Schools' A Bad Thing?" *Current Affairs*, November 30, 2016, https://www.currentaffairs.org/2016/11/why-is-the-decimation-of-public-schools-a-bad-thing.

70. Merrifield, *The School Choice Wars*, 10.

71. Robinson, "Why Is The Decimation."

72. Benjamin Herold, "Northeast Schools: 'Bursting at the Seams,'" The Notebook, June 10, 2011, http://legacy.thenotebook.org/blog/113794/northeast-schools-bursting-seams; Rose Arce, "Does Class Size Matter?" CNN School of Thought, December 6, 2011, http://schoolsofthought.blogs.cnn.com/2011/12/06/does-class-size-matter/.

73. Scott McNealy, "Our Public Education System 'is Failing,'" CNBC, August 9, 2016, http://www.cnbc.com/2016/08/09/our-public-education-system-is-failing-scott-mcnealy-commentary.html.

74. Adam B. Schaeffer, "No, Virginia, There is No Such Thing as School Choice," Cato Institute, October 29, 2006, https://www.cato.org/publications/commentary/no-virginia-there-is-no-such-thing-school-choice.

75. The Friedman Foundation for Educational Choice, "How Does School Choice Affect Public Schools?" undated, 1, http://www.schoolchoicewi.org/files/7114/2064/5055/How-does-school-choice-affect-public-schools.pdf.

76. Schaeffer, "No, Virginia."

77. Milton Friedman, "Why America Needs School Vouchers," *Wall Street Journal*, September 28, 2000, https://www.edchoice.org/who-we-are/our-founders/the-friedmans-on-school-choice/article/why-america-needs-school-vouchers/.

78. Martin Carnoy, "School Vouchers are Not a Proven Strategy for Improving Student Achievement," Report by the Economic Policy Institute, February 28, 2017, 3–7, http://www.epi.org/files/pdf/121635.pdf; Jonathan N. Mills, Anna J. Egalite, and Patrick J. Wolf, "How Has The Louisiana Scholarship Program Affected Students? A Comprehensive Summary of Effects after Two Years," Education Research Alliance, February 22, 2016, 2–7, http://educationresearchalliancenola.org/files/publications/ERA-Policy-Brief-Public-Private-School-Choice-160218.pdf; Atila Abdulkadiroglu, Parag Pathak, and Christopher Walters, "School Vouchers and Student Achievement: First-Year Evidence from the Louisiana Scholarship Program," School Effectiveness & Inequality Initiative Discussion Paper #2015.06, December, 2015, http://seii.mit.edu/wp-content/uploads/2016/01/SEII-Discussion-Paper-2015.06-Abdulkadiro%C4%9Flu-Pathak-Walters.pdf; David Figlio and Krzysztof Karbownik, "Evaluation of Ohio's EdChoice Scholarship Program: Selection, Competition, and Performance Effects," Thomas B. Fordham Institute, July, 2016, 2, 32–38, https://edex.s3-us-west-2.amazonaws.com/publication/pdfs/FORDHAM%20Ed%20Choice%20Evaluation%20Report_online%20edition.pdf.

79. Abdulkadiroglu, Pathak, and Walters, "School Vouchers and Student Achievement," 3.

80. Carnoy, "School Vouchers are Not a Proven Strategy," 6; Figlio and Karbownik, "Evaluation of Ohio's EdChoice," 16.

81. Abdulkadiroglu, Pathak, and Walters, "School Vouchers and Student Achievement," 3; Carnoy, "School Vouchers are Not a Proven Strategy," 3; Stephanie

Mencimer, "Mike Pence's Voucher Program in Indiana Was a Windfall for Religious Schools," *Mother Jones*, December 2, 2016, http://www.motherjones.com/politics/2016/11/mike-pence-voucher-program-religious-schools; Ann Doss Helms, "Praying for Options: Religious Schools Dominate NC Voucher Program," *The Charlotte Observer*, April 8, 2016, http://www.charlotteobserver.com/news/local/education/article70759617.html.

82. Mark Weber, "School Vouchers Are Not a Cure for Segregation," Parts I-V, Jersey Jazzman, May, 2016, http://jerseyjazzman.blogspot.fr/2016/05/school-vouchers-are-not-cure-for.html.

83. Kevin Carey, "DeVos and Tax Credit Vouchers: Arizona Shows What Can Go Wrong," *New York Times*, March 2, 2017, https://www.nytimes.com/2017/03/02/upshot/arizona-shows-what-can-go-wrong-with-tax-credit-vouchers.html?_r=0; Capitol Broadcasting Company, "Editorial: Embezzlement Charge At Fayetteville Private School Exposes Risks of Voucher Abuse," WRAL, February 21, 2017, http://www.wral.com/editorial-embezzlement-charge-at-fayetteville-private-school-exposes-risks-of-voucher-abuse/16541678/; Gus Garcia-Roberts, "McKay Scholarship Program Sparks a Cottage Industry of Fraud and Chaos," *Miami New Times*, June 23, 2011, http://www.miaminewtimes.com/news/mckay-scholarship-program-sparks-a-cottage-industry-of-fraud-and-chaos-6381391.

84. See, for example, Lindsay Wagner, "Tiny Private School Puts Spotlight on Voucher System's Flaws," *NC Policy Watch*, March 1, 2017, http://www.ncpolicywatch.com/2016/03/01/tiny-private-school-puts-spotlight-on-voucher-systems-flaws/; see also Lyndsey Layton, "D.C. School Voucher Program Lacks Oversight, GAO Says," *Washington Post*, November 15, 2013, https://www.washingtonpost.com/local/education/dc-school-voucher-program-lacks-oversight-gao-says/2013/11/15/9bb8c35e-4e3d-11e3-be6b-d3d28122e6d4_story.html?utm_term=.1f6d412969d2.

85. Association of Christian Schools International, "Frequently Asked Questions about School Choice," accessed March 21, 2017, https://www.acsi.org/legal-legislative-pages/school-choice-pages/frequently-asked-questions-about-school-choice.

86. Hadfield, *Rules for a Flat World*, 5.

87. Ibid., 249–264.

88. Ibid., 3.

89. Indeed, in his seminal 1974 article, Marc Galanter demonstrated that when courts charge fees in order allow access and especially if those fees are combined with the need for other resources, such as the funds to hire a lawyer, access to those courts, and thus access to justice, is considerably diminished for those who do not have the required resources. Expanding on Galanter, Hannah Simpson's preliminary work demonstrates that in wealthy countries such as the United States, when the state (that is, the government) seeks to use its "property rights institutions" to generate income used for other functions of the state, the result is enhanced access to justice for wealthy persons who are able to pay the required fees, and diminished access to justice for those who are not. Marc Galanter, "Why the "Haves" Come Out Ahead: Speculations on the Limits of Legal Change," *Law & Society Review* 9 (1974): 95–160, http://jan.ucc.nau.edu/~phelps/Galanter%201974.pdf; Hannah Simpson,

"Access to Justice in Revenue-Seeking Legal Institutions," Working Paper, June 14, 2017, https://static1.squarespace.com/static/5668949cdc5cb47474730d69/t/59417e47f5e231163ce27bbc/1497464393084/Access+to+Justice+Manuscript_Simpson.pdf.

90. Hadfield, *Rules for a Flat World*, 246–248.

91. George Monbiot, "No Country with a McDonald's Can Remain a Democracy," *The Guardian*, December 6, 2016, https://www.theguardian.com/commentisfree/2016/dec/06/mcdonalds-democracy-corporate-globalisation-trump-le-pen-farage; Joel S. Hirschhorn, "America, Welcome to Your Delusional Democracy," Wake Up World, September 16, 2016, https://wakeup-world.com/2016/09/16/welcome-to-your-delusional-democracy/.

92. Martin Gilens and Benjamin I. Page, "Testing Theories of American Politics: Elites, Interest Groups, and Average Citizens," *Perspectives on Politics*, September, 2014, 565, 575–577, https://scholar.princeton.edu/sites/default/files/mgilens/files/gilens_and_page_2014_-testing_theories_of_american_politics.doc.pdf; see also Martin Gilens and Benjamin I. Page, "Critics Argued With Our Analysis of U.S. Political Inequality. Here Are 5 Ways They're Wrong," *Washington Post*, May 23, 2016, https://www.washingtonpost.com/news/monkey-cage/wp/2016/05/23/critics-challenge-our-portrait-of-americas-political-inequality-heres-5-ways-they-are-wrong/?utm_term=.cf83dde48245.

93. Hadfield, *Rules for a Flat World*, 208, 210–212, 248.

94. Barbara Bardes, Mack Shelley, and Steffen Schmidt, *American Government and Politics Today: The Essentials 2009—2010 Edition* (Boston: Wadsworth Cengage Learning, 2010), 10.

95. Hadfield, *Rules for a Flat World*, 271, 253.

96. Ibid., 252, 254, 262, 265, 273–275.

97. Ibid., 252.

98. Ibid., 248, 265, 266–268, 276–277.

99. Ibid., 272, 276.

100. Ibid., 273.

101. Ibid., 271, 277.

102. Ibid., 251, 275–276.

103. "Agenda for Sustainable Development," 25–26.

104. "Declaration on Free Access to Law," Free Access to Law Movement, last amended 2012, http://www.fatlm.org/declaration/.

105. Hadfield, *Rules for a Flat World*, 91–100.

106. Ibid.,90.

107. Ibid., 94.

108. Ibid., 256.

109. In the Public Interest, "How Privatization Increases Inequality," 48.

110. Colin Crouch, *The Strange Non-Death of Neoliberalism* (Cambridge, England: Polity Press, 2011), 180.

Appendix

The Modern (or Modernizing) Regulator

First-hand Insight

Over the course of 2014 through mid-2016 I interviewed a number of persons who either play or have played a significant role in the regulation of legal services in England and Wales, Australia, Canada or the United States. Certain chapters of this book contain brief references to those interviews. Excerpts of selected interviews are provided here in this Appendix, and the full redacted versions of all the interviews are available online at *www.notjustforlawyers.com*. These interviews offer unique, first-hand insight into the outlook and approach of a modern (or a modernizing) regulator.

For more information about the interviews, see "The Story Behind the Stories" at the end of this Appendix.

The following is a listing of the interviews that are available online.

Table A.1

Part	*Location*	*Name*	*Title*	*Affiliation*
II	England and Wales	David Clementi	Author	The Clementi Report*
		Crispin Passmore	Executive Director	Solicitors Regulation Authority
		Elisabeth Davies	Chair	Legal Services Consumer Panel
		Alex Roy	Head of Development and Research	Legal Services Board
III	Australia	Paul Clauson and Scott McLean	Legal Services Commissioner Principal Legal Officer	Queensland Legal Services Commission
		John Briton	Former Legal Services Commissioner	Queensland Legal Services Commission
		Steve Mark and Tahlia Gordon	Former Legal Services Commissioner and Former Research & Projects Manager	Office of the Legal Services Commissioner for New South Wales
IV	Canada	Darrel Pink	Executive Director	Nova Scotia Barristers' Society
		Kristin Dangerfield	CEO	Law Society of Manitoba
		Herman Van Ommen	Chair, Law Firm Regulation Task Force	Law Society of British Columbia
		Ross Earnshaw and Margaret Drent	Chair, Task Force on Compliance-Based Entity Regulation Policy Counsel	Law Society of Upper Canada
		Fred Headon	Chair, CBA Legal Futures Initiative	Canadian Bar Association
V	United States	Hope C. Todd	Assistant Director for Legal Ethics	District of Columbia Bar
		Saul Singer	Senior Legal Ethics Counsel	District of Columbia Bar
		Wallace E. "Gene" Shipp, Jr and Lawrence Bloom	Bar Counsel Senior Staff Attorney	DC Office of Bar Counsel
		James C. Coyle	Attorney Regulation Counsel	Colorado Supreme Court
		James Grogan	Deputy Administrator & Chief Counsel	Illinois Attorney Registration & Disciplinary Commission

*"Review of the Regulatory Framework for Legal Services in England and Wales: Final Report," December, 2004, http://webarchive.nationalarchives.gov.uk/+/http://www.legal-services-review.org.uk/content/report/report-chap.pdf

CRISPIN PASSMORE, EXECUTIVE DIRECTOR, SOLICITORS REGULATION AUTHORITY

The Solicitors Regulation Authority (SRA) is the frontline regulatory body for solicitors in England and Wales. In the excerpt below, Passmore explains how the SRA radically altered its approach to regulation:

> The SRA is the largest regulator of legal services in England and Wales. When it came into existence in 2007, it inherited a traditional and old-fashioned system of regulation that was driven by the needs of the profession and protecting the reputation of solicitors, rather than regulating the market effectively. It was very prescriptive, very controlling, very risk adverse—and there were a lot of rules.
>
> The SRA changed this approach, partly because it saw the need to do so but also because of the requirements of the Legal Services Act, which made it possible for managers and investors in law firms to be nonlawyers for the first time, through the creation of ABSs. In the process it changed its senior management, notably bringing in people with experience in regulation of other sectors, it dismantled old ways of doing things, and it created a new approach to regulating the profession. Today the SRA has been transformed—it now regulates the market with the primary goal of making it work well for consumers and supporting the rule of law. Today we have something that is emerging as a regulatory model fit for the ever changing face of the legal sector, but we still have work to do to fully modernize how we regulate.
>
> Our objective is to create a more liberal market, where lawyers and legal service providers have much more freedom in how they operate, but where consumers and the public interest in the proper administration of justice are protected. The SRA is robust in holding lawyers accountable as individuals for their actions as well as supervising firms pro-actively. Some lawyers resist the changes and others see opportunities to develop and grow their business. We want to encourage businesses to thrive and to support a strong legal profession as that is the best way to help consumers and the public. But of course we also regulate to ensure that firms continue to practice according to the high professional standards required of them and to protect against potential risks to client money, competent services and the risks to the administration of justice and rule of law from unacceptable practices.
>
> We have a robust application process to authorize new law firms, but we are not trying to turn people down. We want new entrants to the market as they bring new ideas, while making sure that we understand what they are doing and that they are able to deliver competent and ethical legal services. The authorization process sets standards that act to deter people from applying who would not meet them—so we don't need to turn down many. Most of all we want innovators, investors and entrepreneurs to feel welcome in the legal market—they will bring the innovation and investment that increases choice and closes the access to justice gap.

The purpose of the application process is to establish boundaries for practice and filter out the few that are not welcome in this market. Historically the focus was only on qualification as a solicitor—because only solicitors could own solicitors firms. Now our application process focuses also on the firm and its owners and managers.

In fact, the authorization process is only a very small part of the regulatory process. We have a large flow of information, complaints and reports into the SRA each year—several thousand in fact. We risk assess these to focus investigations on the most serious ones, working with firms to put things right where they are less serious but still significant, and filtering out the trivial. We use that data to spot patterns, emerging issues and sector wide issues so that we can regulate proactively to improve the legal market for consumers.

Regulators can find it difficult to spot 'future bad practice' and prevent those individuals and firms that might do harm in ten or fifteen years' time from entering the market. It might be possible on the margins, but the history of legal regulation has shown us that despite the heavy focus on individuals, long apprenticeship or education and training requirements and high barriers to entry there are still too many examples of unacceptable behavior such as misusing client money. That's why we try to guide the market away from poor practice and towards high ethical standards.

We publish a 'risk outlook' that sets out what we think the biggest current and emerging risks are. Our proactive approach sees us focus our efforts and resources on problem areas—trying to secure compliance early rather than just waiting for things to go terribly wrong. As we review and shrink our rule book we are refocusing it. Rather than prescribe what is allowed and what must be done we are focusing on the outcomes that need to be achieved and only banning what can be justified with evidence. This is a significant change—the onus is on us to justify restrictions rather than on those that want change to prove it is safe. An example of this is changes to Continuing professional development. We no longer have pages of rules on training requirements including prescribing 16 hours of CPD per year, preferring a simple obligation to deliver competent services. That shifts the focus from us as a regulator telling lawyers the right answer to them taking professional responsibility for the training they need to remain competent.

We do not see ABSs as a different species from law firms. They simply have a different ownership and management structure. Our real interest is in the risks that a legal service provider presents to consumers and to the public. The more complex the business, the more important it is for the regulator to understand what is being delivered, how it is being delivered, and how it will be owned and managed.

As we have become more experienced we have become much quicker at authorizing new entrants—even those with complex ownership models. What is clear is that for many of the issues that do go wrong when delivering legal services a strong redress system (complaints mechanisms, Ombudsman scheme, indemnity insurance and compensation arrangements) is more efficient and effective than trying to avoid all problems ever arising. The biggest challenge is to regulate in a way that grows the legal market and thus improves significantly access to justice for individuals and small business in particular. There are more individuals and small business that lose out by having no access to services than there are by unacceptable practice and that is why we are so focused on innovation and growth.

This is an interesting time in the UK legal market. We've seen a lot of innovation, a lot of dynamism, and there are huge opportunities for people who want to do things in different ways. It's good for customers and it's good for lawyers and firms who want to run profitable business by meeting the needs of more consumers.

In my experience, when huge structural changes take place, like the one taking place in the UK legal services market right now, people tend to overestimate the short-term impact, and massively underestimate the long-term effect. I have no idea what the legal services market will look like in 20 years' time, but I am pretty certain it will look very different from how it looks now.

JOHN BRITON, LEGAL SERVICES COMMISSIONER, QUEENSLAND, 2004—2014

John Briton was the first Legal Services Commissioner for Queensland. He is the author of the paper "Between the Idea and the Reality Falls the Shadow."[1] In the excerpt below, he explains why he was appointed commissioner and his perspective on legal services regulation in Australia.

I am not a lawyer. Before my appointment as the first Legal Services Commissioner for Queensland, I served as Queensland's Anti-Discrimination Commissioner and the State Director of the Human Rights and Equal Opportunity Commission. Prior to that I served in Victoria as the Deputy Public Advocate and Senior Advocate in the Office of the Public Advocate, where I investigated and reconciled alleged abuse, exploitation and neglect of older people and people with disabilities.

In those roles, I acquired significant experience with regulatory matters, complaints and investigations of conduct, and notably experience with respect to human rights. And that's the experience I took into my role of Legal Services Commissioner. To my knowledge, I was the first and, to date, the only, non-lawyer appointed in Australia to a Legal Services Commissioner position.

When I assumed my position, I knew that the Commission would comprise lawyers in the main so I knew I would get the legal advice I would need. That being said, many lawyers are incredibly risk adverse, and they see lawyering as a way not to manage risk but to avoid it altogether. In my opinion, effective regulation requires some risk taking and a willingness to push boundaries and test principles and practices. For that reason, I think it was helpful—an advantage—that I was not a lawyer. It made it easier for me to push boundaries. I could challenge assumptions by playing dumb and asking naïve questions. I think it was particularly helpful to not be a lawyer in the context of setting up an organization from the beginning, which enabled me to establish a certain culture.

When I first saw the regulatory framework for ILPs, I thought it was fantastic. I saw a regulatory framework that looks at management systems and what legal ethicists call "ethical infrastructures," and I saw that it really gives you a way to get to the cultural influences that have an impact on the behavior of lawyers in law firms. The regulation of lawyers that only looks at the conduct of individual lawyers is, in my view, a hangover from when everyone was a sole practitioner or operating in very small firms. Today most lawyers work in large and medium-size firms, and the cultural influences of those firms are just as much if not more important in determining how an individual performs than that individual's knowledge and character.

Lawyers can be influenced by a number of different people, and, yes, that includes shareholders. That is not a reason to exclude shareholders. It is a reason to manage the risk.

Australia's response to this has made sense—yes, allow non-lawyers to own shares of a law firm, but require the firm to appoint at least one Legal Practitioner Director. There needs to be a lawyer who is ultimately responsible for the legal services provided by that firm and that person needs to have specific obligations over and above their obligations as a lawyer. Those obligations need to be that the firm is run in accordance with lawyers' professional obligations and making sure that the firm has an ethical infrastructure (governance arrangements, supervisory systems, training) in place. And that lawyer needs to be personally responsible to the disciplinary regime for that. It's a really good framework, and it works.

During my time as Commissioner, we did not stop with the self-assessments. We had a variety of other programs in place. One example is what we called "ethics checks."[2] Done on an anonymous basis, these provided a framework for a firm to involve everyone (or nearly everyone) in their offices to engage with respect to ethical issues. The purpose of the checks was to foster reflection together with spontaneous and organized discussions. We approached this by explaining to firms that it would only take 30 minutes to respond to an online survey intended to get people thinking on topics like complaints management, billing systems, supervision arrangements, etc. We explained that the surveys enabled a firm to test whether perceptions across that firm were consistent, such as if the partners' perceptions were the same as the other lawyers' perceptions and whether the perceptions in one office were the same as the perceptions in another office. It provided a wealth of information that permitted the partners to understand what was happening and to change things if needed.

When we asked partners in law firms that participated in these programs what they thought of them, they thought they were fantastic. They almost invariably said that the surveys forced them to think, and more than a few of them that because of the surveys they realized there were problems that needed to be fixed, and they fixed them.

I have often argued that all law firms should be subject to the same regulatory regime as ILPs. More specifically, I have argued that the single most effective reform we could make to better promote, monitor and enforce high standards of service in the delivery of legal services and to better protect consumers would be to make all law firms subject to the same regulatory arrangements as ILPs. I argue this because the regime[3] offers the best means to engage with law firms about their ethical infrastructures—their management systems, their governance arrangements, their workplace cultures. . . . We do this with the knowledge that a firm's ethical infrastructure is just as if not more important than a lawyer's character in shaping their conduct. All of a lawyer's obligations are affected by culture. Putting lawyers under unreasonable pressure to meet an unreasonable billing target is hardly ethically neutral, for example.

The ILP regulatory structure[4] gives regulators the capacity to engage with law firms about a whole range of influences that shape their performance as a law firm that you can't do under a regulatory framework that is based solely on reacting to complaints. It permits regulators to be helpful and to be seen as being helpful, rather than be seen as an "enemy" to be feared because they are out to get you.

At this time the regulatory system for legal services in Australia is mixed, in that it is partially self-regulated and partially independently regulated. In my opinion, the legal profession in Australia would be much better off if its representative bodies were freed from their regulatory obligations. That would free them up to fully advocate in favor of their members instead to clinging to the assertion that they are motivated purely by the public interest. Nobody believes that, so why do the professional bodies continue to believe it? Why not fully embrace their status as membership and representative bodies, effectively trade unions? At the same time, a fully independent regulatory regime would remove the inherent conflict of interest. It would promote greater confidence in the regulatory regime—it would promote public confidence that legal services are regulated in the public interest rather than the interests of the profession and mitigate the negative image so many members of the public have about lawyers.

I also believe that the public needs to have a much greater voice in the regulation of legal services. Take the handling of complaints, for example. When you do not involve the public, regulators invariably reflect the profession's view of the purposes of the regulatory regime—of the system for dealing with complaints, for example. It becomes heavily weighted to professional discipline—to "weeding out the bad apples." It grants the regulator extensive powers with respect to discipline but few if any powers to order redress for ordinary mistakes that fall short of disciplinary violations. Those regulations were designed without anyone's head in the consumer space. If you look at the other regulatory bodies in Australia, you'll see that they all have consumer sub-committees, or structured arrangements where they consult with consumers or with consumer advocacy organizations, like the Australian Communications Consumer Action Network. You don't see this with respect to legal services. I think this is an important reason why firms can get away with abusive billing practices. Unfortunately, during my time as Commissioner, I could not get the professional bodies to take these issues seriously.

A body that is essentially a membership body will always find it difficult if not impossible to take regulatory action which its members perceive to be a threat to their livelihoods, no matter how great the benefit to the public may be.

This is why we need independent regulators, as they are able to regulate in the interest of the public without any conflict of interest with a duty to represent members. And with independent regulation, I am not saying that the perspective of the public or of the consumer must or even should prevail—I am simply saying that it needs to be in the mix. It's essential for instilling public confidence in lawyers as well as in the regulation of legal services, and for that matter in our system of justice and the rule of law.

DARREL PINK, EXECUTIVE DIRECTOR, NOVA SCOTIA BARRISTERS' SOCIETY

The Nova Scotia Barristers' Society is the governing body for the legal profession in Nova Scotia. In the excerpt below, Pink explains how the province viewed and has reacted to regulatory changes occurring outside Canada:

> The Law Societies in Canada watched events unfold in England and Wales with great interest. Initially, we saw the establishment of the Legal Services Board and the Solicitors Regulatory Authority as a significant threat to the independence of lawyers, and that was the reason for our early interest. But as we watched what was happening there, and as we, regulators in Canada, established personal relationships with regulators in England, we realized that the sky hasn't fallen, and that it likely won't fall. We also realized that what they were doing made a lot of sense.
>
> We also followed what was happening in Australia. Australia is more similar to Canada than England is. Like Canada, Australia is a federation of states, and geographically of a similar size. As we watched the evolution in Australia, from self-regulation to the creation of Legal Services Commissions and the establishment of co-regulation, we realized again that the sky hadn't fallen.
>
> And we realized that the practice of law has changed substantially. We realized that the premise upon which most lawyer regulation is based—the sole practitioner or small partnership practicing locally—does not reflect the way that many lawyers work—it's a 19th century model and it's an archaic way to regulate. Today we have many in-house corporate and government counsel, many very large law firms with hundreds if not thousands of lawyers, and many lawyers who practice regionally, nationally and internationally. Technology has had a profound impact on how lawyers work and communicate with clients.
>
> All this led us, the Council of the Society, to ask the question: What is the right regulatory model for the 21st century?
>
> We have developed the concept of "Triple P" regulation: We think that regulation needs to be proactive, principled and proportionate.
>
> The first change we are making is to move from reactive to proactive regulation. With the exception of the process of admission to the Bar, everything we do is reactive. To make this change, we have looked carefully at Australia. Its "appropriate management systems," in particular, has had a strong influence on us.

We recognize that law firms dictate in many ways how law is practiced, as do government and corporate legal departments. These organizations prescribe the ethos and the mindset in which legal services are delivered. For that reason, we are also looking at how to better regulate entities.

By proportionate, we mean that we don't need the same rules for every situation. For example, we have very detailed rules about how trust accounts are operated. We apply the same rules to every firm, regardless of its size. But the reality is that a 200-person firm presents much less risk than a 3-person firm. A 200-person firm does not need detailed rules from a regulator because they manage risk quite differently.

By principled, we mean that we need to have fewer directives regarding exactly how something should be done. We are good are creating rules, exceptions to rules, sub-rules, etc. Instead, we should be focused on principles about how to practice and behave rather than dictating specifics.

We are focused on what is in the public interest. We do not think about what we are doing in terms of what is good for the legal profession—we do not want to harm the legal profession because it plays a key role in our society, but our focus is on change for the benefit of the public.

We do not think that it is possible to discuss alternative structures without first addressing the regulation of entities in addition to the regulation of individuals. In addition, a system like the SRA's—that requires a potential owner to go to the regulator and answer a bunch of the regulator's questions and meet the regulator's requirements before they can open the doors—is a system that is difficult to put in place.

We think that a more natural approach is simply to enable law firms and lawyers to expand the ways that they provide services. For a regulator, this is a much easier task because it can be done incrementally.

Studies show that in Canada, only 17% of people who have a justiciable issue seek the assistance of a lawyer to resolve it. This means that 83% of justiciable issues are addressed either by others, or by no one. We know that people get legal advice from online legal providers every day. We know that accountants give legal advice every day. We know that human resource management firms, engineering firms, and consulting firms give legal advice every day. These firms do not harm the public and for the most part the public is quite happy with it. For example, if I am constructing a building and it has huge environmental law issues, I am probably better off getting my environmental law advice from the engineer rather than from a lawyer because the engineer pulls all the information together in order to help make the decision.

Ultimately, as a result of our project, the regulator's job will be to have responsibility for the regulation of legal services in general. The regulator will exercise that responsibility in several ways:

1. By clearly regulating lawyers as well as legal entities,
2. By authorizing the delivery of legal services by others who will be exempt from our specific regulation. By "others," I am referring to people like accountants,

real estate brokers, insurance adjustors and a variety of others who offer legal services in the course of their regular work,

3. By creating a model that allows legal services to be delivered by not-for-profit organizations, with or without lawyers, in areas where there are significant access to justice or legal service needs,
4. By allowing lawyers to offer legal services in conjunction with other services (what are typically referred to as multidisciplinary practices, or MDPs), where the structure and all its professionals (psychologists, financial advisors) are subject to the ethical standards that apply to all law firms,
5. By seeking authority to create regulation for paralegals.

You may have noted that the 5-item list above does not include a reference to anything akin to an ILP or an ABS-type structure. This is not an oversight. To begin, it is nothing that a small province like Nova Scotia could ever influence because any framework for alternative business structures would need to be a national framework that comes from a federal approach. This is because so many of our companies as well as law firms operate across provinces and territories, and they need a single model of regulation. For example, banks are federally chartered in Canada—they could offer legal services under an ABS-type structure only under a national framework.

Further, we've known from the beginning of our project that the language of ABS is highly provocative and controversial. The topic is almost incendiary. When people hear the term, they often respond emotionally rather than rationally. So we took it off the table from the beginning. We are not talking about ABS.

The issue of law firm ownership requires a federal approach. This is because we have so many multi-jurisdictional law firms in Canada. We could not abide by structures which in Nova Scotia, for example, could be owned by nonlawyers but that in other provinces they could only be owned by lawyers. The result could be that lawyers of such a Nova Scotia firm could not practice in the other provinces. That result is unacceptable because much of our work is premised on the need to maintain and enhance the mobility of lawyers and law firms in order that they may offer legal services in multiple jurisdictions. We have a national mobility agreement in Canada, under the Constitution we have mandates that people can work in every place in the country, and there are now inter-provincial and federal agreements in place that support that constitutional protection. It's now a given in discussions among law societies that mobility must be preserved at all costs.

All that being said, for Nova Scotia a debate around law firm ownership would be a false debate. This is because, for example, our new framework will allow accounting firms to provide legal services. Once an accounting firm decides to do this, and notably once they do this using lawyers, they will subject themselves to the regulatory jurisdiction of the Society. We will set the regulatory infrastructure for them, and they will comply. If not, they will fall under our sanctioning powers.

Another example: imagine an organization like the YWCA offering a range of assistance (housing, financial, welfare, legal) to victims of violence. I don't believe anyone can seriously argue that any harm to the public will arise from a not-for-profit organization offering legal services, even if they are not owned by lawyers, and even if the services themselves are not provided by lawyers.

You could ask the question how/why has Nova Scotia been able to make the progress it has, in contrast to some other Canadian provinces? In my opinion, this is because in Nova Scotia we've done a significant amount of background work, beginning as far back as 2000. That work had the unintended consequence of allowing us to do the work we are doing today. That background work was not designed for that specific purpose, but now, in retrospect, we see that is has had that effect. The work encompassed two areas: (i) bringing clarity to the regulatory role, and (ii) improving the quality and the nature of our governance.

More specifically as regards bringing clarity to the regulatory role: the Society got out of the business of doing things that ostensibly are for the benefit of lawyers. In becoming a more rigorous regulator, we no longer do anything which is lawyer-centric. We used to have conferences and formal dinners and a variety of things like that—things that had as their motivation the desire to build collegiality and make lawyers feel good. We stopped doing all that, not because they are not important, but became we determined that as a public interest regulator we must focus on our purpose, which is to regulate in the public interest.

As regards governance, we spent a lot of time and energy creating a solid set of governance policies. In doing so, we created a framework where our Council understands its role to be exclusively that of policy maker, and, further, that as part of good governance, it will use only evidence-based decision making.

So, when the Council decided to undertake our current work (a decision that it made on the basis of what was happening in England and Wales and Australia), the Council looked only at the facts. They looked at our research papers,[5] they decided that the papers made sense, and they decided to use the evidence contained in those papers as the basis for moving in the direction that we are going.

In contrast, many of the other law societies in Canada are not as single-minded. While they say they are public interest regulators, they nevertheless hang on to a variety of activities that are designed to make lawyers feel good: receptions and black-tie dinners, awards . . . things that are about lawyers rather than about protection of the public.

Here is something more we can learn from the experiences of England and Australia: It's not about self-regulation or about self-governance, which are two words we have used as our mantra for generations. Instead, it is about independent and professional regulation. The SRA is nowhere close to a perfect regulator, but it shows us that when you professionalize regulation and you assure that that regulator acts independently, the quality of regulation improves. The Legal Services Commissioners of New South Wales, Queensland and Victoria have also shown this to be true.

Another key learning from England and Australia is the value of research. Regulators often act based upon their experience, but with little historic or prospective analysis of what the information we have means. We don't do research. We don't do much analysis of our experience. We know very little about what is happening in the legal profession. England and Australia show us that a small investment in terms of our overall budgets—an investment to better analyze and study—makes a huge difference. We cannot make the kind of changes that I am talking about based upon an analysis done on the back of a match box. It's got to be done based upon valid research.

It's easy to think that members of the public don't care at all about how lawyers are regulated. But they do care about the impact of the regulation of legal services, and about the availability of legal services.

THE STORY BEHIND THE STORIES

The written interviews referenced in this book and posted online at *www.notjustforlawyers.com* are the work-product of oral interviews I conducted between March 2014 and May 2016.

I conducted the interviews either by phone or Skype, with one exception (Sir David Clementi, with whom I met in person). Most interviews lasted about one hour. A small number were shorter—about 30 minutes—and some were much longer—up to two hours, with some of those taking place over more than one call. When I conducted the first interviews in early 2014, I had no idea what I was doing: I wasn't sure what questions to ask, I wasn't sure in what order to ask them and I wasn't adept at formulating follow-up questions. After the first few interviews, I got the hang of it. The interviews became semi-structured, with the support of a topic guide.

More specifically, I developed a core set of questions. Before each interview, I studied the publicly available information about the regulator and the interviewee and tailored the core set of questions to reflect the specificities of both. As I listened to each interviewee, I got into the habit of noting follow-up questions and I got better at identifying the right moments to ask them. Because I was never sure that I asked all the right questions, my last question became "What should I have asked, but didn't?" Often it was this question that elicited the most interesting comments.

In most instances, the interviews were recorded with the permission of the interviewee, and I also took handwritten notes as needed. After each interview, I prepared a write-up. I quickly recognized that a simple transcript of the interview wouldn't work: hearing the spoken word is one thing—reading the spoken word is something entirely different. Run-on sentences, sentence fragments and the repetition of words and ideas are tolerated and even expected in speech, but not in writing. So, what I did was take the words and ideas that the interviewee expressed orally, and organized them on paper (or, more precisely, on a screen) in way that they could be easily accessed by a reader rather than a listener. Because I wanted the focus of the reader to be on the interviewee and not on the interviewer (me), I excluded from the write-up the questions that I posed and any other limited commentary I occasionally made during the interviews. An unfortunate by-product of this is that sometimes in reading the stories, the transitions can be abrupt.

I sent each write-up back to the interviewee. In doing so, I invited him/her to make comments and corrections. At first, I wasn't sure how "warmly" I should extend this invitation. Naturally I wanted any factual errors to be corrected. More than that, I wanted the interviewee to be comfortable with the write-up. At the same time, however, I didn't want the write-up to be transformed into something that no longer reflected the interview. In progressing with the first few write-ups, I discovered that those fears were mostly unfounded—most interviewees made very few if any substantive changes. And when substantive changes were made, in most cases I felt that they improved the write-up. So, after those first few write-ups, I became comfortable extending what I intended to be a warm invitation to make comments and corrections, saying "please don't feel wedded to what I have typed" and "it is important that you are comfortable." And when I received a write-up back, usually in the form of a mark-up, I did not question or quibble with the changes—instead, in nearly all cases I accepted all of them, and then went back through the revised document simply to correct any spelling or grammatical errors.

As noted above, the interviews were conducted between March 2014 and May 2016. In August 2015, I contacted everyone I had interviewed up to that time, and I invited them to work with me to update their write-ups—most of them did so, if not immediately, then over the course of the following months.

Finally, because of spacing concerns, it was impossible to include all of the interviews in this book. The interviews that are included are excerpts. As noted above, full versions of all the interviews can be accessed at *www.notjustforlawyers.com*.

NOTES

1. John Briton, "Between the Idea and the Reality Falls the Shadow" (paper presented at the fifth bi-annual Australian and New Zealand Legal Ethics Colloquium, Melbourne, Australia, December 3–4, 2015), https://www.monash.edu/__data/assets/pdf_file/0004/374872/Briton-Between-the-Idea-and-the-Reality-Falls-the-Shadow-revised-April-2016.pdf.

2. These checks are posted on the Commission's website: http://www.lsc.qld.gov.au/ethics-checks (last updated October 25, 2013).

3. To clarify, here I am referring to the regime under the Legal Profession Model Laws that is today still in place in Queensland. I am not referring to the modified regime for ILPs recently adopted in New South Wales and Victoria, under the Legal Profession Uniform Law.

4. Again, here I refer to the regime under the Legal Profession Model Laws and not the regime under the Legal Profession Uniform Law.

5. These can be accessed at this link: http://nsbs.org/reports-resources.

Bibliography

ABA Commission on Ethics 20/20. "ABA Commission on Ethics 20/20 Will Not Propose Changes to ABA Policy Prohibiting Nonlawyer Ownership of Law Firms." April 16, 2012. http://www.americanbar.org/content/dam/aba/administrative/ethics_2020/20120416_news_release_re_nonlawyer_ownership_law_firms.authcheckdam.pdf.

———. "Discussion Draft for Comment: Alternative Law Practice Structures." December 2, 2011. http://www.americanbar.org/content/dam/aba/administrative/ethics_2020/20111202-ethics2020-discussion_draft-alps.authcheckdam.pdf.

———. "Minutes." February 4, 2010. http://www.americanbar.org/content/dam/aba/migrated/2011_build/ethics_2020/feb_2010_minutes.authcheckdam.pdf.

———. "Minutes." April 29, 2010. http://www.americanbar.org/content/dam/aba/migrated/2011_build/ethics_2020/apr_2010_minutes.authcheckdam.pdf.

———. "Minutes." February 10, 2011. http://www.americanbar.org/content/dam/aba/administrative/ethics_2020/20110328_ethics2020_minutes_february_10–11–2011-approved.authcheckdam.pdf.

———. "Minutes." April 15–16, 2011. http://www.americanbar.org/content/dam/aba/administrative/ethics_2020/20110812_ethics2020_minutes_april_15_16_2011_approved.authcheckdam.pdf.

———. "Minutes." June 13, 2011. http://www.americanbar.org/content/dam/aba/administrative/ethics_2020/20110812_ethics2020_minutes_june_13_2011_approved.authcheckdam.pdf.

———. "Preliminary Issues Outline." November 19, 2009. http://www.americanbar.org/content/dam/aba/migrated/ethics2020/outline.authcheckdam.pdf.

———. "Report to the House of Delegates: Resolution 105A." August, 2012. http://www.americanbar.org/content/dam/aba/administrative/ethics_2020/2012_hod_annual_meeting_105a_filed_may_2012.authcheckdam.pdf.

ABA Commission on Ethics 20/20 Working Group on Alternative Business Structures. "For Comment: Issues Paper Concerning Alternative Business Structures." April 5, 2011. http://www.americanbar.org/content/dam/aba/administrative/ethics_2020/abs_issues_paper.authcheckdam.pdf.

ABA Commission on the Future of Legal Services, Standing Committee on Professional Discipline, Criminal Justice Section Law Practice Division, Standing Committee on Legal Aid And Indigent Defendants, and Standing Committee on Client Protection. "Report to the House of Delegates (105)." November, 2015. http://www.americanbar.org/content/dam/aba/images/office_president/final_regulatory_objectives_resolution_november_2015.pdf.

ABA Commission on the Future of Legal Services. "For Comment: Issues Paper Regarding Alternative Business Structures." April 8, 2016. http://www.americanbar.org/content/dam/aba/images/office_president/alternative_business_issues_paper.pdf.

———. "Informational Report to the House of Delegates." December 2015. http://www.americanbar.org/content/dam/aba/images/office_president/final_hod_informational_report_midyear.pdf.

———. "Issues Paper Concerning New Categories of Legal Services Providers." October 16, 2015. http://www.americanbar.org/content/dam/aba/images/office_president/delivery_of_legal_services_completed_evaluation.pdf.

———. "Issues Paper Concerning Unregulated LSP Entities." March 31, 2016. https://www.americanbar.org/content/dam/aba/images/office_president/final_unregulated_lsp_entities_issues_paper.pdf.

———. "Issues Paper on the Future of Legal Services." November 3, 2014. http://www.americanbar.org/content/dam/aba/images/office_president/issues_paper.pdf.

———. "Report on the Future of Legal Services in the United States." August, 2016. http://abafuturesreport.com/#1.

ABA Commission on Lawyer Assistance Programs. "Proposed Resolution Regarding Model Regulatory Objectives." October 28, 2015. http://www.americanbar.org/content/dam/aba/images/office_president/lawyer_assistance_programs.pdf.

———. "Proposed Resolution Regarding Model Regulatory Objectives." January 11, 2016. http://www.americanbar.org/content/dam/aba/images/office_president/lawyer_assistance_programs_b%20.pdf.

ABA Solo Small Firm and General Practice Division. Memo to ABA Commission on the Future of Legal Services. Undated. http://www.americanbar.org/content/dam/aba/images/office_president/solo_small_firm.pdf.

———. Memo to ABA Commission on the Future of Legal Services. December 30, 2015. http://www.americanbar.org/content/dam/aba/images/office_president/lspcomments_solo_small_firm_and_general_practice_division.pdf.

ABA Standing Committee on the Delivery of Legal Services. "Issues Paper on 'Unregulated Legal LSP Entities.'" May 2, 2016. https://www.americanbar.org/content/dam/aba/images/office_president/delivery_of_legal_services_unregulated.pdf.

ABA Standing Committee on Ethics and Professional Responsibility. "Formal Opinion 464: Division of Legal Fees With Other Lawyers Who May Lawfully Share Fees with Nonlawyers." August 19, 2013. http://www.americanbar.org/content/dam/aba/publications/YourABA/fo_464.authcheckdam.pdf.

ABA Standing Committee on Professionalism. "Comment on Issues Paper Concerning Unregulated LSP Entities." April 28, 2016. https://www.americanbar.

org/content/dam/aba/images/office_president/professionalism_standing_committee_unregulated.pdf.

Abbott, Tony, Barbara Bradshaw, Joe Catanzariti, Harold Cottee, Noela L'Estrange, Martyn Hagan, Philip Selth, and Dudley Stow. "Response to Taskforce Discussion Paper on Business Structures 'Law Practices.'" Undated. http://web.archive.org/web/20110607140350/https://www.ag.gov.au/www/agd/rwpattach.nsf/VAP/(8AB0BDE05570AAD0EF9C283AA8F533E3)~Abbott,+Tony;+Bradshaw,+Barbara;+Catanzariti,+Joe;+Cottee,+Harold;+L+Estrange,+Noela;+Hagan,+Martyn;+Selth,+Philip;+and+Stow,+Dudley+-+Business+Structures.PDF/$file/Abbott,+Tony;+Bradshaw,+Barbara;+Catanzariti,+Joe;+Cottee,+Harold;+L+Estrange,+Noela;+Hagan,+Martyn;+Selth,+Philip;+and+Stow,+Dudley+-+Business+Structures.PDF.

Abdulkadiroglu, Atila, Parag Pathak, and Christopher Walters. "School Vouchers and Student Achievement: First-Year Evidence from the Louisiana Scholarship Program." School Effectiveness & Inequality Initiative Discussion Paper #2015.06. December, 2015. http://seii.mit.edu/wp-content/uploads/2016/01/SEII-Discussion-Paper-2015.06-Abdulkadiro%C4%9Flu-Pathak-Walters.pdf.

Abel, Richard L. *American Lawyers*. New York: Oxford University Press, 1989.

———. "United States: The Contradictions of Professionalism." In *Lawyers in Society: The Common Law World*, edited by Richard L. Abel and Philip S.C. Lewis, 205–222. Washington DC: Beard Books, 2005.

———. "Why Does the ABA Promulgate Ethical Rules?" *Texas Law Review* 59 (1981): 639–688.

Adams, Edward S. and John H. Matheson. "Law Firms on the Big Board?: A Proposal for Nonlawyer Investment in Law Firms." *California Law Review* 86 (1998): 1–40. http://scholarship.law.umn.edu/cgi/viewcontent.cgi?article=1100&context=faculty_articles.

Alternative Business Structures Working Group. "Alternative Business Structures and the Legal Profession in Ontario: A Discussion Paper." September, 2014. http://www.lsuc.on.ca/uploadedFiles/abs-discussion-paper.pdf.

Ambrogi, Bob. "Perlman: ABA Future Commission Not Out to Regulate 'Entire Legal Tech Industry.'" Catalyst. April 26, 2016. https://www.catalystsecure.com/blog/2016/04/perlman-aba-future-commission-not-out-to-regulate-entire-legal-tech-industry/.

Ambrogi, Robert. "ABA Future Panel Calls for Broad Changes in Legal Services." Above the Law. August 8, 2016. http://abovethelaw.com/2016/08/this-week-in-legal-tech-aba-future-panel-calls-for-broad-changes-in-legal-services/.

———. "Washington State Moves Around UPL, Using Legal Technicians to Help Close the Justice Gap." *ABA Journal*. January 1, 2015. http://www.abajournal.com/magazine/article/washington_state_moves_around_upl_using_legal_technicians_to_help_close_the/.

American Antitrust Institute. "AAI Says Legal Profession's Recommendations on Multidisciplinary Practices May Violate Antitrust Laws." February 8, 2000. http://www.antitrustinstitute.org/content/aai-says-legal-professions-recommendations-multidisciplinary-practices-may-violate-antitrust.

American Bar Association. "Resolution 105 Revised and Amended." February 2016. http://www.americanbar.org/content/dam/aba/images/abanews/2016mymres/105.pdf.

"America's Neglected Water Systems Face a Reckoning." Knowledge@Wharton. June 10, 2015. http://knowledge.wharton.upenn.edu/article/americas-neglected-water-systems-face-a-reckoning/.

American Water Works Association. "Buried No Longer: Confronting America's Water Infrastructure Challenge." February 27, 2012. http://www.awwa.org/Portals/0/files/legreg/documents/BuriedNoLonger.pdf.

Andersson, Edward and Richard Wilson. "Globalised Democracy." In *Focus on Citizens: Public Engagement for Better Policy and Services*. OECD Studies on Public Engagement, 299–302. Paris: OECD Publishing, 2009. http://www19.iadb.org/intal/intalcdi/pe/2009/03785.pdf.

Andrews, Thomas R. "Nonlawyers in the Business of Law: Does the One Who Has the Gold Really Make the Rules." *The Hastings Law Journal* 40 (1989): 577–656.

Arce, Rose. "Does Class Size Matter?" CNN School of Thought. December 6, 2011. http://schoolsofthought.blogs.cnn.com/2011/12/06/does-class-size-matter/.

"Are We Better Off Privatizing Water?" *Wall Street Journal*. October 8, 2012. https://www.wsj.com/articles/SB10000872396390443816804578002280926253750.

Arnold, Craig Anthony. "Water Privatization Trends in the United States: Human Rights, National Security, and Public Stewardship." *William & Mary Environmental Law and Policy Review* 33 (2009): 785–849. http://scholarship.law.wm.edu/wmelpr/vol33/iss3/4/.

Association of Christian Schools International. "Frequently Asked Questions about School Choice." Accessed March 21, 2017. https://www.acsi.org/legal-legislative-pages/school-choice-pages/frequently-asked-questions-about-school-choice.

Avvo, Inc. "Unregulated Legal Service Provider Entities." April 28, 2016. https://www.americanbar.org/content/dam/aba/images/office_president/avvo_unregulated.pdf.

Baldwin, Robert, Martin Cave and Martin Lodge. *Understanding Regulation: Theory, Strategy and Practice*. Toronto: Oxford University Press, 2011. https://webcampus.unamur.be/claroline/backends/download.php?url=L0EuX0Rlc21ldF9fMV9CYWxkd2luXyZhbXA7X2NvX1VuZGVyc3RhbmRpbmdfcmVndWxhdGlvbi0xLnBkZg%3D%3D&cidReset=true&cidReq=ECONM864.

Bardes, Barbara, Mack Shelley, and Steffen Schmidt. *American Government and Politics Today: The Essentials 2009–2010 Edition*. Boston: Wadsworth Cengage Learning, 2010.

Barlow, Maude and Wenonah Hauter. "The Dangerous Return of Water Privatization." Utne Reader. January/February 2014. http://www.utne.com/politics/water-privatization-zm0z14jfzros?pageid=2#PageContent2.

Barton, Benjamin H. "Do Judges Systematically Favor the Interests of the Legal Profession?" University of Tennessee Legal Studies Research Paper No. 1. October, 2007. http://ssrn.com/abstract=976478.

———. "An Institutional Analysis of Lawyer Regulation: Who Should Control Lawyer Regulation-Courts, Legislatures, or the Market?" *Georgia Law Review* 37 (2003): 1167–1250.

———. *The Lawyer-Judge Bias in the American Legal System*. New York: Cambridge University Press 2011.

———. "The Lawyer's Monopoly—What Goes and What Stays." *Fordham Law Review* 82 (2014): 3067–90. http://ir.lawnet.fordham.edu/cgi/viewcontent.cgi?article=5008&context=flr.

———. "Why Do We Regulate Lawyers?: An Economic Analysis of the Justifications for Entry and Conduct Regulation." *Arizona State Law Journal* 33 (2001): 429–490.

Batlan, Felice. *Women and Justice for the Poor: A History of Legal Aid, 1863–1945*. New York: Cambridge University Press, 2015.

Beck, Susan. "Divided ABA Adopts Resolution on Nonlawyer Legal Services." *The American Lawyer*. February 8, 2016. http://www.americanlawyer.com/id=1202749202171/Divided-ABA-Adopts-Resolution-on-Nonlawyer-Legal-Services#ixzz3zlhUQwOI.

Bee, Sacramento and Andy Furillo. "California's Prisons Bursting at Seams and Understaffed." *East Bay Times*. November 26, 2005. http://www.eastbaytimes.com/2005/11/26/californias-prisons-bursting-at-seams-and-understaffed/.

Behrens, Mark and Christopher Appel. "Controversial ABA Alternative Business Structures Proposal Stalls . . . Again." IADC Committee Newsletter. June, 2016.

Bernabe, Alberto. "ABA Commission on Future of Legal Services issues Its Final Report; I Am Not Particularly Impressed—UPDATED." *Professional Responsibility Blog*. August 11, 2016. http://bernabepr.blogspot.fr/2016/08/aba-commission-on-future-of-legal.html.

Betke, Christopher G. "Proposal for ABS." April 27, 2016. http://www.americanbar.org/content/dam/aba/images/office_president/christopher_g_betke_abs.pdf.

Bindman, Dan. "Cypriot Construction Consultancy Becomes ABS for its International Kudos." *Legal Futures*. January 17, 2014. http://www.legalfutures.co.uk/latest-news/cypriot-construction-consultancy-becomes-abs-international-kudos.

Bishop, Todd. "Amazon Board Adds Jamie Gorelick, Former Fannie Mae and DOJ Official." *Geekwire*. February 10, 2012. http://www.geekwire.com/2012/amazon-board-adds-fannie-mae-doj-official-jamie-gorelick/.

Black, Julia and Robert Baldwin. "Really Responsive Risk-Based Regulation." *Law & Policy* 32 (2010): 181–213. http://ssrn.com/abstract=1571808.

Black, Julia. "Risk-Based Regulation: Choices, Practices and Lessons Being Learnt." In *Risk and Regulatory Policy: Improving the Governance of Risk*. OECD, 185–236. Paris: OECD Publishing, 2010. http://dx.doi.org/10.1787/9789264082939-en.

Bourgon, Jocelyne. "Why Should Governments Engage Citizens in Service Delivery and Policy Making?" In *Focus on Citizens: Public Engagement for Better Policy and Services*, OECD Studies on Public Engagement, 199–205. Paris: OECD Publishing, 2009. http://www19.iadb.org/intal/intalcdi/pe/2009/03785.pdf.

Boyd, Tony. "High Court Judge Warns of Conflicts Facing Listed Law Firms." *Australian Financial Review*. February 2, 2016. http://www.afr.com/brand/chanticleer/high-court-judge-warns-of-conflicts-facing-listed-law-firms-20160202-gmjues.

Breyer, Stephen. *Breaking the Vicious Circle: Toward Effective Risk Regulation*. Cambridge, Massachusetts: Harvard University Press, 1993.

Briton, John. "Between the Idea and the Reality Falls the Shadow." Paper presented at the fifth bi-annual Australian and New Zealand Legal Ethics Colloquium,

Melbourne, Australia, December 3–4, 2015. http://www.monash.edu/__data/assets/pdf_file/0004/374872/Briton-Between-the-Idea-and-the-Reality-Falls-the-Shadow-1.pdf.

———. "Between The Idea And The Reality Falls The Shadow: A Case Study In Lawyer Regulation." October, 2015. Unpublished paper on file with author.

———. "National Legal Profession Reform and the Regulation of the Future." Paper presented at the St. Vincents' 48th Annual Queensland Law Society Symposium, Brisbane, Australia, March 27, 2010. https://www.lsc.qld.gov.au/__data/assets/pdf_file/0015/106080/national-legal-profession-reform-and-the-regulation-of-the-future.pdf.

———. "A Response to the Business Structures Paper of 25 November 2009." December 15, 2009. http://web.archive.org/web/20110607011704/https://www.ag.gov.au/www/agd/agd.nsf/Page/Consultationsreformsandreviews_NationalLegalProfessionReform-TaskforcePapers-ConsultativeGroupSubmissions.

Broome County Bar Association. "Issues Paper Concerning Unregulated LSP Entities." June 29, 2016. https://www.americanbar.org/content/dam/aba/images/office_president/broome_county_bar_association.pdf.

Broussard, Meredith. "Why Poor Schools Can't Win at Standardized Testing." *The Atlantic*. July 15, 2014. https://www.theatlantic.com/education/archive/2014/07/why-poor-schools-cant-win-at-standardized-testing/374287/.

Buckley, Neil. Letter to David W. Rivkin. September 23, 2016. http://www.legalservicesboard.org.uk/news_publications/speeches_presentations/2016/20160923_LSB_Letter_Re_Draft_Report_IBA_Pres_Task_Force_Independance_Of_Legal_Prof.pdf.

Camp, Scott D. and Gerald G. Gaes, "Growth and Quality of U.S. Private Prisons: Evidence from a National Survey." Paper prepared for Federal Bureau of Prisons, Office of Research and Evaluation. September 21, 2001. https://www.bop.gov/resources/research_projects/published_reports/pub_vs_priv/oreprres_note.pdf.

Capitol Broadcasting Company. "Editorial: Embezzlement Charge At Fayetteville Private School Exposes Risks of Voucher Abuse." WRAL. February 21, 2017. http://www.wral.com/editorial-embezzlement-charge-at-fayetteville-private-school-exposes-risks-of-voucher-abuse/16541678/.

Carey, Kevin. "DeVos and Tax Credit Vouchers: Arizona Shows What Can Go Wrong." *New York Times*. March 2, 2017. https://www.nytimes.com/2017/03/02/upshot/arizona-shows-what-can-go-wrong-with-tax-credit-vouchers.html?_r=0.

Carrigan, Christopher. "Captured by Disaster? Reinterpreting Regulatory Behavior in the Shadow of the Gulf Oil Spill." In *Preventing Regulatory Capture: Special Interest Influence and How to Limit It*, edited by Daniel Carpenter and David A. Moss, 239–291. New York: Cambridge University Press, 2014.

Carissimo, Justin. "Jeff Sessions Reverses Obama Order to Phase Out Private Prisons." *Independent*. February 23, 2017. http://www.independent.co.uk/news/world/americas/jeff-sessions-signals-support-for-private-prisons-a7596661.html.

Carnoy, Martin. "School Vouchers are Not a Proven Strategy for Improving Student Achievement." Report by the Economic Policy Institute. February 28, 2017. http://www.epi.org/files/pdf/121635.pdf.

Cavicchia, Marilyn. "Which Way Forward?: National Conference of Bar Presidents Discusses Possible Futures for the Profession and for Bar Associations." *Bar Leader* 39. March-April 2015. http://www.americanbar.org/publications/bar_leader/2014–15/march-april/which-way-forward-national-conference-bar-presidents-discusses-possible-futures-profession-bar-associations.html.

CBA Legal Futures Initiative. "Futures: Transforming the Delivery of Legal Services in Canada." August, 2014. http://www.cba.org/CBAMediaLibrary/cba_na/PDFs/CBA%20Legal%20Futures%20PDFS/Futures-Final-eng.pdf.

Center for International Environmental Law. "The Ebb and Flow of the Water Privatization Debate Briefing Paper for the Fourth World Water Forum." March 2006. http://www.ciel.org/Publications/EbbFlow_Mar06.pdf.

Chambliss, Elizabeth and David B. Wilkins. "A New Framework for Law Firm Discipline." *Georgetown Journal of Legal Ethics* 16 (2002): 335–351. http://heinonline.org/HOL/LandingPage?handle=hein.journals/geojlege16&div=18&id=&page=.

Chandler, Mark, Charles J. Kalil, Thomas L. Sager, Brackett B. Denniston III, Robert C. Weber, A. Douglas Melamed, Glenn E. Bost II, Randal S. Milch, and Frank R. Jimenez. "Comments of Nine General Counsel on the ABA Commission on Ethics 20/20's Discussion Paper on Alternative Law Practice Structures." February 29, 2012. http://www.americanbar.org/content/dam/aba/administrative/ethics_2020/ethics_20_20_comments/ninegeneralcounselcomments_alpschoiceoflawinitial-draftproposal.authcheckdam.pdf.

Chaserant, Camille and Sophie Harnay, "The Regulation of Quality in the Market for Legal Services: Taking the Heterogeneity of Legal Services Seriously." *The European Journal of Comparative Economics* 10 (2013): 267–291. http://eaces.liuc.it/18242979201302/182429792013100208.pdf.

Christensen, Barlow F. "The Unauthorized Practice of Law: Do Good Fences Really Make Good Neighbors—or Even Good Sense?" *American Bar Foundation Research Journal* 5 (Spring, 1980): 159–216.

Clark, Gerard J. "Internet Wars: The Bar Against the Websites." *Journal of High Technology Law* XIII (2013): 247–296. https://www.suffolk.edu/documents/jhtl_publications/CLARKMACRO-FINALFINAL.pdf.

Clearwater, Karen. "President's Report: The Map Followed . . ." *The Law Society of Manitoba Communiqué 2.0*. May, 2015, 1–2. http://www.lawsociety.mb.ca/publications/communique/May%202015.pdf.

Clementi, David. "Consultation Paper on the Review of the Regulatory Framework for Legal Services in England and Wales." March, 2004. http://webarchive.nationalarchives.gov.uk/+/http://www.legal-services-review.org.uk/content/consult/review.htm.

———. "Review of the Regulatory Framework for Legal Services in England and Wales: Final Report." December, 2004. http://webarchive.nationalarchives.gov.uk/+/http://www.legal-services-review.org.uk/content/report/report-chap.pdf.

"CMA Final Report: Demand for Better Price and Service Transparency from Law Firms, and Review of Legal Regulation." *Legal Futures*. December 15, 2016. http://www.legalfutures.co.uk/latest-news/cma-final-report-demand-better-price-service-transparency-law-firms-review-legal-regulation.

Coglianese, Cary. "Management-Based Regulation: Implications for Public Policy." In *Risk and Regulatory Policy: Improving the Governance of Risk*. OECD, 159–183. Paris: OECD Publishing, 2010. http://dx.doi.org/10.1787/9789264082939-en.

Colorado Cross-Disability Coalition. "Comments on Civil Legal Service Providers." April 24, 2016. https://www.americanbar.org/content/dam/aba/images/office_president/julie_reiskin.pdf.

Colorado Supreme Court Attorney Regulation Advisory Committee Subcommittee on Proactive Management-Based Program. "Meeting Minutes." October 19, 2016. http://www.coloradosupremecourt.com/PDF/AboutUs/PMBR/PMBP%20Subcommittee%20Minutes%2010–19–16.pdf.

———. "Meeting Minutes." January 18, 2017. http://www.coloradosupremecourt.us/PDF/AboutUs/PMBR/PMBP%20Subcommittee%20Minutes%201–18–17.pdf.

Columbia Law School Human Rights Institute and Northeastern University School of Law Program on Human Rights and the Global Economy. "Equal Access to Justice: Ensuring Meaningful Access to Counsel in Civil Cases, Including Immigration Proceedings—Response to the Seventh and Ninth Periodic Reports of the United States to the Committee on the Elimination of All Forms of Racial Discrimination." July, 2014. http://web.law.columbia.edu/sites/default/files/microsites/human-rights-institute/files/equal_access_to_justice_-_cerd_shadow_report.pdf.

Committee on Privatization of Water Services in the United States, National Research Council. *Privatization of Water Services in the United States: An Assessment of Issues and Experience*. Washington, DC: National Academy Press, 2002. https://doi.org/10.17226/10135.

Committee on Standards in Public Life. "Striking the Balance: Upholding the Seven Principles of Public Life in Regulation." September, 2016. https://www.gov.uk/government/uploads/system/uploads/attachment_data/file/554817/Striking_the_Balance__web__-_v3_220916.pdf.

Competition & Markets Authority. "Legal Services Market Study: Final Report." December 15, 2016. https://assets.publishing.service.gov.uk/media/58518dc1ed915d0aeb0000a4/legal-services-market-study-final-report.pdf.

Conference of Chief Justices. "Resolution 9: Recommending Consideration of ABA Model Regulatory Objectives for the Provision of Legal Services." February 3, 2016. http://ccj.ncsc.org/~/media/Microsites/Files/CCJ/Resolutions/02012016-Recommending-Consideration-ABA-Model-Regulatory-Objectives-Provision-Legal-Services.ashx.

"Consultative Group—Summary of Key Issues." July 23, 2010. http://web.archive.org/web/20110408032839/http://ag.gov.au/www/agd/rwpattach.nsf/VAP/(9A5D88DBA63D32A661E6369859739356)~CG+key+issue+summary+-+as+at+11+August+2010.PDF/$file/CG+key+issue+summary+-+as+at+11+August+2010.PDF.

Cordova-Novion, Cesar and Stéphane Jacobzone. "Strengthening the Institutional Setting for Regulatory Reform: The Experience from OECD Countries." OECD Working Papers on Public Governance, No. 19. OECD Publishing, 2011. http://dx.doi.org/10.1787/5kgglrpvcpth-en.

Corporate Accountability International. "Public Water Works! The Case for Prioritizing our Most Essential Public Service." 2012. https://www.stopcorporateabuse.org/sites/default/files/resources/public-water-works.pdf.

Coyle, Jim. "Subcommittee Turns to Proactive Regulation." Colorado Supreme Court. Winter 2016. http://www.coloradosupremecourt.com/newsletters/winter2016/Subcommittee%20turns%20to%20proactive%20regulation.htm.

Craig, Susanne. "Trump's Empire: A Maze of Debts and Opaque Ties." *New York Times*. August 20, 2016. http://www.nytimes.com/2016/08/21/us/politics/donald-trump-debt.html.

Crews, Clyde Wayne. "Donald Trump Promises to Eliminate Two Regulations for Every One Enacted." *Forbes*. November 22, 2016. http://www.forbes.com/sites/waynecrews/2016/11/22/donald-trump-promises-to-eliminate-two-regulations-for-every-one-enacted/#413314902b87.

Cross, Michael. "IBA 2016: Legal Independence in E&W Under Attack." *The Law Society Gazette*. September 22, 2016. https://www.lawgazette.co.uk/news/iba-2016-legal-independence-in-eandw-under-attack/5057851.article.

Cross, Robert. "Balancing Regulatory Risk." Presentation at UCL International Access to Justice Conference, London, England, June 20, 2014. https://research.legalservicesboard.org.uk/wp-content/media/UCL-AtoJ-Conference-presentation-20-June-2014.pdf.

Crouch, Colin. *The Knowledge Corrupters: Hidden Consequences of the Financial Takeover of Public Life*. Cambridge, UK: Polity Press, 2016.

———. *The Strange Non-Death of Neoliberalism*. Cambridge, England: Polity Press, 2011.

Curry, Greg and Thompson & Knight, LLP. Untitled and undated. https://www.americanbar.org/content/dam/aba/images/office_president/greg_curry_and_thompson_and_knight_abs.pdf.

"Declaration on Free Access to Law." Free Access to Law Movement. Last amended 2012. http://www.fatlm.org/declaration/.

Department for Constitutional Affairs. "The Future of Legal Services: Putting Consumers First." October, 2005. http://webarchive.nationalarchives.gov.uk/+/http://www.dca.gov.uk/legalsys/folwp.pdf.

Devlin, Richard and Ora Morison. "Access to Justice and the Ethics and Politics of Alternative Business Structures." *The Canadian Bar Review* 91 (2012): 483–553. http://ssrn.com/abstract=2437035.

Devlin, Richard F. and Porter Heffernan. "The End(S) Of Self-Regulation?" *Alberta Law Review* 45 (2008): 169–214. http://ssrn.com/abstract=2101801.

Director General of Fair Trading. "Competition in Professions." March, 2001. http://webarchive.nationalarchives.gov.uk/20140402142426/http:/www.oft.gov.uk/shared_oft/reports/professional_bodies/oft328.pdf.

"Donald Trump Says 70 Percent of Federal Regulations 'Can Go.'" *The Telegraph*. October 7, 2016. http://www.telegraph.co.uk/news/2016/10/07/donald-trump-says-70-percent-of-federal-regulations-can-go/.

"[Draft] Regulatory Objectives of the Supreme Court of Colorado." November 12, 2015. http://www.americanbar.org/content/dam/aba/images/office_president/supreme_court_of_colorado.pdf.

DRI—The Voice of the Defense Bar. "Issues Paper Regarding Alternative Business Structures." May 4, 2016. http://www.americanbar.org/content/dam/aba/images/office_president/dri_the_voice_of_the_defense_bar_abs.pdf.

Duroni, Lance. "US Law Firms Still Flirting with Going Public." *Law 360*, July 15, 2015. http://www.law360.com/articles/671281/us-law-firms-still-flirting-with-going-public.

Dyck, Karen. "Innovating Regulation on the Prairies." *Slaw*. January 20, 2016. http://www.slaw.ca/2016/01/20/innovating-regulation-on-the-prairies/.

Earnshaw, Ross. "Promoting Better Practices—a Proactive Approach to Lawyer and Paralegal Regulation." *Slaw*. February 1, 2016. http://www.slaw.ca/2016/02/12/promoting-better-practices-a-proactive-approach-to-lawyer-and-paralegal-regulation/.

Edwards, Blake. "The Debate Over Non-Lawyer Firm Ownership Is Officially Closed, For Now." *Bloomberg Law*. May 17, 2016. https://bol.bna.com/the-debate-over-non-lawyer-firm-ownership-is-officially-closed-for-now/.

Ehrhardt, Sara and Maude Barlow. "A Debate on Water Privatization, Part Six. *Grist*. July 17, 2004. http://grist.org/article/barlow2/.

EM. May 5, 2015 (11:33 am). Comment on Alice Woolley, "Bencher Elections—The Challenge to Self-Regulations Legitimacy." *Slaw*. April 30, 2015. http://www.slaw.ca/2015/04/30/bencher-elections-the-challenge-to-self-regulations-legitimacy/.

Evans, Adrian, Francesca Bartlett, Maxine Evers, Kath Hall, Linda Haller, Vivien Holmes, Suzanne Le Mire, Mary Anne Noone and Christine Parker. "Submission to National Legal Profession Reform Consultation on Proposed National Law." June 22, 2010. http://web.archive.org/web/20110603165707/http://www.ema.gov.au/www/agd/rwpattach.nsf/VAP/(9A5D88DBA63D32A661E6369859739356)~134+Christine+Parker+Submission+to+NLP+Project+Consultation+22062010.pdf/$file/134+Christine+Parker+Submission+to+NLP+Project+Consultation+22062010.pdf.

Federal Trade Commission and US Department of Justice. Letter to Kansas Bar Association, February 4, 2005. https://www.ftc.gov/sites/default/files/documents/advocacy_documents/ftc-and-department-justice-comment-kansas-bar-association-concerning-proposed-definition-practice/v050002.pdf.

Figlio, David and Krzysztof Karbownik. "Evaluation of Ohio's EdChoice Scholarship Program: Selection, Competition, and Performance Effects." Thomas B. Fordham Institute. July, 2016. https://edex.s3-us-west-2.amazonaws.com/publication/pdfs/FORDHAM%20Ed%20Choice%20Evaluation%20Report_online%20edition.pdf.

Food & Water Watch. "Has Water Privatization Gone Too Far in New Jersey?" June, 2010. https://www.inthepublicinterest.org/wp-content/uploads/FWW_PrivatizationInNewJersey.pdf.

———. "The Public Works How the Remunicipalization of Water Services Saves Money." December, 2010. http://www.foodandwaterwatch.org/sites/default/files/The%20Public%20Works%20FS%20Dec%202010.pdf.

———. "The State of Public Water in the United States." February, 2016. http://www.foodandwaterwatch.org/sites/default/files/report_state_of_public_water.pdf.

———. "Water Privatization: Facts and Figures." August 31, 2015. http://www.foodandwaterwatch.org/insight/water-privatization-facts-and-figures.

Fortney, Susan and Tahlia Gordon. "Adopting Law Firm Management Systems to Survive and Thrive: A Study of the Australian Approach to Management-Based

Regulation." *University of St. Thomas Law Journal* 10 (2013): 152–194. http://ir.stthomas.edu/ustlj/vol10/iss1/4/.

Fortney, Susan Saab. "Promoting Public Protection through an 'Attorney Integrity' System: Lessons from the Australian Experience with Proactive Regulation of Lawyers." *The Professional Lawyer* 23 (2015): 1–12. http://www.americanbar.org/content/dam/aba/publications/professional_lawyer/volume_23_number_1/ABA_PLN_v023n01_001_promoting_public_protection_through_an_attorney_integrity_system_lessons_from_the_australian_experience_with_proactive_regulation_of_lawyers.authcheckdam.pdf.

———. "The Role of Ethics Audits in Improving Management Systems and Practices: An Empirical Examination of Management-Based Regulation of Law Firms." *St. Mary's Journal on Legal Malpractice and Ethics* 4 (2015): 112–149. http://ssrn.com/abstract=2660358.

Forum on the Entertainment and Sports Law Industries. "ABA Commission on the Future of Legal Services—Issues Paper on Alternative Business Structures/Comments Requested." May 3, 2016. http://www.americanbar.org/content/dam/aba/images/office_president/entertainment_and_sports_abs.pdf.

Foster, Danny. "World Justice Project Describes the Failure of America's Legal Services Marketplace." *Responsive Law Blog*. March 14, 2014. http://responsivelaw.org/index.php/blog/item/100-world-justice-project-report?highlight=WyJ3b3JsZCIsIndvcmxkJ3MiLCJqdXN0aWNlIiwiJ2p1c3RpY2UiLCJwcm9qZWN0IiwicHJvamVjdCdzIiwicnVsZSIsIm9mIiwibGF3IiwibGF3J3MiLCJpbmRleCIsIndvcmxkIGp1c3RpY2UiLCJ3b3JsZCBqdXN0aWNlIHByb2plY3QiLCJqdXN0aWNlIHByb2plY3QiLCJydWxlIG9mIiwicnVsZSBvZiBsYXciLCJvZiBsYXciLCJvZiBsYXcgaW5kZXgiLCJsYXcgaW5kZXgiXQ.

Fouzder, Monidipa. "SRA Says 'Sorry' Over ABS Application Delays." *The Law Society Gazette*. April 27, 2015. http://www.lawgazette.co.uk/practice/sra-says-sorry-over-abs-application-delays/5048340.fullarticle.

Fox, Lawrence J. "Burying the Lede." 2015. http://www.americanbar.org/content/dam/aba/images/office_president/larry_fox.pdf.

———. "What Would Bob MacCrate Think?", n.d. http://www.americanbar.org/content/dam/aba/images/office_president/lawrence_j_fox_abs.pdf.

"Framework Document: Agreement between the Ministry of Justice and the Legal Services Board." June, 2011. http://www.legalservicesboard.org.uk/about_us/lsb_framework_document/pdf/moj_framework_agreement_june_2011.pdf.

The Friedman Foundation for Educational Choice. "How Does School Choice Affect Public Schools?" Undated. http://www.schoolchoicewi.org/files/7114/2064/5055/How-does-school-choice-affect-public-schools.pdf.

Friedman, Ken. "Could Dental-Board Decision Unlock Lawyer Control of State Bar Regulations?" *Forbes,* March 4, 2015. http://www.forbes.com/sites/danielfisher/2015/03/04/dental-board-decision-could-unlock-lawyer-control/#75de2e7b68cf.

Friedman, Milton. "Why America Needs School Vouchers." *Wall Street Journal*. September 28, 2000. https://www.edchoice.org/who-we-are/our-founders/the-friedmans-on-school-choice/article/why-america-needs-school-vouchers/.

Fung, Archon. "Participate, but Do So Pragmatically." In *Focus on Citizens: Public Engagement for Better Policy and Services*. OECD Studies on Public Engagement, 227–230. Paris: OECD Publishing, 2009. http://www19.iadb.org/intal/intalcdi/pe/2009/03785.pdf.

Furlong, Jordan. "Watershed: The CBA Futures Report." Law21. August 14, 2014. http://www.law21.ca/2014/08/watershed-cba-futures-report/.

Galanter, Marc. "Why the "Haves" Come Out Ahead: Speculations on the Limits of Legal Change." *Law & Society Review* 9 (1974): 95–160. http://jan.ucc.nau.edu/~phelps/Galanter%201974.pdf.

Gallivan, Henry Mills. "ABA Proposal on Alternative Business Structures." April 28, 2016. http://www.americanbar.org/content/dam/aba/images/office_president/henry_mills_gallivan_abs.pdf.

Garcia-Roberts, Gus. "McKay Scholarship Program Sparks a Cottage Industry of Fraud and Chaos." *Miami New Times*. June 23, 2011. http://www.miaminewtimes.com/news/mckay-scholarship-program-sparks-a-cottage-industry-of-fraud-and-chaos-6381391.

Gibeaut, John. "'It's a Done Deal': House of Delegates Vote Crushes Chances for MDP." *ABA Journal* 9 (2000): 92–93. http://www.jstor.org/stable/27841689.

Gilens, Martin and Benjamin I. Page. "Critics Argued With Our Analysis of U.S. Political Inequality. Here Are 5 Ways They're Wrong." *Washington Post*. May 23, 2016. https://www.washingtonpost.com/news/monkey-cage/wp/2016/05/23/critics-challenge-our-portrait-of-americas-political-inequality-heres-5-ways-they-are-wrong/?utm_term=.cf83dde48245.

———. "Testing Theories of American Politics: Elites, Interest Groups, and Average Citizens." *Perspectives on Politics*. September, 2014. https://scholar.princeton.edu/sites/default/files/mgilens/files/gilens_and_page_2014_-testing_theories_of_american_politics.doc.pdf.

Goldsmith, Jonathan. "Endangered Lawyers." *Law Society Gazette*. January 26, 2015. http://www.lawgazette.co.uk/analysis/comment%E2%80%94%20and%E2%80%94%20opinion/endangered%E2%80%94%20lawyers/5046285.article.

Goodwin, James. "Racism, Cost-Benefit Analysis, and Trump Advisor Steve Bannon." *CPR Blog*. November 29, 2016. http://www.progressivereform.org/CPRBlog.cfm?idBlog=BD292079-CA1F-3304-A41D96F4C6D2A68F.

Gordon, David. "An Analysis of the Privatization of Drinking Water Facilities in the United States." Masters project submitted in partial fulfillment of the requirements for the Masters of Environmental Management degree in the Nicholas School of the Environment of Duke University, May, 2011. http://dukespace.lib.duke.edu/dspace/bitstream/handle/10161/3708/Gordon_David_Final_MP.pdf;sequence=1.

Gordon, Thomas M. "Comments on: Alternative Business Structures." May 31, 2011. http://www.americanbar.org/content/dam/aba/administrative/ethics_2020/ethics_20_20_comments/responsivelaw_issuespaperconcerningalternativebusinessstructures.authcheckdam.pdf.

———. "Comments on: Alternative Law Practice Structures." January 30, 2012. http://www.americanbar.org/content/dam/aba/administrative/ethics_2020/ethics_20_20_comments/responsivelaw_alpsdiscussiondraft.authcheckdam.pdf.

———. "Comments On: Issues Paper Regarding Alternative Business Structures." May 2, 2016. http://www.americanbar.org/content/dam/aba/images/office_president/responsive_law_abs.pdf.

Gordon, Tahlia and Paddy Oliver. "The Demise of Appropriate Management Systems for Australian Law Firms." May 11, 2015. https://www.linkedin.com/pulse/demise-appropriate-management-systems-australian-law-firms-gordon.

Gorelick, Jamie S. and Michael Traynor. "For Comment: Discussion Paper on Alternative Law Practice Structures." December 2, 2011. http://www.americanbar.org/content/dam/aba/administrative/ethics_2020/20111202-ethics2020-discussion_draft-alps.authcheckdam.pdf.

"Government Conclusions—Competition and Regulation in the Legal Services Market: A Report Following the Consultation 'In the Public Interest?'" July 2003. http://webarchive.nationalarchives.gov.uk/+/http://www.dca.gov.uk/consult/general/oftreptconc.htm.

Grady, Kenneth. Video Testimony to the ABA Commission on the Future of Legal Services. February, 2015. http://bcove.me/x9hwfqsq.

Graham, D. John. "Why Governments Need Guidelines for Risk Assessment and Management." In *Risk and Regulatory Policy: Improving the Governance of Risk*, OECD, 237–247. Paris: OECD Publishing, 2010. http://dx.doi.org/10.1787/9789264082939-en.

Greenhouse, Linda. "Outsourcing the Constitution." *New York Times*. March 1, 2017. https://www.nytimes.com/2017/03/01/opinion/outsourcing-the-constitution.html.

Gregson, Joseph Shannon. "Comparing Public and Private Prison Systems." Paper presented to the Public Administration Faculty at the University of Michigan-Flint In Partial Fulfillment of the Requirements for the Master of Public Administration, Fall, 2000. https://deepblue.lib.umich.edu/bitstream/handle/2027.42/117712/Gregson.pdf?sequence=1&isAllowed=y.

Hadfield, Gillian K. and Deborah L. Rhode. "How to Regulate Legal Services to Promote Access, Innovation, and the Quality of Lawyering." *Hastings Law Journal* 67 (2016): 1191–1223. http://www.hastingslawjournal.org/wp-content/uploads/Hadfield_Rhode-67.5.pdf.

Hadfield, Gillian K. and Jamie Heine. "Life in the Law-Thick World: The Legal Resource Landscape for Ordinary Americans." USC CLASS Research Papers Series No. CLASS15-2; USC Law Legal Studies Paper No. 15–2. January 9, 2015. http://dx.doi.org/10.2139/ssrn.2547664.

Hadfield, Gillian. "The Cost of Law: Promoting Access to Justice through the (Un) Corporate Practice of Law." *International Review of Law and Economics* 38 (2014): 43–63. http://ssrn.com/abstract=2333990.

———. "Legal Barriers to Innovation: The Growing Economic Cost of Professional Control Over Corporate Legal Markets." *Stanford Law Review* 60 (2008): 101–146. http://ssrn.com/abstract=1104902.

———. "Legal Infrastructure and the New Economy." *I/S: A Journal of Law and Policy for the Information Society* 8 (2012): 1–59. http://ssrn.com/abstract=1567712.

———. *Rules for a Flat World: Why Humans Invented Law and How to Reinvent It For a Complex Global Economy*. New York: Oxford University Press, 2016.

Harris, Dan. Comment on Renee Knake, "ABA Commission on Future of Legal Services Responds." *Lexblog*. August 24, 2016. http://kevin.lexblog.com/2016/08/24/aba-future-delivery-legal-services-responds/.

Hasselback, Drew. "Why the Law Society of Upper Canada's Move Toward 'Entity Regulation' Matters." *Financial Post*. May 31, 2016. http://business.financialpost.com/legal-post/drew-hasselback-why-the-law-society-of-upper-canadas-move-toward-entity-regulation-matters.

Hawthorne, Michael. "EPA Warns of Lead in Water in East Chicago," *Chicago Tribune*, March 2, 2017, http://www.chicagotribune.com/suburbs/ct-east-chicago-lead-water-20170302-story.html.

Helms, Ann Doss. "Praying for Options: Religious Schools Dominate NC Voucher Program." *The Charlotte Observer*. April 8, 2016. http://www.charlotteobserver.com/news/local/education/article70759617.html.

Hempling, Scott. *Preside or Lead? The Attributes and Actions of Effective Regulators*. Silver Spring, MD: Scott Hempling Attorney at Law LLC, 2013.

Hepburn, Glen. "Alternatives to Traditional Regulation." OECD Report. 2006. http://www.oecd.org/gov/regulatory-policy/42245468.pdf.

Herold, Benjamin. "Northeast Schools: 'Bursting at the Seams.'" The Notebook. June 10, 2011. http://legacy.thenotebook.org/blog/113794/northeast-schools-bursting-seams.

Hilborne, Nick. "Business Services Giant Blames SRA Rules for Scuppering ABS Plans." *Legal Futures*. July 31, 2015. http://www.legalfutures.co.uk/latest-news/business-services-giant-blames-sra-rules-for-scuppering-abs-plans.

———. "Competition and Markets Authority to Investigate Legal Services." *Legal Futures*. January 13, 2016. http://www.legalfutures.co.uk/latest-news/competition-and-markets-authority-to-investigate-legal-services.

———. "COLPs Failing to Report Problems to SRA, Groundbreaking Study Finds." *Legal Futures*. March 3, 2016. http://www.legalfutures.co.uk/latest-news/colps-failing-to-report-problems-to-sra-groundbreaking-study-finds.

———. "Government Promises to Clear Way for Supermarket and Estate Agent ABSs." *Legal Futures*. November 30, 2015. http://www.legalfutures.co.uk/latest-news/government-promises-to-clear-way-for-supermarket-and-estate-agent-abss.

———. "Not So Slow: SRA Approving Alternative Business Structures in Only Two Weeks." *Legal Futures*. February 17, 2016. http://www.legalfutures.co.uk/latest-news/not-so-slow-sra-approving-alternative-business-structures-in-only-two-weeks.

———. "Philip: If It's a New Law Firm, It Should Be an ABS." *Legal Futures*. October 15, 2015. http://www.legalfutures.co.uk/latest-news/philip-if-its-a-new-law-firm-it-should-be-an-abs.

———. "Rules Forcing Local Authorities to Set Up ABSs 'Risk Privatisation of Public Sector Legal Services.'" *Legal Futures*. August 3, 2015. http://www.legalfutures.co.uk/latest-news/rules-forcing-local-authorities-to-set-up-abss-risk-privatisation-of-public-sector-legal-services.

Hill, Benjamin H., III. "Non-Lawyer Ownership of Law Firms." April 25, 2016. http://www.americanbar.org/content/dam/aba/images/office_president/benjamin_j_hill_abs.pdf.

Hill, Louise Lark. "The Preclusion of Nonlawyer Ownership of Law Firms: Protecting the Interest of Clients or Protecting the Interest of Lawyers?" *Capital University Law Review* 42 (2014): 907–949. http://ssrn.com/abstract=2546886.

Hirschhorn, Joel S. "America, Welcome to Your Delusional Democracy." Wake Up World. September 16, 2016. https://wakeup-world.com/2016/09/16/welcome-to-your-delusional-democracy/.

Holderman, Paula Hudson. "Commentary on the Report from the ABA's Commission on the Future of Legal Services." April 27, 2016. http://www.americanbar.org/content/dam/aba/images/office_president/paula_hudson_holderman_abs.pdf.

Holmwood, Monika. "The New Legal Profession Uniform Law Takes Effect from 1 July 2015. Be Prepared." Law Graduate in Pink. June 17, 2015. http://lawgradinpink.blogspot.fr/2015/06/the-new-legal-profession-uniform-law.html.

Hunter, Pierce G. "Constitutional Law— Unauthorized Practice of Law: Driving Legal Business Without a License, LegalZoom, Inc., and Campbell v. Asbury Automotive, Inc., 2011 Ark. 157, 381 S.W.3d 21." *University of Arkansas at Little Rock Law Review* 36 (2014): 201–228. http://lawrepository.ualr.edu/lawreview/vol36/iss2/5.

Hurst, James Willard. *The Growth of American Law: The Law Makers*. Boston: Little, Brown and Company, 1950.

Iacobucci, Edward M. and Michael J. Trebilcock. "An Economic Analysis of Alternative Business Structures for the Practice of Law." Paper presented at the Law Society of Upper Canada's symposium for the Alternative Business Structures. October 4, 2013. http://www.lsuc.on.ca/uploadedFiles/ABS-report-Iacobucci-Trebilcock-september-2014.pdf.

Illinois Criminal Justice Information Authority. "Blueprint for the Future: Final Report of Trends & Issues for the 1990s." January, 1991.

Illinois State Bar Association. "Issues Paper Regarding Alternative Business Structures: Request for Comments." 2016. http://www.americanbar.org/content/dam/aba/images/office_president/illinois_state_bar_association_abs.pdf.

"Incorporation: Why are Law Firms Reluctant to Move Away from the Partnership Model?" *Lawyers Weekly*. August 18, 2011. http://www.lawyersweekly.com.au/features/9018-incorporation-why-are-law-firms-reluctant-to-move.

In re Co-operative Law Co. 198 NY 479 (1910) 479–486. https://casetext.com/case/matter-of-co-operative-law-co.

International Association of Defense Counsel. "ABA Commission on the Future of Legal Services—Alternative Business Structures." May 3, 2016. http://www.americanbar.org/content/dam/aba/images/office_president/international_association_of_defense_counsel_abs.pdf.

Johnson, Carrie. "Rights Advocates See 'Access to Justice' Gap in U.S." NPR, March 10, 2014. http://www.npr.org/sections/thetwo-way/2014/03/10/288225649/rights-advocates-see-access-to-justice-gap-in-u-s.

Johnson, Gene. "Washington Experiments with More Affordable Legal Advice." *The Seattle Times*. September 27, 2015. http://www.seattletimes.com/seattle-news/washington-experiments-with-more-affordable-legal-advice/.

Johnstone, Quintin. "Unauthorized Practice Controversy: A Struggle Among Power Groups." *Kansas Law Review* 4 (1955): 1–57. http://digitalcommons.law.yale.edu/fss_papers/1912.

Jones, Daniel Stedman. *Masters of the Universe: Hayek, Friedman, and the Birth of Neoliberal Politics*. Princeton, New Jersey: Princeton University Press, 2012.

Kanno-Youngs, Zolan. "Tenants in Maze of New York Courts Get a Helping Hand: The Court Navigator Program Guides People Who Don't Have An Attorney Through Their Civil Case." *The Wall Street Journal*. February 15, 2016. http://www.wsj.com/articles/tenants-in-maze-of-new-york-courts-get-a-helping-hand-1455591801.

Karmel, Roberta S. "Will Law Firms Go Public?" *University of Pennsylvania Journal of International Law* 35 (2014): 487–539. http://scholarship.law.upenn.edu/jil/vol35/iss2/4.

Kashin, Oleg. "Rex Tillerson's Special Friend in the Kremlin." *New York Times*. December 22, 2016. http://www.nytimes.com/2016/12/22/opinion/rex-tillersons-special-friend-in-the-kremlin.html?_r=0.

Knake, Renee Newman. "Democratizing the Delivery of Legal Services." *Ohio State Law Journal* 73 (2012): 1–46. http://dx.doi.org/10.2139/ssrn.1800258.

Kowalski, Mitch. "Anti-ABS Arguments Continue to Be Based on Emotion—Not Fact." *Slaw*, December 30, 2014. http://www.slaw.ca/2014/12/30/anti-abs-arguments-continue-to-be-based-on-emotion-not-fact/.

———. "Axiom Gobbles Up Canadian Market Share in Fascinating Deal with Cognition." *Financial Post*. January 20, 2016. http://business.financialpost.com/legal-post/mitch-kowalski-axiom-gobbles-up-canadian-market-share-in-fascinating-deal-with-cognition.

———. "What if the Western Provinces Saved the Profession?" *Slaw*. February 7, 2013. http://www.slaw.ca/2013/02/07/what-if-the-western-provinces-saved-the-profession/.

———. "Why One Scandal Shouldn't Doom a New Twist on Law Firm Ownership." *Financial Post*, August 17, 2015. http://business.financialpost.com/legal-post/why-one-scandal-shouldnt-doom-a-new-twist-on-law-firm-ownership.

Krager, Ted. *Skullduggery: The True Causes of the Financial Crisis*. Bloomington, IN: Authorhouse, 2012.

Kuczajda, Thomas A. "Self Regulation, Socialization, and the Role of *Model Rule* 5.1." *Georgetown Journal of Legal Ethics* 12 (1998–1999): 119–149. http://heinonline.org/HOL/LandingPage?handle=hein.journals/geojlege12&div=13&id=&page=.

Laird, Lorelei. "ABA House Approves Model Regulatory Objectives for Nontraditional Legal Services." *ABA Journal*. February 8, 2016. http://www.abajournal.com/news/article/house_approves_proposed_model_regulatory_objectives_for_nontraditional_lega/.

Law Firm Regulation Task Force. "Interim Report of the Law Firm Regulation Task Force." October 3, 2016. https://www.lawsociety.bc.ca/docs/publications/reports/LawFirmRegulation-2016.pdf.

———. "Law Firm Regulation Consultation Brief." October 26, 2015. https://www.lawsociety.bc.ca/docs/newsroom/highlights/FirmRegulation-brief.pdf.

———. "Law Firm Regulation Survey Report." Undated. https://www.lawsociety.bc.ca/docs/publications/survey/LawFirmRegulation.pdf.

The Law Society of British Columbia. "2015—2017 Strategic Plan." https://www.lawsociety.bc.ca/docs/about/StrategicPlan_2015–17.pdf.

The Law Society of Upper Canada. "Report to Convocation: Treasurer's Report." June 25, 2015. https://www.lsuc.on.ca/uploadedFiles/For_the_Public/About_the_Law_Society/Convocation_Decisions/2015/convocation-june-2015-treasurer.pdf.

———. Video "Promoting Better Legal Practices." February 8, 2016. https://www.youtube.com/watch?v=Wz2lPSyfqbI.

The Law Society of Upper Canada Compliance-Based Entity Regulation Task Force. "Call for Input Consultation Paper: 'Promoting Better Legal Practices.'" January, 2016. https://www.lsuc.on.ca/uploadedFiles/compliance-based-entity-regulation-consultation-paper.pdf.

———. "Report to Convocation." December 4, 2015. https://www.lsuc.on.ca/uploadedFiles/For_the_Public/About_the_Law_Society/Convocation_Decisions/2015/convocation%20december%202015%20compliance.pdf

———. "Report to Convocation." May 26, 2016. http://www.lsuc.on.ca/uploadedFiles/For_the_Public/About_the_Law_Society/Convocation_Decisions/2016/convocation_may_2016_cber.pdf.

The Law Society of Upper Canada Professional Regulations Committee. "First Report to Convocation." February 27, 2014, 1442–1507. http://www.lsuc.on.ca/uploadedFiles/ABS-report-to-Convocation-feb-2014.pdf.

———. "Report to Convocation." September 24, 2015, 110–132. http://www.lsuc.on.ca/uploadedFiles/For_the_Public/About_the_Law_Society/Convocation_Decisions/2015/convocation-september-2015-prc.pdf.

Layton, Lyndsey. "D.C. School Voucher Program Lacks Oversight, GAO Says." *Washington Post*. November 15, 2013. https://www.washingtonpost.com/local/education/dc-school-voucher-program-lacks-oversight-gao-says/2013/11/15/9bb8c35e-4e3d-11e3-be6b-d3d28122e6d4_story.html?utm_term=.1f6d412969d2.

Lee, Michelle Ye Hee. "Yes, U.S. Locks People Up at a Higher Rate than Any Other Country." *The Washington Post*. July 7, 2015. https://www.washingtonpost.com/news/fact-checker/wp/2015/07/07/yes-u-s-locks-people-up-at-a-higher-rate-than-any-other-country/?utm_term=.854bffd0aa07.

Leef, George. "Why The Legal Profession Says LegalZoom Is Illegal." *Forbes*. October 14, 2014. http://www.forbes.com/sites/georgeleef/2014/10/14/why-the-legal-profession-says-legalzoom-is-illegal/#580de4037664.

Legal Services Board. "The Regulatory Objectives: Legal Services Act 2007." Undated. http://www.legalservicesboard.org.uk/news_publications/publications/pdf/regulatory_objectives.pdf

———. "Research Strategy." June 14, 2010. http://www.legalservicesboard.org.uk/what_we_do/Research/pdf/lsb_research_strategy_2010_formatted_version.pdf.

Legal Services Consumer Panel. "Consumer Impact Report 2014." December 5, 2014. http://www.legalservicesconsumerpanel.org.uk/publications/research_and_reports/documents/Consumer%20Impact%20Report%203.pdf.

Lenihan, Donald G. "Public Engagement Is a Must in a Multi-Stakeholder World." In *Focus on Citizens: Public Engagement for Better Policy and Services*. OECD

Studies on Public Engagement, 207–212. Paris: OECD Publishing, 2009. http://www19.iadb.org/intal/intalcdi/pe/2009/03785.pdf.

Levi, John. "Civil Legal Aid: Ensuring Equal Access to Justice." Legal Services Corporation Blog. January 26, 2015. http://www.lsc.gov/media-center/blog/2015/01/26/civil-legal-aid-ensuring-equal-access-justice.

Li, Victor. "ABA's New Center for Innovation Will Drive Efforts for New Methods of Delivering Legal Services." *ABA Journal*. November 1, 2016. http://www.abajournal.com/magazine/article/aba_center_for_innovation.

Libhart, Stephanie S. Letter to ABA Commission on Ethics 20/20. October 4, 2012. http://www.americanbar.org/content/dam/aba/administrative/ethics_2020/ethics_20_20_comments/pa_iolta_board_of_the_supreme_court_comments_pro_hac_vice_admission.authcheckdam.pdf.

Lichtblau, Eric. "Jamie S. Gorelick." *New York Times*. November 9, 2008. http://www.nytimes.com/2008/11/08/us/politics/08gorelick.html.

Lobina, Emanuele with Corporate Accountability International. "Troubled Waters: Misleading Industry PR and the Case for Public Water." November, 2014. https://www.stopcorporateabuse.org/sites/default/files/resources/troubledwaters_webres.pdf.

Lockwood, Sally Evans. Letter to ABA Commission on Ethics 20/20 Working Group on Inbound Foreign Lawyers. July 5, 2010. http://www.americanbar.org/content/dam/aba/administrative/ethics_2020/ethics_20_20_comments/supremecourtofgeorgiaofficeofbaradmissions_inboundforeignlawyersmemorandaandtemplate.authcheckdam.pdf.

Lombardo, Crystal. "Water Privatization Pros and Cons." Vision Launch. January 7, 2015. http://visionlaunch.com/water-privatization-pros-and-cons/#.

Lord Falconer of Thoroton. "Legal Services: Clementi Report." Written statement to House of Lords. December 15, 2004. http://hansard.millbanksystems.com/written_statements/2004/dec/15/legal-services-clementi-report#column_83ws.

Los Angeles County Bar Association. "Comment of the Los Angeles County Bar Association to the American Bar Association's Commission on the Future of Legal Services Regarding Alternative Business Structures." April 29, 2016. https://www.americanbar.org/content/dam/aba/images/office_president/los_angeles_county_bar_association_abs.pdf.

Loughrey, Joan and Sundeep Aulakh. "Framing Regulation and Compliance in Legal Services Firms: the Role of the Compliance Officer for Legal Practice." Paper presented at Georgetown University Law Center, "Authorized Revolution: Regulatory Disruption of the Legal Services Market," Washington, D.C., April 24, 2015. http://www.law.georgetown.edu/continuing-legal-education/programs/academic-conferences/regulating-legal-services.cfm.

"LSB Could Pose Risk to Independence of Legal Profession, Warns Law Society President." *Legal Futures*. May 25, 2010. http://www.legalfutures.co.uk/latest-news/lsb-could-pose-risk-to-independence-of-legal-profession-warns-law-society-president.

"LSB Underplaying Needs of 'Vulnerable' In Favour of Business, Warns Bar Regulator." *Legal Futures*. March 3, 2015. http://www.legalfutures.co.uk/latest-news/lsb-underplaying-needs-of-vulnerable-in-favour-of-business-warns-bar-regulator.

Luoma, Jon R. "Water for Profit." *Mother Jones*. November/December, 2002. http://www.motherjones.com/politics/2002/11/water-profit.

Macey, Jonathan. "Occupation Code 541110: Lawyers, Self-Regulation, and the Idea of a Profession." *Fordham Law Review* 74 (2005): 1079–1103. http://digitalcommons.law.yale.edu/cgi/viewcontent.cgi?article=2352&context=fss_papers.

Maher, Frank. "PII Renewal: The Insurance Issues Facing Law Firms." *LexisNexis Future of Law Blog*. May 28, 2013. http://blogs.lexisnexis.co.uk/futureoflaw/2013/05/pii-renewal-the-insurance-issues-facing-law-firms/.

Mark, Steven and Georgina Cowdroy. "Incorporated Legal Practices—A New Era in the Provision of Legal Services in the State of New South Wales." *Penn State International Law Review* 22 (2004): 671–693. http://ssrn.com/abstract=673021.

Mark, Steven and Tahlia Gordon. "Innovations in Regulation—Responding to a Changing Legal Services Market." *Georgetown Journal of Legal Ethics* 22 (2009): 501–533. http://www.olsc.nsw.gov.au/Documents/innovations_regulation_geo_journal.pdf.

Mark, Steve, Tahlia Gordon, Marlene Le Brun, and Gary Tamsitt. "Preserving the Ethics and Integrity of the Legal Profession in an Evolving Market: A Comparative Regulatory Response." Undated. http://www.olsc.nsw.gov.au/Documents/preserving%20ethics%20integrity%20legal%20profession%20uk_paper.pdf.

Mark, Steve. "The Regulatory Framework in Australia." Paper presented at the ABA Center for Professional Responsibility 40th National Conference on Professional Responsibility, Long Beach, California, May 29, 2014. http://www.americanbar.org/content/dam/aba/events/professional_responsibility/2014/05/40th-aba-national-conference-on-professional-responsibility/session1_02_mark_the_regulatory_framework_in_australia_final.authcheckdam.pdf.

Mason, Cody. "Too Good to Be True: Private Prisons in America." Report prepared for The Sentencing Project. January, 2012. http://sentencingproject.org/wp-content/uploads/2016/01/Too-Good-to-be-True-Private-Prisons-in-America.pdf.

Matheson, John H. and Edward S. Adams. "Not 'If' but 'How:' Reflecting on the ABA Commission's Recommendations on Multidisciplinary Practice." *Minnesota Law Review* 84 (2000): 1269–1358. http://scholarship.law.umn.edu/cgi/viewcontent.cgi?article=1098&context=faculty_articles.

Mathewson, Mark. "Illinois Supreme Court Adopts 'Proactive Management-Based Regulation.'" *Illinois Lawyer Now*. January 27, 2017. https://iln.isba.org/blog/2017/01/25/illinois-supreme-court-adopts-proactive-management-based-regulation.

Maute, Judith L. "Global Continental Shifts in a New Governance Paradigm in Lawyer Regulation and Consumer Protection: Riding the Wave." In *Alternative Perspectives on Lawyers and Legal Ethics: Reimagining the Profession*, edited by Francesca Bartlett, Reid Mortensen and Kieran Tranter, 11–55. London: Routledge, 2011.

McCarty, Nolan. "Complexity, Capacity and Capture." In *Preventing Regulatory Capture: Special Interest Influence and How to Limit It*, edited by Daniel Carpenter and David A. Moss, 99–123. New York: Cambridge University Press, 2014.

McLaren, Michael and Marianne Butler. "Origins of the Legal Services Act 2007." In *Guide to the Legal Services Act 2007*, edited by James Thorne and Iain Miller, 1–12. UK: LexisNexis, 2009.

McNealy, Scott. "Our Public Education System 'is Failing.'" CNBC. August 9, 2016. http://www.cnbc.com/2016/08/09/our-public-education-system-is-failing-scott-mcnealy-commentary.html.

Mercer, Malcolm. May 18, 2015 (10:15 am). Comment on Alice Woolley, "Bencher Elections—The Challenge to Self-Regulations Legitimacy." *Slaw*. April 30, 2015. http://www.slaw.ca/2015/04/30/bencher-elections-the-challenge-to-self-regulations-legitimacy/.

Memorandum by the General Council of the Bar." *Joint Committee on the Draft Legal Services Bill Minutes of Evidence*. June, 2006. http://www.publications.parliament.uk/pa/jt200506/jtselect/jtlegal/232/6060812.htm.

"Memorandum by the Law Society of England and Wales." *Joint Committee on the Draft Legal Services Bill Minutes of Evidence*. June 2006. http://www.publications.parliament.uk/pa/jt200506/jtselect/jtlegal/232/6060802.htm.

Merrifield, John. *The School Choice Wars*. Lanham, Maryland: Scarecrow Press, 2001.

Merritt, Chris. "Incorporation could be `Ethical Minefield.'" *The Australian Financial Review*. May 19, 2000.

———. "Integrated Legal Holdings Calls for Reprieve on $12.6m Loan Repayments." *The Australian*, September 12, 2014. http://www.theaustralian.com.au/business/legal-affairs/integrated-legal-holdings-calls-for-reprieve-on-126m-loan-repayments/story-e6frg97x-1227055657940.

Merrow, Ivan Mitchell. "In Futuro: What the CBA's Legal Futures Report Means for You." *Juris Diction*. November 18, 2014. http://juris-diction.ca/in-futuro-what-the-cbas-legal-futures-report-means-for-you/.

Mezrani, Leanne. "Rules to Govern NSW and Vic Lawyers Locked In." *Lawyers Weekly*. May 28, 2015. http://www.lawyersweekly.com.au/news/16582-rules-to-govern-lawyers-in-nsw-and-victoria-locked-in.

Middlesex County Bar Association. "Issues Paper Regarding Alternative Business Structures." May 6, 2016. http://www.americanbar.org/content/dam/aba/images/office_president/middlesex_county_bar_association_abs.pdf.

———. Letter to Katy Englehart. December 3, 2015. http://www.americanbar.org/content/dam/aba/images/office_president/lspcomments_middlesex_county_bar_association.pdf.

"Mike Pence's Voucher Program in Indiana Was a Windfall for Religious Schools." *Mother Jones*. December 2, 2016. http://www.motherjones.com/politics/2016/11/mike-pence-voucher-program-religious-schools.

Milliner, Robert. "LLFG Limited Response." December 22, 2009. http://web.archive.org/web/20110607140759/https://www.ag.gov.au/www/agd/rwpattach.nsf/VAP/(8AB0BDE05570AAD0EF9C283AA8F533E3)~Milliner,+Robert+(Chair+,+LLFG+Limited+(Large+Law+Firm+Group))+-+Business+Structures.PDF/$file/Milliner,+Robert+(Chair+,+LLFG+Limited+(Large+Law+Firm+Group))+-+Business+Structures.PDF.

———. "Regulatory Framework, Consumer Protection, Business Structures, Liability of Principals, Fidelity Cover and General Observations." December 22, 2009. http://web.archive.org/web/20110607140747/https://www.ag.gov.au/www/agd/rwpattach.nsf/VAP/(8AB0BDE05570AAD0EF9C283AA8F533E3)~Milliner,+Robert+(Chair,+LLFG+Limited+(Large+~+Regulatory+Framework,+Consumer+Protection,+Business+Structures,+Liability+of+Principals,+Fidelity+Cover+and+General+Observations.PDF/$file/Milliner,+Robert+(Chair,+LLFG+Limited+(Large+

~+Regulatory+Framework,+Consumer+Protection,+Business+Structures,+Liability+of+Principals,+Fidelity+Cover+and+General+Observations.PDF.

Mills, Jonathan N., Anna J. Egalite, and Patrick J. Wolf. "How Has The Louisiana Scholarship Program Affected Students? A Comprehensive Summary of Effects after Two Years." Education Research Alliance. February 22, 2016. http://educationresearchalliancenola.org/files/publications/ERA-Policy-Brief-Public-Private-School-Choice-160218.pdf.

Moliterno, James E. *The American Legal Profession in Crisis: Resistance and Responses to Change*. New York: Oxford University Press, 2013.

Monbiot, George. "Neoliberalism—The Ideology at the Root of all Our Problems." *The Guardian*. April 15, 2016. https://www.theguardian.com/books/2016/apr/15/neoliberalism-ideology-problem-george-monbiot.

———. "No Country with a McDonald's Can Remain a Democracy." *The Guardian*. December 6, 2016. https://www.theguardian.com/commentisfree/2016/dec/06/mcdonalds-democracy-corporate-globalisation-trump-le-pen-farage.

"More Than 40% of Low-Income Schools Don't Get a Fair Share of State and Local Funds, Department of Education Research Finds." US Department of Education. November 30, 2011. https://www.ed.gov/news/press-releases/more-40-low-income-schools-dont-get-fair-share-state-and-local-funds-department-.

Murphy, James T. "Comment: Issues Paper Regarding Alternative Business Stuctures [sic]." April 26, 2016. http://www.americanbar.org/content/dam/aba/images/office_president/james_t_murphy_abs.pdf.

Murrell, Larry D. "Ethics 20/20 Non-lawyer Ownership of Law Firms." March 2, 2012. http://www.americanbar.org/content/dam/aba/administrative/ethics_2020/ethics_20_20_comments/murrell_alpsdiscussiondraft.authcheckdam.pdf.

National Legal Profession Reform Taskforce."Interim Report on Key Issues and Funding." October, 2010. http://www.justice.nsw.gov.au/Documents/LPR_Documents/pdf/Interim_Report_on_Key_Issues_and_Funding_PDF.pdf.

———. "National Legal Profession Reform—Consultative Group Paper: Business Structures—'Law Practices.'" November 25, 2009. http://www.justice.nsw.gov.au/Documents/LPR_Documents/pdf/NationalLegalProfessionReformTaskforce-Paper-BusinessStructures-December2009.pdf.

———. "National Legal Profession Reform Project—Consultation Regulation Impact Statement." May, 2010. http://www.justice.nsw.gov.au/Documents/LPR_Documents/pdf/National+Legal+Profession+Reform+Project+-+Consultation+Regulation+Impact+Statement+(including+Attachments+A-C).pdf.

National Organization of Bar Counsel. "Comments to 'Issues Paper Concerning New Categories of Legal Services Providers.'" December 21, 2015. http://www.americanbar.org/content/dam/aba/images/office_president/lspcomments_national_organization_of_bar_counsel.pdf.

New England Litigation Technology Professionals. "For Comment: Issues Paper Concerning Unregulated LSP Entities." April 28, 2016. https://www.americanbar.org/content/dam/aba/images/office_president/new_england_litigation_technology_professionals_board_of_directors.pdf.

New Jersey State Bar Association. "Comments on Issues Paper Unregulated LSP Entities." April 28, 2016. https://www.americanbar.org/content/dam/aba/images/office_president/new_jersey_state_bar_association_unregulated.pdf.

———. Letter to ABA Commission on the Future of Legal Services. October 27, 2015. http://www.americanbar.org/content/dam/aba/images/office_president/new_jersey_state_bar_association.pdf.

———. Letter to Katy Englehart. December 28, 2015. http://www.americanbar.org/content/dam/aba/images/office_president/lspcomments_new_jersey_state_bar_association.pdf.

New South Wales, Legislative Council, Official Report of Debates (Hansard), 52nd Parl, 2nd Sess. October 12, 2000. https://www.parliament.nsw.gov.au/prod/parlment/hansart.nsf/V3Key/LC20001012006?open&refNavID=.

New York State Bar Association, Letter to Katy Englehart, December 22, 2015, http://www.americanbar.org/content/dam/aba/images/office_president/lspcomments_new_york_state_bar_association.pdf.

New York State Bar Association. "New York State Bar Association's Comments on the ABA Commission on the Future of Legal Services' Issues Papers On Legal Checkups, Unregulated LSP Entities and Alternative Business Structures." April 28, 2016. https://www.americanbar.org/content/dam/aba/images/office_president/new_york_state_bar.pdf.

New York Times Editorial Board. "How a Budget Chief Can Wreak Havoc." *New York Times*. December 27, 2016. http://www.nytimes.com/2016/12/27/opinion/how-a-budget-chief-can-wreak-havoc.html?_r=0.

———. "Under Mr. Trump, Private Prisons Thrive Again." *New York Times*. February 24, 2017. https://www.nytimes.com/2017/02/24/opinion/under-mr-trump-private-prisons-thrive-again.html?_r=0.

North Carolina State Board of Dental Examiners v. Federal Trade Commission. February 25, 2015. http://www.supremecourt.gov/opinions/14pdf/13–534_19m2.pdf.

Nova Scotia Barristers' Society. "2016–2019 Strategic Framework." Accessed March 20, 2017, http://cdn2.nsbs.org/sites/default/files/cms/menu-pdf/2016–2019_strat-framework.pdf.

———. "Council Highlights." November 25, 2016. http://nsbs.org/sites/default/files/ftp/CouncilMaterials/2016–11–25_CouncilHighlights.pdf.

———. Council Meeting Materials. November 25, 2016. http://nsbs.org/sites/default/files/ftp/CouncilMaterials/2016–11–25_CouncilPkg.pdf.

———. "NSBS Seeks Your Assistance: Transforming Regulation—Consultation Document." 2014. http://nsbs.org/sites/default/files/ftp/InForumPDFs/2014–02–03_TransformingRegulation_Consultation.pdf.

O'Sullivan, Julie R. "Professional Discipline for Law Firms? A Response to Professor Schneyer's Proposal." *Georgetown Journal of Legal Ethics* 16 (2002): 1–90. http://scholarship.law.georgetown.edu/cgi/viewcontent.cgi?article=1900&context=facpub.

OECD CleanGovBiz. "Regulatory Policy: Improving Governance." July, 2012. http://www.oecd.org/cleangovbiz/toolkit/49256979.pdf.

OECD. *Being an Independent Regulator*. Paris: OECD Publishing, 2016. http://dx.doi.org/10.1787/9789264255401-en.

———. *The Governance of Regulators*. Paris: OECD Publishing, Paris, 2014. http://dx.doi.org/10.1787/9789264209015-en.

———. *Managing Conflict of Interest in the Public Service: OECD Guidelines and Overview*. Paris: OECD Publishing, 2003. http://www.oecd.org/corruption/ethics/48994419.pdf.

———. *OECD Regulatory Policy Outlook 2015*. Paris: OECD Publishing, 2015. http://dx.doi.org/10.1787/9789264238770-en.

———. *Regulatory Policy and Governance: Supporting Economic Growth and Serving the Public Interest*. Paris: OECD Publishing, 2011. http://www.oecd.org/gov/regulatory-policy/regulatorypolicyandgovernancesupportingeconomicgrowthandservingthepublicinterest.htm.

———.*Regulatory Policy in Perspective: A Reader's Companion to the OECD Regulatory Policy Outlook* 2015. Paris: OECD Publishing, 2015. http://dx.doi.org/10.1787/9789264241800-en.

———. "Regulatory Policy and the Road to Sustainable Growth." 2010. https://www.oecd.org/regreform/policyconference/46270065.pdf.

———. *Risk and Regulatory Policy: Improving the Governance of Risk*. Paris: OECD Publishing, 2010. http://dx.doi.org/10.1787/9789264082939-en.

OECD Initiative on Inclusive Growth. *All On Board: Making Inclusive Growth Happen*. Paris: OECD Publishing, 2014. https://www.oecd.org/inclusive-growth/All-on-Board-Making-Inclusive-Growth-Happen.pdf.

OECD Post-2015. "Building More Effective, Accountable, and Inclusive Institutions for All." Element 6, Paper 1, n.d. http://www.oecd.org/dac/_POST-2015%20effective%20and%20accountable%20institutions.pdf.

OECD Public Governance and Territorial Development Directorate Public Governance Committee. "Revolving Doors, Accountability and Transparency—Emerging Regulatory Concerns and Policy Solutions in the Financial Crisis." Expert Group on Conflict of Interest Discussion Paper. May 5, 2009. http://www.oecd.org/officialdocuments/publicdisplaydocumentpdf/?cote=GOV/PGC/ETH(2009)2&docLanguage=En.

OECD Studies on Public Engagement. *Focus on Citizens: Public Engagement for Better Policy and Services*. Paris: OECD Publishing, 2009. http://www19.iadb.org/intal/intalcdi/pe/2009/03785.pdf.

Office of the Inspector General, US Department of Justice. "Review of the Federal Bureau of Prisons' Monitoring of Contract Prisons." August, 2016. https://oig.justice.gov/reports/2016/e1606.pdf#page=2.

"Office for Legal Complaints (OLC) Operating Framework." July, 2012. http://www.legalombudsman.org.uk/wp-content/uploads/2014/08/OLC-Operating-framework-20121.pdf.

Oleson, J.C. "The Punitive Coma." *California Law Review* 90 (2002): 829–901. http://dx.doi.org/doi:10.15779/Z38HH7S.

Oliver, Paddy. "ILP Forum: Incorporated Legal Practices & Legal Profession Uniform Law." June 24, 2015. http://www.lexcel.com.au/wp-content/uploads/2015/07/

Paddy-Oliver-ILP-Forum-Legal-Profession-Uniform-Law-Session-24-June-2015.pdf.

Paddock, Richard C., Eric Lipton, Ellen Barry, Rod Nordland, Danny Hakim, and Simon Romero. “Potential Conflicts Around the Globe for Trump, the Businessman President.” *New York Times*. November 26, 2016. http://www.nytimes.com/2016/11/26/us/politics/donald-trump-international-business.html.

Parker, Christine, Tahlia Ruth Gordon, and Steve A. Mark. “Regulating Law Firm Ethics Management: An Empirical Assessment of the Regulation of Incorporated Legal Practices in NSW.” *Journal of Law and Society* 37 (2010): 466–500. http://dx.doi.org/10.2139/ssrn.1527315.

Parker, Christine. “Peering Over the Ethical Precipice: Incorporation, Listing, and the Ethical Responsibilities of Law Firms.” May 13, 2008. http://dx.doi.org/10.2139/ssrn.1132926.

Parker, David and Colin Kirkpatrick. “Measuring Regulatory Performance -The Economic Impact of Regulatory Policy: A Literature Review of Quantitative Evidence.” OECD Expert Paper No.3. August, 2012. https://www.oecd.org/gov/regulatory-policy/3_Kirkpatrick%20Parker%20web.pdf.

“Partnerships of ILPs & the Legal Profession Uniform Law—Lexcel Consulting.” The Profitable Lawyer Blog. March 21, 2016. http://www.lexcel.com.au/partnership-of-ilps-legal-profession-uniform-law/.

Paterson, Alan, Lindsay Farmer, Frank Stephen and James Love. “Competition and the Market for Legal Services.” *Journal of Law and Society* 15 (1988): 361–373.

Paterson, Alan. *Lawyers and the Public Good.* New York: Cambridge University Press, 2012.

Paterson, Alan A. “Professionalism and the Legal Services Market.” *International Journal of the Legal Profession* 3 (1996): 137–168.

Paton, Paul D. “Between a Rock and a Hard Place: The Future of Self-Regulation—Canada between the United States and the English /Australian Experience.” *Journal of the Professional Lawyer* (2008): 87–118. https://ssrn.com/abstract=1226802.

———. “Multidisciplinary Practice Redux: Globalization, Core Values, and Reviving the MDP Debate in America.” *Fordham Law Review* 78 (2010): 2193–2244. http://ir.lawnet.fordham.edu/cgi/viewcontent.cgi?article=4527&context=flr.

Peacock, Nicholas. “The Office for Legal Complaints.” In *Guide to the Legal Services Act 2007*, edited by James Thorne and Iain Miller, 75–88. UK: LexisNexis, 2009.

Pearce, Russell G. and Eli Wald. “Rethinking Lawyer Regulation: How a Relational Approach Would Improve Professional Rules and Roles.” *Michigan State Law Review* 2012 (2012): 513–536. http://digitalcommons.law.msu.edu/cgi/viewcontent.cgi?article=1034&context=lr.

Perlman, Andrew M. “A Bar Against Competition: The Unconstitutionality of Admission Rules for Out-of-State Lawyers.” *Georgetown Journal of Legal Ethics* 18 (2004): 135–178. http://ssrn.com/abstract=664194.

———. “Towards the Law of Legal Services.” *Cardozo Law Review* 37 (2015): 49–112. http://ssrn.com/abstract=2561014.

———. “Toward a Unified Theory of Professional Regulation.” *Florida Law Review* 55 (2003): 977–1041. http://dx.doi.org/10.2139/ssrn.449200.

Potanovic, George. "Take Back Our Water: How Trump's Appetite for Privatization Threatens Your Drinking Water." *Salon*. January 23, 2017. http://www.salon.com/2017/01/23/take-back-our-water-how-trumps-appetite-for-privatization-threatens-your-drinking-water_partner/.

Prairie Law Societies. "Consultation Report." September, 2016. http://www.lawsocietylistens.ca/.

———. "Consultation Report: Appendix—Paper Responses." September, 2016. http://www.lawsocietylistens.ca/.

———. "Innovating Regulation: A Collaboration of the Prairie Law Societies." November, 2015. http://www.lawsociety.sk.ca/media/127107/INNOVATING-REGULATION.pdf.

Public Citizen. "Top 10 Reasons to Oppose Water Privatization." Undated. https://www.citizen.org/documents/Top10-ReasonsToOpposeWaterPrivatization.pdf.

In the Public Interest. "How Privatization Increases Inequality." September, 2016. https://www.inthepublicinterest.org/wp-content/uploads/InthePublicInterest_InequalityReport_Sept2016.pdf.

Queensland Law Society. "Information Kit for Multi-Disciplinary Partnerships (MDPs)." June 28, 2011. http://www.qls.com.au/For_the_profession/Practice_support/Resources/Law_practice_structures/Multi-disciplinary_partnerships_MDPs.

Queensland Legal Services Commission. "Incorporated Legal Practices Self-Assessment Audit." Version 4.0. June 1, 2012. https://www.lsc.qld.gov.au/__data/assets/pdf_file/0005/97781/ILP-Self-Assessment-Audit-Form-Version-4.pdf.

Reardon, Jayne. "ABA Commission's Future of Legal Services Report: A Clarion Call for Action." *2Civility*. August 11, 2016. https://www.2civility.org/aba-commissions-future-of-legal-services-report-a-clarion-call-for-action/.

Rees, Victoria and Gabriela Quintanilla. "Nova Scotia Barristers' Society: A Journey Towards a New Model of Regulation and Governance of Legal Services in the Public Interest." June 24, 2015. http://nsbs.org/sites/default/files/ftp/ERU_Newsletter/2015–06–24-IBATransformingRegulation.pdf.

Rees, Victoria. "Transforming Regulation and Governance in the Public Interest." Paper prepared for Council of the Nova Scotia Barristers' Society. October 15, 2013. https://nsbs.org/sites/default/files/cms/news/2013–10–30transformingregulation.pdf.

Renda, Andrea. "Regulatory Impact Assessment and Regulatory Policy." In *Regulatory Policy in Perspective: A Reader's Companion to the OECD Regulatory Policy Outlook 2015*, OECD, 35–114. Paris: OECD Publishing, 2015. http://dx.doi.org/10.1787/9789264241800-en.

Responsive Law. "Comments on: Issues Paper Concerning New Categories of Legal Services

Providers." January 8, 2016. http://www.americanbar.org/content/dam/aba/images/office_president/lspcomments_responsive_law.pdf.

———. "Issues Paper Concerning Unregulated Legal Service Providers." April 28, 2016. https://www.americanbar.org/content/dam/aba/images/office_president/responsive_law_unregulated.pdf.

Rhode, Deborah L., and Lucy Buford Ricca. "Protecting the Profession or the Public? Rethinking Unauthorized-Practice Enforcement." *Fordham Law Review* 82

(2014): 2587–2610. http://fordhamlawreview.org/assets/pdfs/Vol_82/No_6/RhodeRicca_May.pdf.

Rhode, Deborah L. and Alice Woolley. "Comparative Perspectives on Lawyer Regulation: An Agenda for Reform in the United States and Canada." *Fordham Law Review* 80 (2012): 2761–2790. http://ir.lawnet.fordham.edu/cgi/viewcontent.cgi?article=4808&context=flr.

Richmond, Douglas R. "Discussion Paper on Alternative Law Practice Structures." January 6, 2012. http://www.americanbar.org/content/dam/aba/administrative/ethics_2020/ethics_20_20_comments/richmond_alpsdiscussiondraft.authcheckdam.pdf.

Rickman, Jess C. "ABS Survey--Rejection of the Proposal." April 27, 2016. http://www.americanbar.org/content/dam/aba/images/office_president/jess_c_rickman_abs.pdf.

Rigertas, Laurel A. "The Legal Profession's Monopoly: Failing to Protect Consumers." *Fordham Law Review* 82 (2014): 2683–2703. http://fordhamlawreview.org/assets/pdfs/Vol_82/No_6/Rigertas_May.pdf.

Robertson, Patricia and Katherine Watt. "The LSB's Role in the Regulatory Framework." In *Guide to the Legal Services Act 2007*, edited by James Thorne and Iain Miller, 39–58. UK: LexisNexis, 2009.

———. "The Regulatory Framework." In *Guide to the Legal Services Act 2007*, edited by James Thorne and Iain Miller, 13–38. UK: LexisNexis, 2009.

Robinson, Nathan J. "Why Is 'The Decimation of Public Schools' A Bad Thing?" *Current Affairs*. November 30, 2016. https://www.currentaffairs.org/2016/11/why-is-the-decimation-of-public-schools-a-bad-thing.

Rose, Neil. "Profession Set on Collision Course with Government over Independent Regulation." *Legal Futures*. December 1, 2015. http://www.legalfutures.co.uk/latest-news/profession-set-on-collision-course-with-government-over-independent-regulation.

———. "Reform of In-House Lawyer Regulation Could Improve Consumer Access to Justice, Says LSB." *Legal Futures*. July 30, 2015. http://www.legalfutures.co.uk/latest-news/reform-of-in-house-lawyer-regulation-could-improve-consumer-access-to-justice-says-lsb.

———. "The Sorry Tale of a Fallen Giant." *Legal Futures*. March 2, 2016. http://www.legalfutures.co.uk/blog/the-sorry-tale-of-a-fallen-giant.

———. "SRA's Approach to Licensing ABSs 'Damaging Competition, Consumers and Access to Justice.'" *Legal Futures*. April 9, 2014. http://www.legalfutures.co.uk/latest-news/sras-approach-licensing-abss-damaging-competition-consumers-access-justice.

———. "SRA Finally Taken Off Report Over Way It Handles ABS Applications." *Legal Futures*. May 20, 2015. http://www.legalfutures.co.uk/latest-news/sra-finally-taken-off-report-over-way-it-handles-abs-applications.

Rubenstein, Edwin S. "The Untapped Potential of Water Privatization." A Hudson Institute Report for American Water Works, Inc. October, 2000. http://www.esr-research.com/Theprivatewaterindustry.htm.

Ryan, Emma. "Multidisciplinary Legal Services Firm Announces ASX Listing." *Lawyers Weekly*. December 21, 2016. http://www.lawyersweekly.com.au/news/20275-multidisciplinary-legal-services-firm-announces-asx-listing?utm_ source=lawyersweekly&utm_campaign=newsflash21_12_2016&utm_medium=email.

Salyzyn, Amy. "From Colleague to Cop to Coach: Contemporary Regulation of Lawyer Competence." *Canadian Bar Review* forthcoming, Ottawa Faculty of Law Working Paper No. 2016–2043. October 24, 2016. https://ssrn.com/abstract=2858332.

———. "Law Society of Upper Canada to Move Forward with Proactive Entity Regulation," Canadian Association for Legal Ethics. May 28, 2016. https://ethicsincanada.com/2016/05/28/law-society-of-upper-canada-to-move-forward-with-proactive-entity-regulation/.

———. "What If We Didn't Wait?: Canadian Law Societies and the Promotion of Effective Ethical Infrastructure in Law Practices." *Canadian Bar Review*. April, 2015. http://ssrn.com/abstract=2533229.

Schaeffer, Adam B. "No, Virginia, There is No Such Thing as School Choice." Cato Institute. October 29, 2006. https://www.cato.org/publications/commentary/no-virginia-there-is-no-such-thing-school-choice.

Schmitz, Cristin. "ABS Issue Dominating Bencher Vote." *The Lawyers Weekly*. April 17, 2015. http://www.lawyersweekly.ca/articles/2362.

Schneyer, Ted. "Professional Discipline for Law Firms." *Cornell Law Review* 77 (1991): 1–46. http://scholarship.law.cornell.edu/cgi/viewcontent.cgi?article=3509&context=clr.

——— "The Case for Proactive Management-Based Self-Regulation to Improve Professional Self-Regulation for US Lawyers." *Hofstra Law Review* 42 (2013): 233–265.

Semple, Noel. "Access to Justice: Is Legal Services Regulation Blocking the Path?" *International Journal of the Legal Profession* 20 (2013): 267–283. http://scholar.uwindsor.ca/cgi/viewcontent.cgi?article=1004&context=lawpub.

———. "Legal Services Regulation in Canada: Plus Ça Change?" Invited submission to international volume on comparative legal services regulation, ed. Andy Boon. Hart Publishing, 2017 Forthcoming, (September 1, 2016). https://ssrn.com/abstract=2833336.

———. *Legal Services Regulation at the Crossroads: Justitia's Legions*. Cheltenham, UK: Edward Elgar Publishing, 2015.

Schwarcz, Daniel. "Preventing Capture Through Consumer Empowerment Programs: Some Evidence from Insurance Regulation." In *Preventing Regulatory Capture: Special Interest Influence and How to Limit It*, edited by Daniel Carpenter and David A. Moss, 365–396. New York: Cambridge University Press, 2014.

Semuels, Alana. "Aging Pipes Are Poisoning America's Tap Water." *The Atlantic*. July 29, 2015. https://www.theatlantic.com/business/archive/2015/07/dont-drink-the-water/399803/.

Shafer, Jack. "Fannie Mae and the Vast Bipartisan Conspiracy: A List of Villains in Boldface." *Slate*. September 16, 2008. http://www.slate.com/articles/news_and_politics/press_box/2008/09/fannie_mae_and_the_vast_bipartisan_conspiracy.html.

Sharp, Laura Bellegie. "Comments Regarding the Alternative Business Solutions Issues Paper." April 28, 2016. http://www.americanbar.org/content/dam/aba/images/office_president/laura_sharp_abs.pdf.

Simpson, Hannah. "Access to Justice in Revenue-Seeking Legal Institutions." Working Paper. June 14, 2017. https://static1.squarespace.com/static/5668949cdc5cb47474730d69/t/59417e47f5e231163ce27bbc/1497464393084/Access+to+Justice+Manuscript_Simpson.pdf.

Simpson, James. "Why is Swamp Queen Jamie Gorelick Advising Jared Kushner?" *Canada Free Press*. March 26, 2017. http://canadafreepress.com/article/why-is-swamp-queen-jamie-gorelick-advising-jared-kushner.

Smith, D. Clark. "Response to Commission's Issues Paper Regarding Alternative Business Structures dated April 8, 2016." April 29, 2016. https://www.americanbar.org/content/dam/aba/images/office_president/d_clark_smith_jr_abs.pdf.

Smith, Clint. "Why the U.S. Is Right to Move Away from Private Prisons." *The New Yorker*. August 24, 2016. http://www.newyorker.com/news/news-desk/why-the-u-s-is-right-to-move-away-from-private-prisons.

Smith, Reginald Heber. *Justice and the Poor*. New York: Carnegie Foundation, 1919.

Smith, Sean. "Administrators Called in to ILH." *West Australian*, December 18, 2014. https://au.news.yahoo.com/thewest/a/25810173/administrators-called-in-to-ilh/.

Snook, Terrence T. "Proposal to Allow ABS (Non Lawyer Ownership of Law Firms) and MDPs (Multi Disciplinary Programs)." April 28, 2016. https://www.americanbar.org/content/dam/aba/images/office_president/terry_snook_abs.pdf.

Snyder, Laura. *Democratizing Legal Services: Obstacles and Opportunities*. Lanham, Maryland: Lexington Books, 2016.

———. "Does the UK Know Something We Don't About Alternative Business Structures?" *ABA Journal*, January 1, 2015. http://www.abajournal.com/magazine/article/does_the_uk_know_something_we_dont_about_alternative_business_structures.

———. "WJP Rule of Law Index: Rankings for Four Subfactors." *Not Just for Lawyers*. April 17, 2017. http://notjustforlawyers.com/wjp-rule-of-law-index-rankings/.

Solicitors Regulation Authority. "Outcomes-Focused Regulation at a Glance: Your Quick Guide to Getting Started with OFR and the New Handbook." Undated. http://c.ymcdn.com/sites/ncbp.org/resource/collection/F9556696-FF20–442A-B922–0FE6CFD2FB3E/Outcomes_focused_regulation_Redacted.pdf.

"SRA Backs Call for Independent Legal Regulators." Solicitors Regulation Authority. December 2, 2015. http://www.sra.org.uk/sra/news/press/government-independence-plans-backed.page.

"SRA Unveils Its First Three ABSs." *Legal Futures*. March 28, 2012. http://www.legalfutures.co.uk/latest-news/breaking-news-sra-unveils-its-first-three-abss.

Stephen, Frank H. *Lawyers, Markets and Regulation*. Cheltenham, UK: Edward Elgar, 2013.

Strickler, Andrew. "Ill. Likely Set Trend for New Professional Conduct Training." *Law360*. January 27, 2017. https://www.law360.com/articles/885424/ill-likely-set-trend-for-new-professional-conduct-training.

Sullivan, Michael J. "Alternative Business Structures. April 26, 2016. https://www.americanbar.org/content/dam/aba/images/office_president/michel_j_sullivan_abs.pdf.

"Supermarket 'Law Shops' to Sell Legal Services." *BBC News*. October 6, 2011. http://www.bbc.co.uk/news/uk-15187154.

Supreme Court of Illinois. "Illinois Becomes First State to Adopt Proactive Management Based Regulation." January 25, 2017. http://www.illinoiscourts.gov/Media/PressRel/2017/012417.pdf.

Susskind, Richard. *The End of Lawyers? Rethinking the Nature of Legal Services.* Oxford: Oxford University Press, 2010.

Tabo, Tamara. "What Lawyers Must Learn From Dentists About The Unauthorized Practice Of Law." *Above the Law*, March 2, 2015. http://abovethelaw.com/2015/03/what-lawyers-must-learn-from-dentists-about-the-unauthorized-practice-of-law/?rf=1.

Tani, Maxwell. "Trump: I'm a 'Smart Person,' Don't Need Intelligence Briefings Every Single Day." *Business Insider UK*. December 11, 2016. http://uk.businessinsider.com/donald-trump-intelligence-briefings-skip-2016–12?r=US&IR=T.

Tartaglia, Mike. "Private Prisons, Private Records." *Boston University Law Review* 94 (2014): 1689–1744. http://www.bu.edu/bulawreview/files/2014/10/TARTAGLIA.pdf.

Terry, Laurel S., Steve Mark, and Tahlia Gordon. "Adopting Regulatory Objectives for the Legal Profession." *Fordham Law Review* 80 (2012): 2685–2760. http://ssrn.com/abstract=2085003.

Terry, Laurel S. "Globalization and the ABA Commission on Ethics 20/20: Reflections on Missed Opportunities and the Road Not Taken." *Hofstra Law Review* 43 (2014): 95–137. http://www.hofstralawreview.org/wp-content/uploads/2015/01/BB.3.Terry_.final2_.pdf.

———. "Trends in Global and Canadian Lawyer Regulation." *Saskatchewan Law Review* 76 (2013): 145–184. http://www.personal.psu.edu/faculty/l/s/lst3/Terry_Canada_Trends_Lawyer_Regulation.pdf.

Texas Association of Defense Counsel, Texas Trial Lawyers Association, and Texas Chapters of the American Board of Trial Advocates. "Comment and Opposition by Texas Association of Defense Counsel, Texas Trial Lawyers Association, and Texas Chapters of the American Board of Trial Advocates on Alternate Business Structures." May 4, 2016. http://www.americanbar.org/content/dam/aba/images/office_president/texas_association_of_defense_counsel_abs.pdf.

Thies, Richard L. Letter to the ABA Commission on Ethics 20/20. February 23, 2012. http://www.americanbar.org/content/dam/aba/administrative/ethics_2020/ethics_20_20_comments/thies_alpsdiscussiondraft.authcheckdam.pdf.

Thompson, Christie. "Everything You Ever Wanted to Know About Private Prisons . . . is None of your Damn Business." The Marshall Project. December 18, 2014. https://www.themarshallproject.org/2014/12/18/everything-you-ever-wanted-to-know-about-private-prisons#.nQOGdI8Gw.

Tort Trial & Insurance Practice Section. "ABA Commission on the Future of Legal Services / Issue Paper Regarding Alternative Business Structures." May 6, 2016. http://www.americanbar.org/content/dam/aba/images/office_president/tips_abs.pdf.

"UN Adopts New Global Goals, Charting Sustainable Development for People and Planet by 2030." United Nations News Centre, September 25, 2015. http://www.un.org/apps/news/story.asp?NewsID=51968#.Vgo773qqqko.

United Nations Summit for the Adoption of the Post-2015 Development Agenda. "Transforming Our World: The 2030 Agenda for Sustainable Development." October 21, 2015. http://www.un.org/ga/search/view_doc.asp?symbol=A/RES/70/1&Lang=E.

United Nations Economic and Social Commission for Asia and the Pacific. "What is Good Governance?" 2009. http://www.unescap.org/sites/default/files/good-governance.pdf.

United States Government Accountability Office. "Water Infrastructure: Information on Selected Midsize and Large Cities with Declining Populations." Report to the Ranking Member, Subcommittee on Environment and the Economy, Committee on Energy and Commerce, House of Representatives. September, 2016. http://gao.gov/assets/680/679783.pdf.

Van Ommen, Herman. "Law Firm Regulation." *Slaw*. February 16, 2016. http://www.slaw.ca/2016/02/16/law-firm-regulation/.

Varghese, Shiney. "Privatizing U.S. Water." Paper prepared by the Institute for Agriculture and Trade Policy Trade and Global Governance Program. July, 2007. http://www.iatp.org/files/451_2_99838.pdf.

Wagner, Lindsay. "Tiny Private School Puts Spotlight on Voucher System's Flaws." *NC Policy Watch*. March 1, 2017. http://www.ncpolicywatch.com/2016/03/01/tiny-private-school-puts-spotlight-on-voucher-systems-flaws/.

Walker, Edward T., Michael McQuarrie and Caroline W. Lee. "Rising Participation and Declining Democracy." In *Democratizing Inequalities: Dilemmas of the New Public Participation*, edited by Caroline W. Lee, Michael McQuarrie and Edward T. Walker, 3–23. New York: New York University Press, 2015.

Walko, Matthew. "Comment on ABA's Issues Paper Regarding Alternative Business Structures dated April 8, 2016." April 25, 2016. http://www.americanbar.org/content/dam/aba/images/office_president/matthew_walko_abs.pdf.

Walsh, Mark. "Dental Board Ruling May Drill into State Bar Associations' Immunity." *ABA Journal*. May 1, 2015. http://www.abajournal.com/magazine/article/dental_board_ruling_may_drill_into_state_bar_associations_immunity.

Weber, Mark. "School Vouchers Are Not a Cure for Segregation," Parts I-V. Jersey Jazzman. May, 2016. http://jerseyjazzman.blogspot.fr/2016/05/school-vouchers-are-not-cure-for.html.

"Welcoming The ABA's New President." *Metropolitan Corporate Counsel*. August 22, 2014. http://www.metrocorpcounsel.com/articles/29818/welcoming-aba%E2%80%99s-new-president.

Weston, J. Michael. "ABA Commission on the Future of Legal Services—Alternative Business Structures." April 27, 2016. http://www.americanbar.org/content/dam/aba/images/office_president/lederer_weston_craig_abs.pdf.

Whealing, Justin. "ILH's Future under a Cloud." *Lawyers Weekly*, December 19, 2014. http://www.lawyersweekly.com.au/news/15962-ILH-s-future-under-a-cloud.

"Why America's Schools Have A Money Problem." *NPR*. April 18, 2016. http://www.npr.org/2016/04/18/474256366/why-americas-schools-have-a-money-problem.

Woolley, Alice."Bencher Elections—The Challenge to Self-Regulations Legitimacy." *Slaw*. April 30, 2015. http://www.slaw.ca/2015/04/30/bencher-elections-the-challenge-to-self-regulations-legitimacy/.

Wright, Bradley. December 30, 2014 (6:28 pm), January 2, 2015 (1:43 pm), January 7, 2015 (10:31 am), and January 23, 2015 (5:38 pm). Comments on Mitch Kowalski, "Anti-ABS Arguments Continue to Be Based on Emotion—Not Fact." *Slaw*. December 30, 2014. http://www.slaw.ca/2014/12/30/anti-abs-arguments-continue-to-be-based-on-emotion-not-fact/comment-page-1/#comments.

Yates, Sally Q. "Memorandum for the Acting Director, Federal Bureau of Prisons." August 18, 2016. https://www.justice.gov/opa/file/886311/download.

———. "Phasing Out Our Use of Private Prisons." The United States Department of Justice. August 18, 2016. https://www.justice.gov/opa/blog/phasing-out-our-use-private-prisons.

Zacharias, Fred C. "The Myth of Self-Regulation." *Minnesota Law Review* 93 (2009): 1147–1190. http://www.minnesotalawreview.org/wp-content/uploads/2012/01/Zacharias_MLR.pdf.

Zapotosky, Matt and Chico Harlan. "Justice Department Says It Will End Use of Private Prisons." *The Washington Post*. August 18, 2016. https://www.washingtonpost.com/news/post-nation/wp/2016/08/18/justice-department-says-it-will-end-use-of-private-prisons/?amp;tid=ss_tw&utm_term=.57f0149acafa&postshare=9221471534255226&utm_term=.0b4001c3b3f9.

Zorza, Richard. "Does the Concept of "Entity Regulation" Provide an Entry Point for Access Contribution Requrements [sic]." April 2, 2016. https://www.americanbar.org/content/dam/aba/images/office_president/richard_zorza_unregulated.pdf.

———. "Good News from the ABA—Regulatory Objectives Adopted." Richard Zorza's Access to Justice Blog. February 9, 2016. http://accesstojustice.net/.

Index

Note: Page references for figures and tables are italicized

About the Author

During the more than twenty years since she graduated from law school, **Laura Snyder** has had the opportunity to experience legal services from multiple perspectives: as a law firm associate, as in-house counsel, and as a consumer for herself and on behalf of family members. She has also had the opportunity to experience legal services on an international basis: in the United States, the United Kingdom and France, as well as in a host of other countries in Europe, the Middle East, Central Asia and Africa. These experiences taught her both that the regulation and the delivery of legal services are universal concepts and that neither their limitations nor their potential are constrained by borders.

Born and raised in the United States, Snyder holds a JD from the University of Illinois College of Law, a DEA in *droit privé* from the University of Paris I (Panthéon-Sorbonne) and she completed the TRIUM Executive MBA program (an alliance of the London School of Economics, New York University Stern School of Business and HEC School of Management). Snyder is a member of the bars of Illinois, New York and Paris. She is based in France.

www.ingramcontent.com/pod-product-compliance
Ingram Content Group UK Ltd.
Pitfield, Milton Keynes, MK11 3LW, UK
UKHW041127071026
15587UKWH00009B/286

9 781498 530064